SHINOBU OHTAKA

Enjoy Magi volume 24!!!

MAGI

Volume 24
Shonen Sunday Edition

Story and Art by
SHINOBU OHTAKA

MAGI Vol.24
by Shinobu OHTAKA
© 2009 Shinobu OHTAKA
All rights reserved.
Original Japanese edition published by SHOGAKUKAN.
English translation rights in the United States of America, Canada, the United Kingdom,
Ireland, Australia and New Zealand arranged with SHOGAKUKAN.

ORIGINAL COVER DESIGN / Yasuo SHIMURA+Bay Bridge Studio

Translation & English Adaptation ◇ John Werry
Touch-up Art & Lettering ◇ Stephen Dutro
Editor ◇ Mike Montesa

Printed in the U.S.A.

Published by VIZ Media, LLC
P.O. Box 77010
San Francisco, CA 94107

10 9 8 7 6 5 4 3 2 1
First printing, June 2017

www.viz.com

MAGI
The labyrinth of magic

24

Story & Art by
SHINOBU OHTAKA

MAGI
The labyrinth of magic

24

CONTENTS

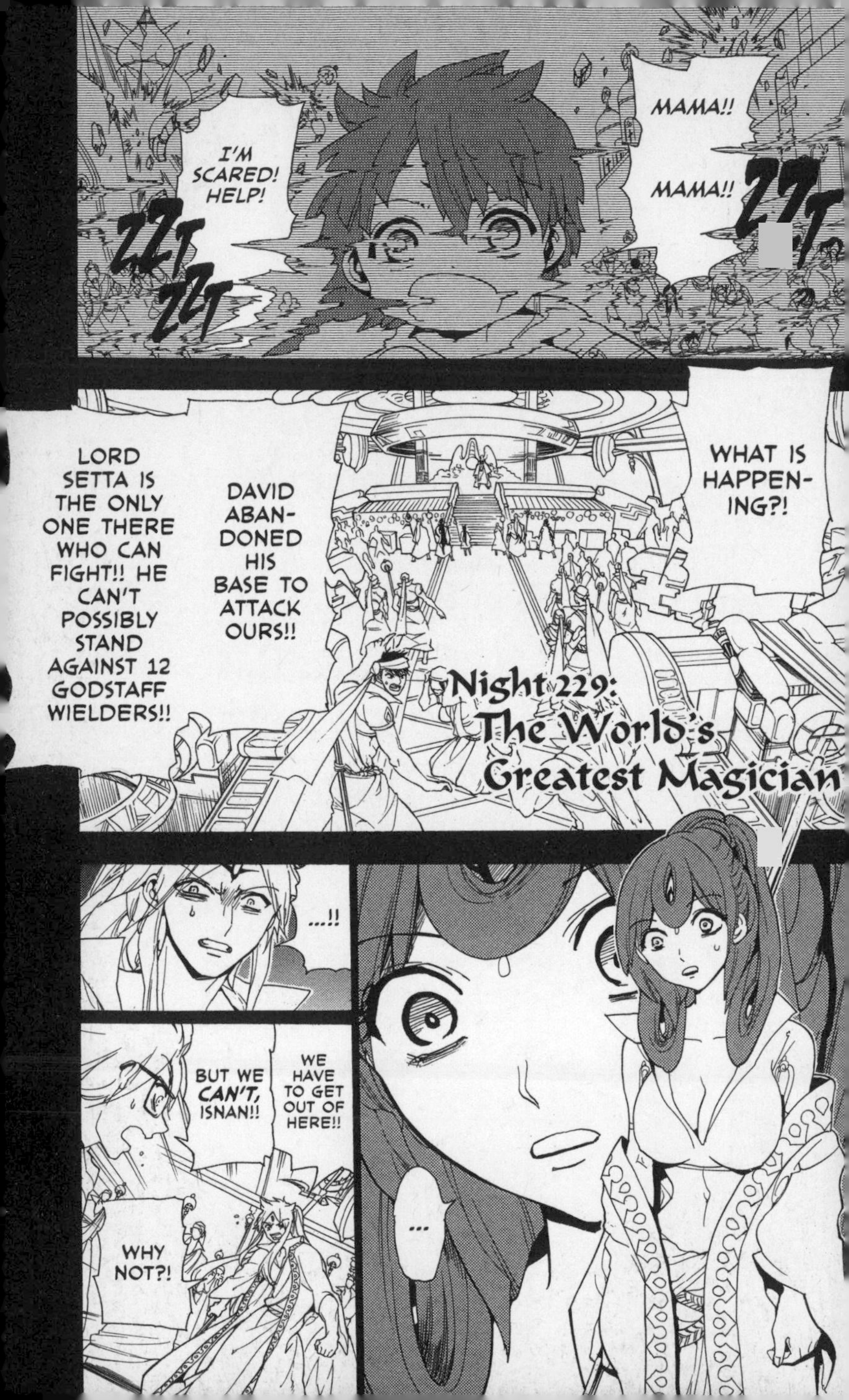
MAMA!!
MAMA!!
ZZT
I'M SCARED! HELP!
ZZT
ZZT
WHAT IS HAPPEN-ING?!
DAVID ABAN-DONED HIS BASE TO ATTACK OURS!!
LORD SETTA IS THE ONLY ONE THERE WHO CAN FIGHT!! HE CAN'T POSSIBLY STAND AGAINST 12 GODSTAFF WIELDERS!!
Night 229: The World's Greatest Magician
...
...!!
WE HAVE TO GET OUT OF HERE!!
BUT WE CAN'T, ISNAN!!
WHY NOT?!

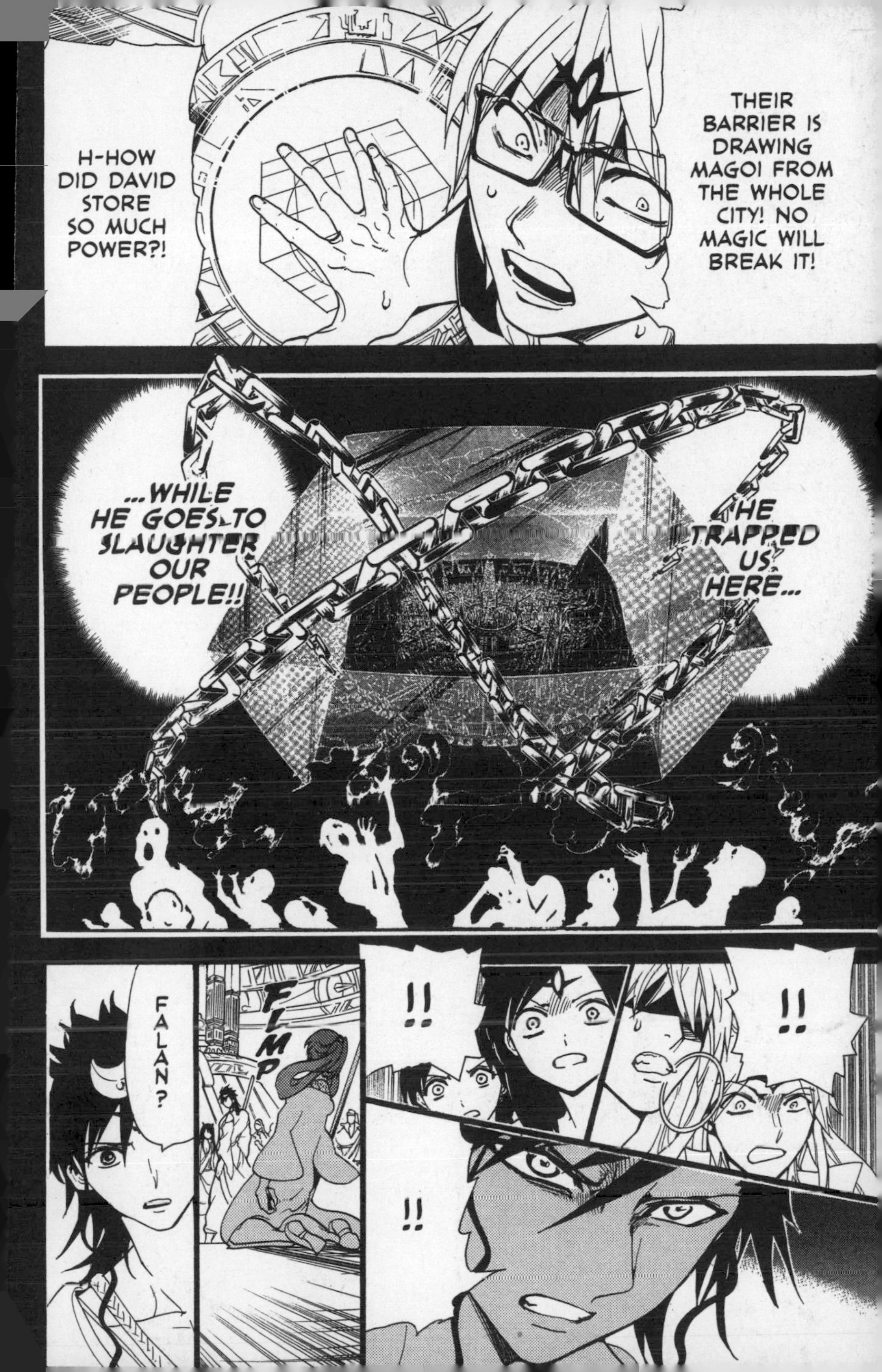
THEIR BARRIER IS DRAWING MAGOI FROM THE WHOLE CITY! NO MAGIC WILL BREAK IT!
H-HOW DID DAVID STORE SO MUCH POWER?!
HE TRAPPED US HERE...
...WHILE HE GOES TO SLAUGHTER OUR PEOPLE!!
!!
!!
!!
FLMP
FALAN?

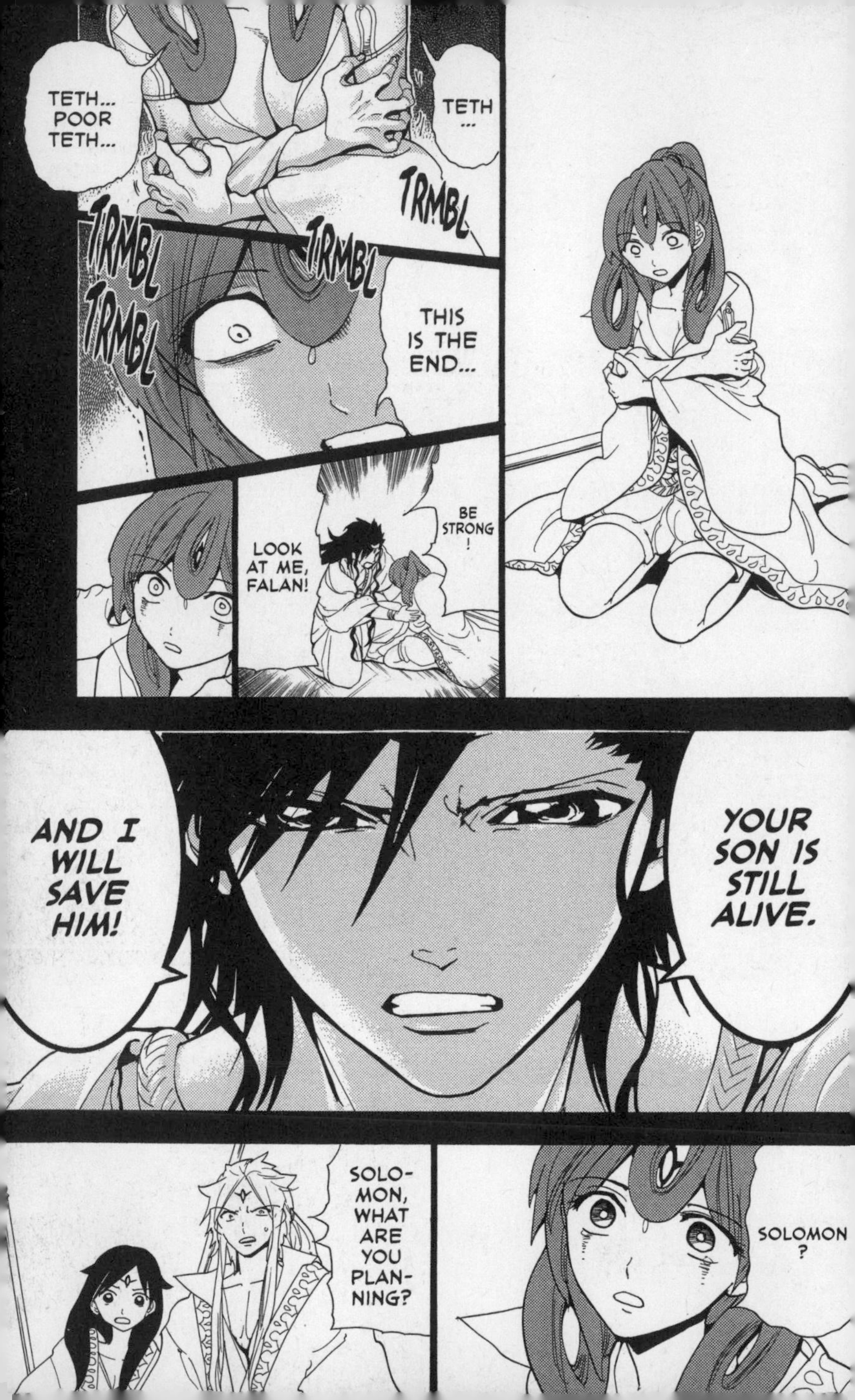
TETH ...
TRMBL
TETH... POOR TETH...
THIS IS THE END...
TRMBL
TRMBL
TRMBL
BE STRONG!
LOOK AT ME, FALAN!
YOUR SON IS STILL ALIVE.
AND I WILL SAVE HIM!
SOLOMON?
SOLO-MON, WHAT ARE YOU PLAN-NING?

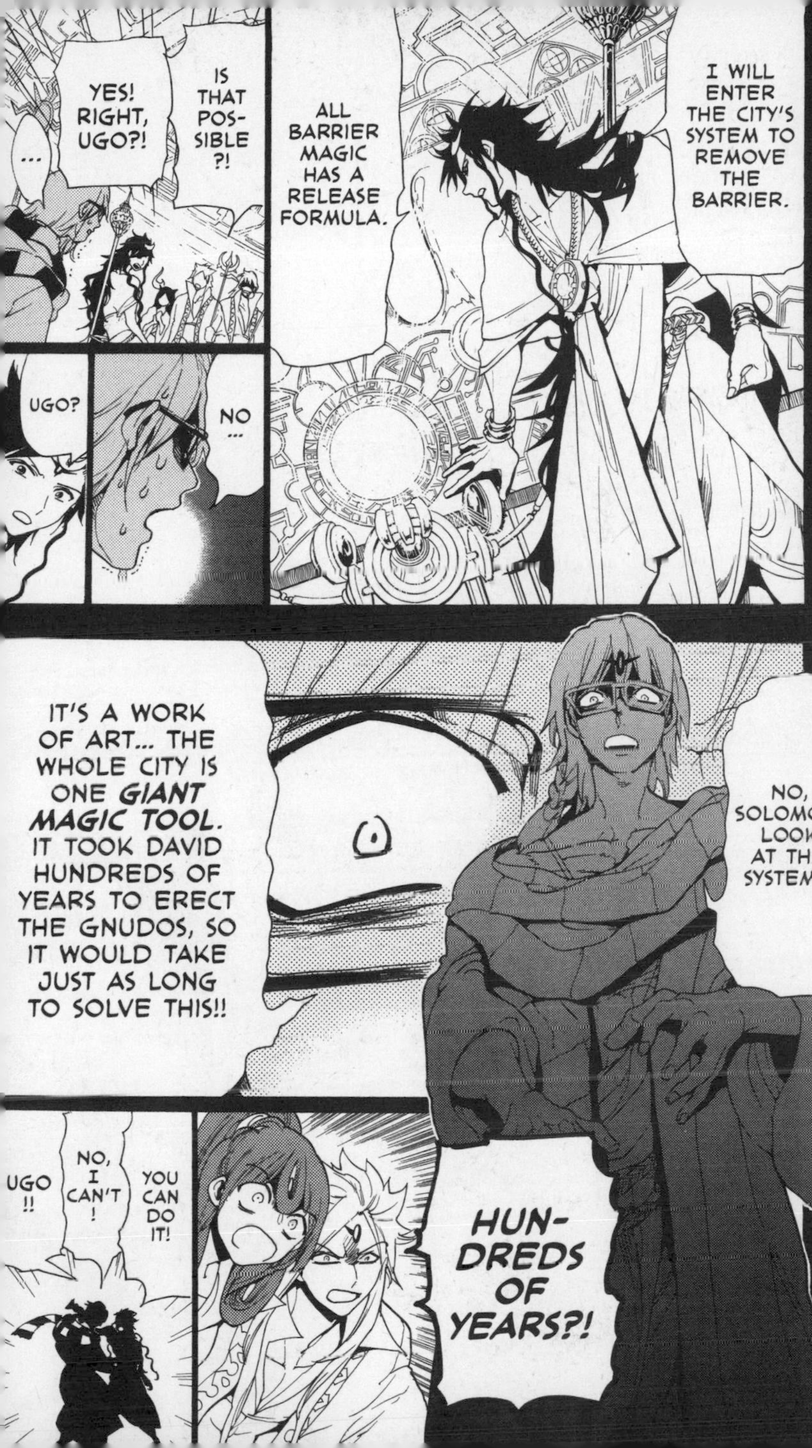
I WILL ENTER THE CITY'S SYSTEM TO REMOVE THE BARRIER.
ALL BARRIER MAGIC HAS A RELEASE FORMULA.
IS THAT POS-SIBLE?!
YES! RIGHT, UGO?!
...
NO ...
UGO?
NO, SOLOMON. LOOK AT THIS SYSTEM...
IT'S A WORK OF ART... THE WHOLE CITY IS ONE *GIANT MAGIC TOOL*. IT TOOK DAVID HUNDREDS OF YEARS TO ERECT THE GNUDOS, SO IT WOULD TAKE JUST AS LONG TO SOLVE THIS!!
HUN-DREDS OF YEARS?!
YOU CAN DO IT!
NO, I CAN'T!
UGO !!

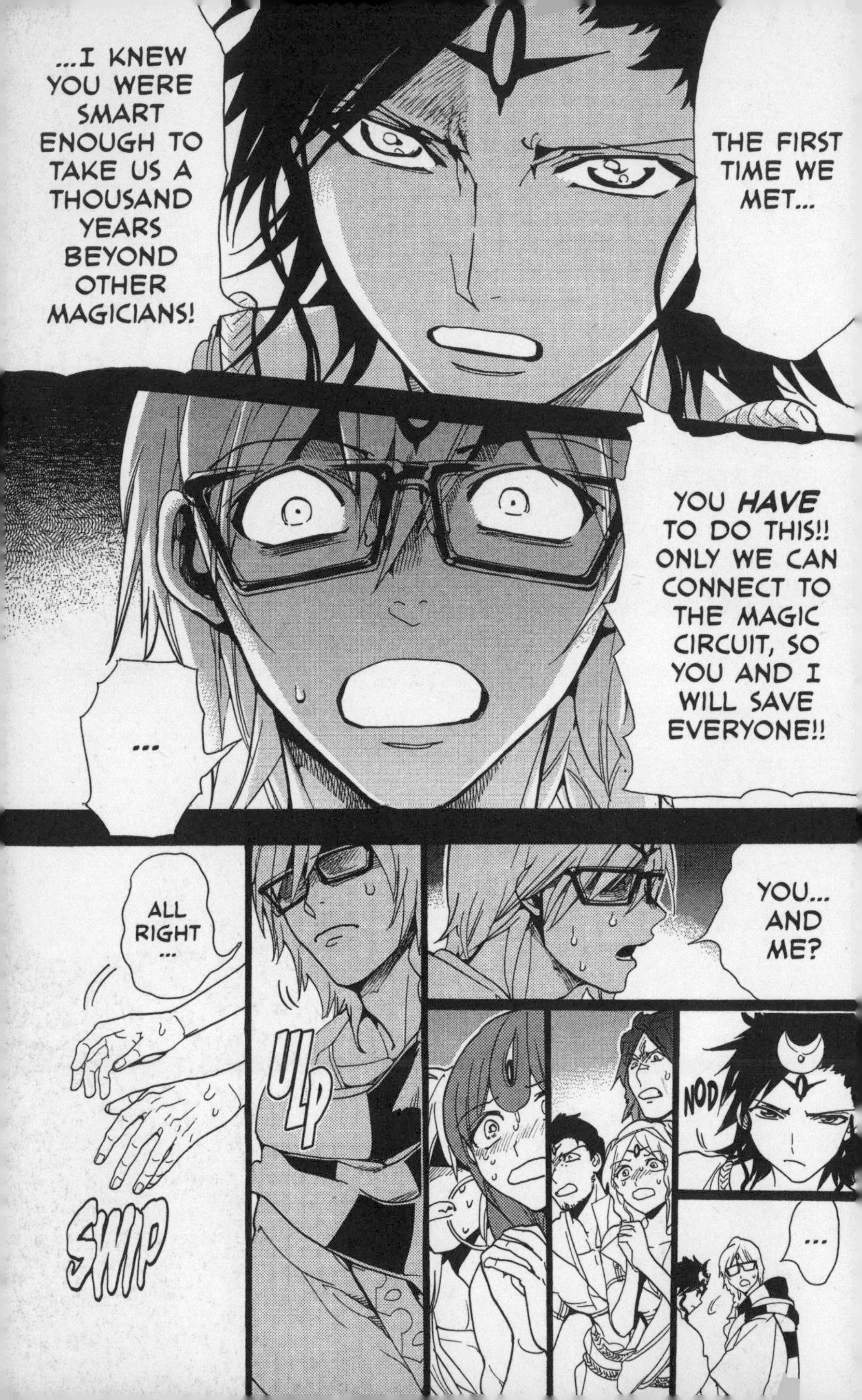
THE FIRST TIME WE MET...
...I KNEW YOU WERE SMART ENOUGH TO TAKE US A THOUSAND YEARS BEYOND OTHER MAGICIANS!
YOU *HAVE* TO DO THIS!! ONLY WE CAN CONNECT TO THE MAGIC CIRCUIT, SO YOU AND I WILL SAVE EVERYONE!!
...
YOU... AND ME?
NOD
...
ALL RIGHT...
ULP
SHIP

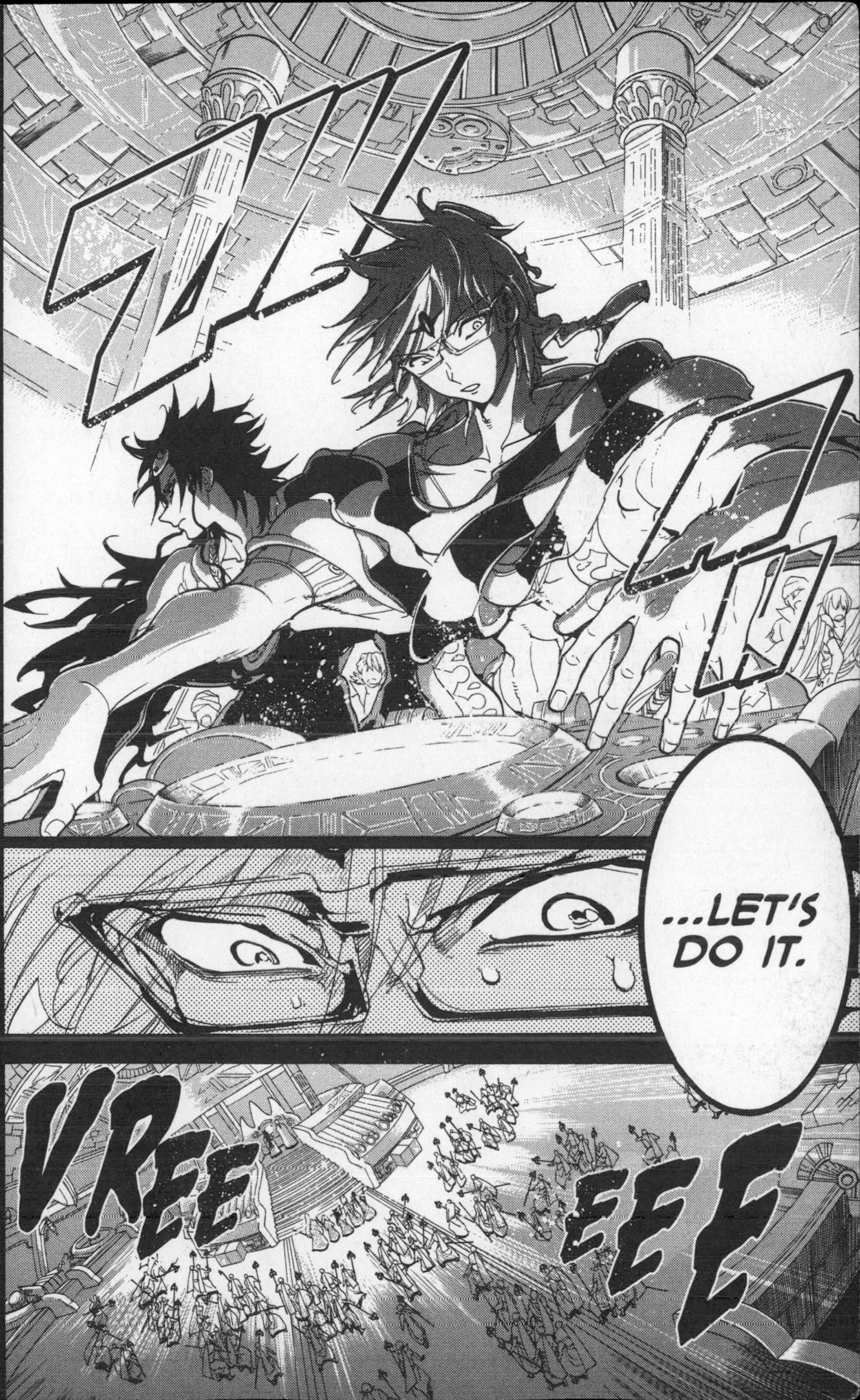
...LET'S DO IT.
VREEEEEE

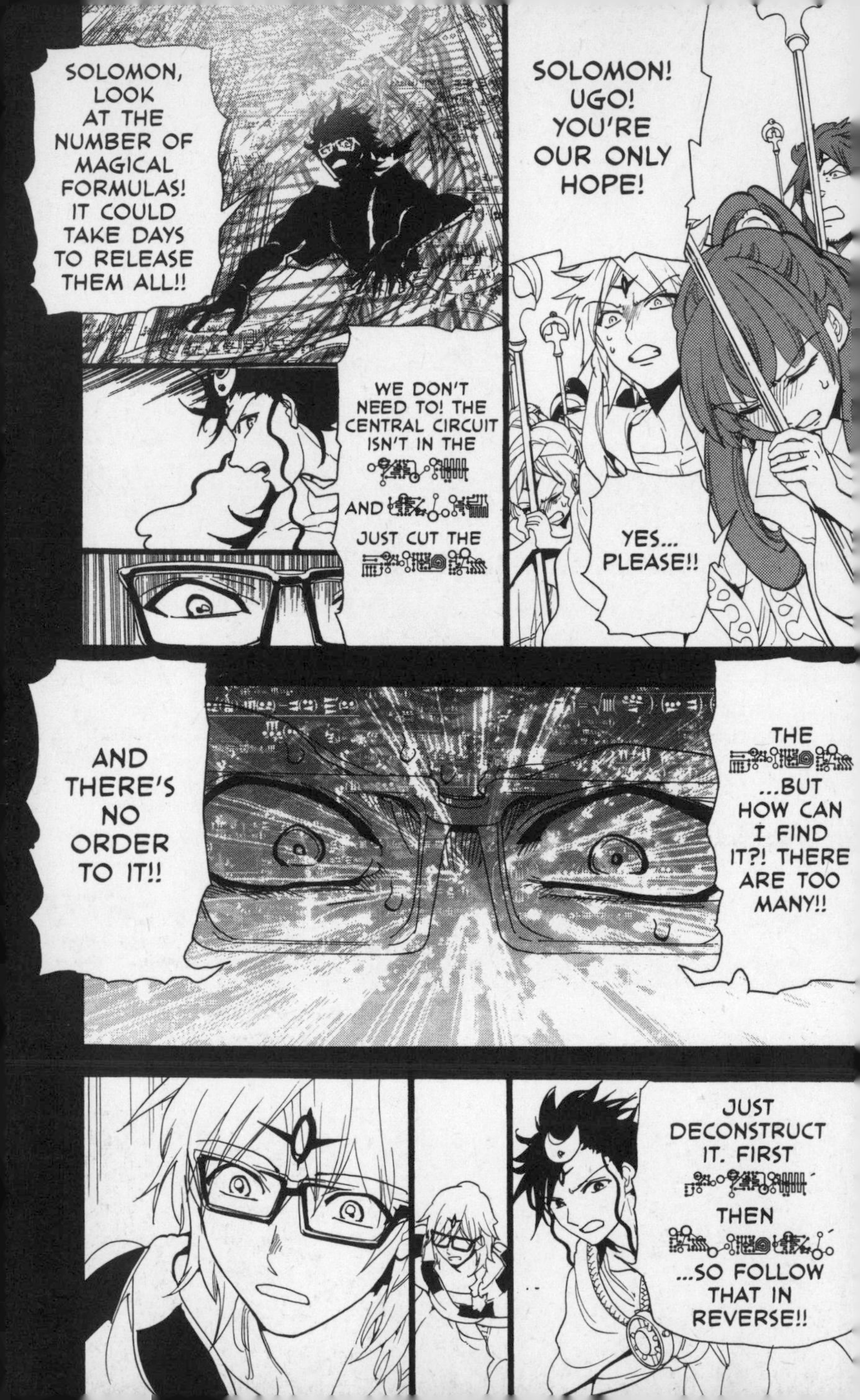
SOLOMON! UGO! YOU'RE OUR ONLY HOPE!
YES... PLEASE!!
SOLOMON, LOOK AT THE NUMBER OF MAGICAL FORMULAS! IT COULD TAKE DAYS TO RELEASE THEM ALL!!
WE DON'T NEED TO! THE CENTRAL CIRCUIT ISN'T IN THE
AND
JUST CUT THE
THE
...BUT HOW CAN I FIND IT?! THERE ARE TOO MANY!!
AND THERE'S NO ORDER TO IT!!
JUST DECONSTRUCT IT. FIRST
THEN
...SO FOLLOW THAT IN REVERSE!!

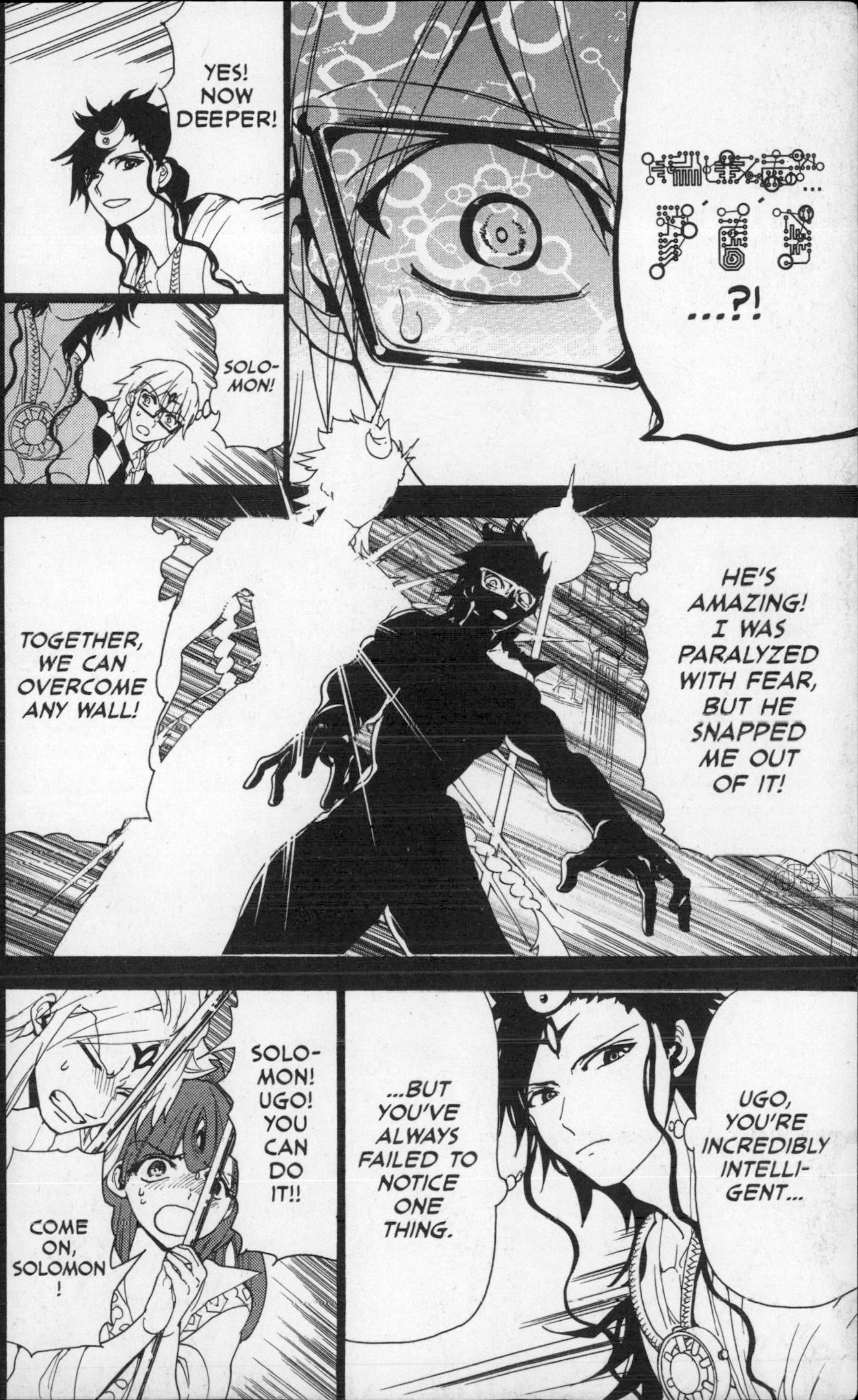
...?!
YES! NOW DEEPER!
SOLO-MON!
HE'S AMAZING! I WAS PARALYZED WITH FEAR, BUT HE SNAPPED ME OUT OF IT!
TOGETHER, WE CAN OVERCOME ANY WALL!
UGO, YOU'RE INCREDIBLY INTELLI-GENT...
...BUT YOU'VE ALWAYS FAILED TO NOTICE ONE THING.
SOLO-MON! UGO! YOU CAN DO IT!!
COME ON, SOLOMON!

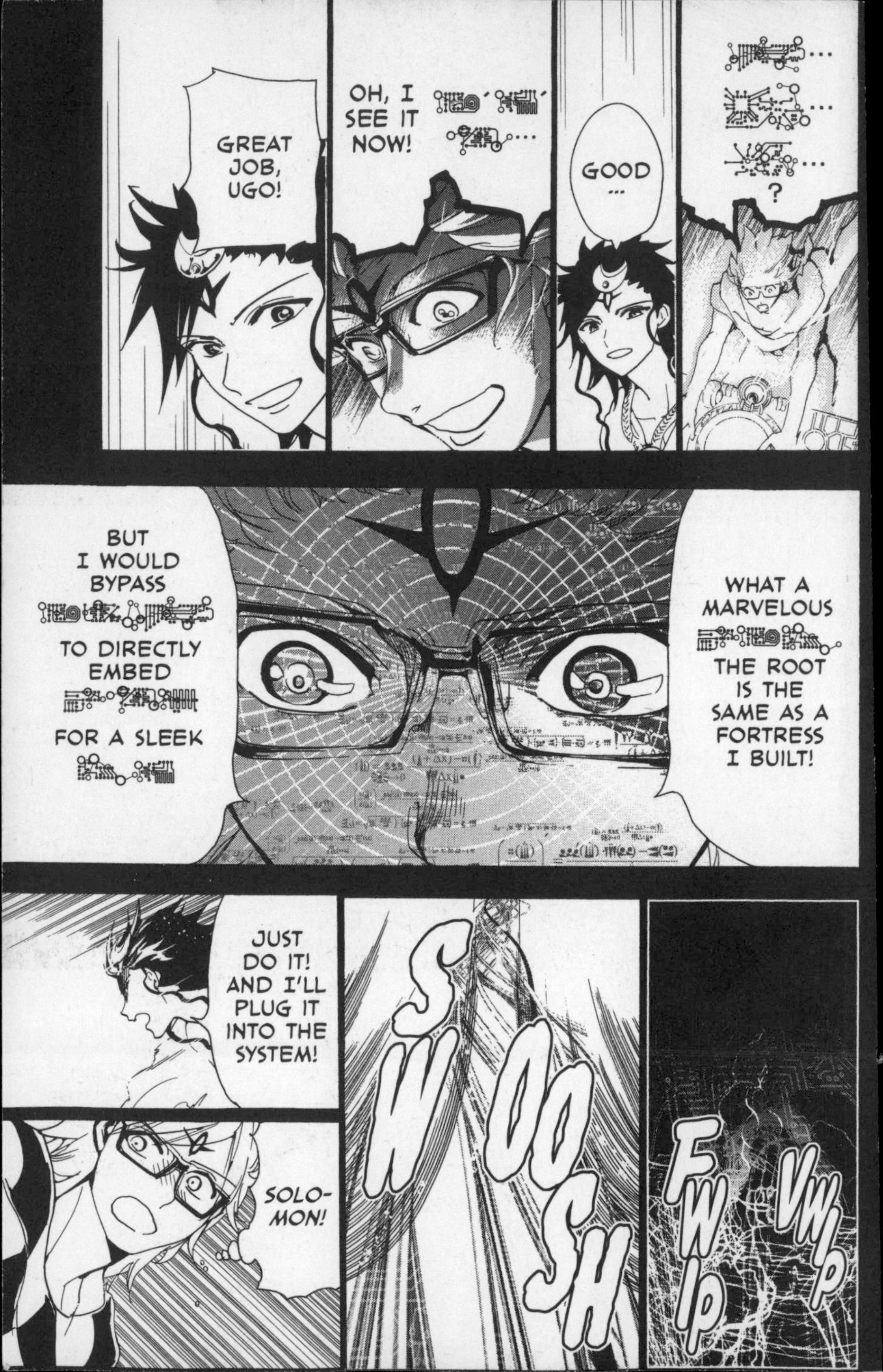
?
GOOD ...
OH, I SEE IT NOW!
GREAT JOB, UGO!
WHAT A MARVELOUS
THE ROOT IS THE SAME AS A FORTRESS I BUILT!
BUT I WOULD BYPASS
TO DIRECTLY EMBED
FOR A SLEEK
FWIP VWIP
SWOOSH
JUST DO IT! AND I'LL PLUG IT INTO THE SYSTEM!
SOLO-MON!

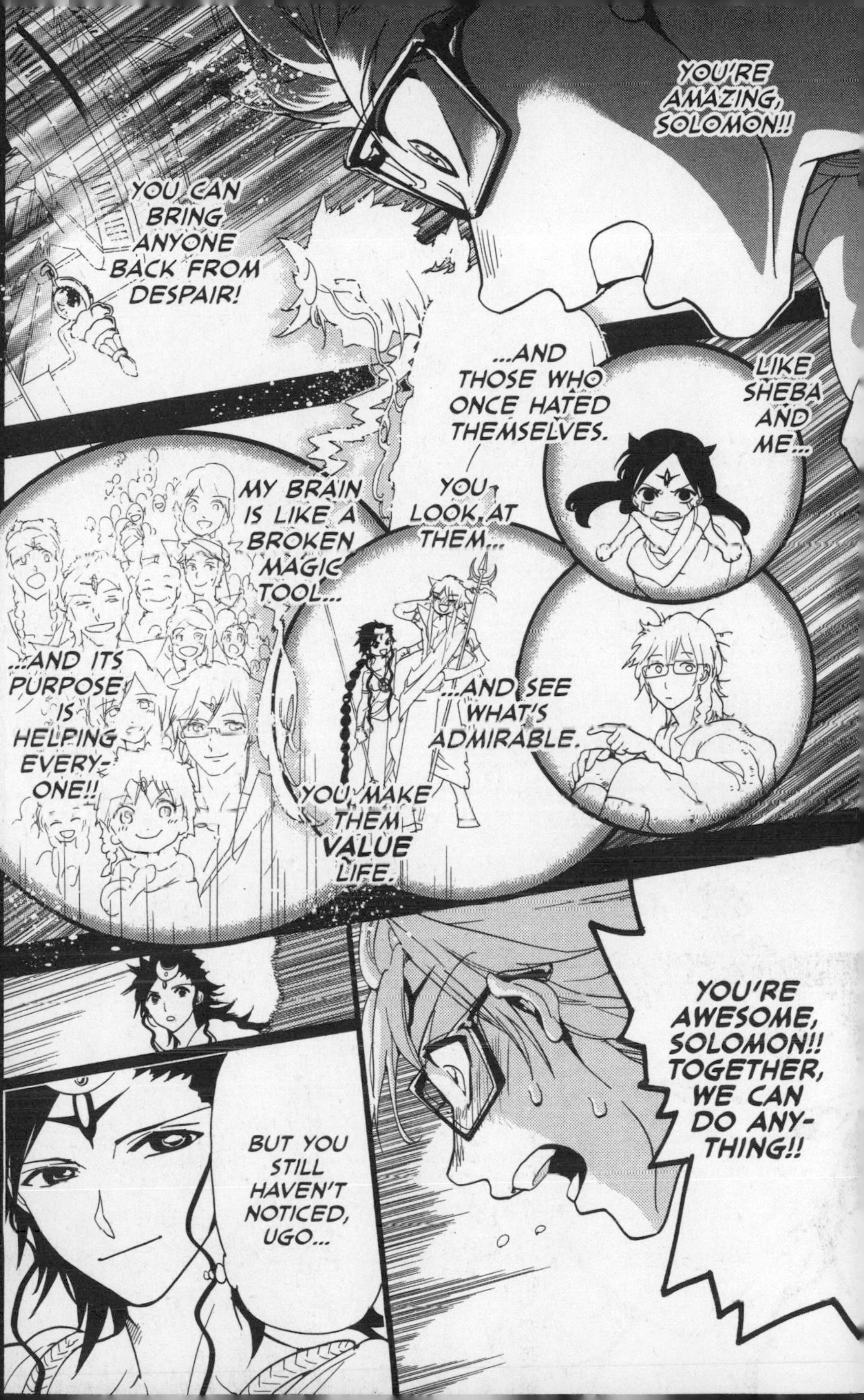
YOU'RE AMAZING, SOLOMON!!
YOU CAN BRING ANYONE BACK FROM DESPAIR!
LIKE SHEBA AND ME...
...AND THOSE WHO ONCE HATED THEMSELVES.
YOU LOOK AT THEM...
...AND SEE WHAT'S ADMIRABLE.
YOU MAKE THEM VALUE LIFE.
MY BRAIN IS LIKE A BROKEN MAGIC TOOL...
...AND ITS PURPOSE IS HELPING EVERY-ONE!!
YOU'RE AWESOME, SOLOMON!! TOGETHER, WE CAN DO ANY-THING!!
BUT YOU STILL HAVEN'T NOTICED, UGO...

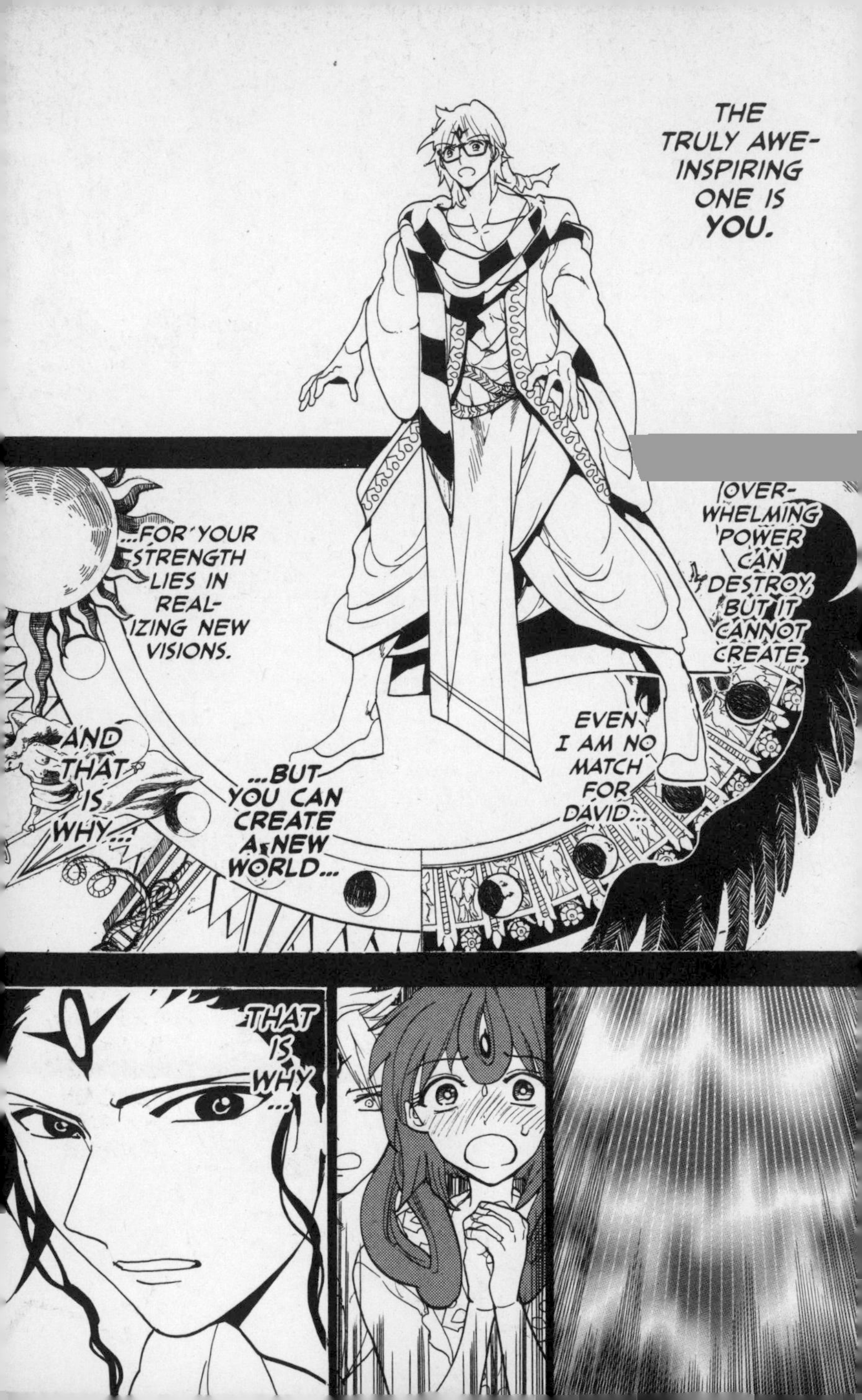
THE TRULY AWE-INSPIRING ONE IS YOU.
OVER-WHELMING POWER CAN DESTROY, BUT IT CANNOT CREATE.
EVEN I AM NO MATCH FOR DAVID...
...BUT YOU CAN CREATE A NEW WORLD...
...FOR YOUR STRENGTH LIES IN REAL-IZING NEW VISIONS.
AND THAT IS WHY...
THAT IS WHY...

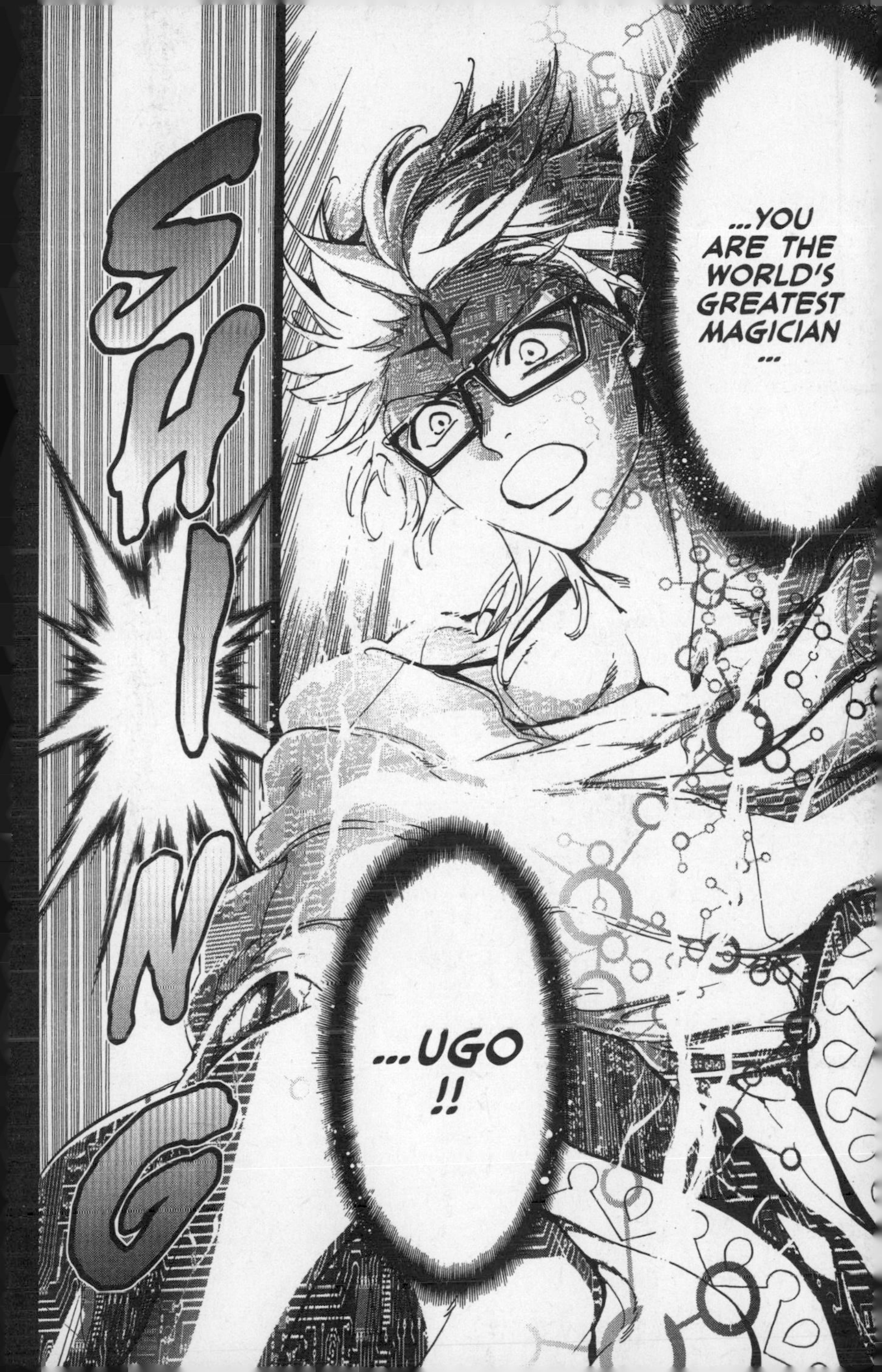
...YOU ARE THE WORLD'S GREATEST MAGICIAN ...
...UGO !!
SHING

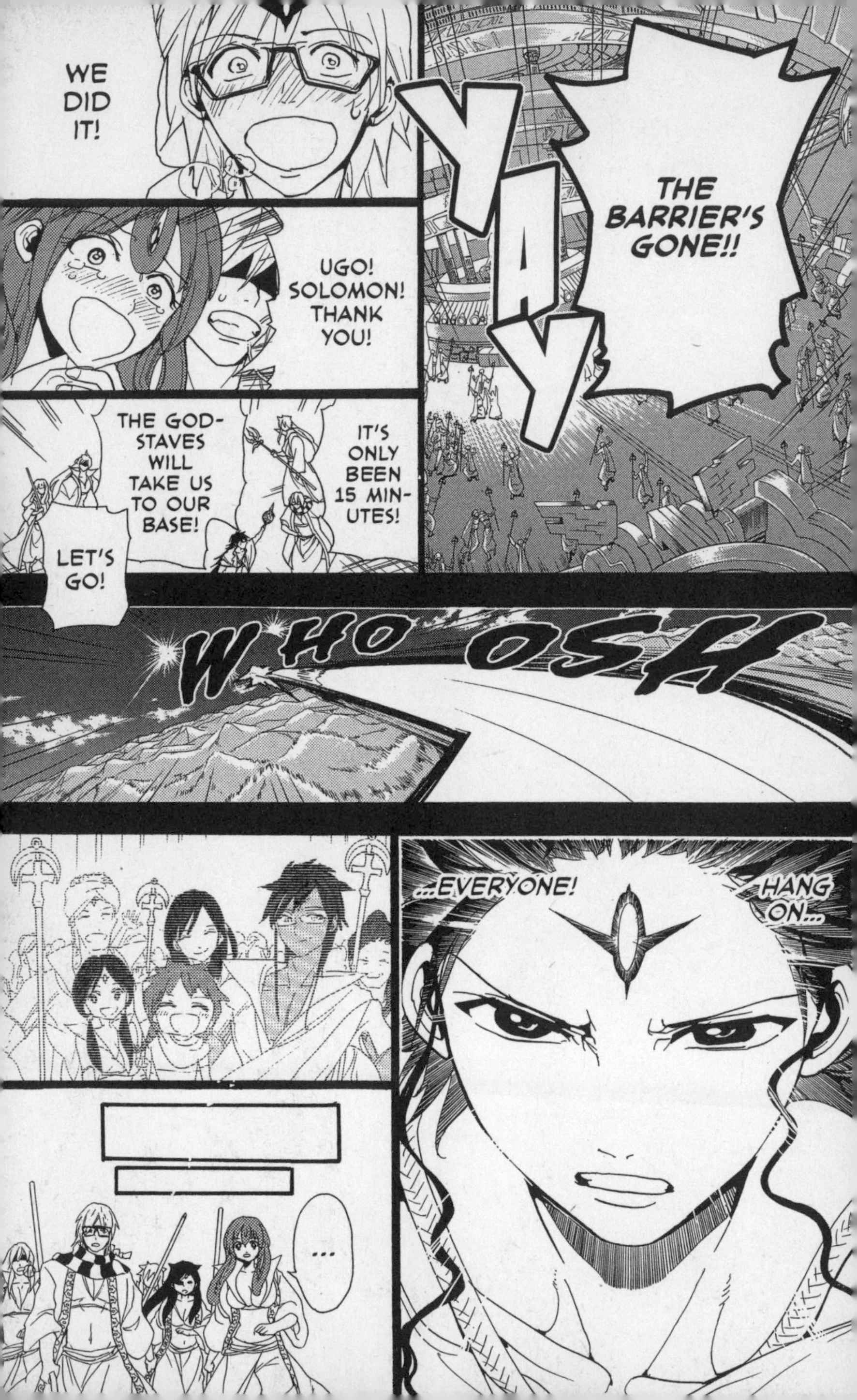
YAY
THE BARRIER'S GONE!!
WE DID IT!
UGO! SOLOMON! THANK YOU!
IT'S ONLY BEEN 15 MINUTES!
THE GOD-STAVES WILL TAKE US TO OUR BASE!
LET'S GO!
WHOOSH
HANG ON...
...EVERYONE!
...

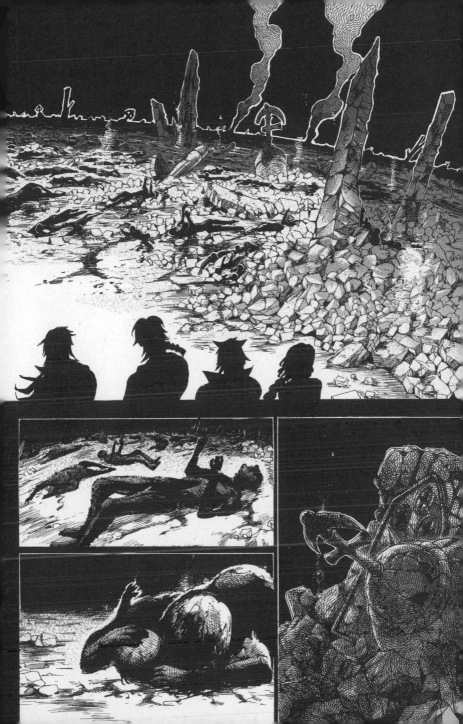

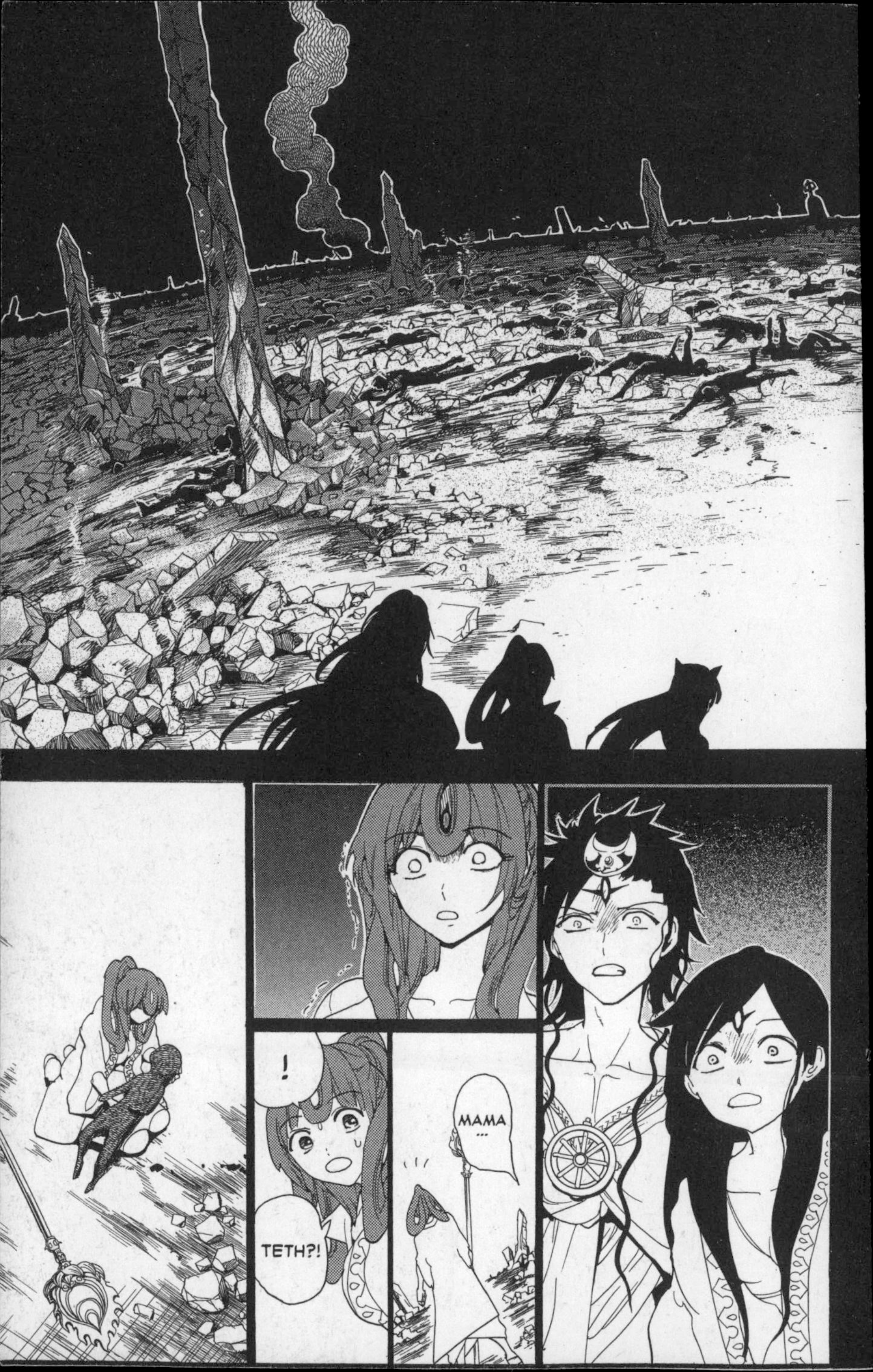
MAMA ...
!
TETH?!

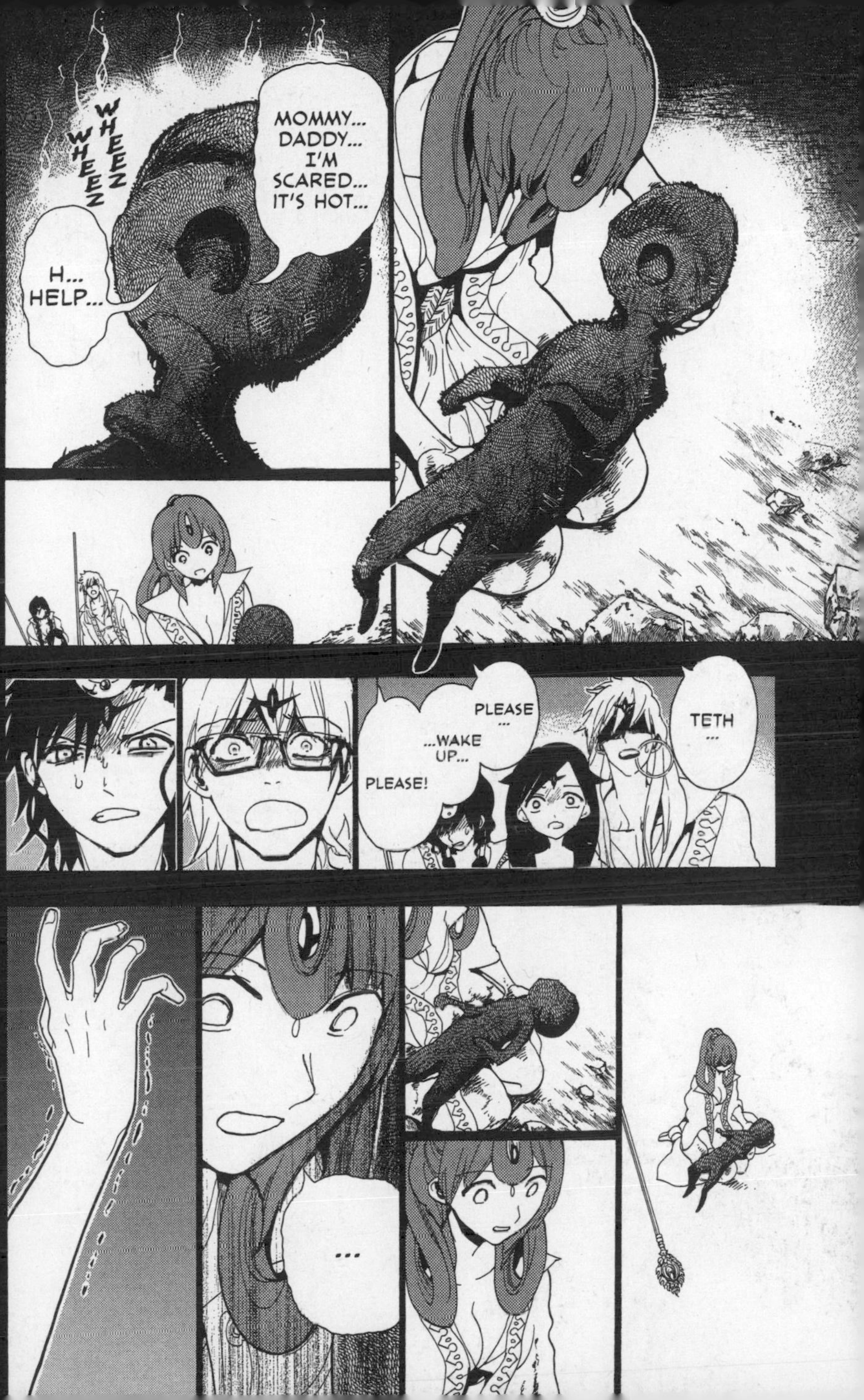
MOMMY... DADDY... I'M SCARED... IT'S HOT...
WHEEZ WHEEZ
H... HELP...
TETH ...
PLEASE ...
...WAKE UP...
PLEASE!
...

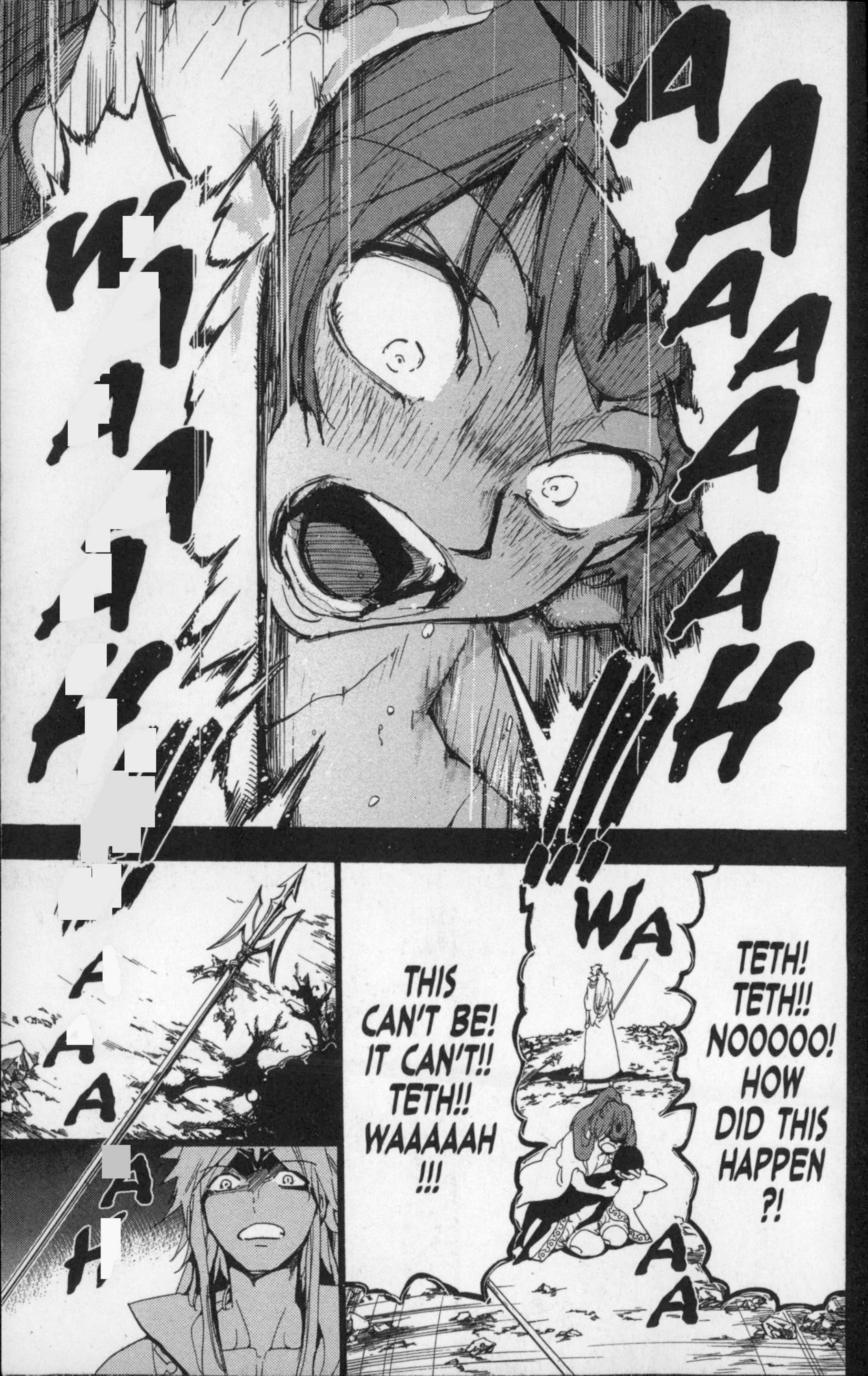
AAAAAAAH!!!!
WA
TETH! TETH!! NOOOOO! HOW DID THIS HAPPEN?!
THIS CAN'T BE! IT CAN'T!! TETH!! WAAAAAH!!!
AAA

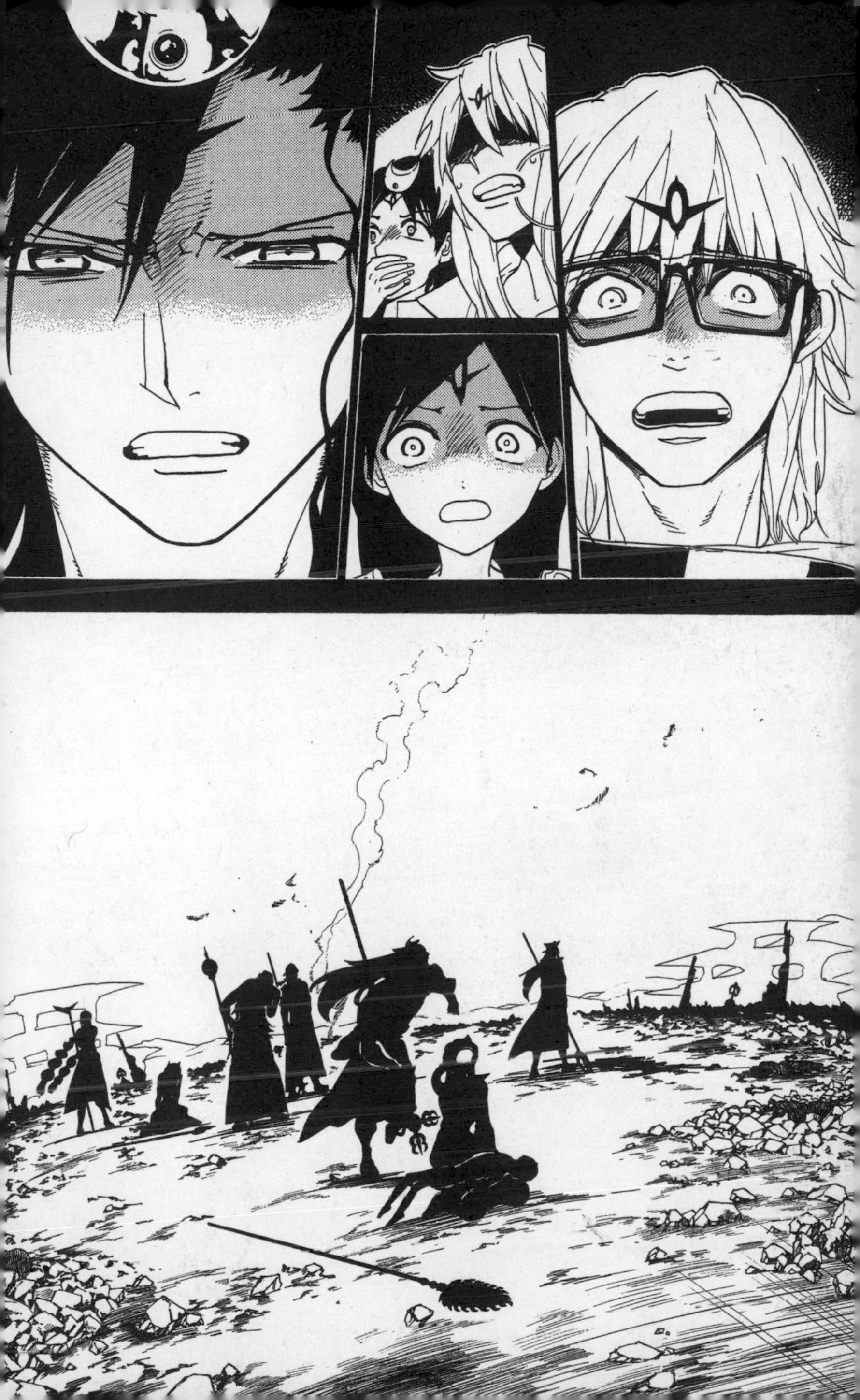

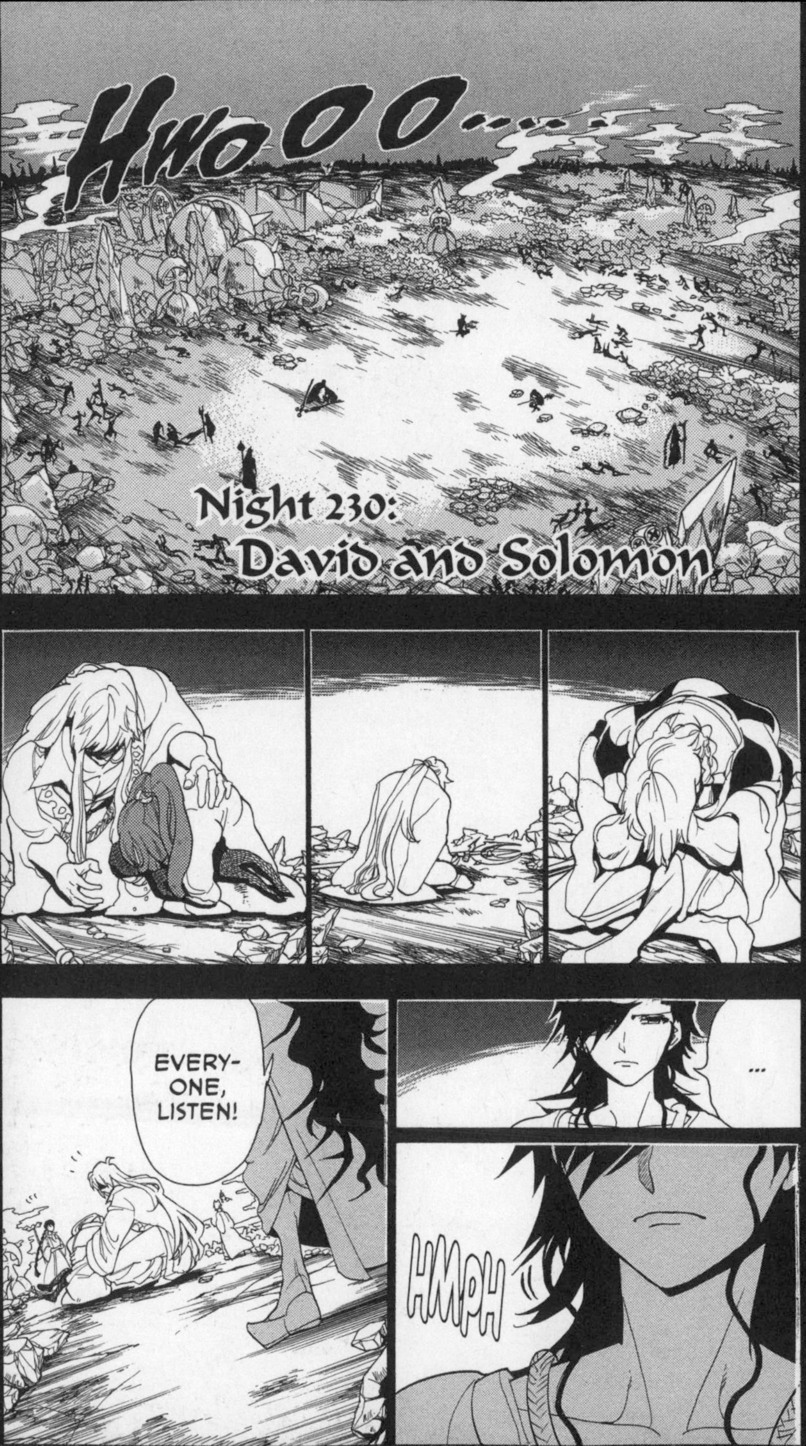
HWOOO.....
Night 230:
David and Solomon
...
HMPH
EVERY-ONE, LISTEN!

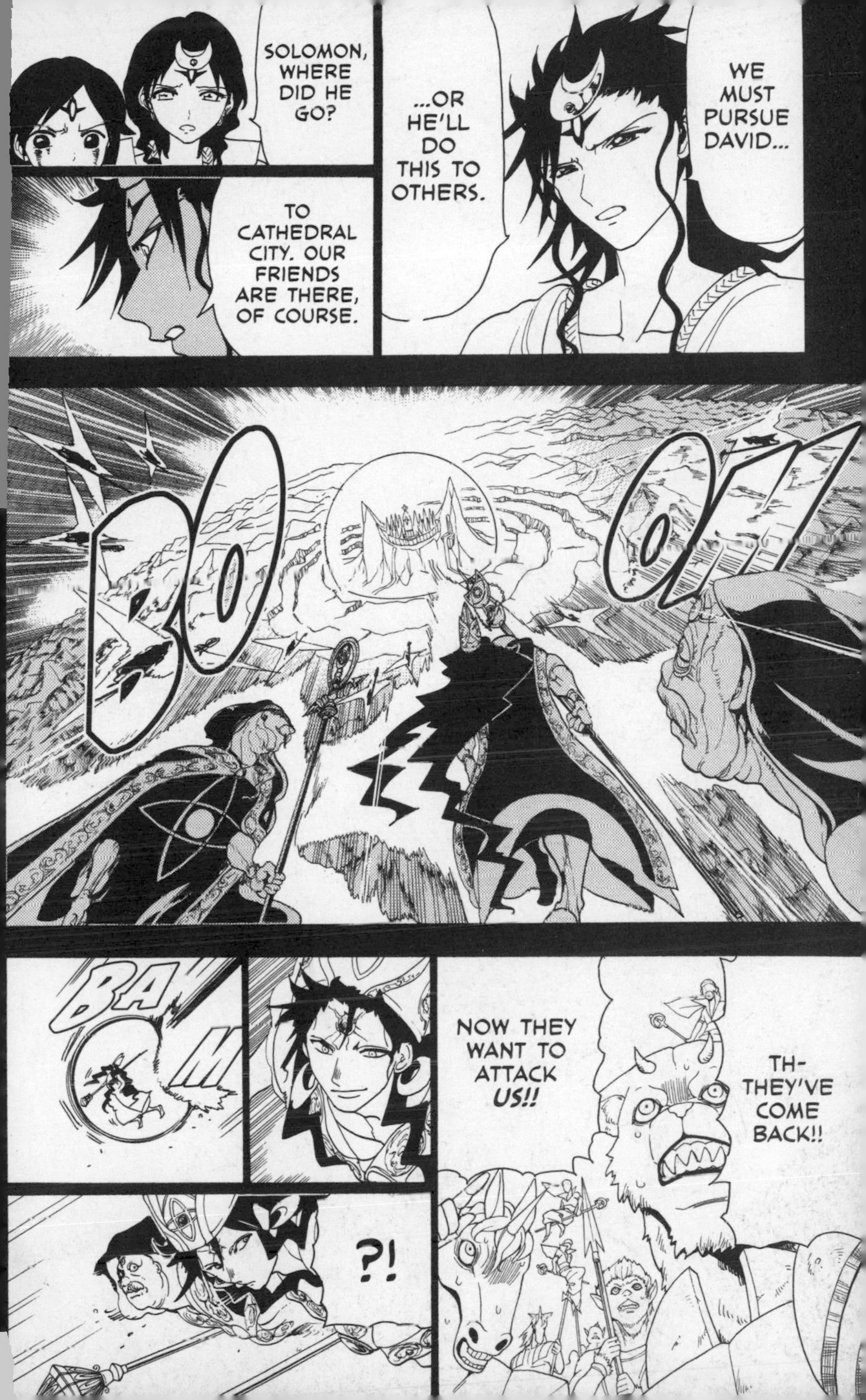

WE MUST PURSUE DAVID...
...OR HE'LL DO THIS TO OTHERS.
SOLOMON, WHERE DID HE GO?
TO CATHEDRAL CITY. OUR FRIENDS ARE THERE, OF COURSE.
BOOM
TH- THEY'VE COME BACK!!
NOW THEY WANT TO ATTACK *US!!*
BAM
?!

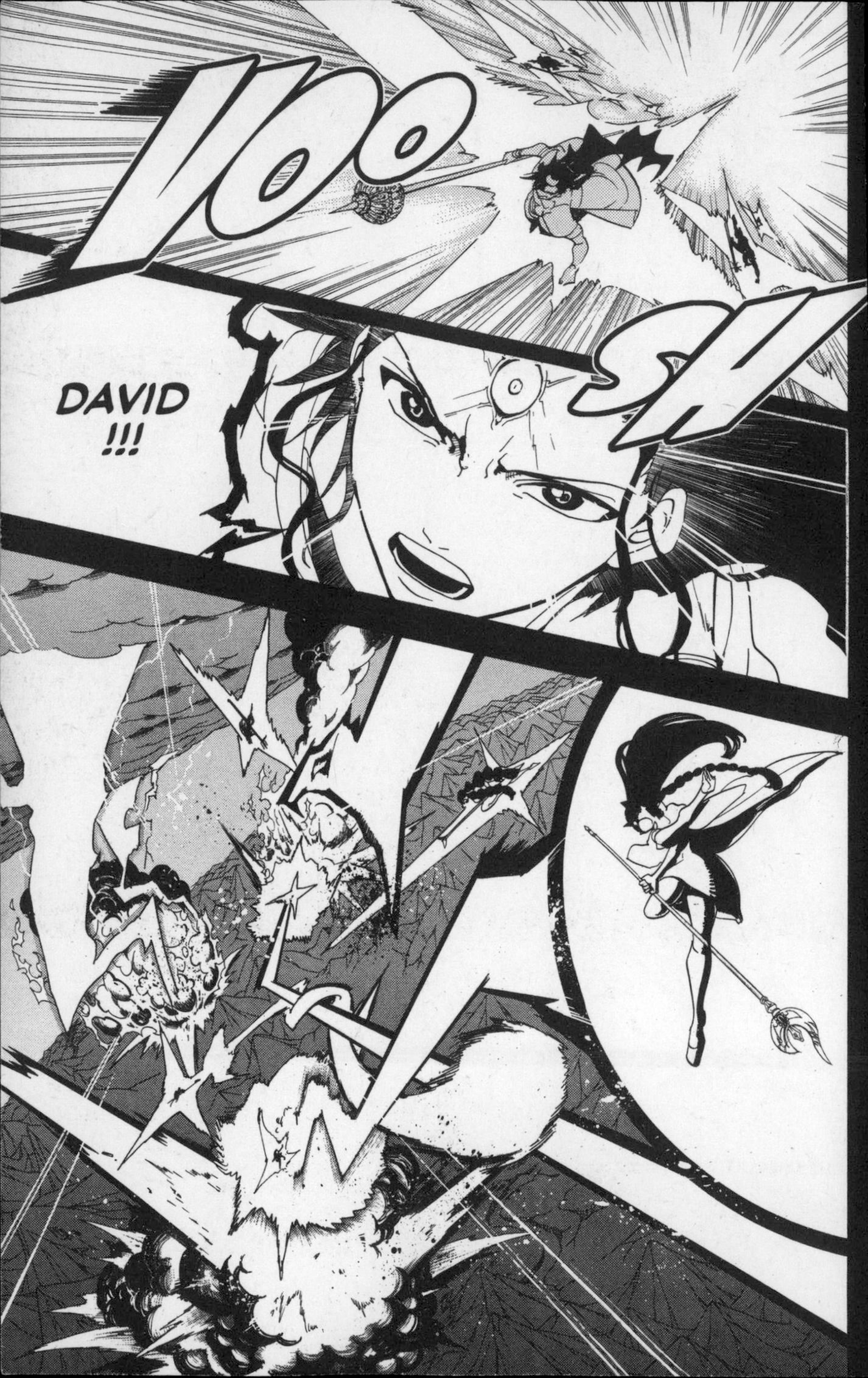
WOOSH
DAVID !!!

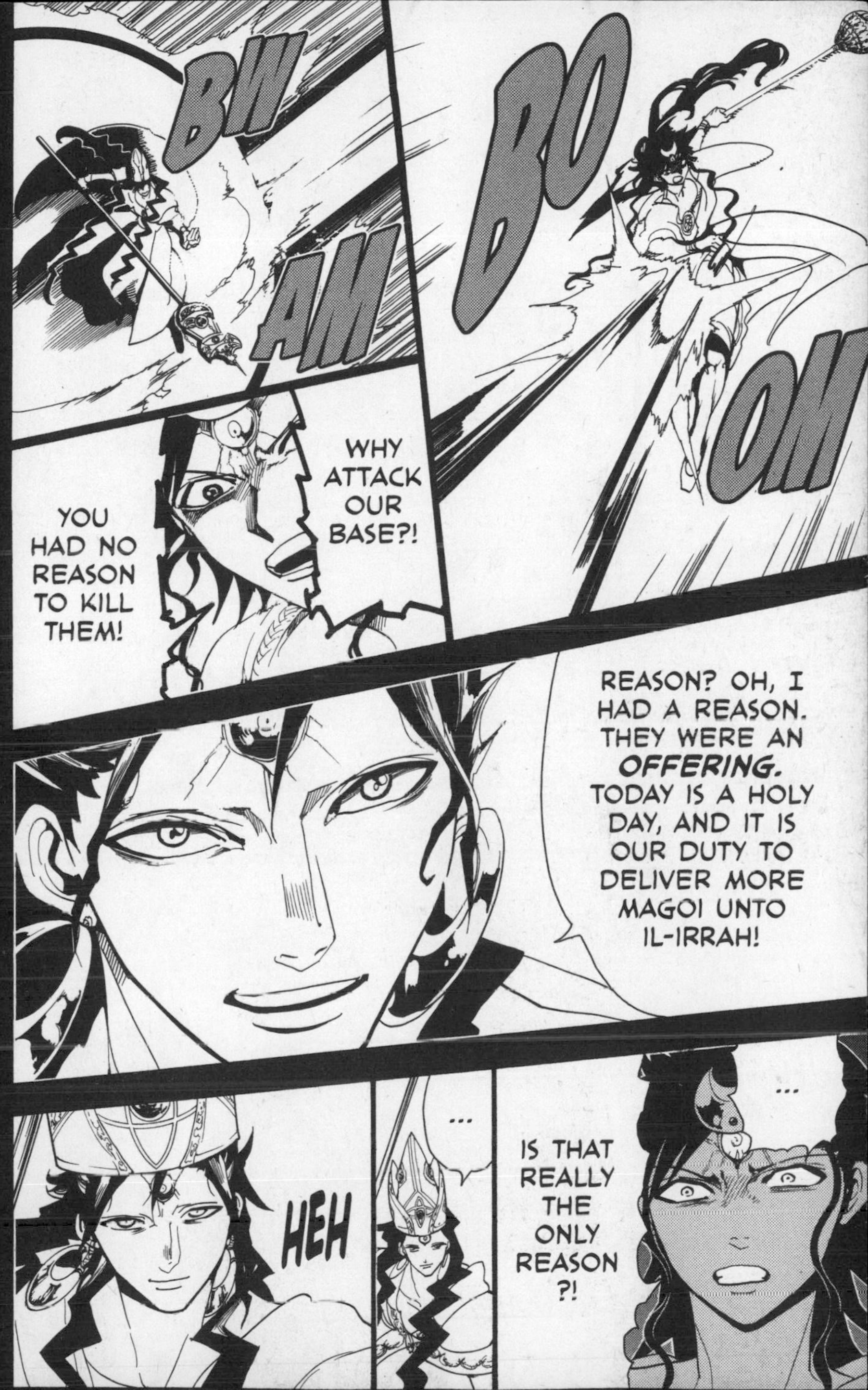
BOOOM
BWAM
WHY ATTACK OUR BASE?!
YOU HAD NO REASON TO KILL THEM!
REASON? OH, I HAD A REASON. THEY WERE AN *OFFERING.* TODAY IS A HOLY DAY, AND IT IS OUR DUTY TO DELIVER MORE MAGOI UNTO IL-IRRAH!
...
IS THAT REALLY THE ONLY REASON?!
...
HEH

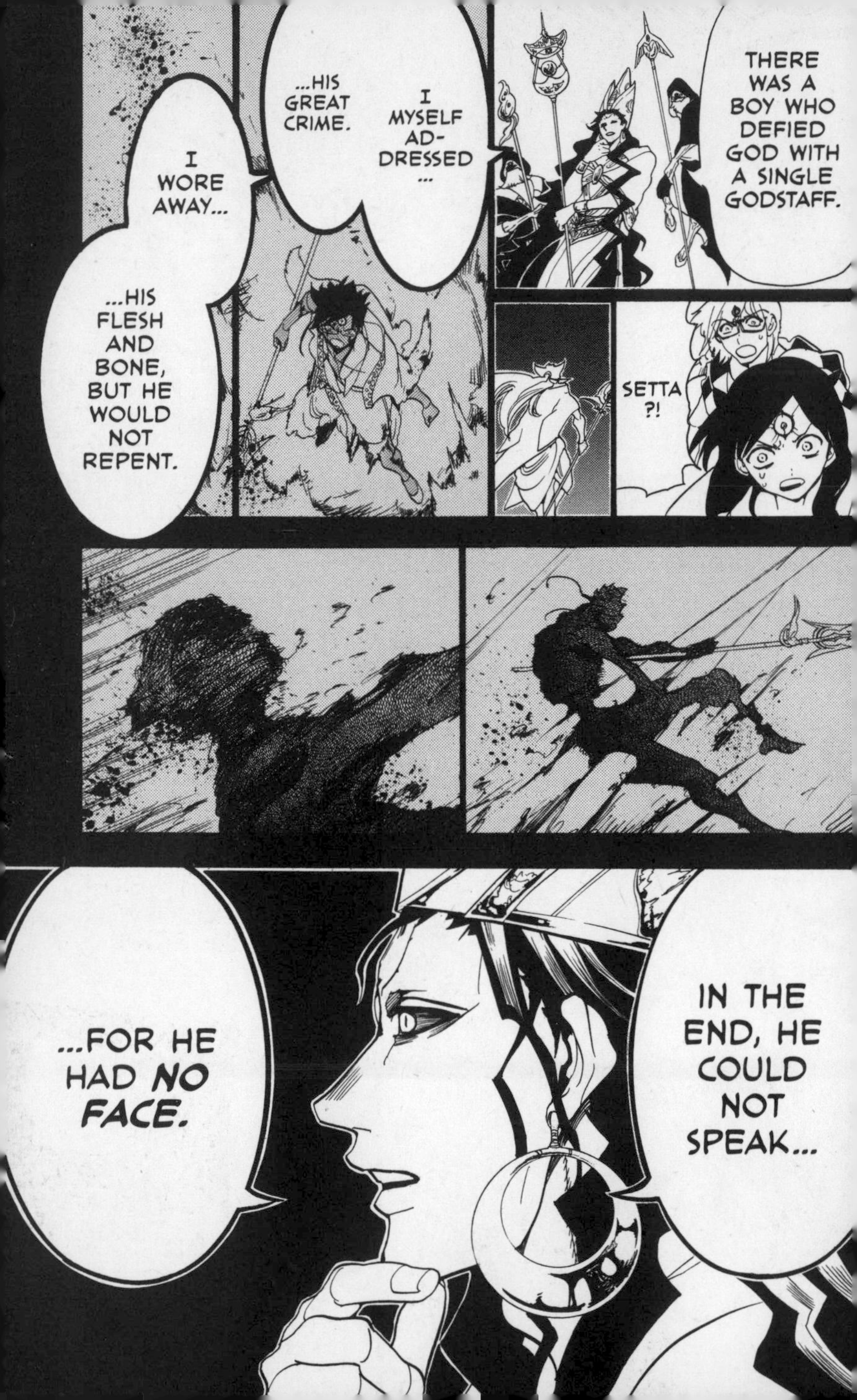
THERE WAS A BOY WHO DEFIED GOD WITH A SINGLE GODSTAFF.
SETTA?!
I MYSELF AD-DRESSED...
...HIS GREAT CRIME.
I WORE AWAY...
...HIS FLESH AND BONE, BUT HE WOULD NOT REPENT.
IN THE END, HE COULD NOT SPEAK...
...FOR HE HAD **NO** ***FACE.***

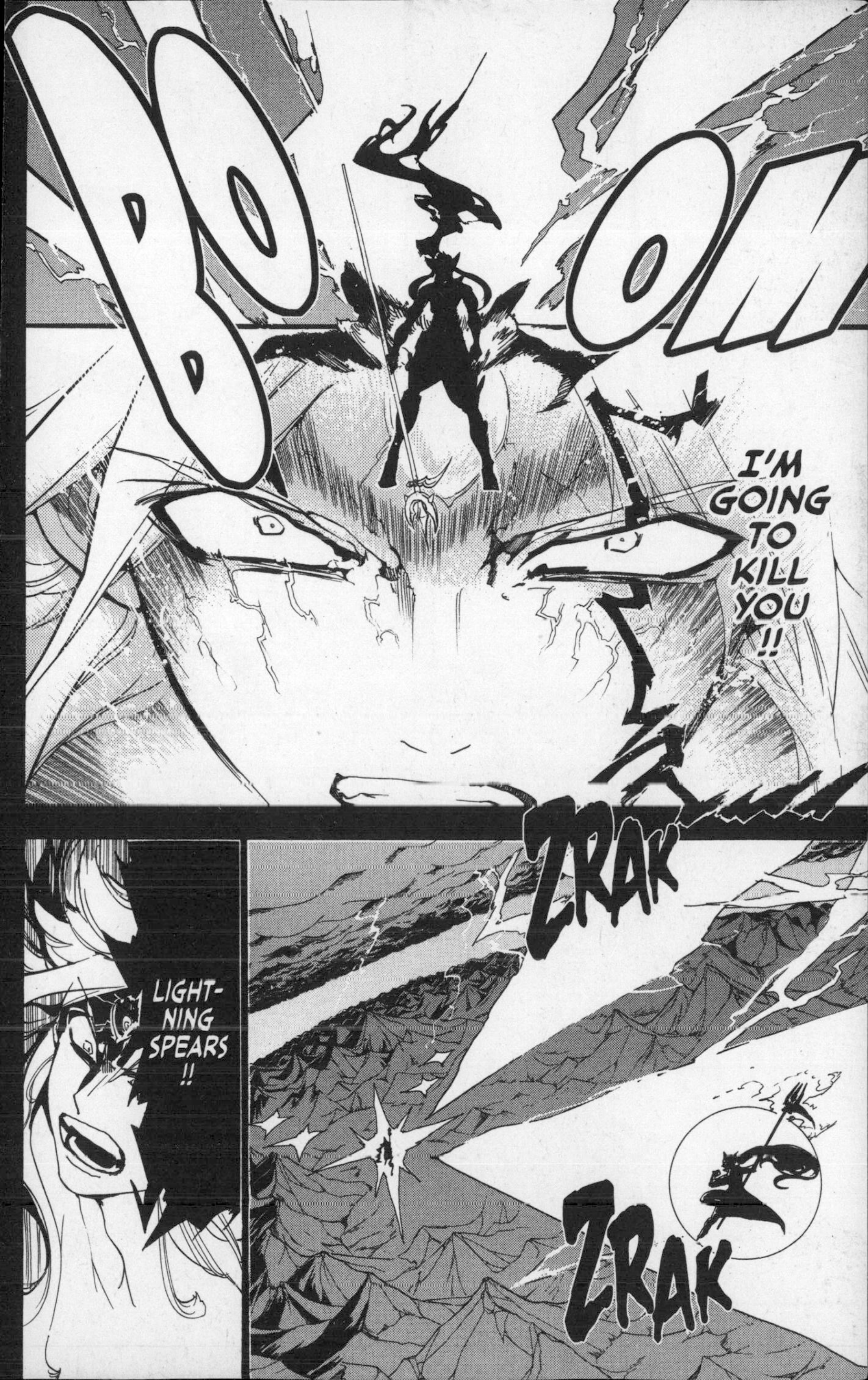
I'M GOING TO KILL YOU !!
ZRAK
ZRAK
LIGHT-NING SPEARS !!

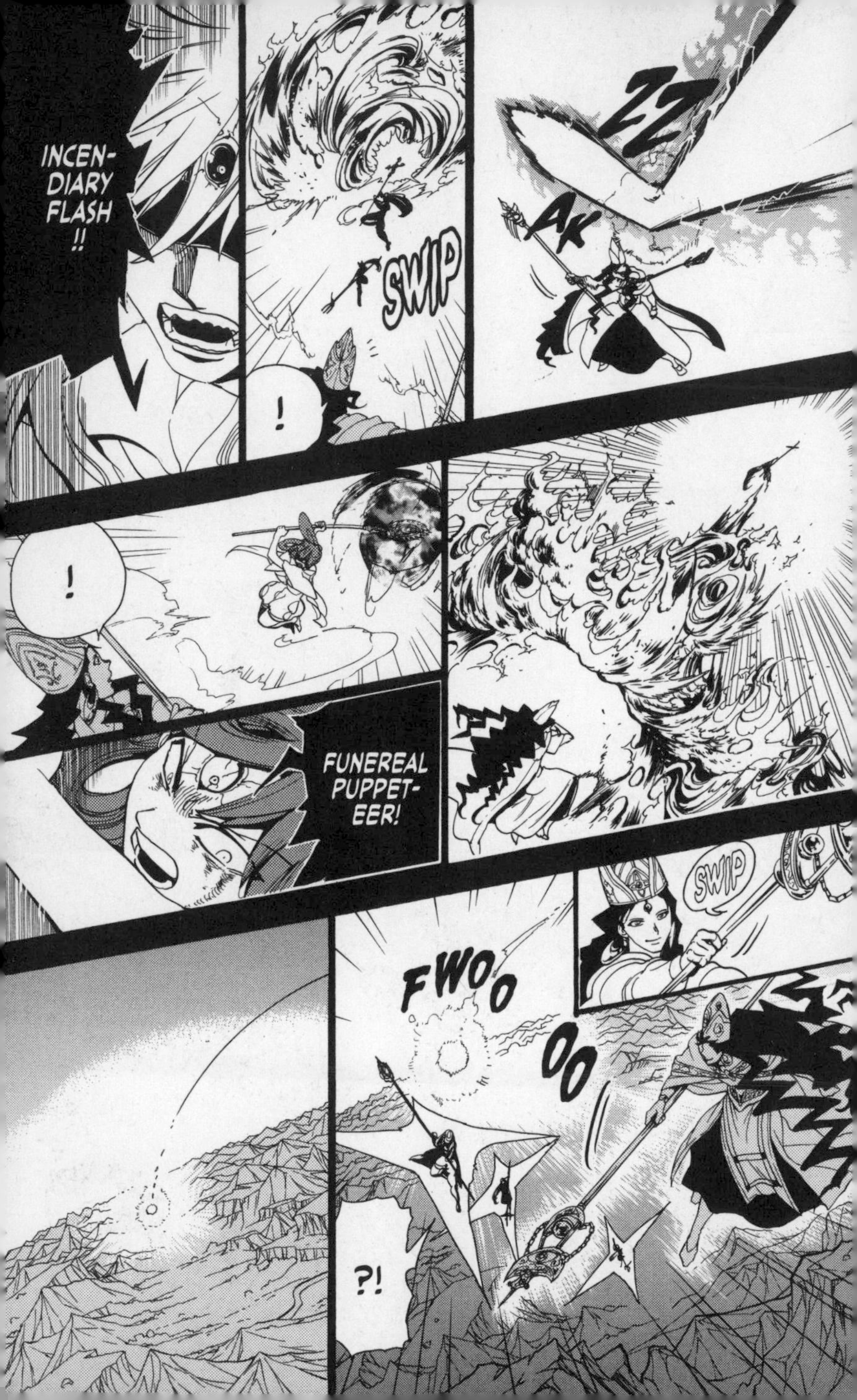
ZZ
AK
SWIP
!
INCEN-
DIARY
FLASH
!!
!
FUNEREAL
PUPPET-
EER!
SWIP
FWOO
OO
?!

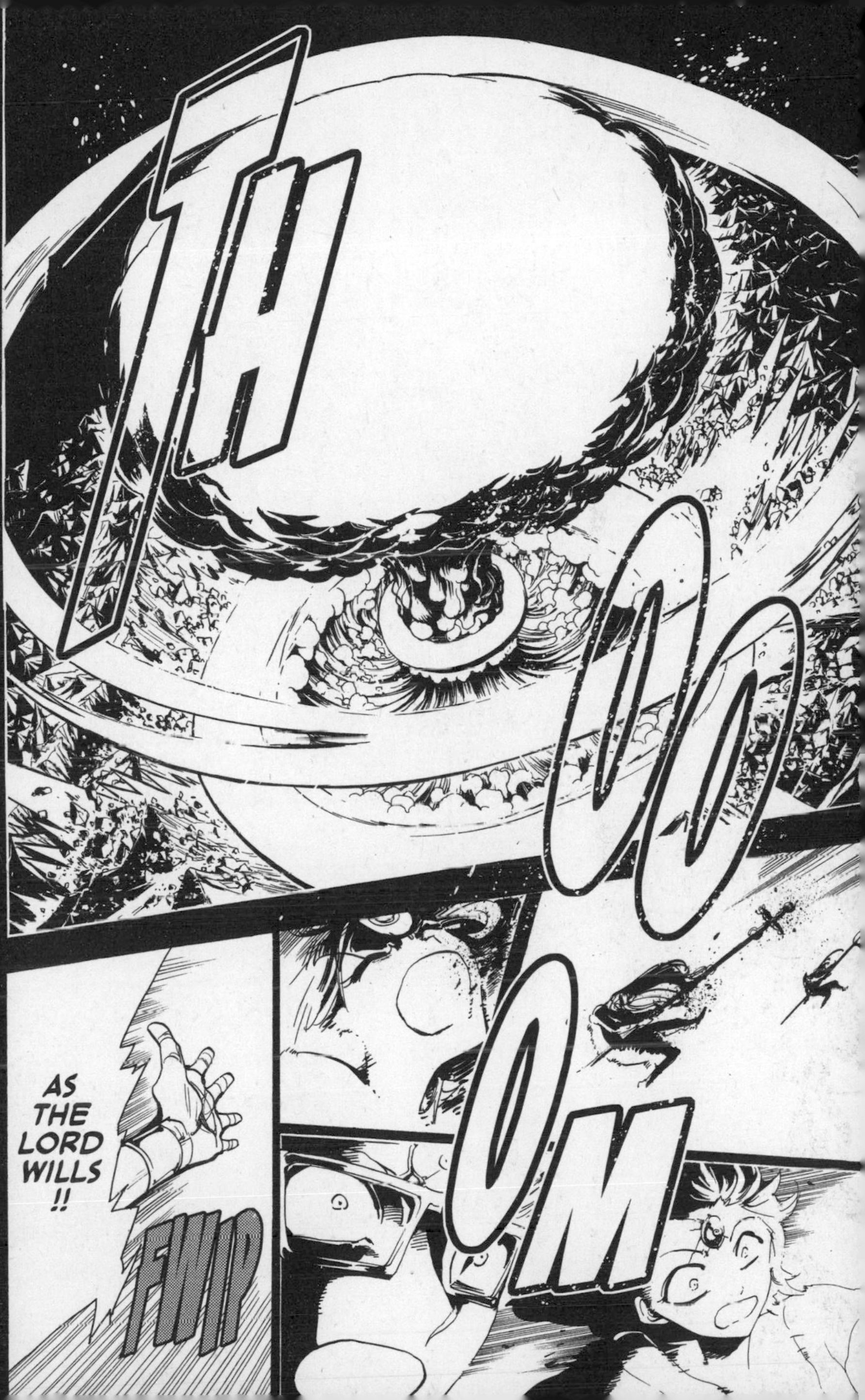
THOOOM
AS THE LORD WILLS!!
FWIP

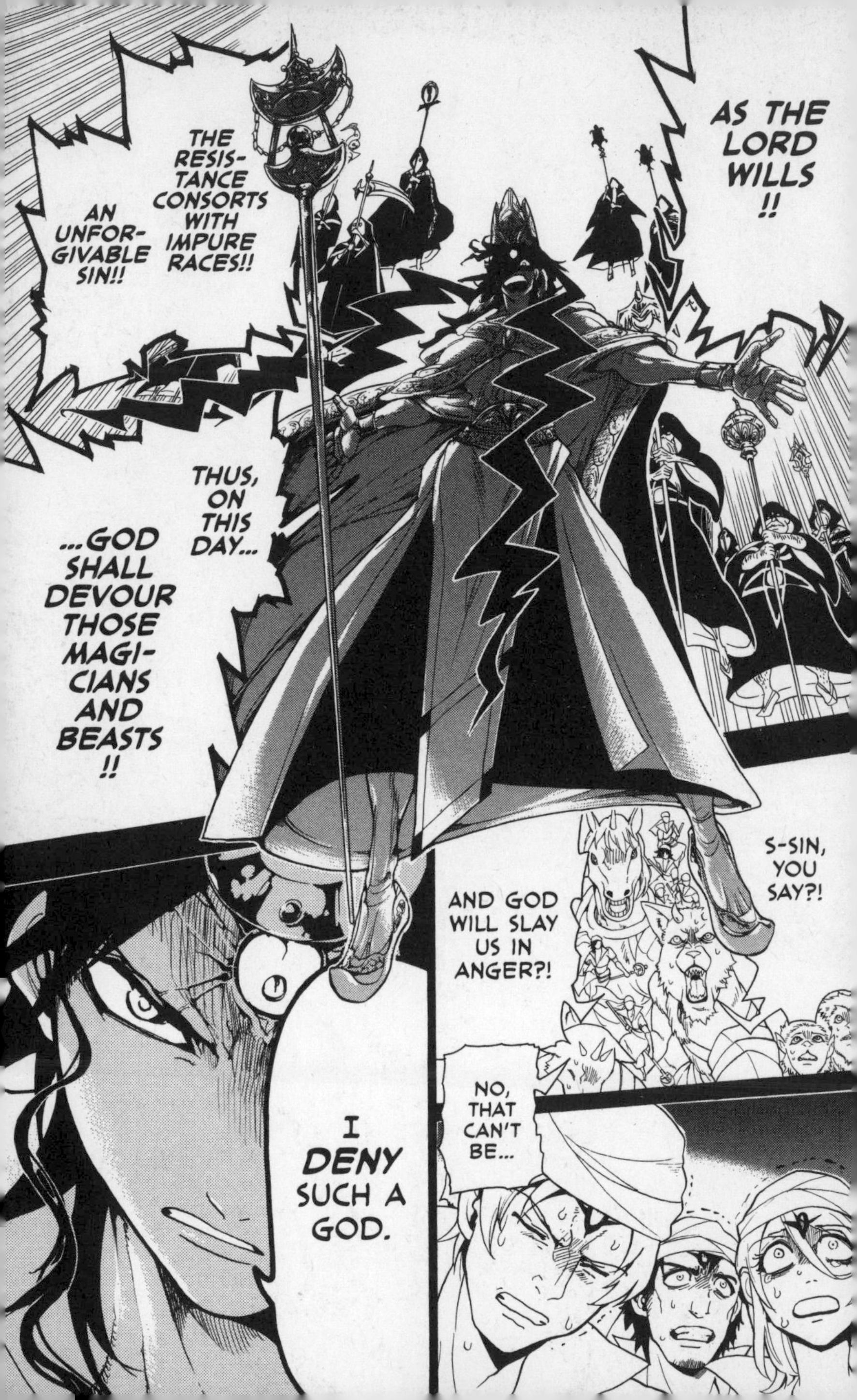
AS THE LORD WILLS!!
THE RESISTANCE CONSORTS WITH IMPURE RACES!!
AN UNFORGIVABLE SIN!!
THUS, ON THIS DAY...
...GOD SHALL DEVOUR THOSE MAGICIANS AND BEASTS!!
S-SIN, YOU SAY?!
AND GOD WILL SLAY US IN ANGER?!
NO, THAT CAN'T BE...
I DENY SUCH A GOD.

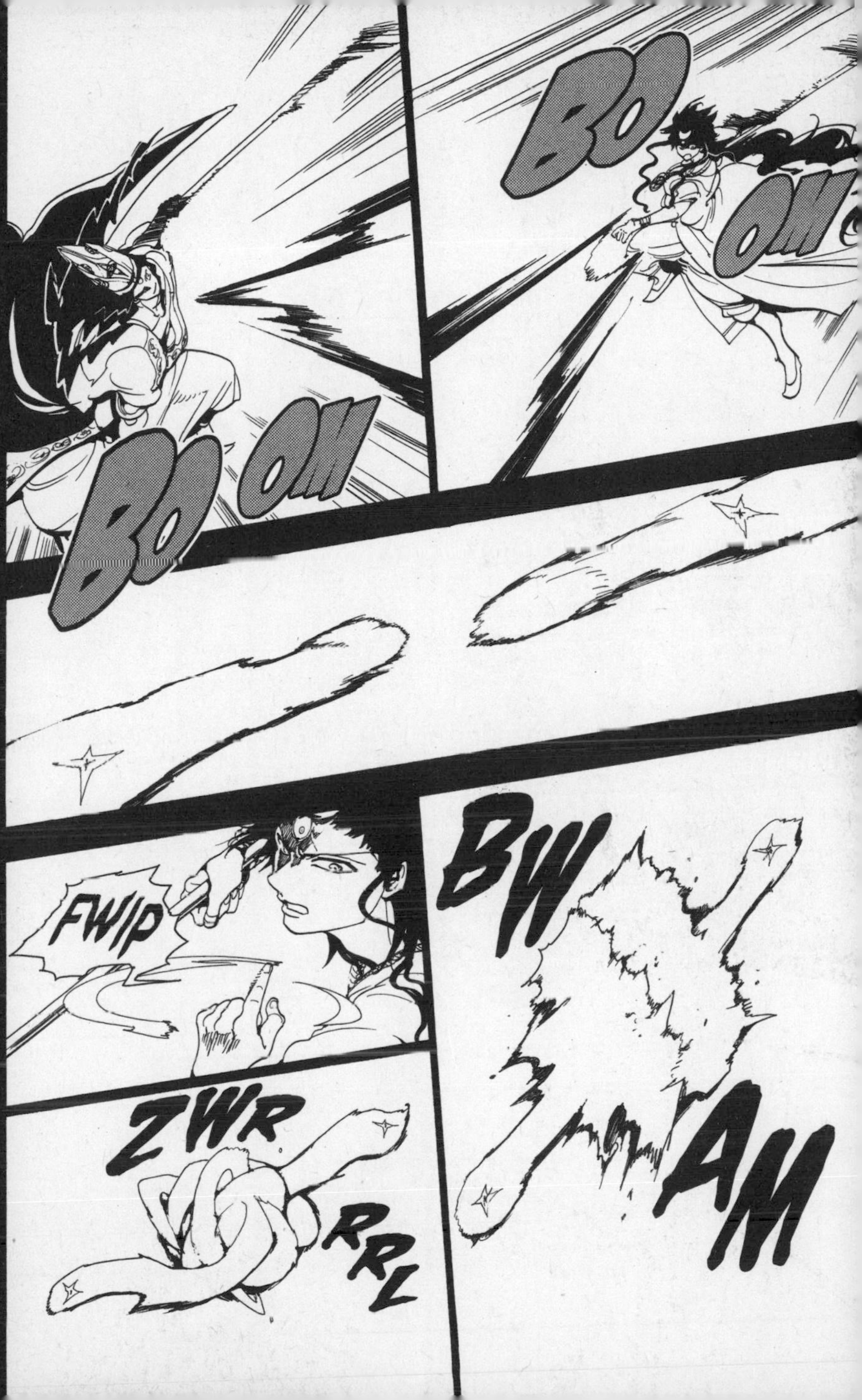
BOOM
BOOM
BWAM
FWIP
ZWRRRL

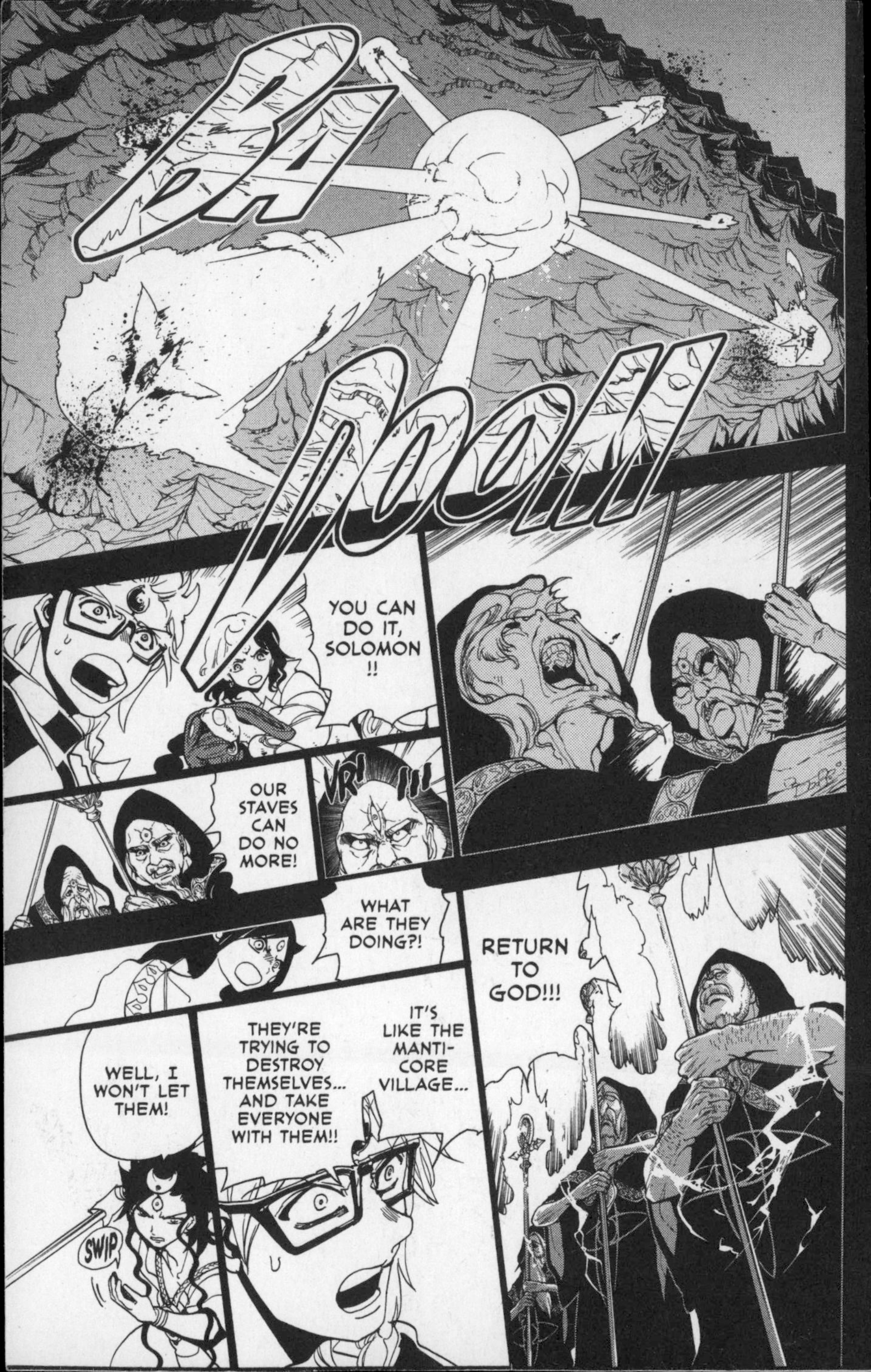
YOU CAN DO IT, SOLOMON!!
OUR STAVES CAN DO NO MORE!
RETURN TO GOD!!!
WHAT ARE THEY DOING?!
IT'S LIKE THE MANTI-CORE VILLAGE...
THEY'RE TRYING TO DESTROY THEMSELVES... AND TAKE EVERYONE WITH THEM!!
WELL, I WON'T LET THEM!
SWIP

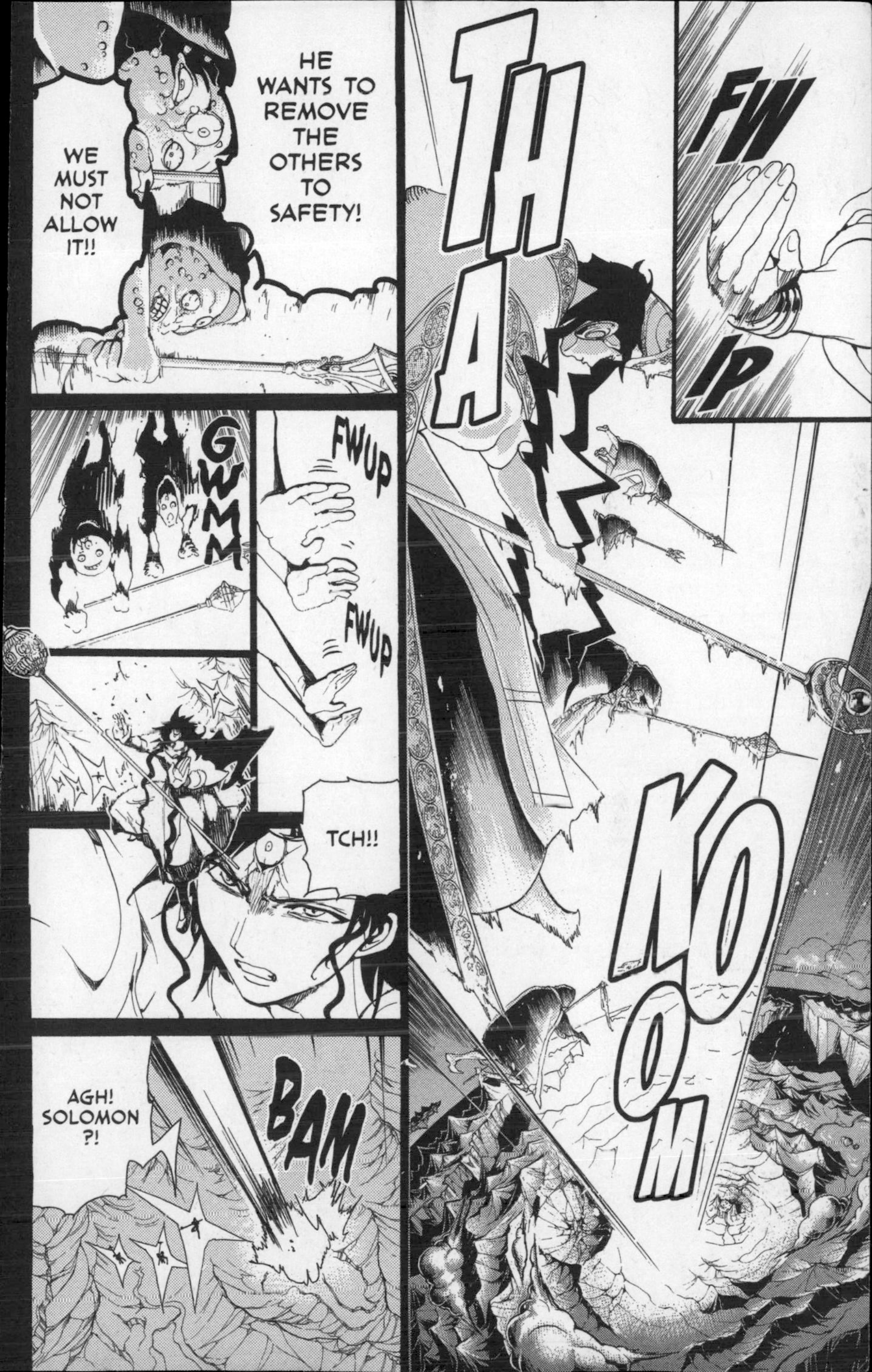
FWIP
THA
KOOOM
HE WANTS TO REMOVE THE OTHERS TO SAFETY!
WE MUST NOT ALLOW IT!!
FWUP
FWUP
GWMM
TCH!!
BAM
AGH! SOLOMON ?!

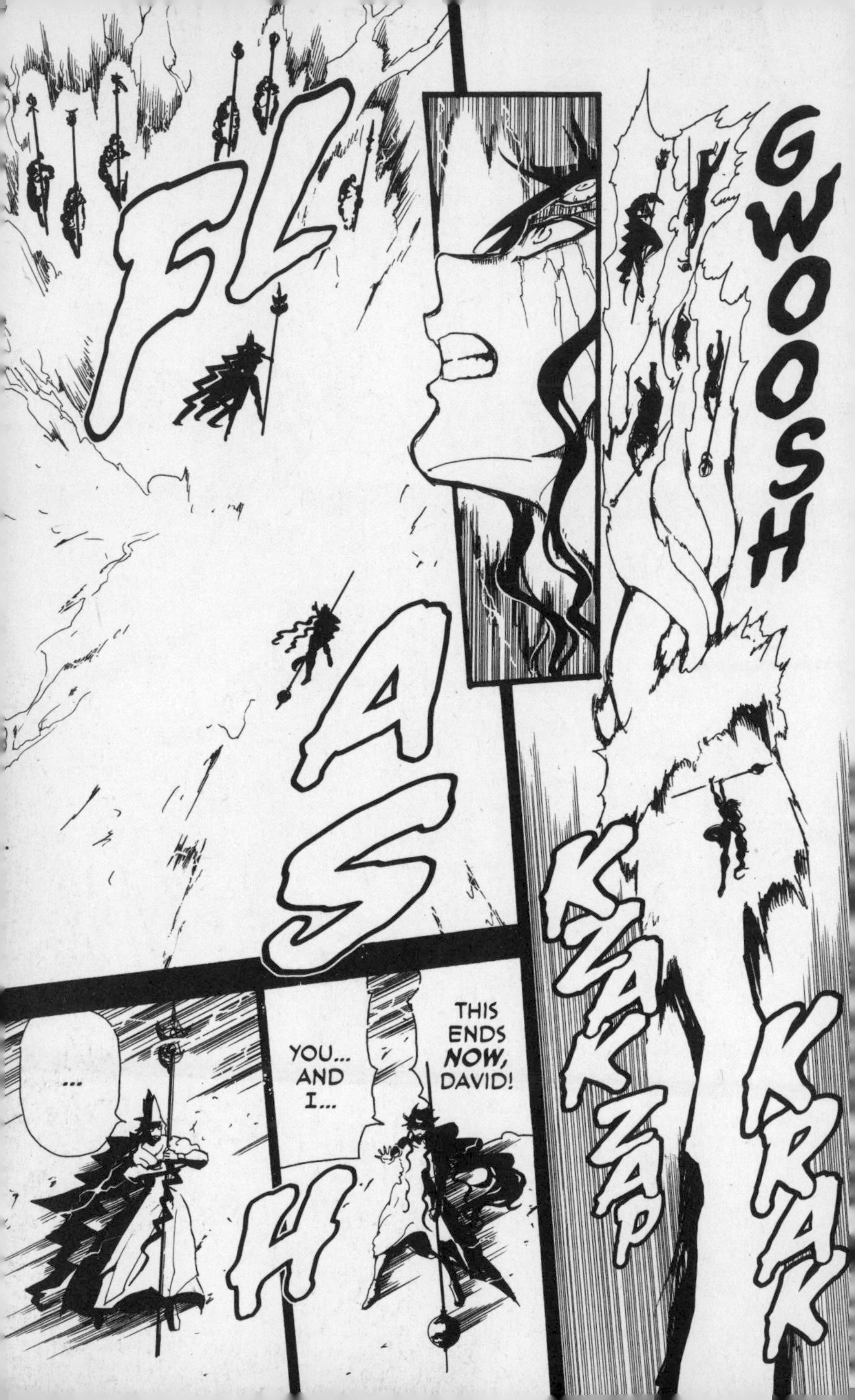
GWOOSH
KRAK
FLASH
THIS ENDS NOW, DAVID!
YOU... AND I...
...

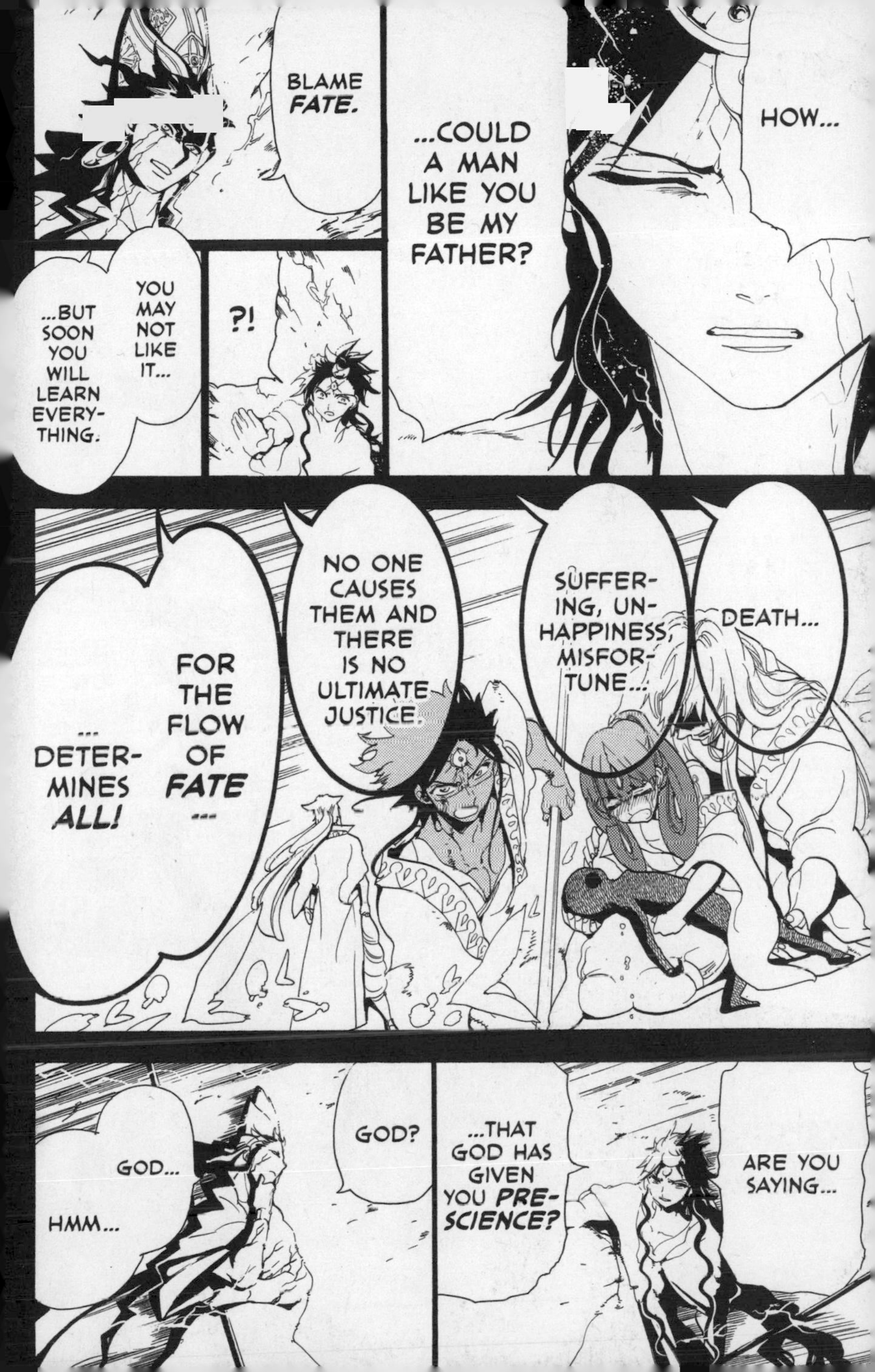
HOW...
...COULD A MAN LIKE YOU BE MY FATHER?
BLAME *FATE.*
?!
YOU MAY NOT LIKE IT...
...BUT SOON YOU WILL LEARN EVERYTHING.
DEATH...
SUFFERING, UNHAPPINESS, MISFORTUNE...
NO ONE CAUSES THEM AND THERE IS NO ULTIMATE JUSTICE.
FOR THE FLOW OF *FATE* ---
--- DETERMINES *ALL!*
ARE YOU SAYING...
...THAT GOD HAS GIVEN YOU *PRESCIENCE?*
GOD?
GOD...
HMM...

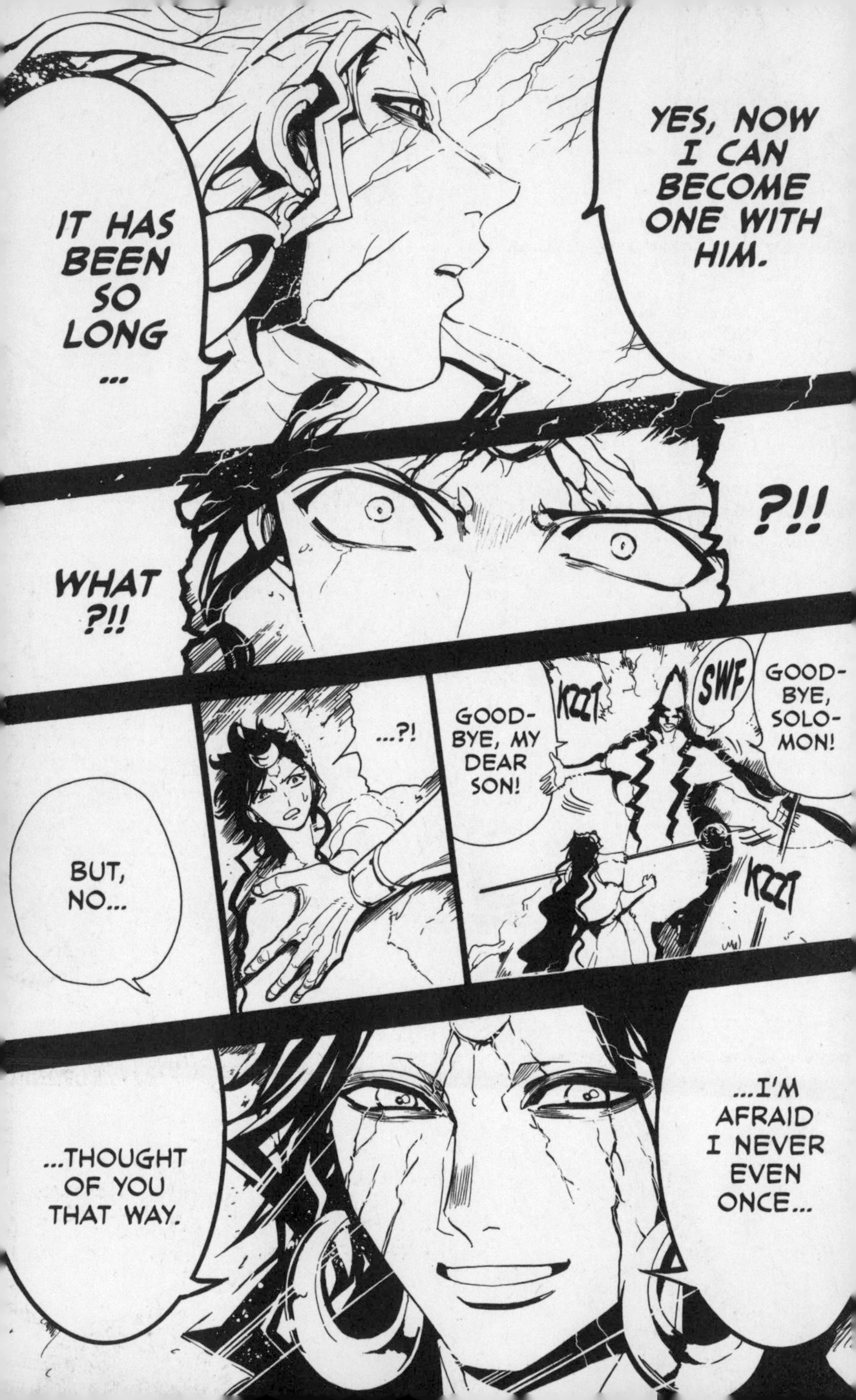
YES, NOW I CAN BECOME ONE WITH HIM.
IT HAS BEEN SO LONG...
?!!
WHAT ?!!
GOOD-BYE, SOLOMON!
SWF
KZZT
GOOD-BYE, MY DEAR SON!
KZZT
...?!
BUT, NO...
...I'M AFRAID I NEVER EVEN ONCE...
...THOUGHT OF YOU THAT WAY.

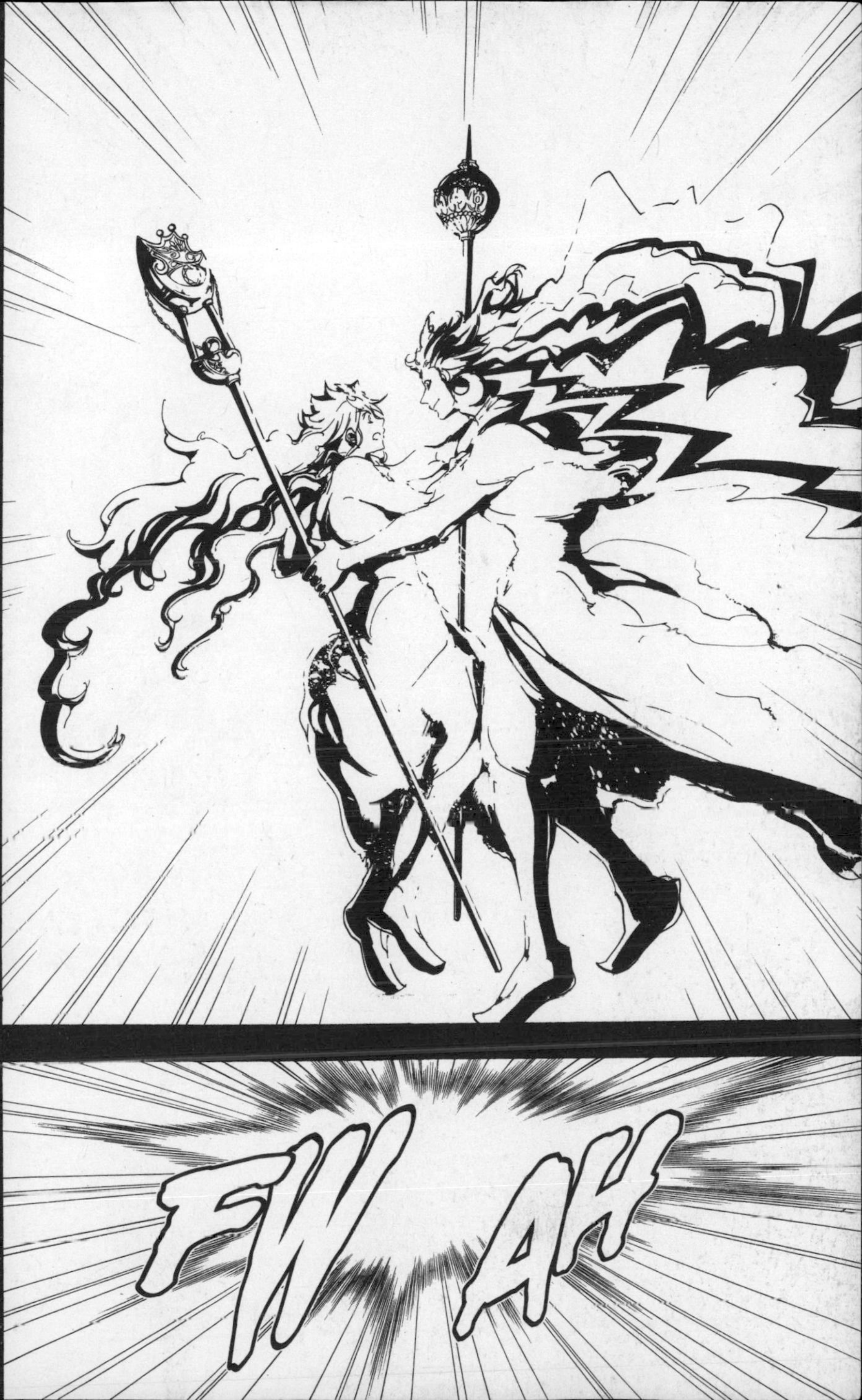
FWAH

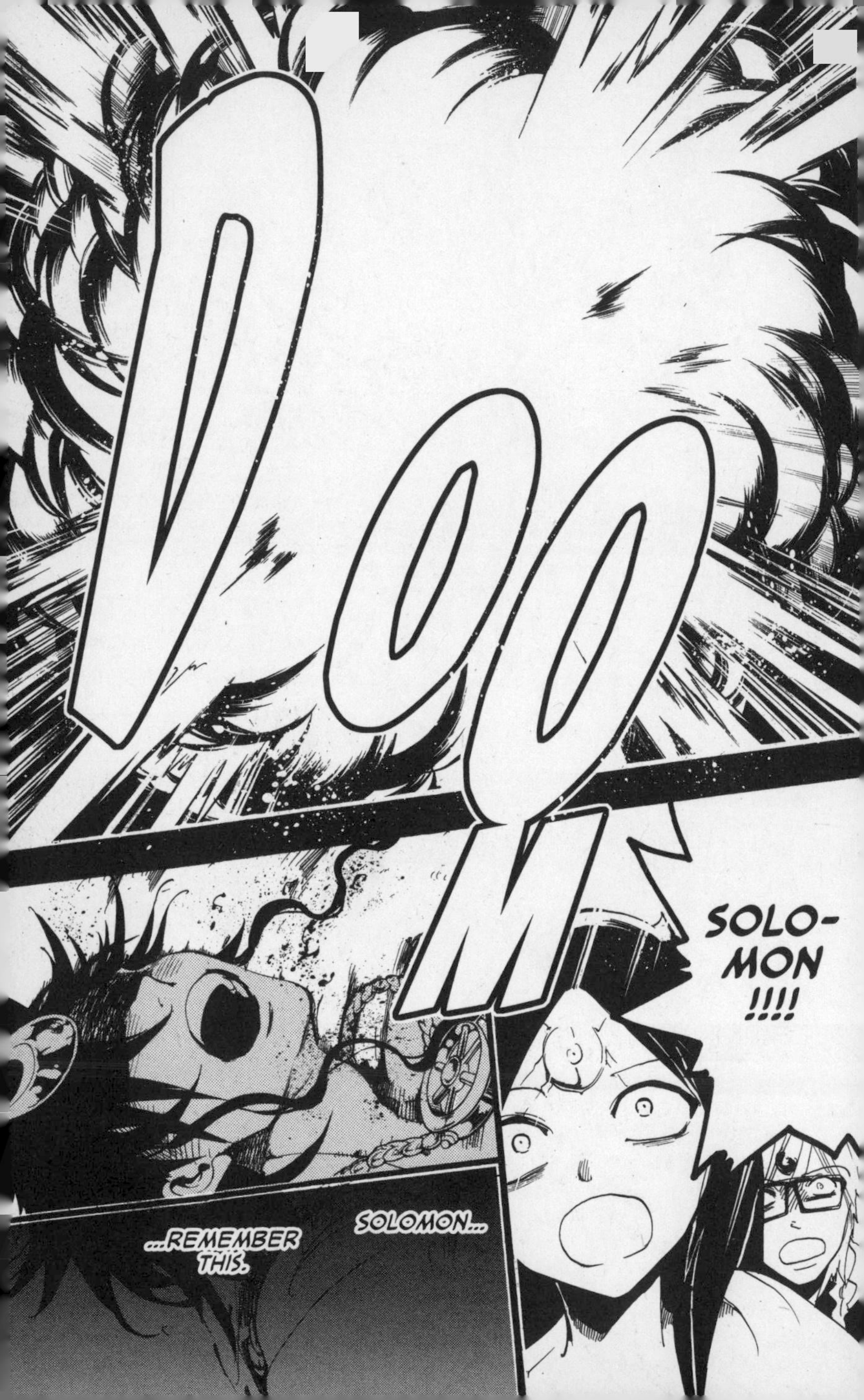
DOOM
SOLO-MON!!!!
SOLOMON...
...REMEMBER THIS.

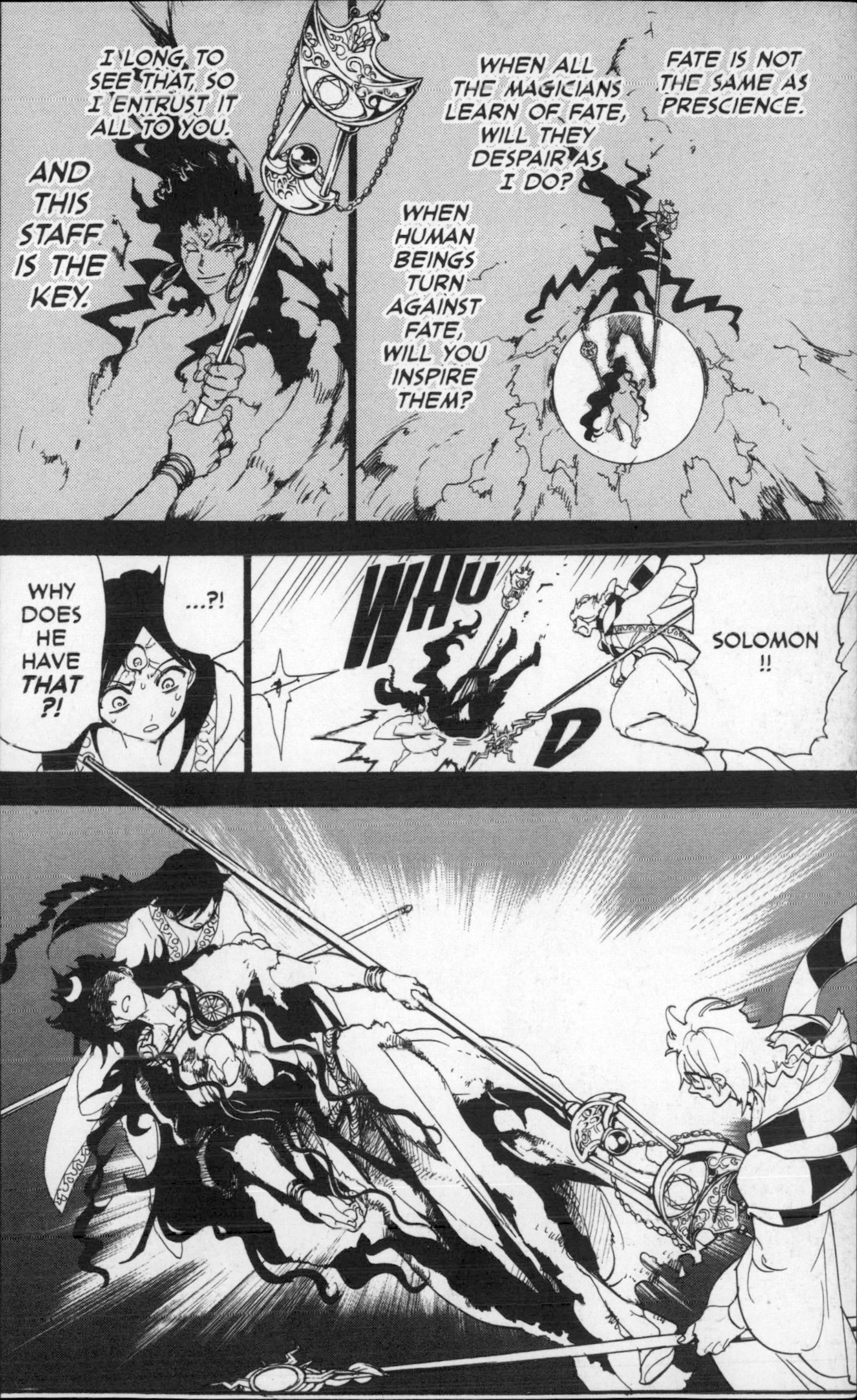

FATE IS NOT THE SAME AS PRESCIENCE.
WHEN ALL THE MAGICIANS LEARN OF FATE, WILL THEY DESPAIR AS I DO?
WHEN HUMAN BEINGS TURN AGAINST FATE, WILL YOU INSPIRE THEM?
I LONG TO SEE THAT, SO I ENTRUST IT ALL TO YOU.
AND THIS STAFF IS THE KEY.
SOLOMON !!
WHUD
...?!
WHY DOES HE HAVE *THAT* ?!

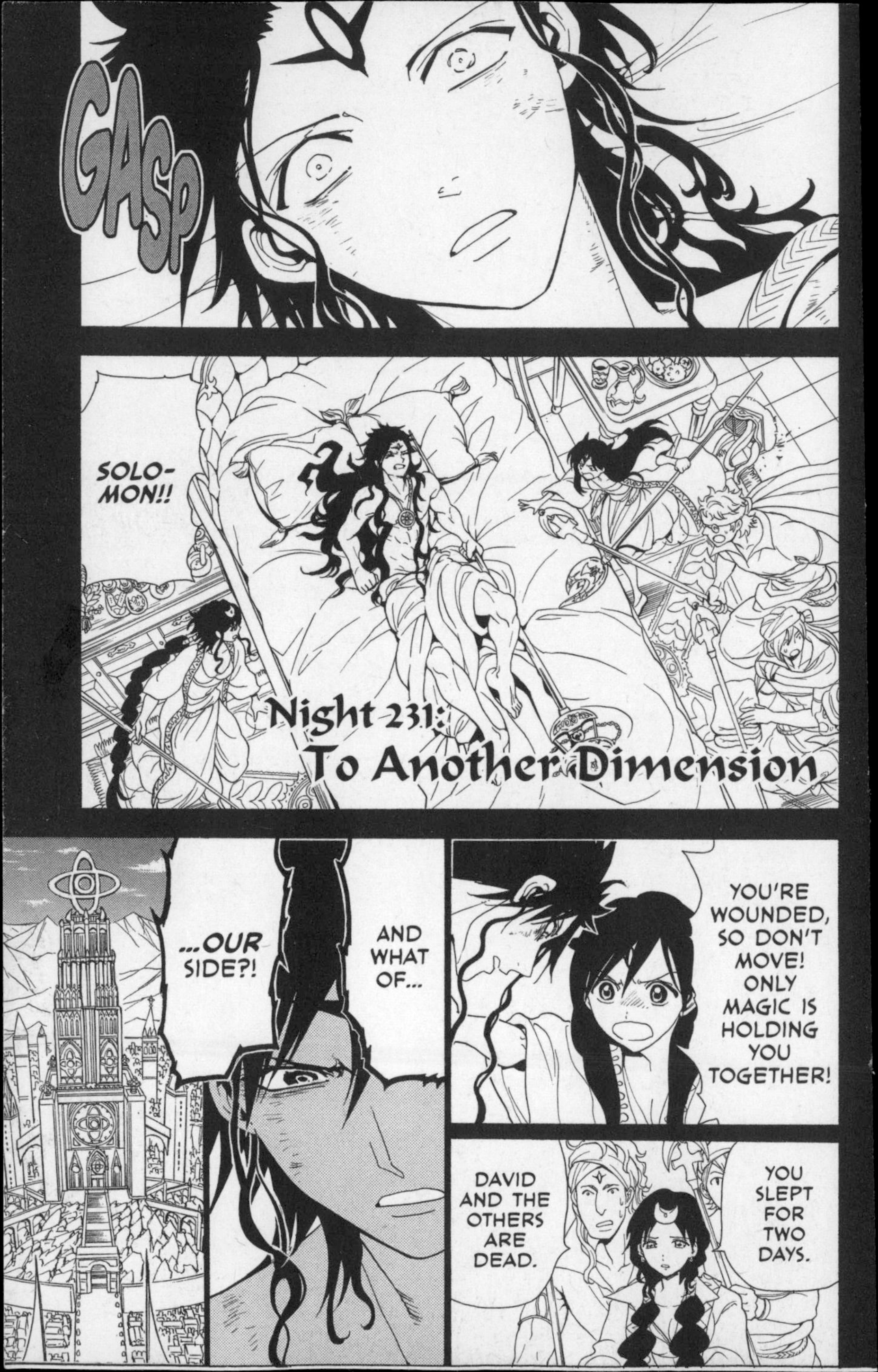
GASP
SOLO-MON!!
Night 231: To Another Dimension
YOU'RE WOUNDED, SO DON'T MOVE! ONLY MAGIC IS HOLDING YOU TOGETHER!
YOU SLEPT FOR TWO DAYS.
DAVID AND THE OTHERS ARE DEAD.
AND WHAT OF...
...OUR SIDE?!

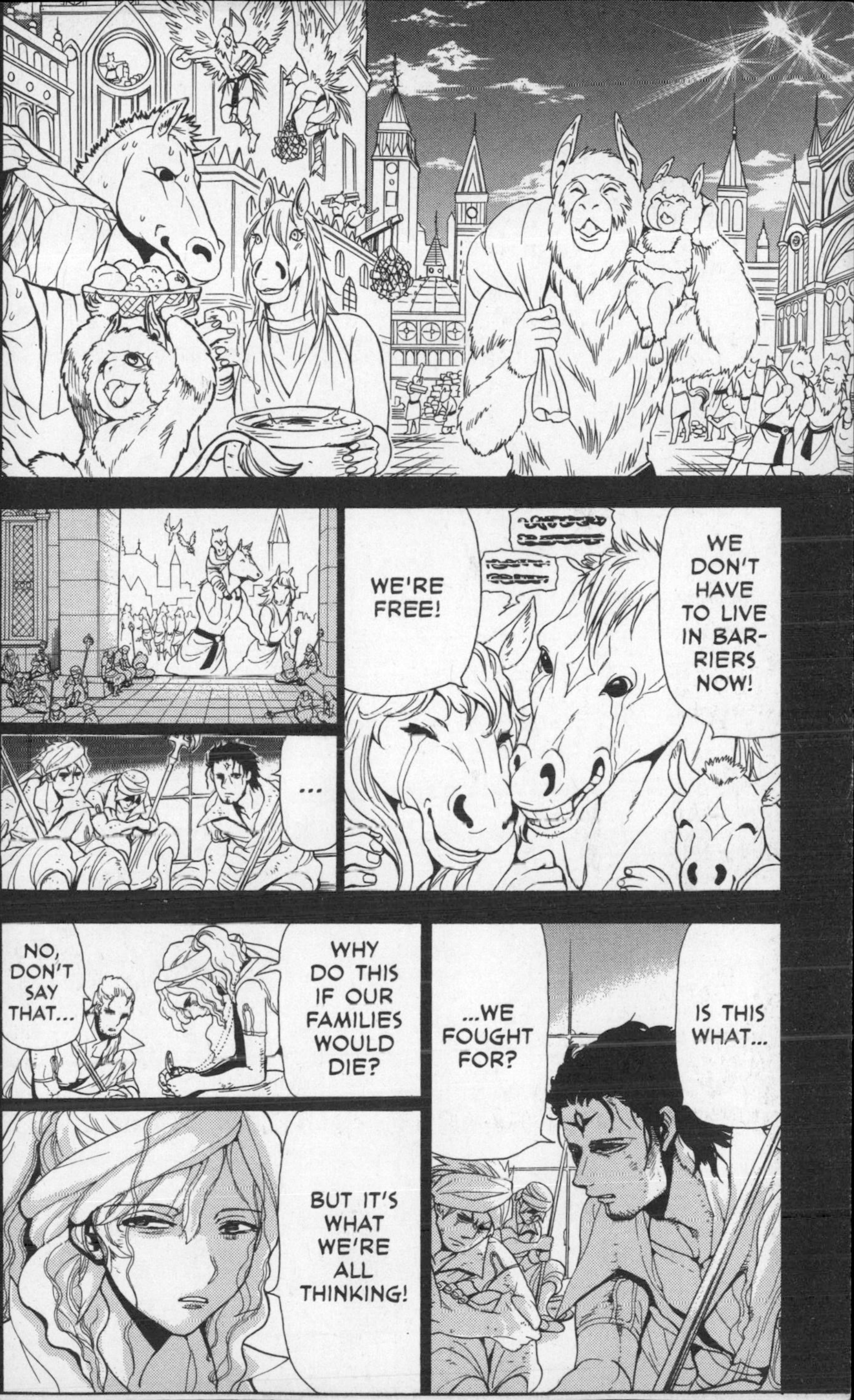
WE DON'T HAVE TO LIVE IN BARRIERS NOW!
WE'RE FREE!
...
IS THIS WHAT...
...WE FOUGHT FOR?
WHY DO THIS IF OUR FAMILIES WOULD DIE?
NO, DON'T SAY THAT...
BUT IT'S WHAT WE'RE ALL THINKING!

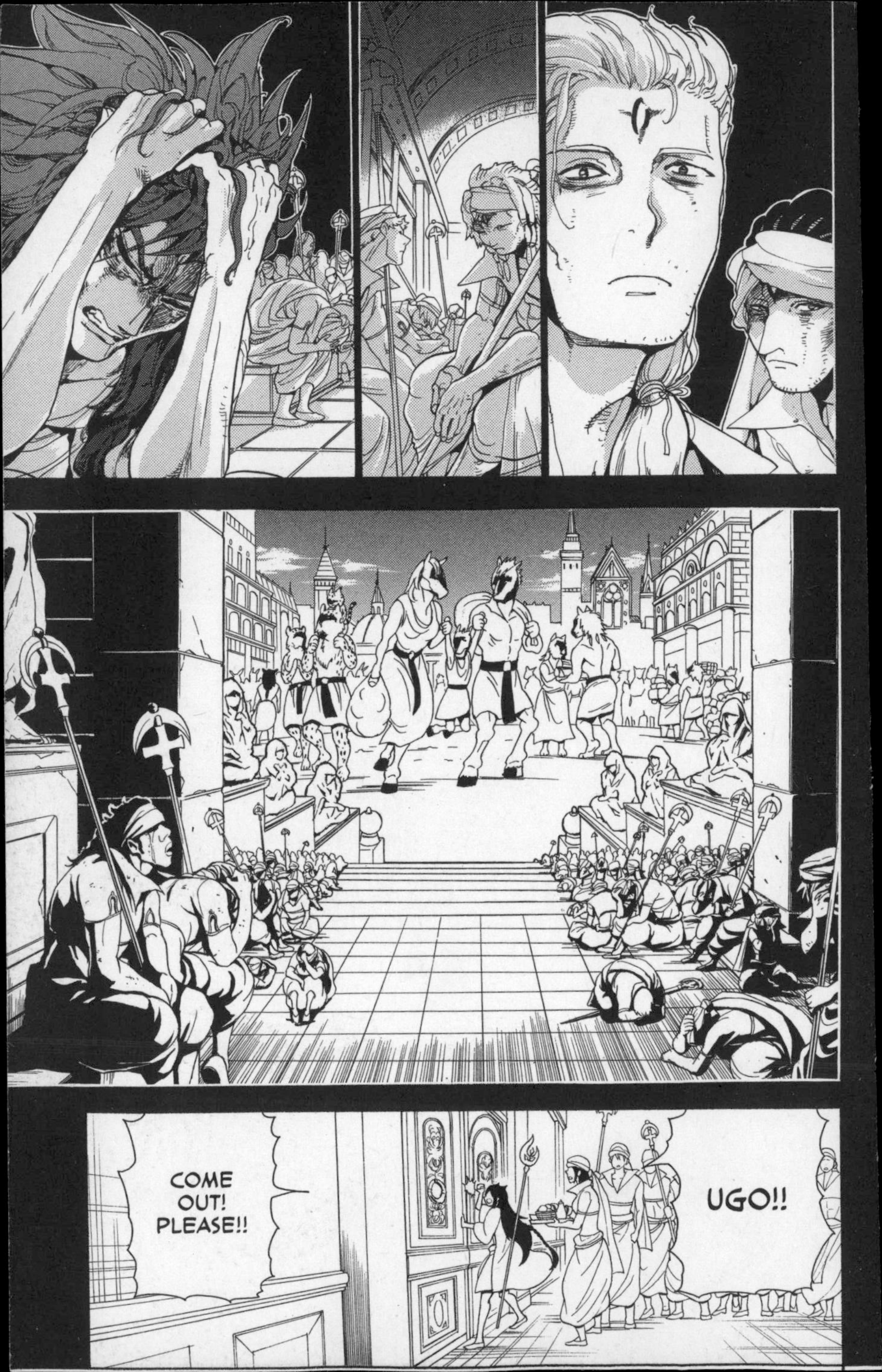
UGO!!
COME OUT! PLEASE!!

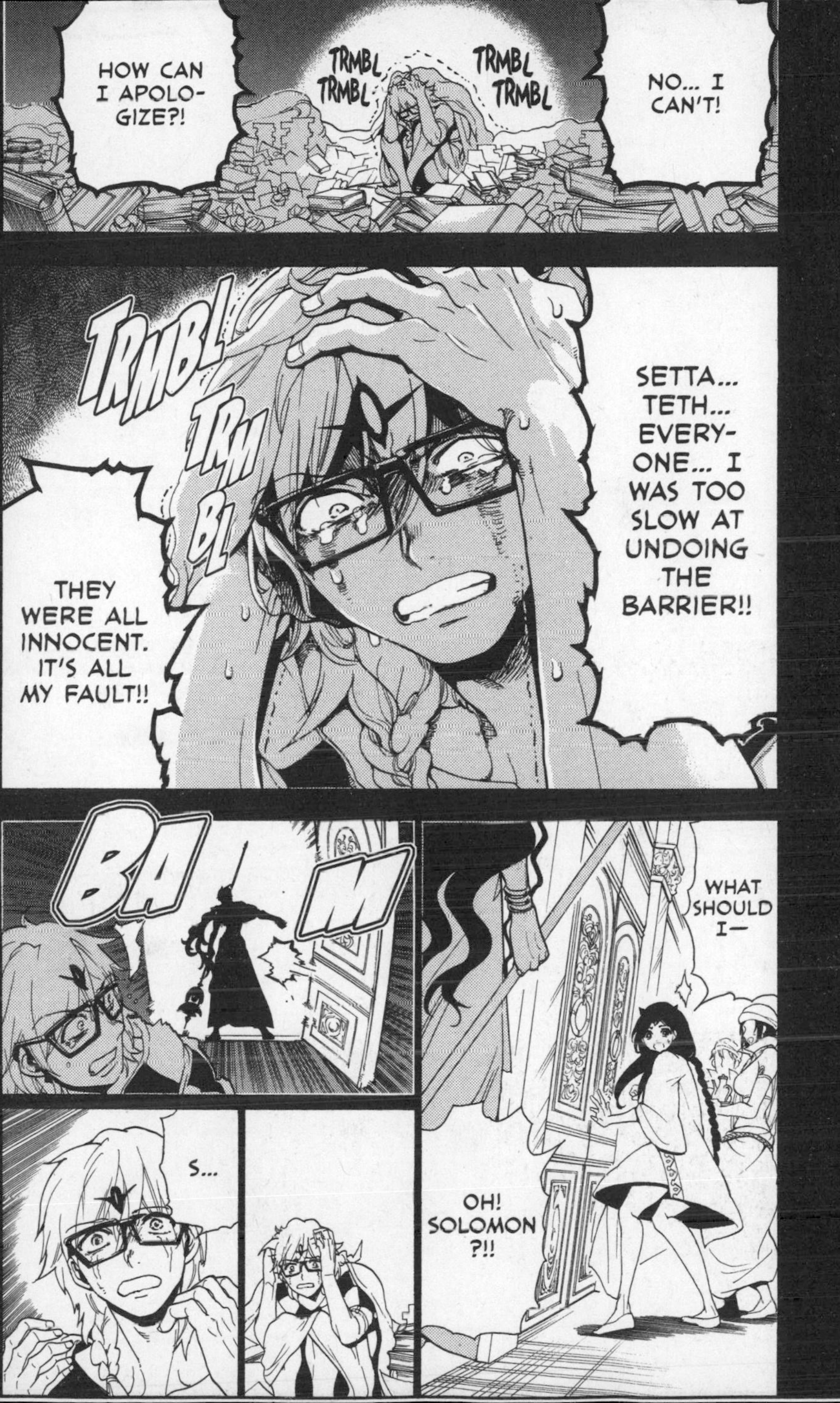
NO... I CAN'T!
TRMBL TRMBL
TRMBL TRMBL
HOW CAN I APOLOGIZE?!
SETTA... TETH... EVERYONE... I WAS TOO SLOW AT UNDOING THE BARRIER!!
TRMBL TRM BL
THEY WERE ALL INNOCENT. IT'S ALL MY FAULT!!
WHAT SHOULD I—
OH! SOLOMON ?!!
BAM
S...

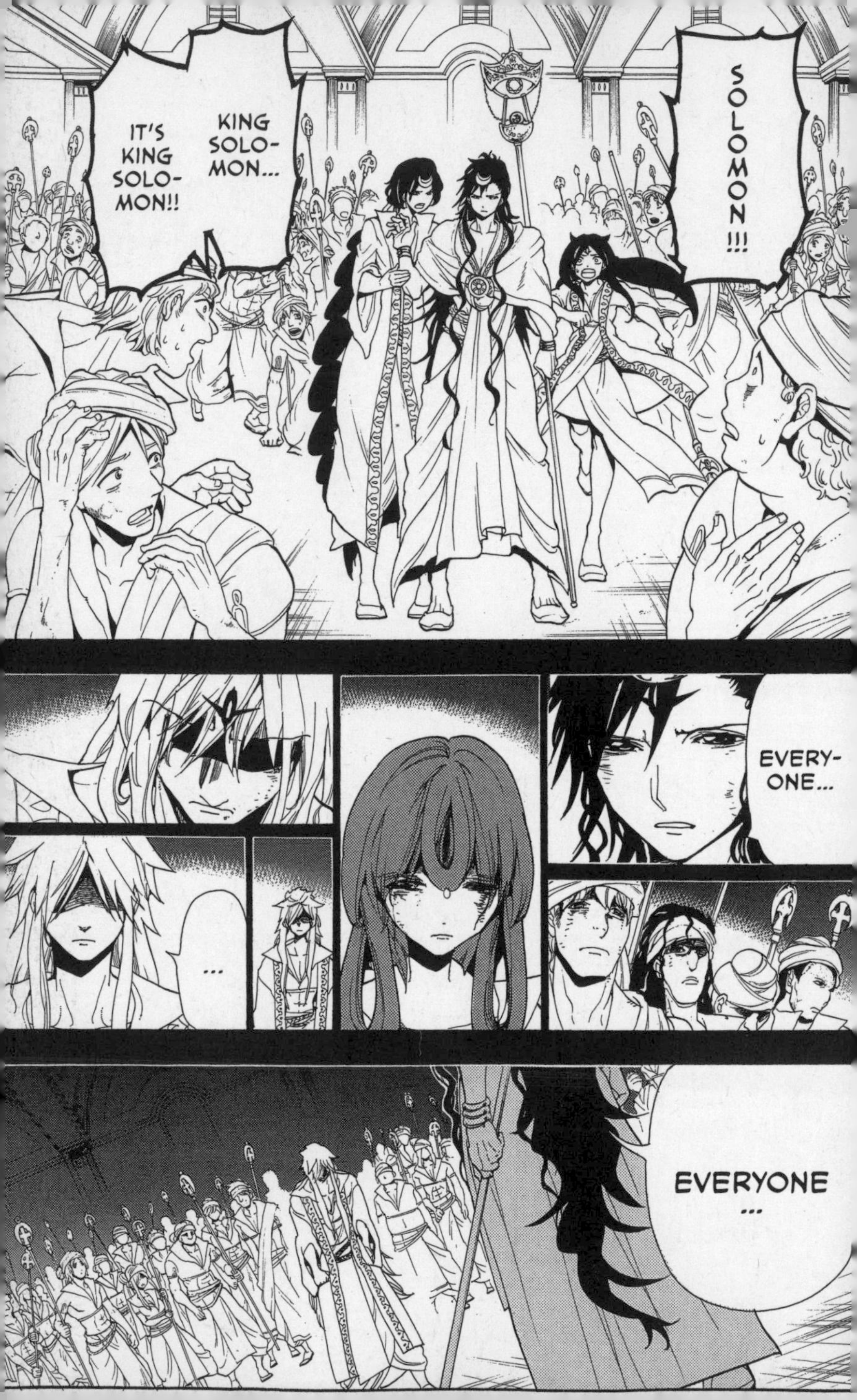
SOLOMON!!!
KING SOLO-MON...
IT'S KING SOLO-MON!!
EVERY-ONE...
...
EVERYONE ...

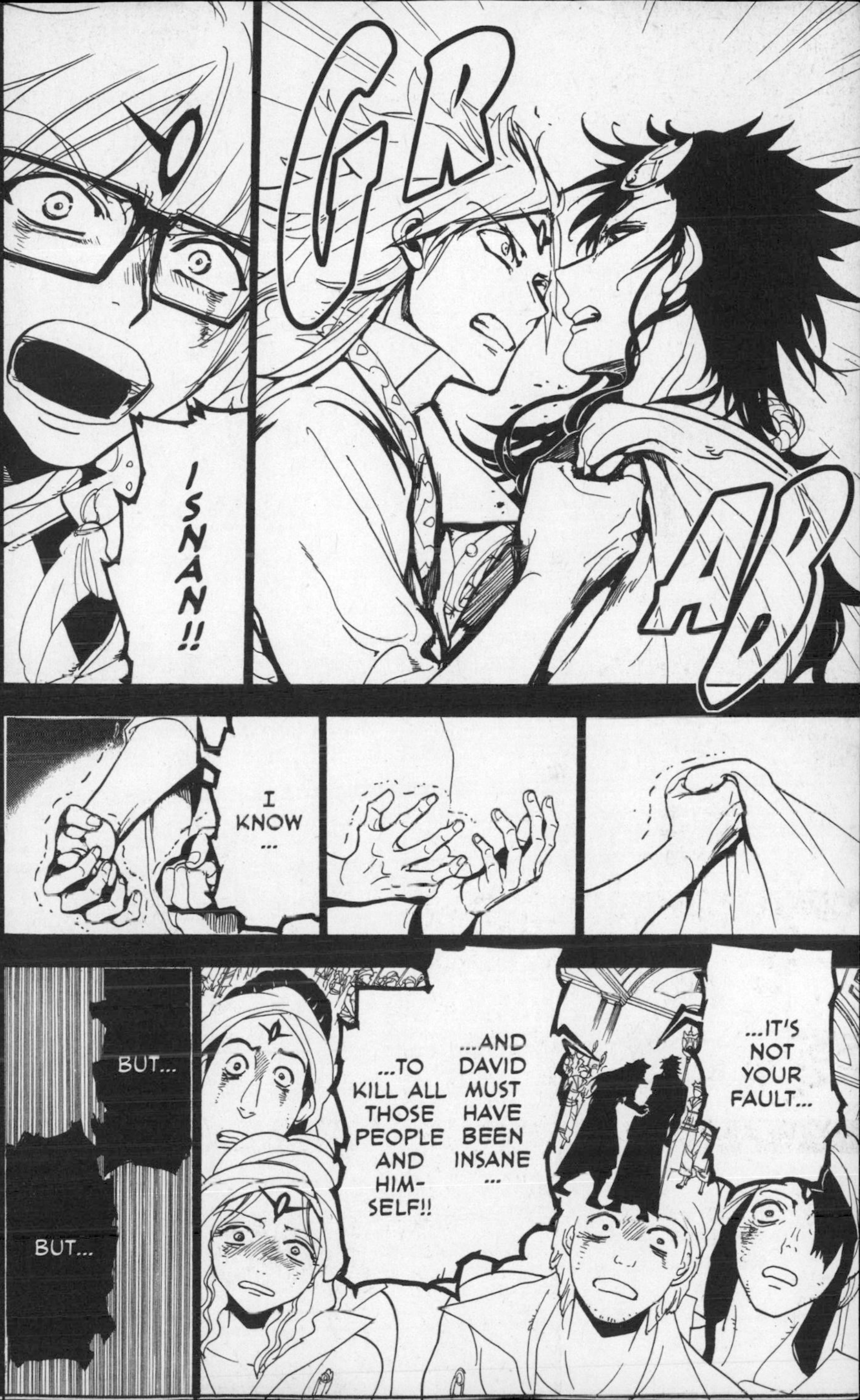
GR
AB
ISNAN!!
I KNOW...
...IT'S NOT YOUR FAULT...
...AND DAVID MUST HAVE BEEN INSANE...
...TO KILL ALL THOSE PEOPLE AND HIMSELF!!
BUT...
BUT...

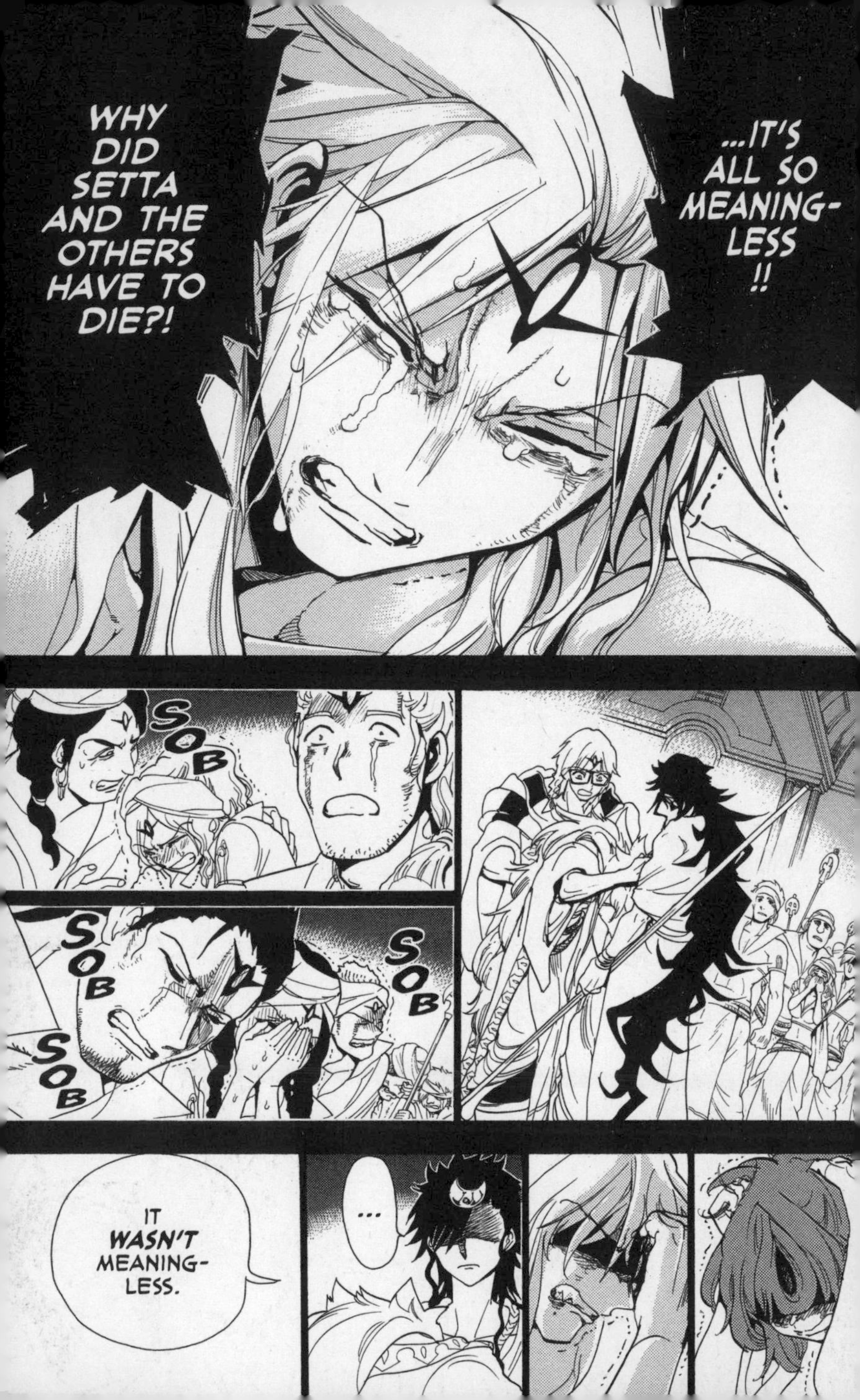
...IT'S ALL SO MEANING-LESS!!
WHY DID SETTA AND THE OTHERS HAVE TO DIE?!
SOB
SOB
SOB
SOB
...
IT WASN'T MEANING-LESS.

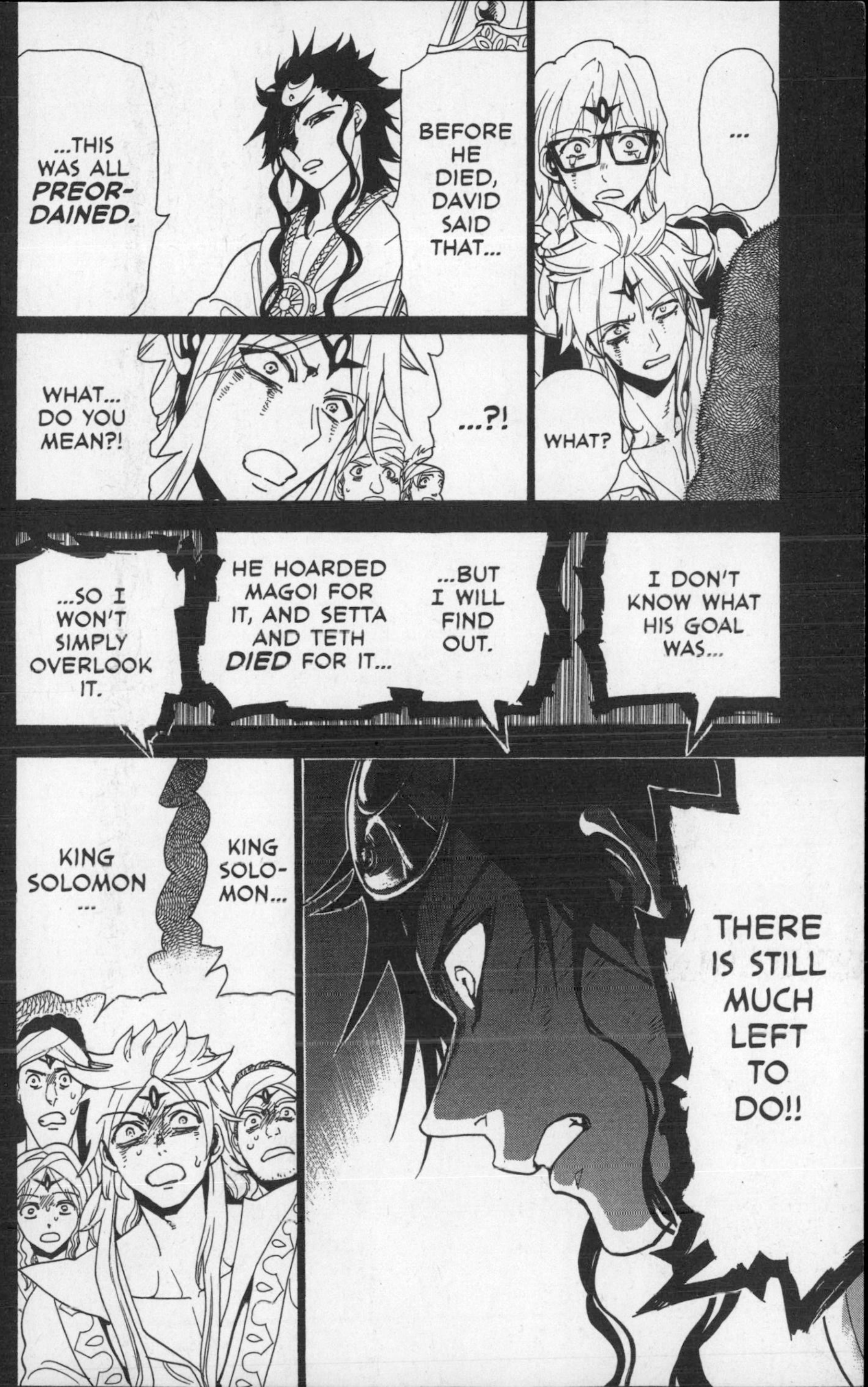
...
WHAT?
BEFORE HE DIED, DAVID SAID THAT...
...THIS WAS ALL PREORDAINED.
...?!
WHAT... DO YOU MEAN?!
I DON'T KNOW WHAT HIS GOAL WAS...
...BUT I WILL FIND OUT.
HE HOARDED MAGOI FOR IT, AND SETTA AND TETH DIED FOR IT...
...SO I WON'T SIMPLY OVERLOOK IT.
THERE IS STILL MUCH LEFT TO DO!!
KING SOLOMON...
KING SOLOMON...

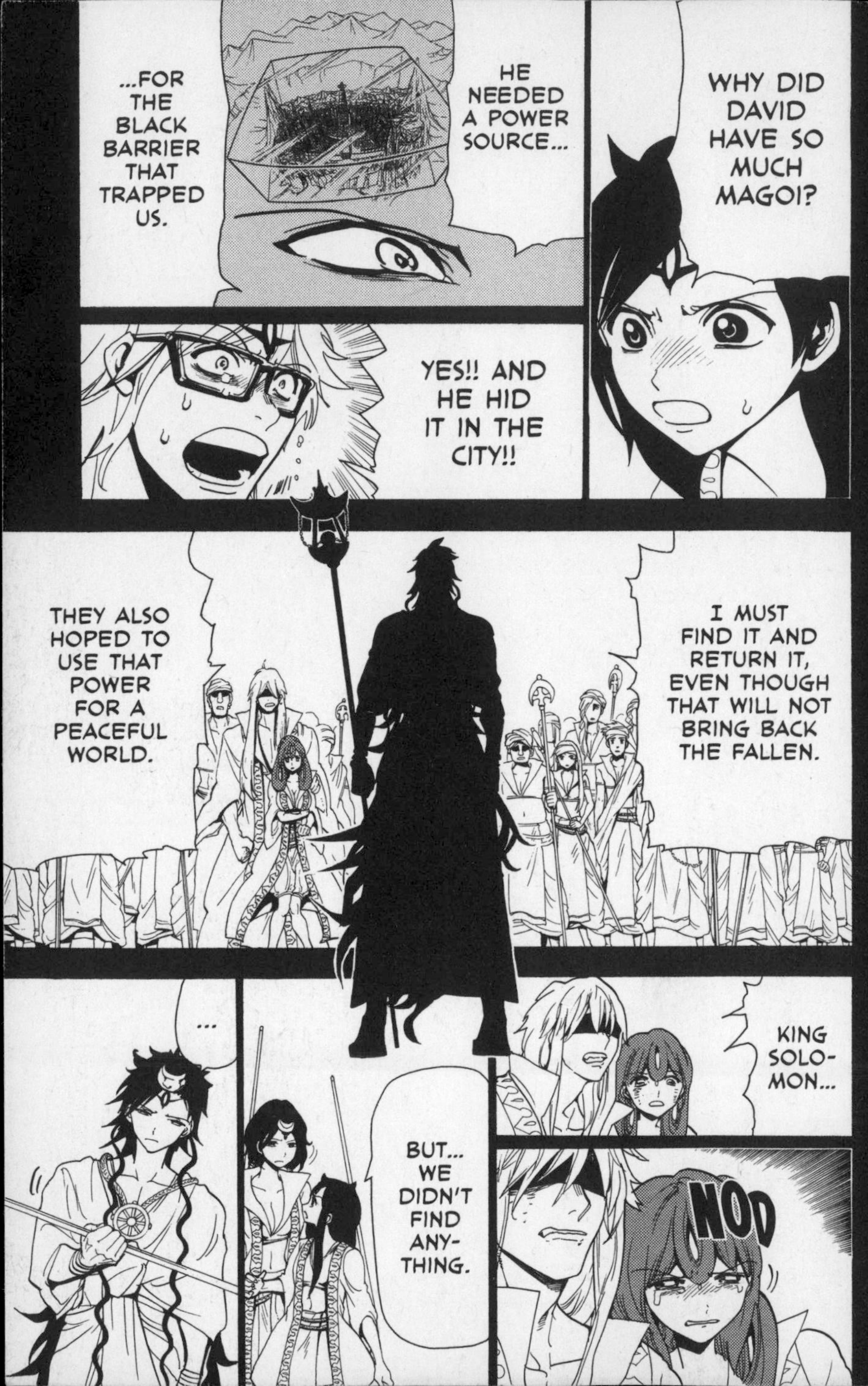
WHY DID DAVID HAVE SO MUCH MAGOI?
HE NEEDED A POWER SOURCE...
...FOR THE BLACK BARRIER THAT TRAPPED US.
YES!! AND HE HID IT IN THE CITY!!
I MUST FIND IT AND RETURN IT, EVEN THOUGH THAT WILL NOT BRING BACK THE FALLEN.
THEY ALSO HOPED TO USE THAT POWER FOR A PEACEFUL WORLD.
KING SOLOMON...
NOD
BUT... WE DIDN'T FIND ANYTHING.
...

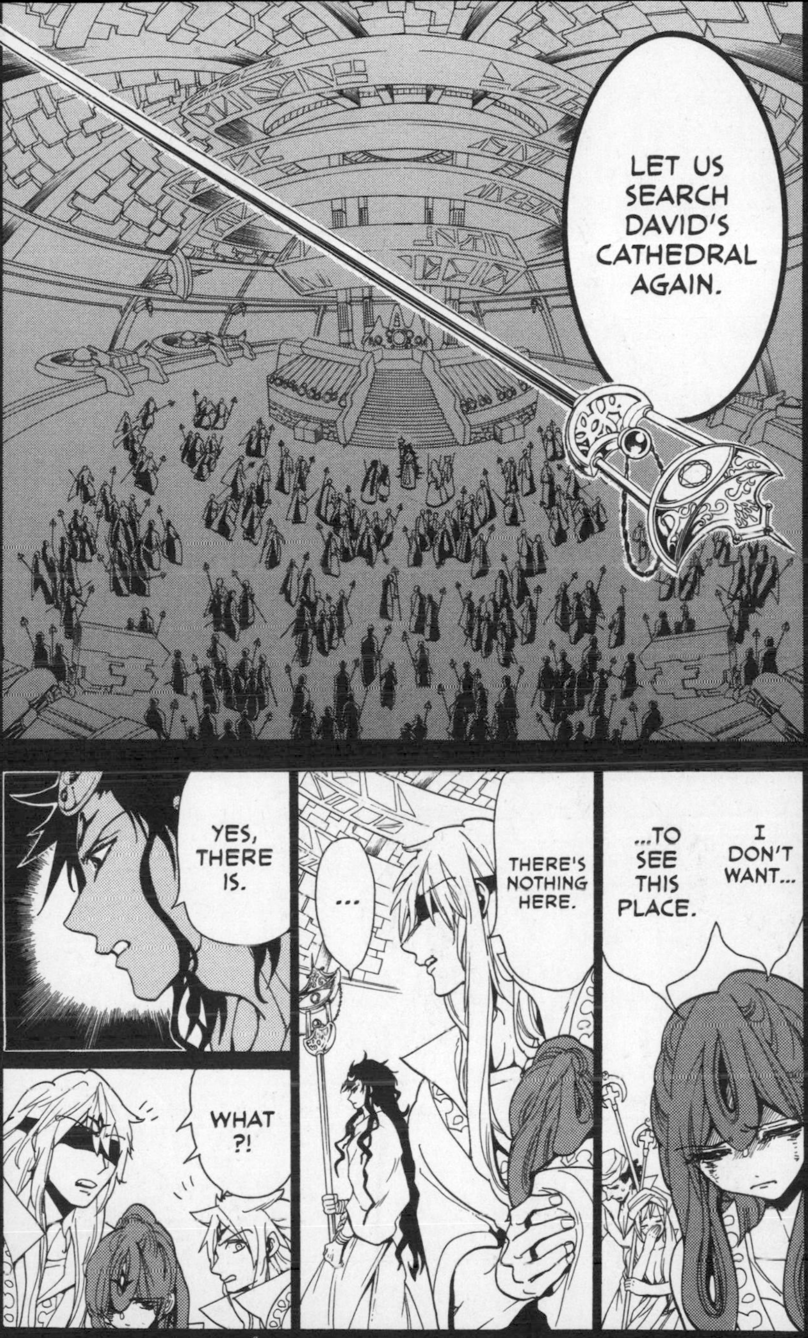
LET US SEARCH DAVID'S CATHEDRAL AGAIN.
I DON'T WANT...
...TO SEE THIS PLACE.
THERE'S NOTHING HERE.
...
YES, THERE IS.
WHAT ?!

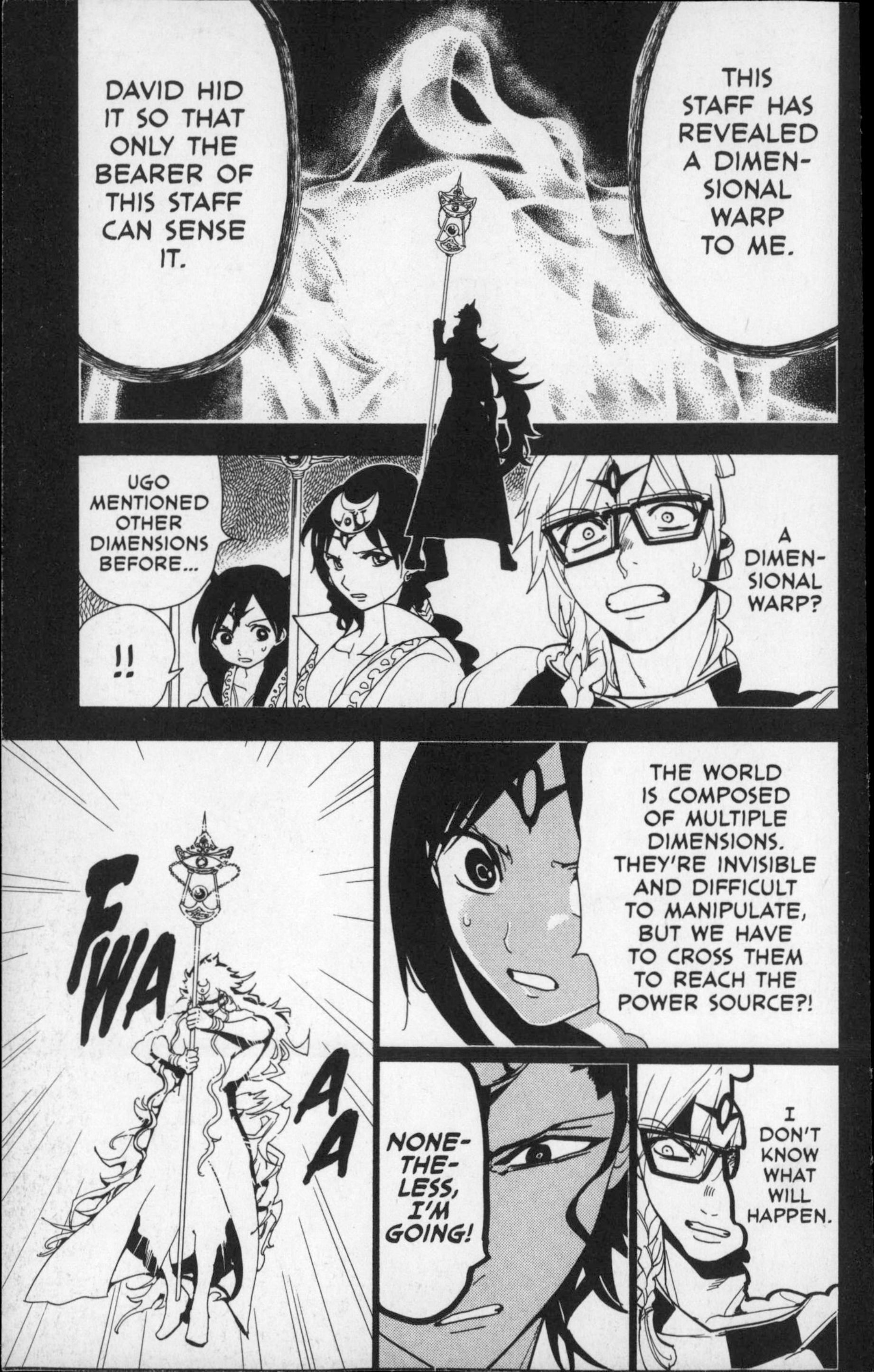
THIS STAFF HAS REVEALED A DIMEN- SIONAL WARP TO ME.
DAVID HID IT SO THAT ONLY THE BEARER OF THIS STAFF CAN SENSE IT.
A DIMEN- SIONAL WARP?
UGO MENTIONED OTHER DIMENSIONS BEFORE...
!!
THE WORLD IS COMPOSED OF MULTIPLE DIMENSIONS. THEY'RE INVISIBLE AND DIFFICULT TO MANIPULATE, BUT WE HAVE TO CROSS THEM TO REACH THE POWER SOURCE?!
I DON'T KNOW WHAT WILL HAPPEN.
NONE- THE- LESS, I'M GOING!
FWAAA

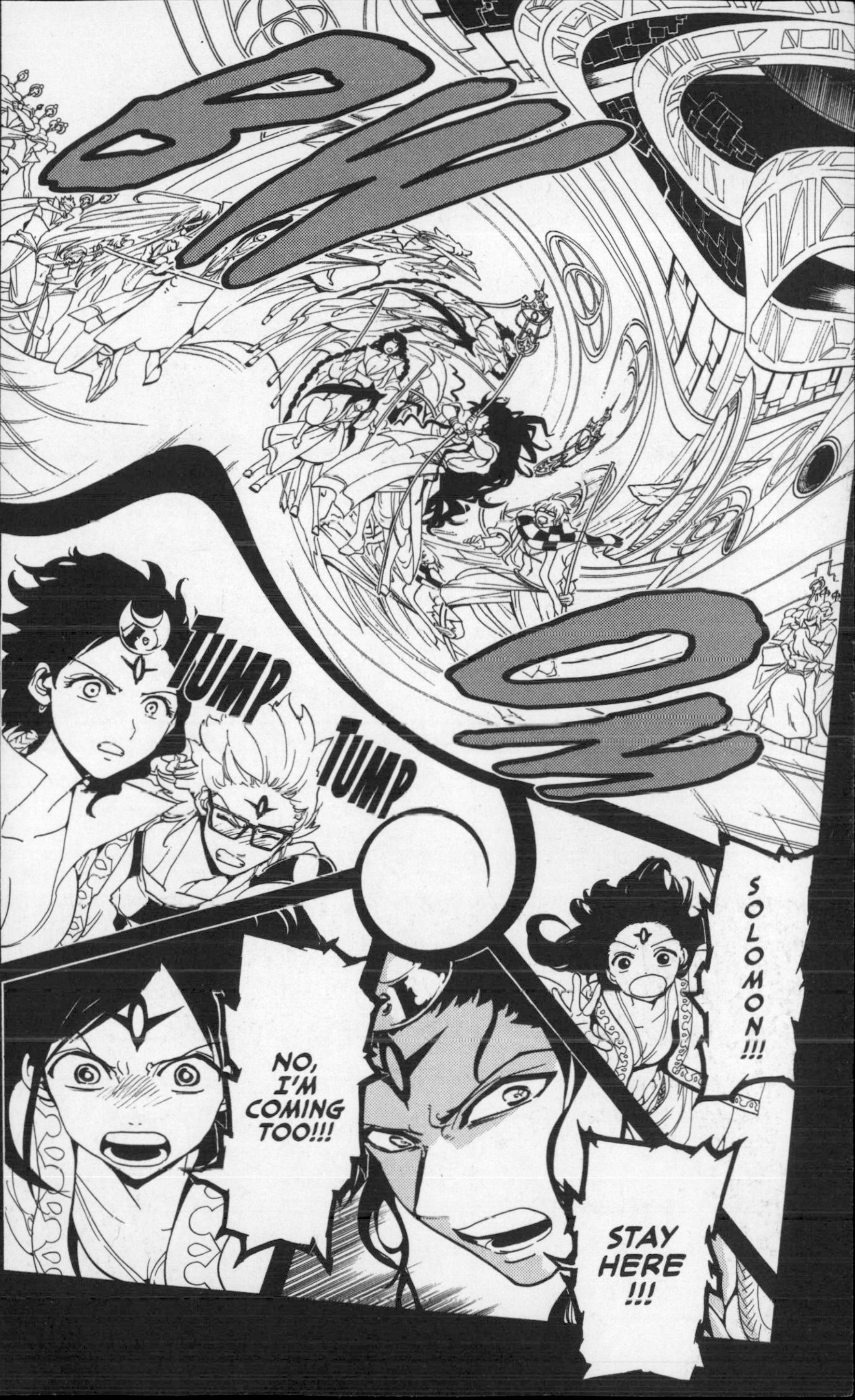
TUMP
TUMP
SOLOMON!!!
STAY HERE!!!
NO, I'M COMING TOO!!!

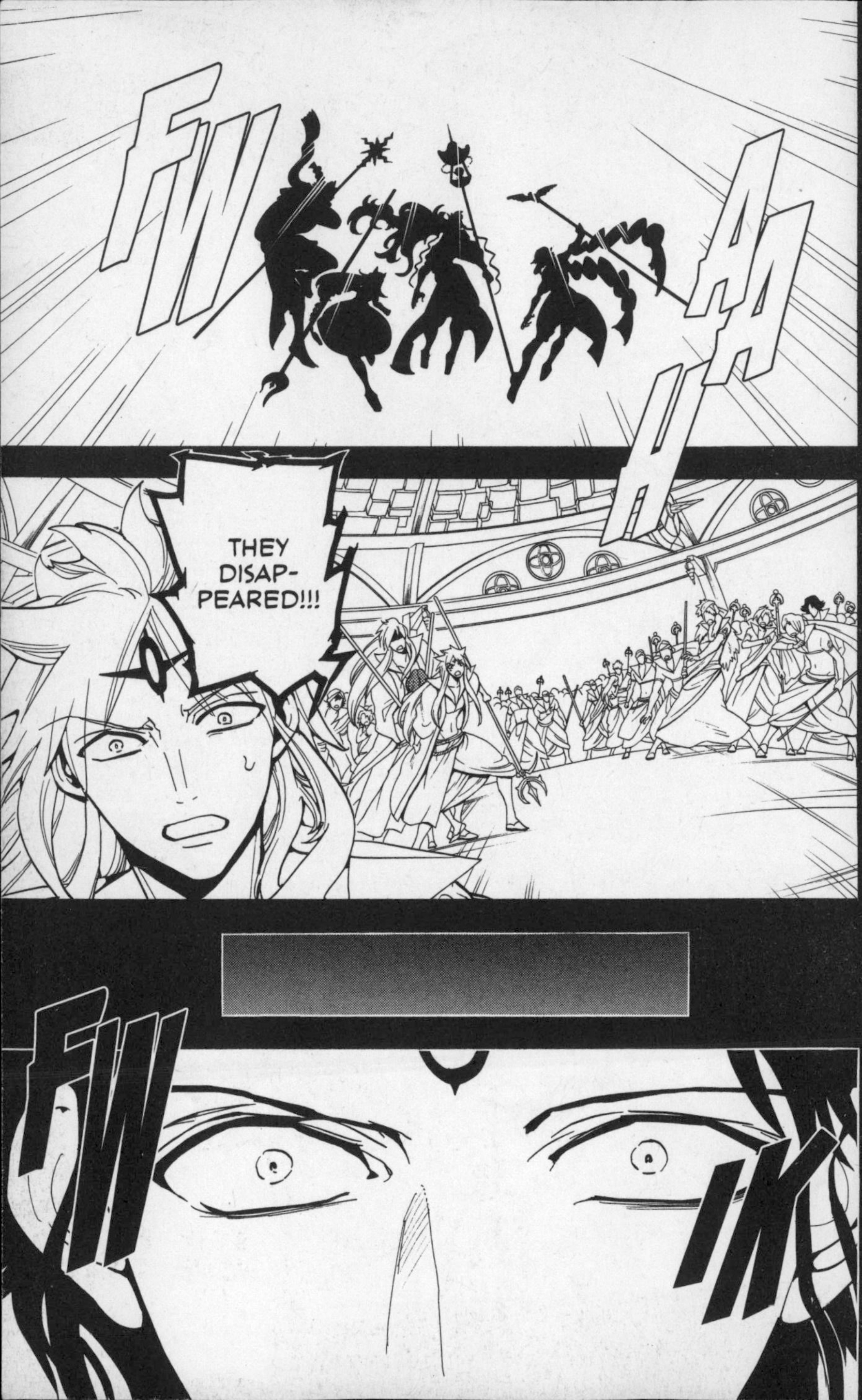
THEY DISAP- PEARED!!!

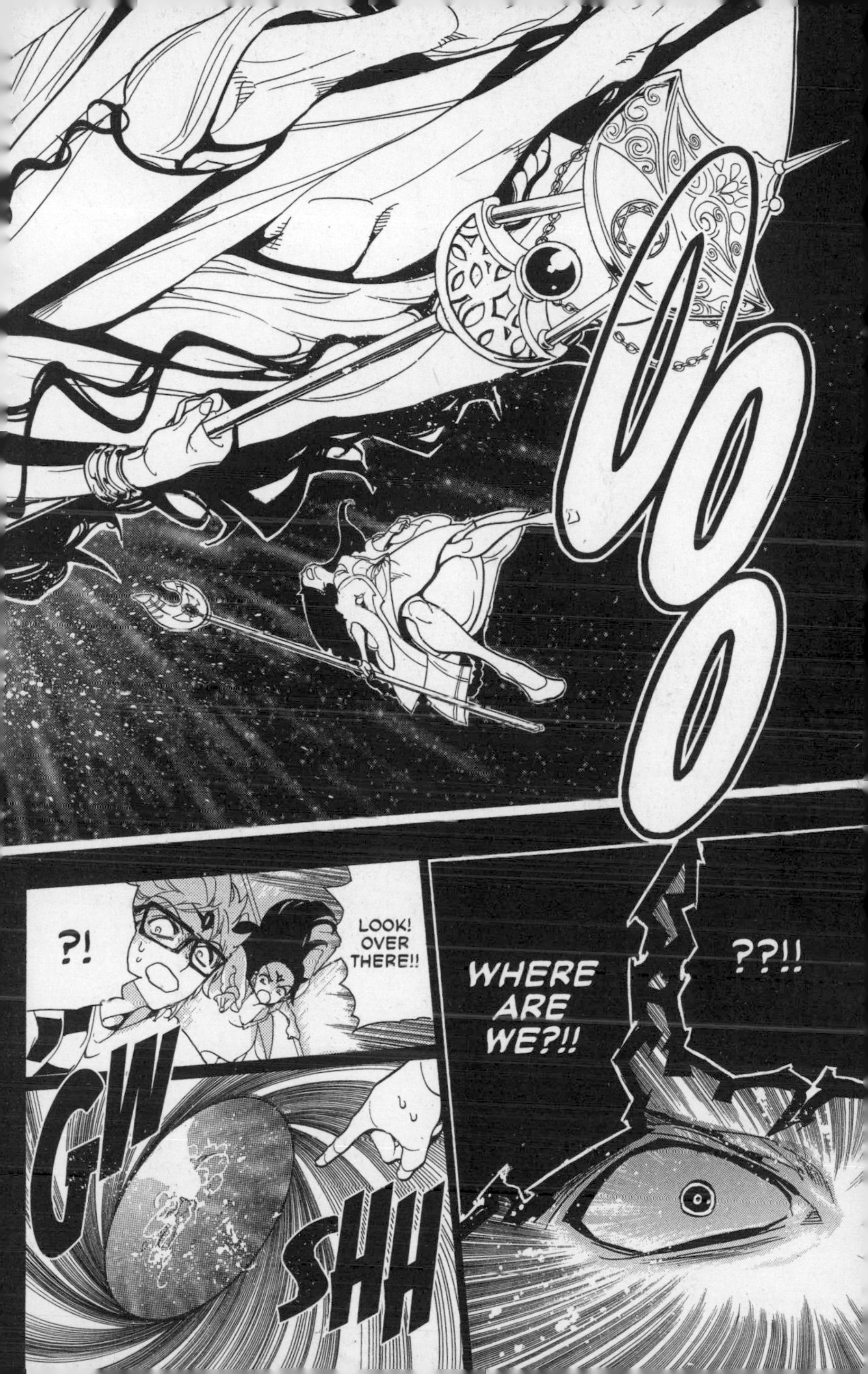
??!!
WHERE ARE WE?!!
LOOK! OVER THERE!!
?!
GW SHH

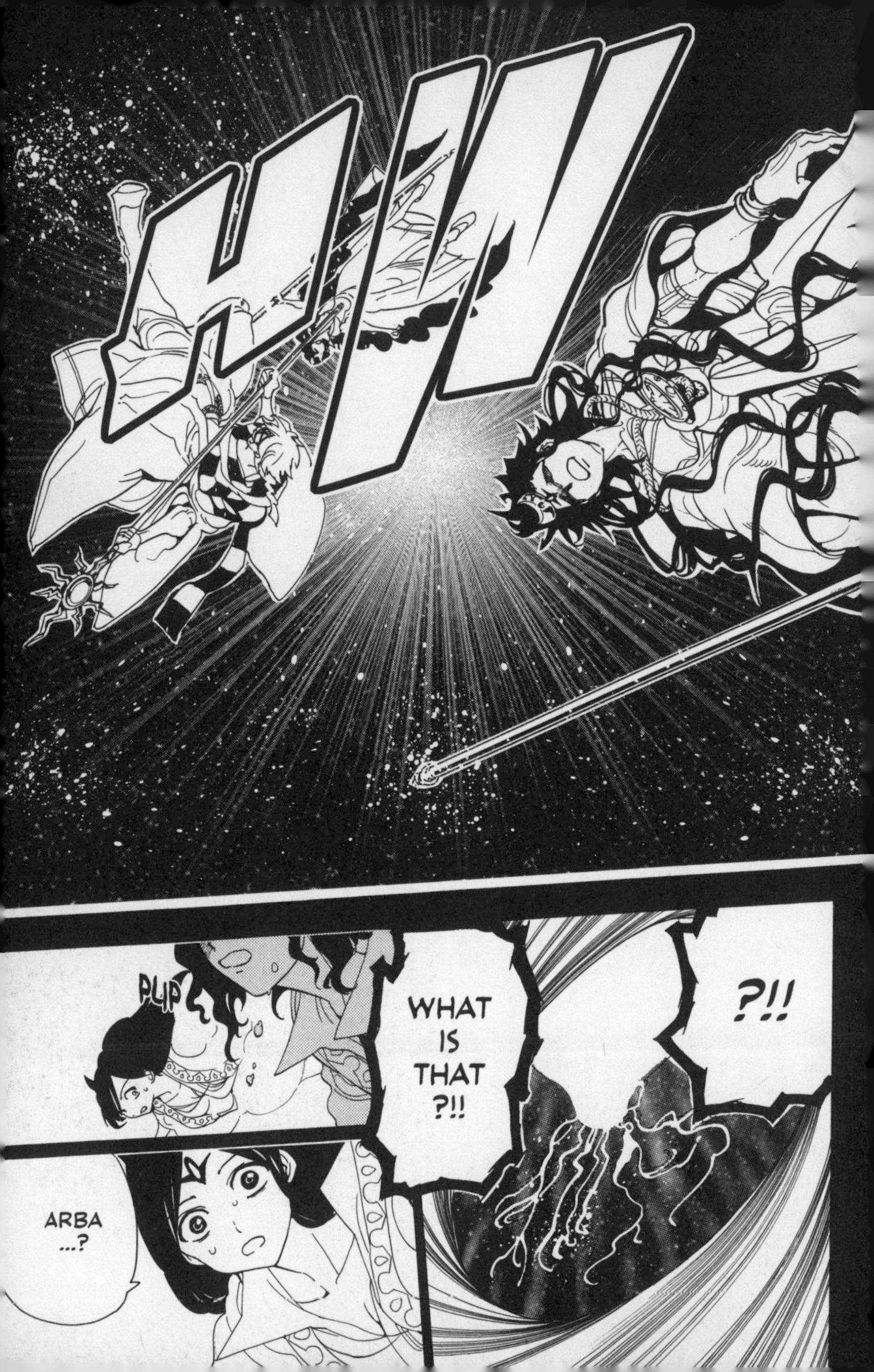
?!!
WHAT IS THAT ?!!
PLIP
ARBA ...?

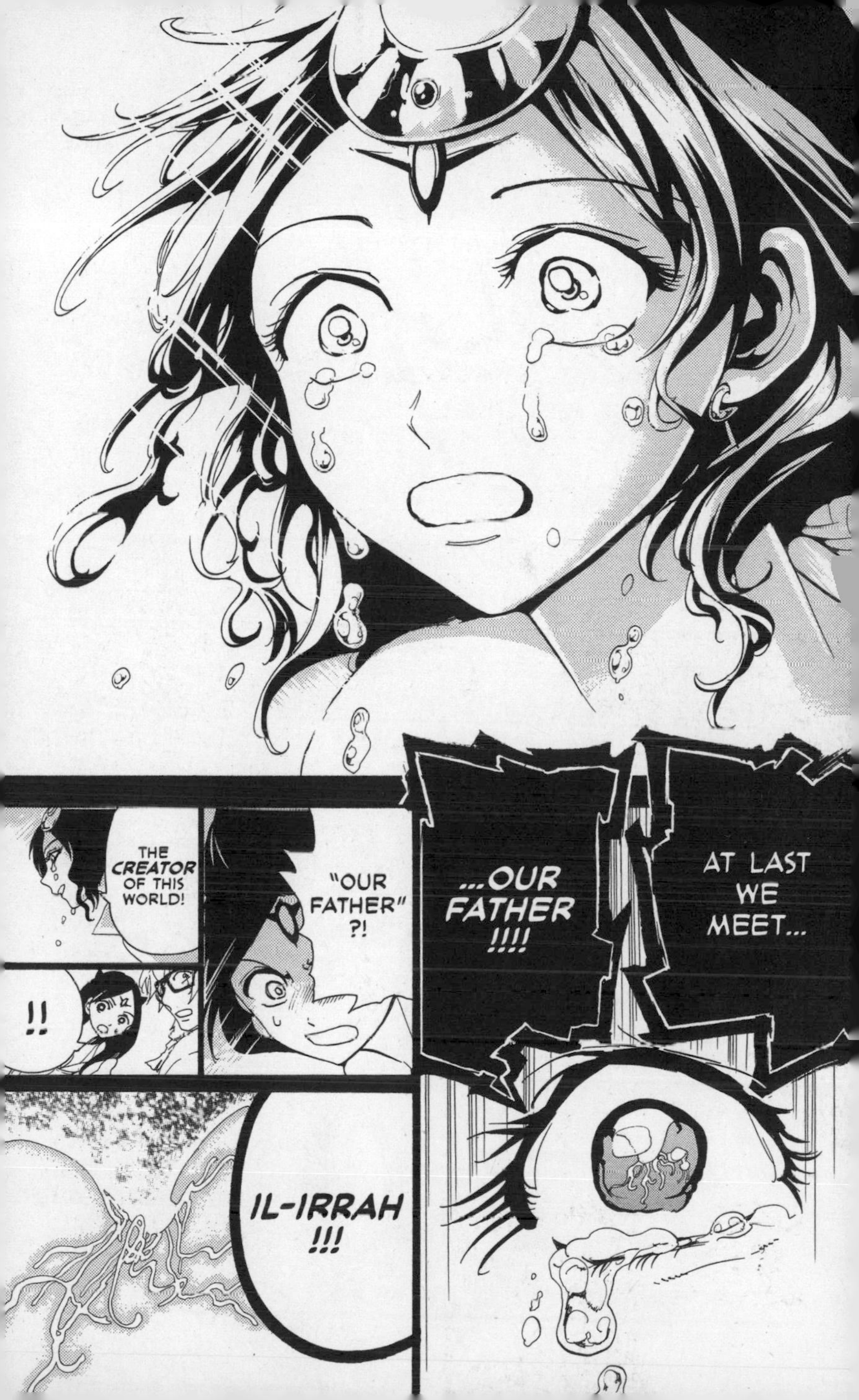
AT LAST WE MEET...
...OUR FATHER !!!!
"OUR FATHER" ?!
THE CREATOR OF THIS WORLD!
!!
IL-IRRAH !!!

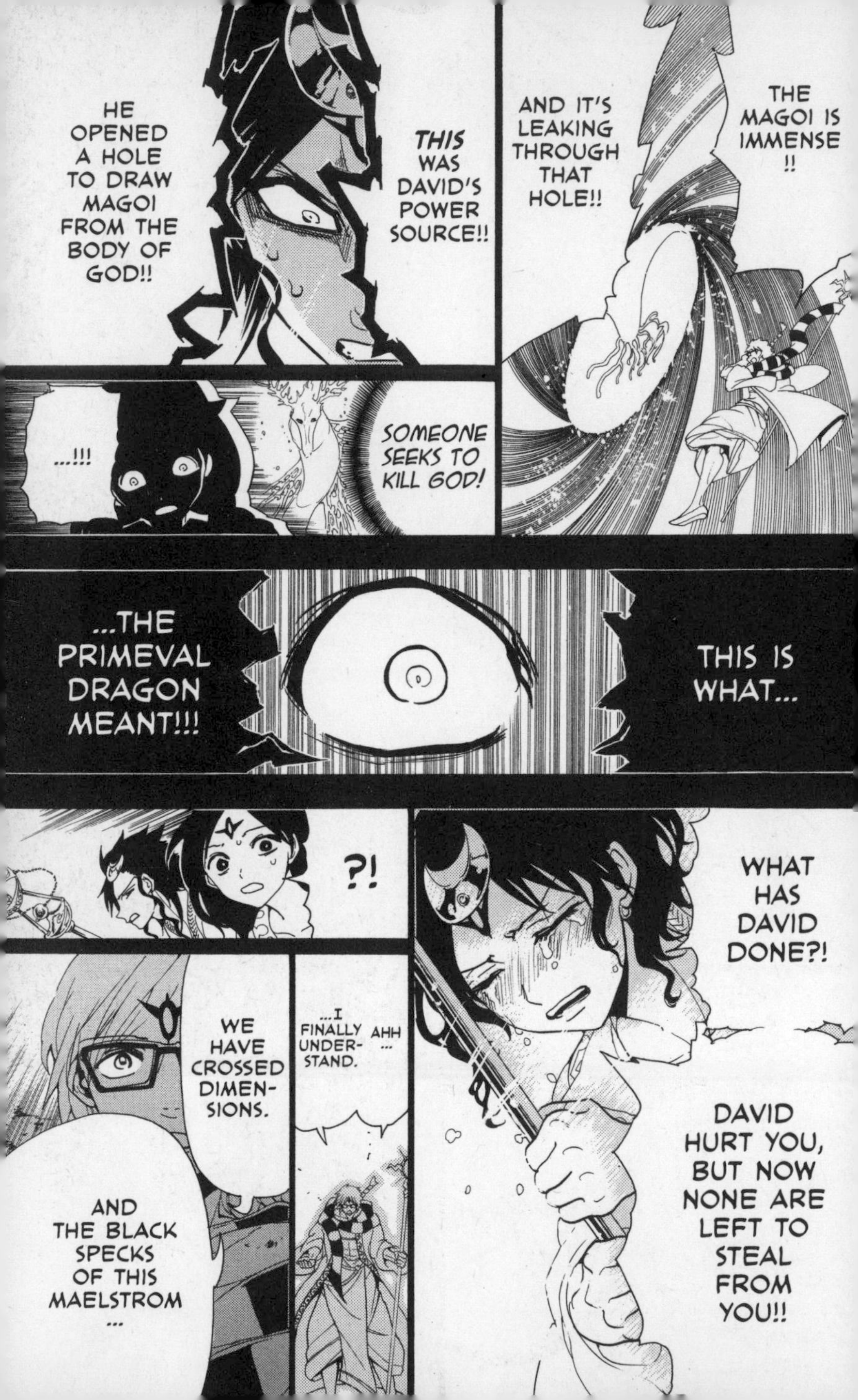
THE MAGOI IS IMMENSE!!
AND IT'S LEAKING THROUGH THAT HOLE!!
THIS WAS DAVID'S POWER SOURCE!!
HE OPENED A HOLE TO DRAW MAGOI FROM THE BODY OF GOD!!
SOMEONE SEEKS TO KILL GOD!
...!!!
THIS IS WHAT...
...THE PRIMEVAL DRAGON MEANT!!!
WHAT HAS DAVID DONE?!
DAVID HURT YOU, BUT NOW NONE ARE LEFT TO STEAL FROM YOU!!
?!
AHH ...
...I FINALLY UNDER-STAND.
WE HAVE CROSSED DIMEN-SIONS.
AND THE BLACK SPECKS OF THIS MAELSTROM ...

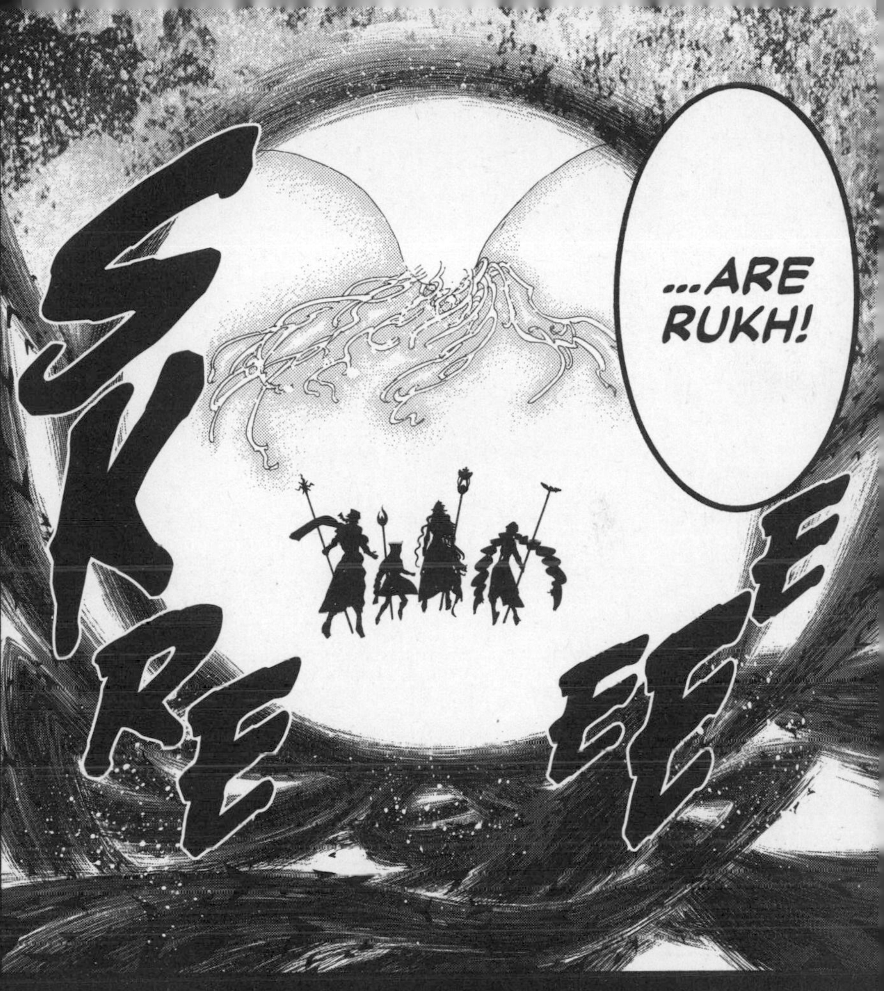
...ARE RUKH!
SKREEEE

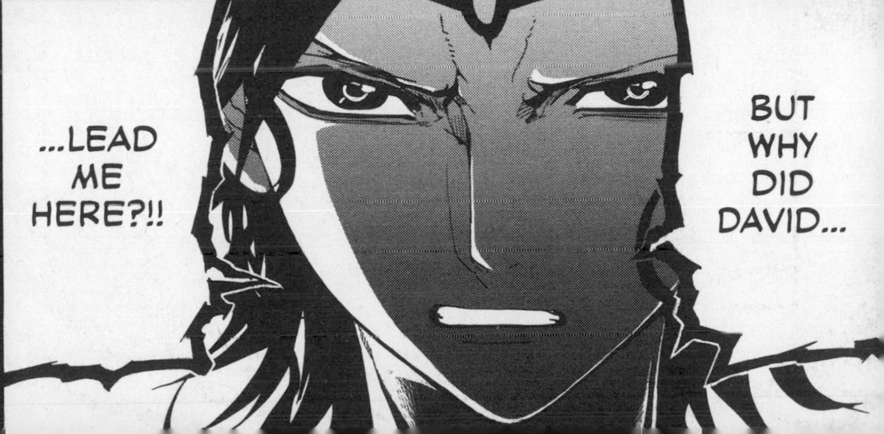
BUT WHY DID DAVID...
...LEAD ME HERE?!!

Night 232: Solomon's World

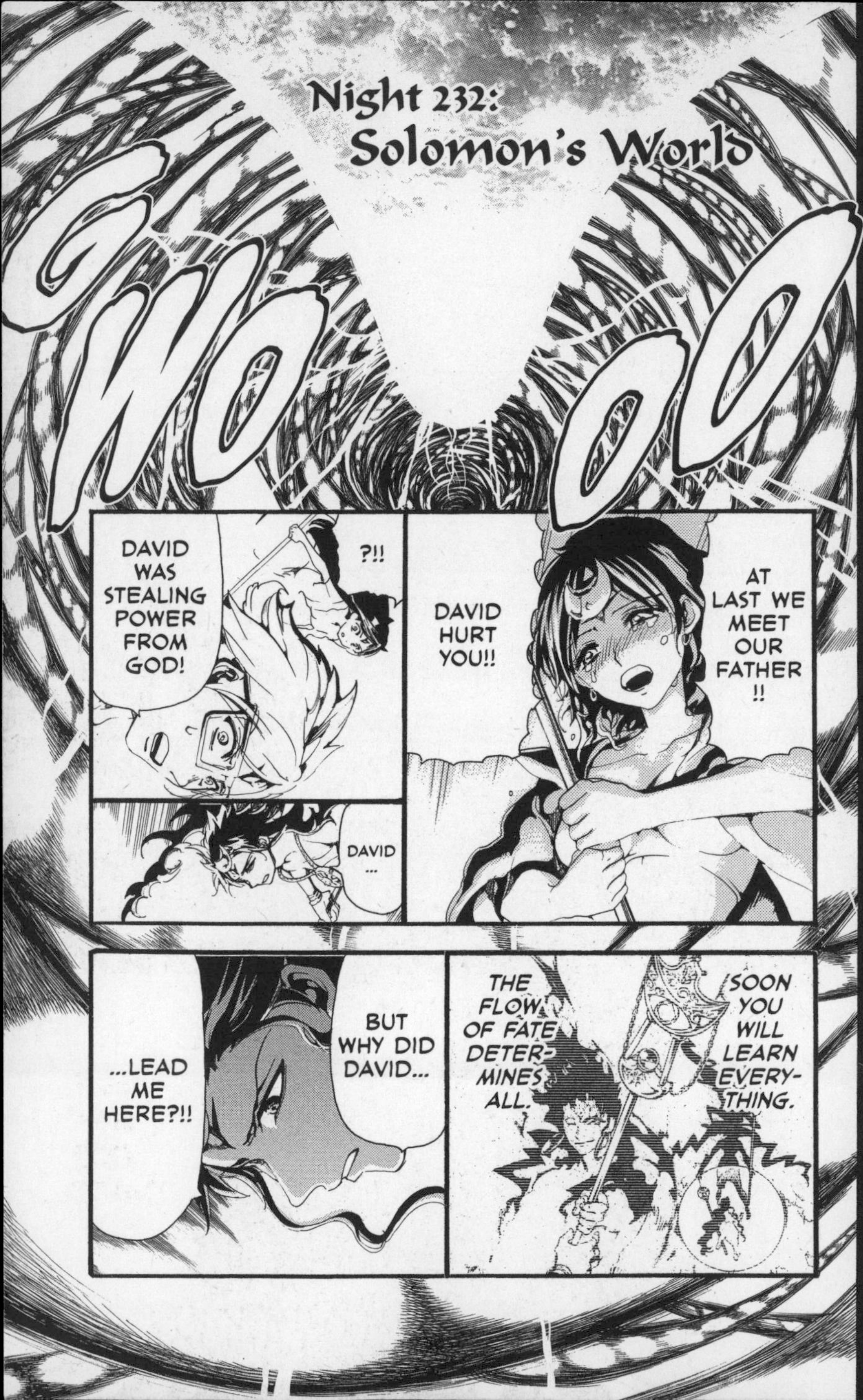
WHOOO
AT LAST WE MEET OUR FATHER!!
DAVID HURT YOU!!
?!!
DAVID WAS STEALING POWER FROM GOD!
DAVID...
SOON YOU WILL LEARN EVERYTHING.
THE FLOW OF FATE DETERMINES ALL.
BUT WHY DID DAVID...
...LEAD ME HERE?!!

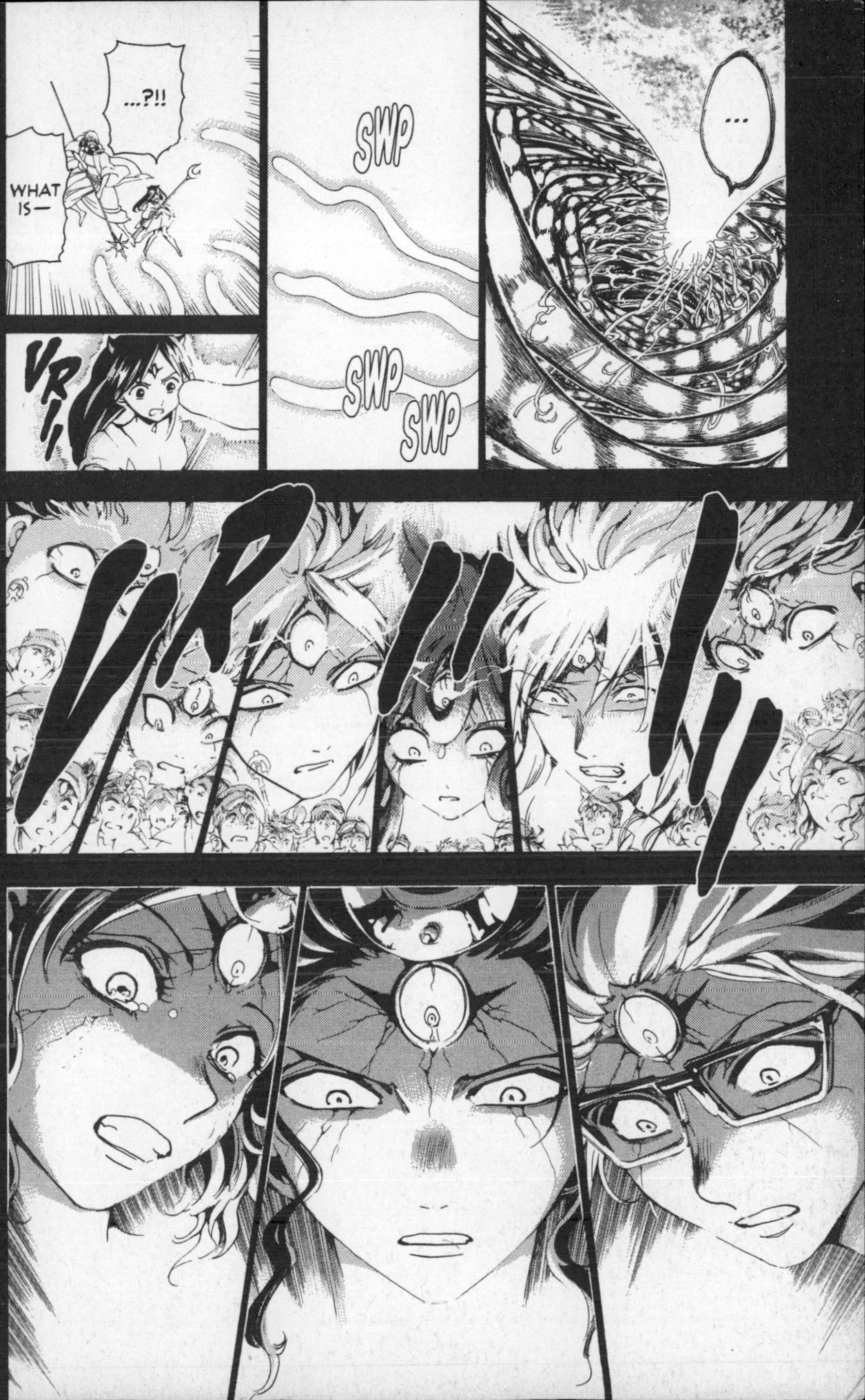
...
SWP
SWP
SWP
...?!!
WHAT IS—
VR!!

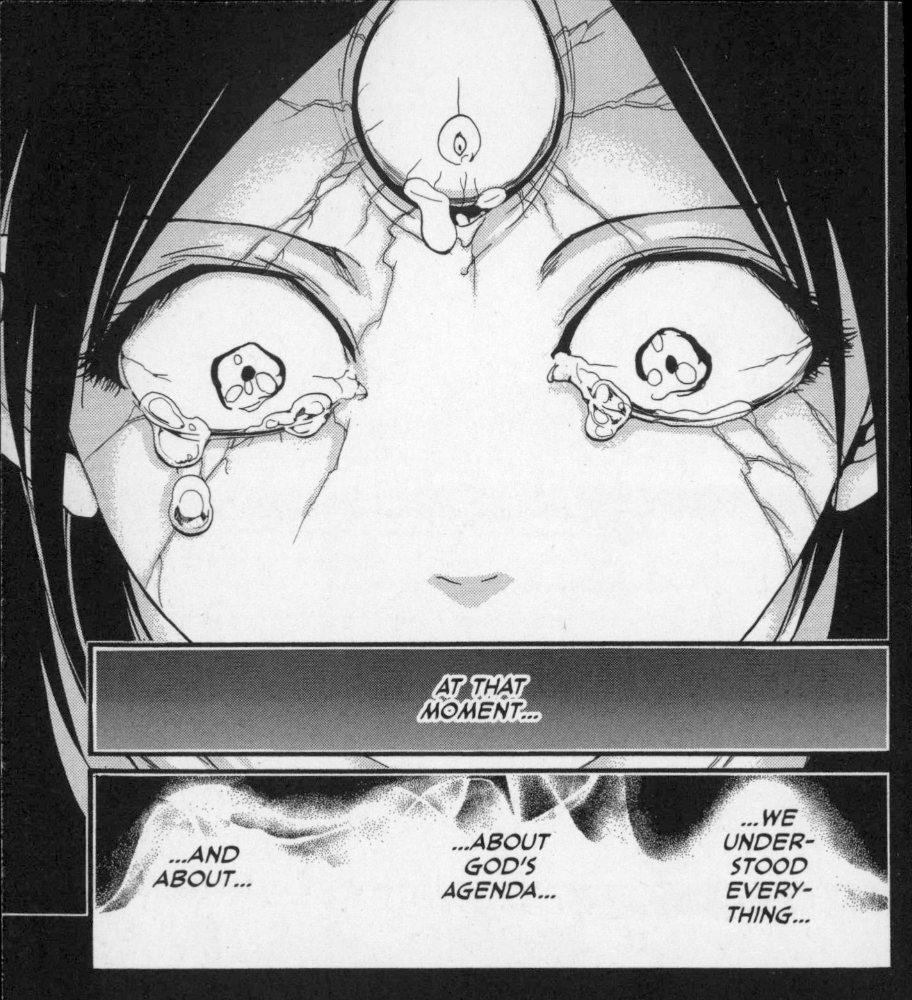
AT THAT MOMENT...
...WE UNDER-STOOD EVERY-THING...
...ABOUT GOD'S AGENDA...
...AND ABOUT...

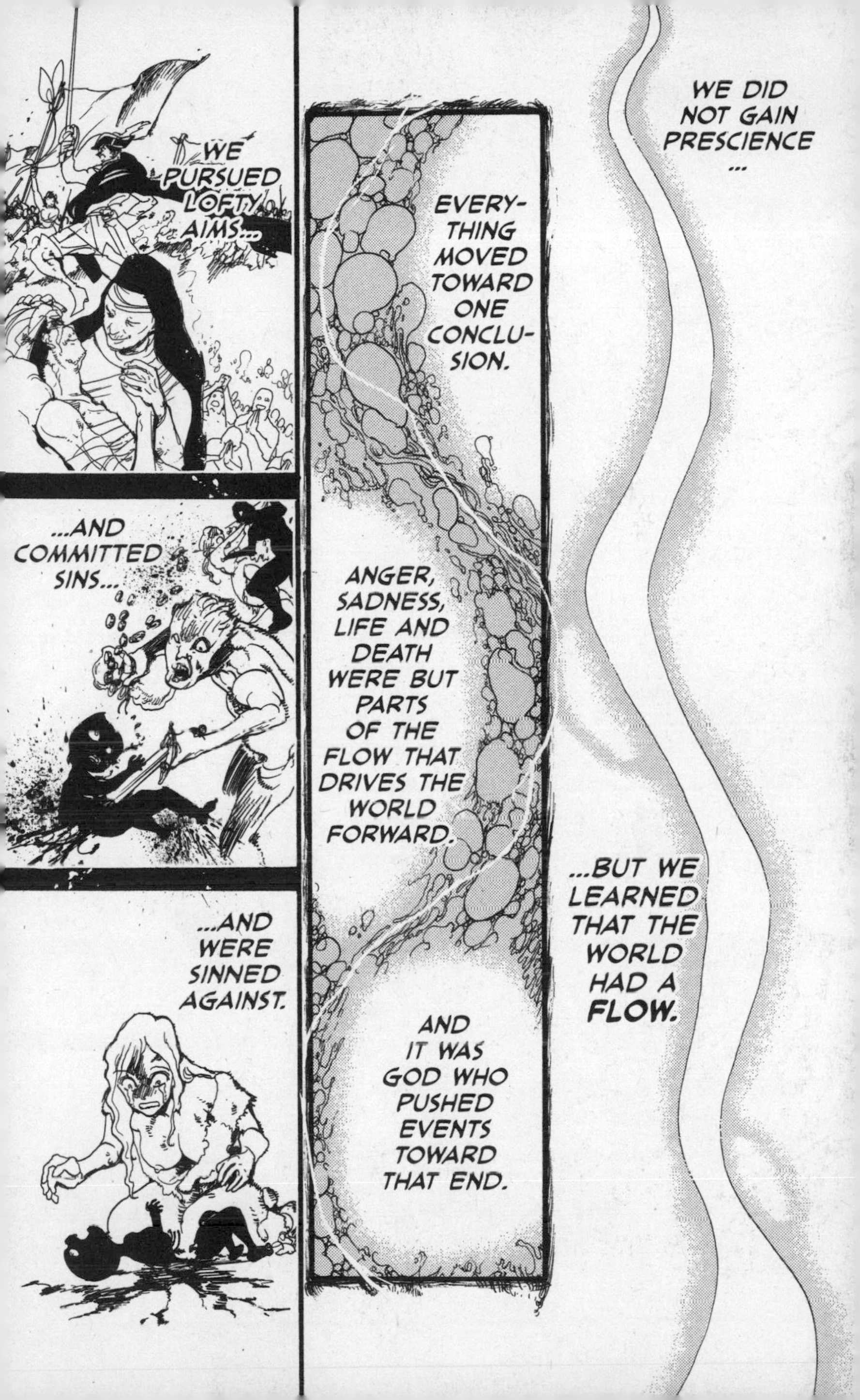

WE DID NOT GAIN PRESCIENCE...
...BUT WE LEARNED THAT THE WORLD HAD A **FLOW.**
EVERYTHING MOVED TOWARD ONE CONCLUSION.
ANGER, SADNESS, LIFE AND DEATH WERE BUT PARTS OF THE FLOW THAT DRIVES THE WORLD FORWARD.
AND IT WAS GOD WHO PUSHED EVENTS TOWARD THAT END.
WE PURSUED LOFTY AIMS...
...AND COMMITTED SINS...
...AND WERE SINNED AGAINST.

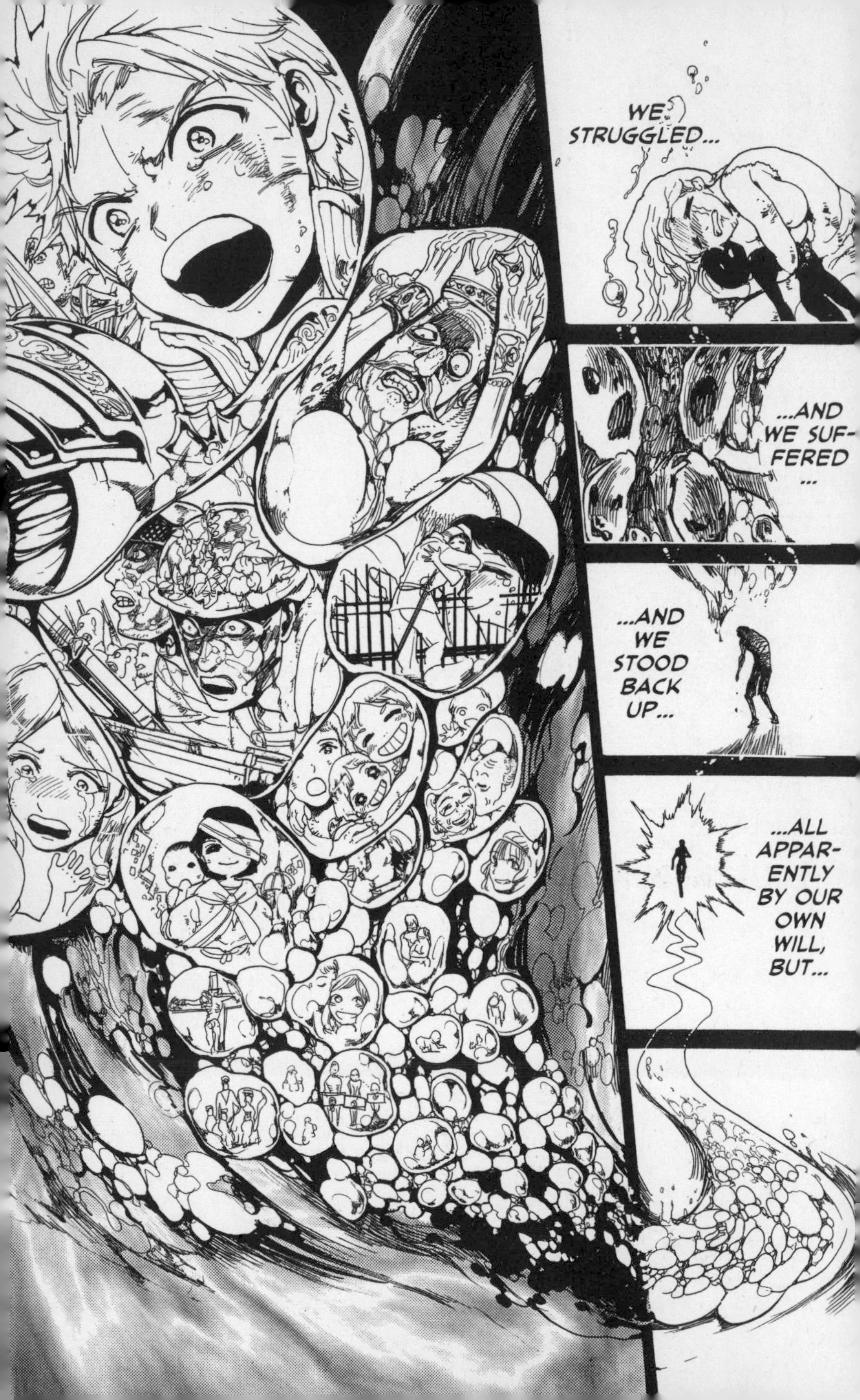
WE STRUGGLED...
...AND WE SUFFERED...
...AND WE STOOD BACK UP...
...ALL APPARENTLY BY OUR OWN WILL, BUT...

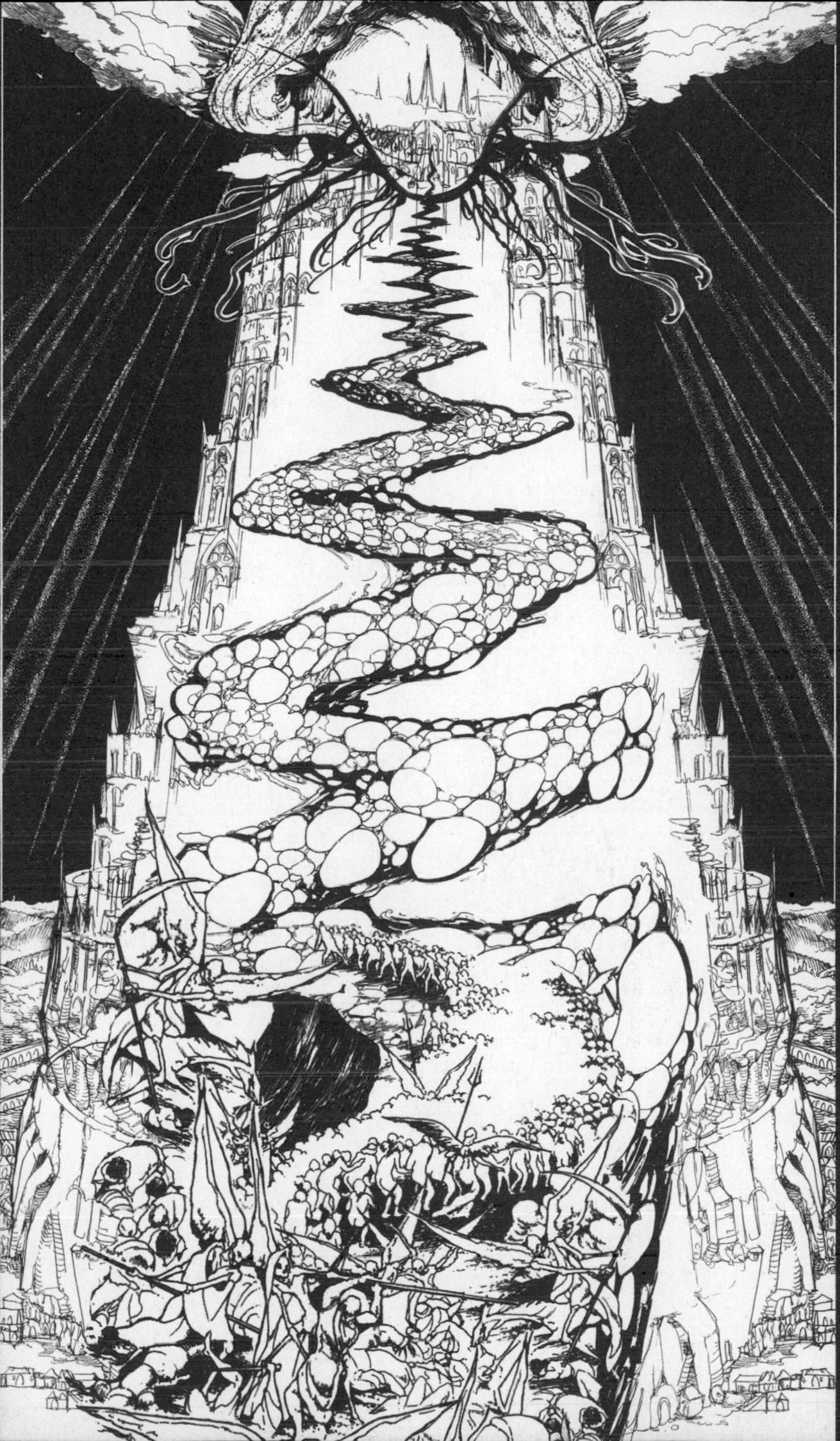

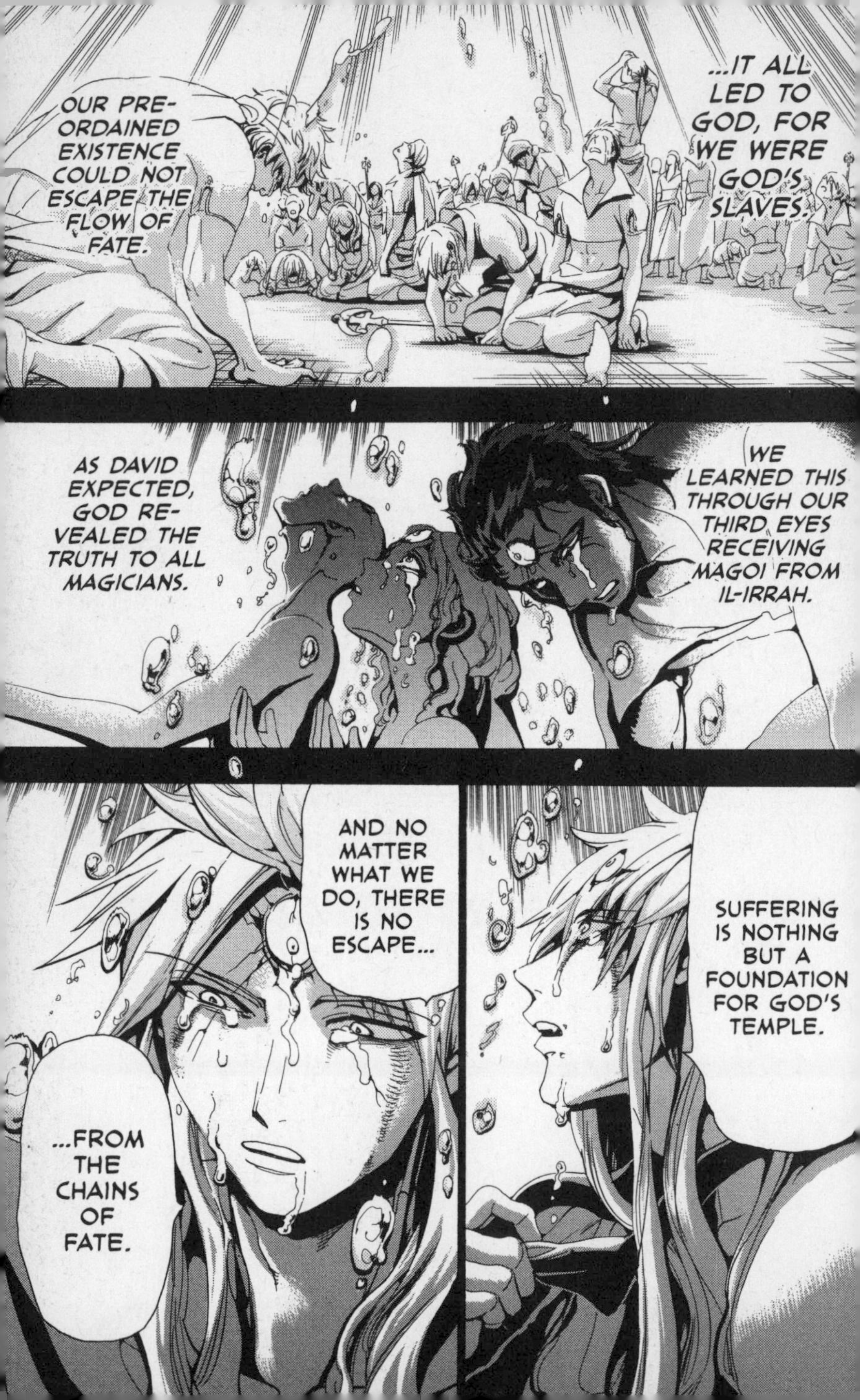
...IT ALL LED TO GOD, FOR WE WERE GOD'S SLAVES.
OUR PRE-ORDAINED EXISTENCE COULD NOT ESCAPE THE FLOW OF FATE.
WE LEARNED THIS THROUGH OUR THIRD EYES RECEIVING MAGOI FROM IL-IRRAH.
AS DAVID EXPECTED, GOD RE-VEALED THE TRUTH TO ALL MAGICIANS.
SUFFERING IS NOTHING BUT A FOUNDATION FOR GOD'S TEMPLE.
AND NO MATTER WHAT WE DO, THERE IS NO ESCAPE...
...FROM THE CHAINS OF FATE.

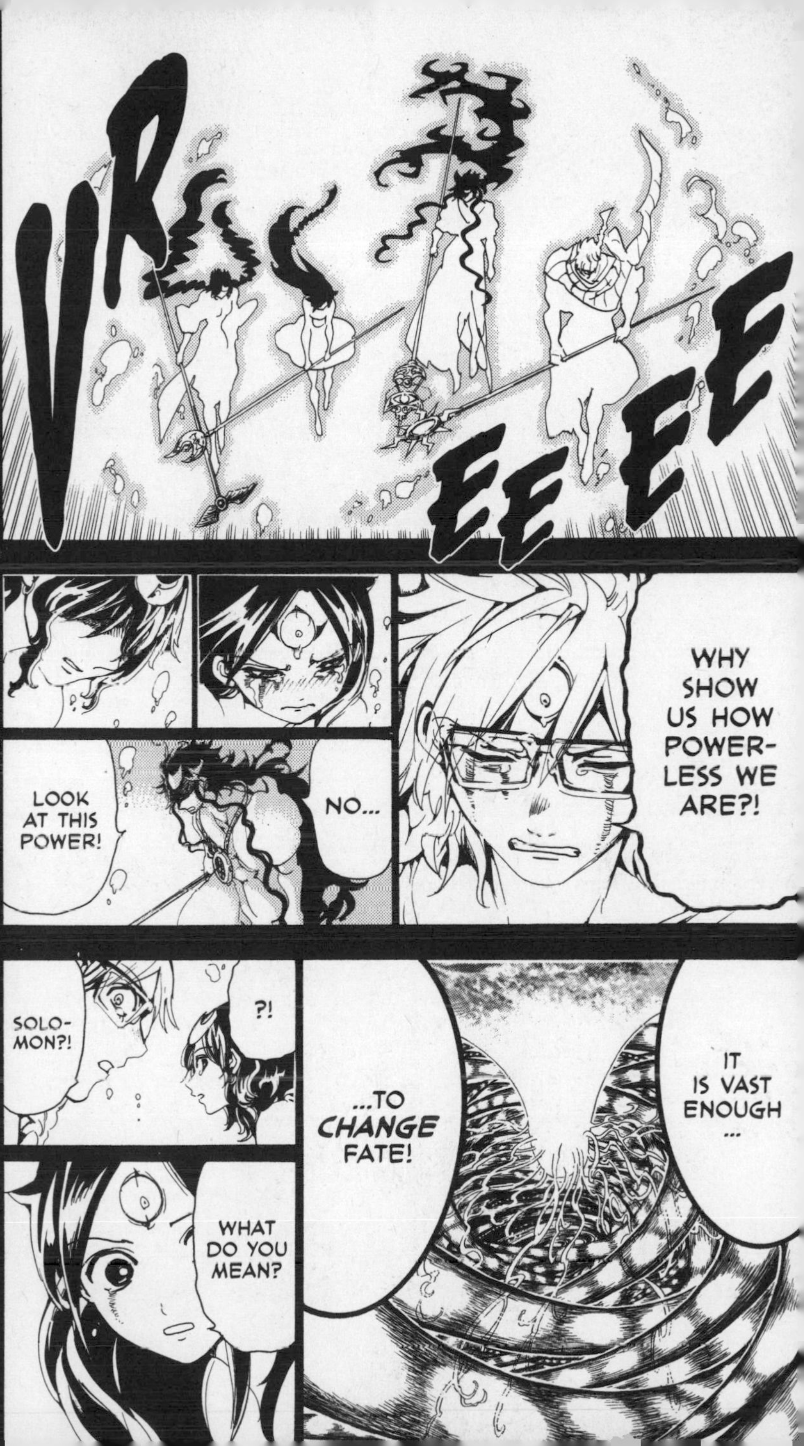
VREEEEEE
WHY SHOW US HOW POWERLESS WE ARE?!
NO...
LOOK AT THIS POWER!
IT IS VAST ENOUGH...
...TO *CHANGE* FATE!
?!
SOLOMON?!
WHAT DO YOU MEAN?

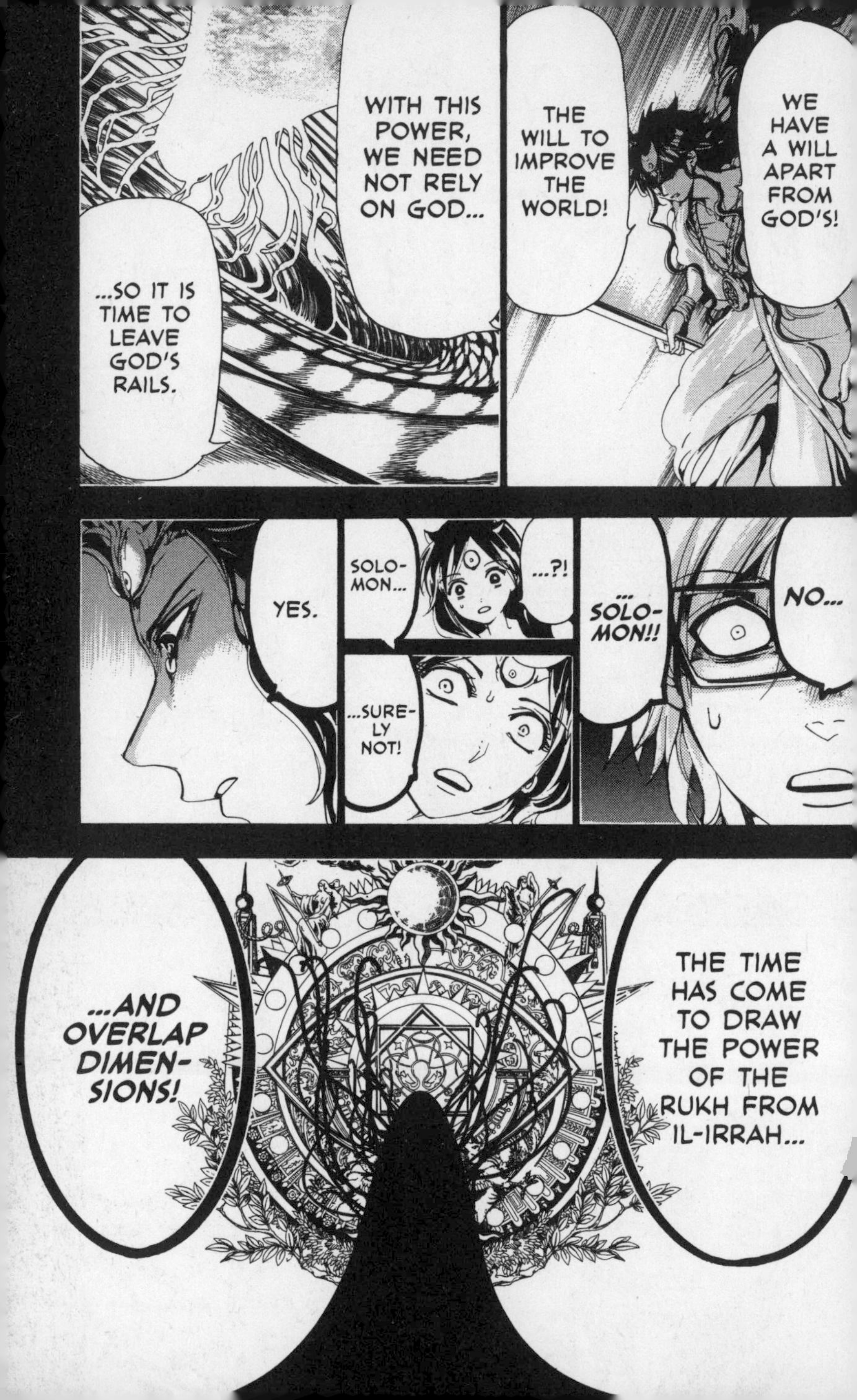
WE HAVE A WILL APART FROM GOD'S!
THE WILL TO IMPROVE THE WORLD!
WITH THIS POWER, WE NEED NOT RELY ON GOD...
...SO IT IS TIME TO LEAVE GOD'S RAILS.
NO...
...SOLO-MON!!
...?!
SOLO-MON...
...SURE-LY NOT!
YES.
THE TIME HAS COME TO DRAW THE POWER OF THE RUKH FROM IL-IRRAH...
...AND OVERLAP DIMEN-SIONS!

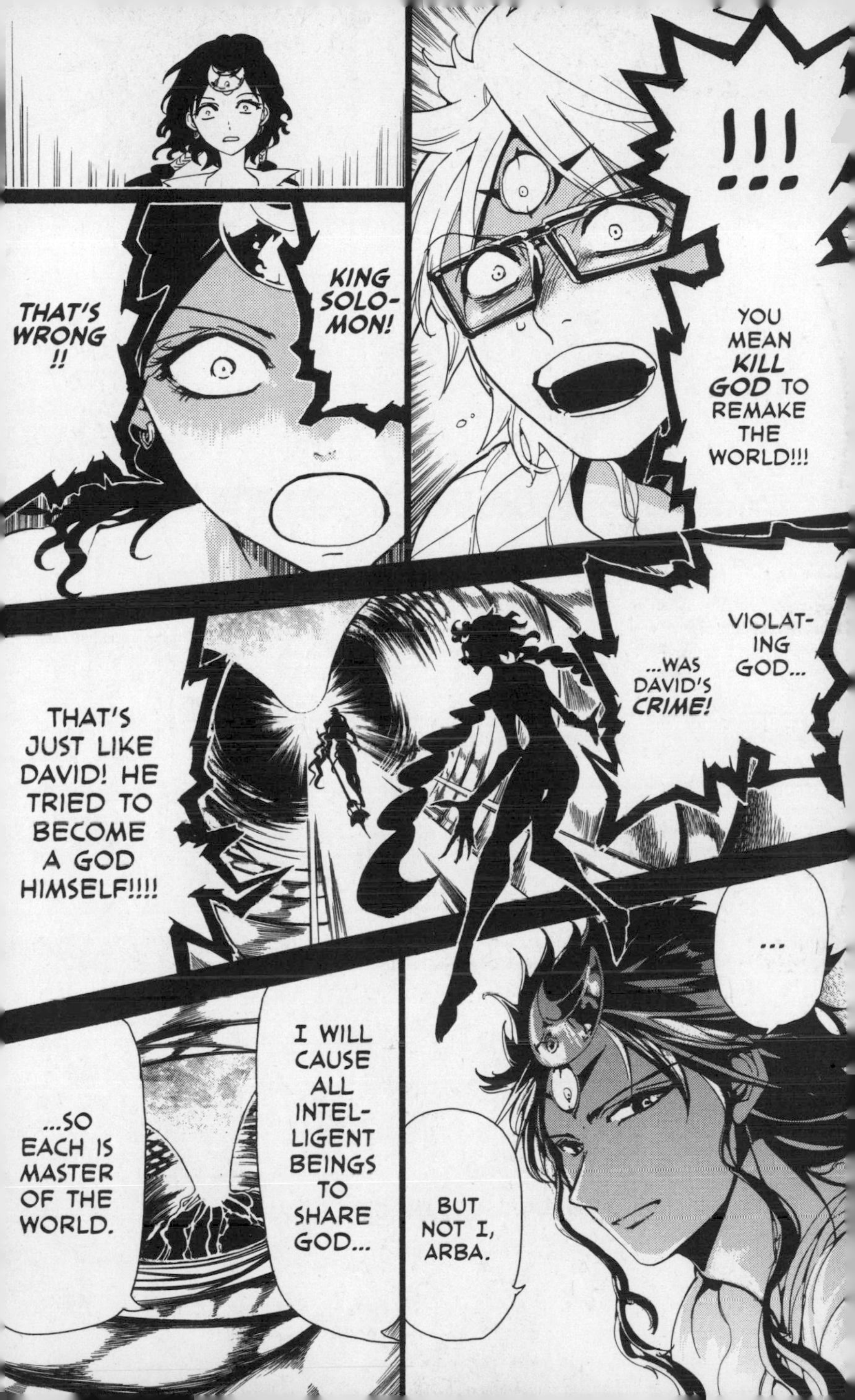
!!!...
YOU MEAN KILL GOD TO REMAKE THE WORLD!!!
KING SOLOMON!
THAT'S WRONG!!
VIOLATING GOD...
...WAS DAVID'S CRIME!
THAT'S JUST LIKE DAVID! HE TRIED TO BECOME A GOD HIMSELF!!!!
...
BUT NOT I, ARBA.
I WILL CAUSE ALL INTELLIGENT BEINGS TO SHARE GOD...
...SO EACH IS MASTER OF THE WORLD.

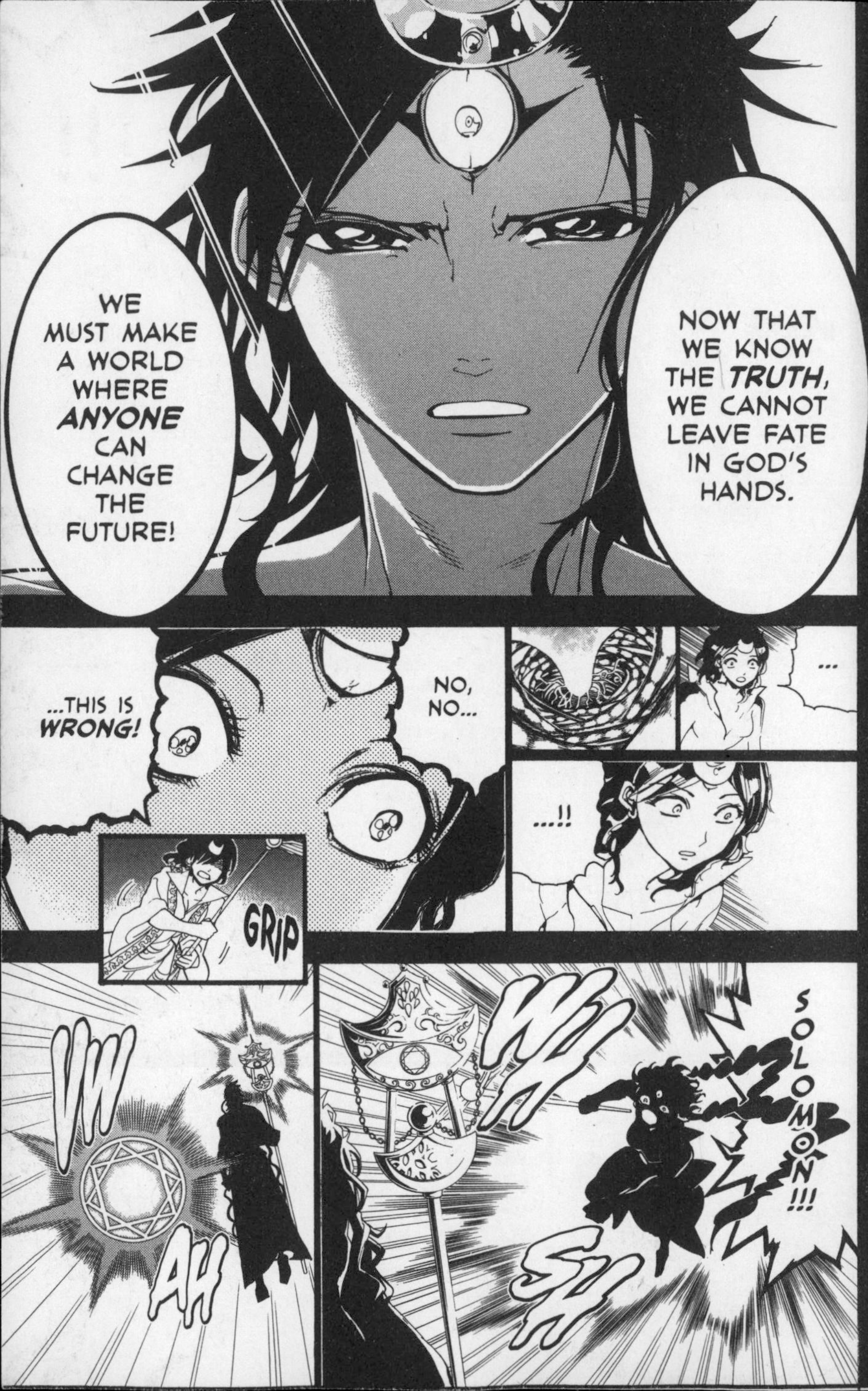
NOW THAT WE KNOW THE *TRUTH*, WE CANNOT LEAVE FATE IN GOD'S HANDS.
WE MUST MAKE A WORLD WHERE *ANYONE* CAN CHANGE THE FUTURE!
...
...!!
NO, NO...
...THIS IS *WRONG!*
GRIP
SOLOMON!!!
WH
SH
VW
AH

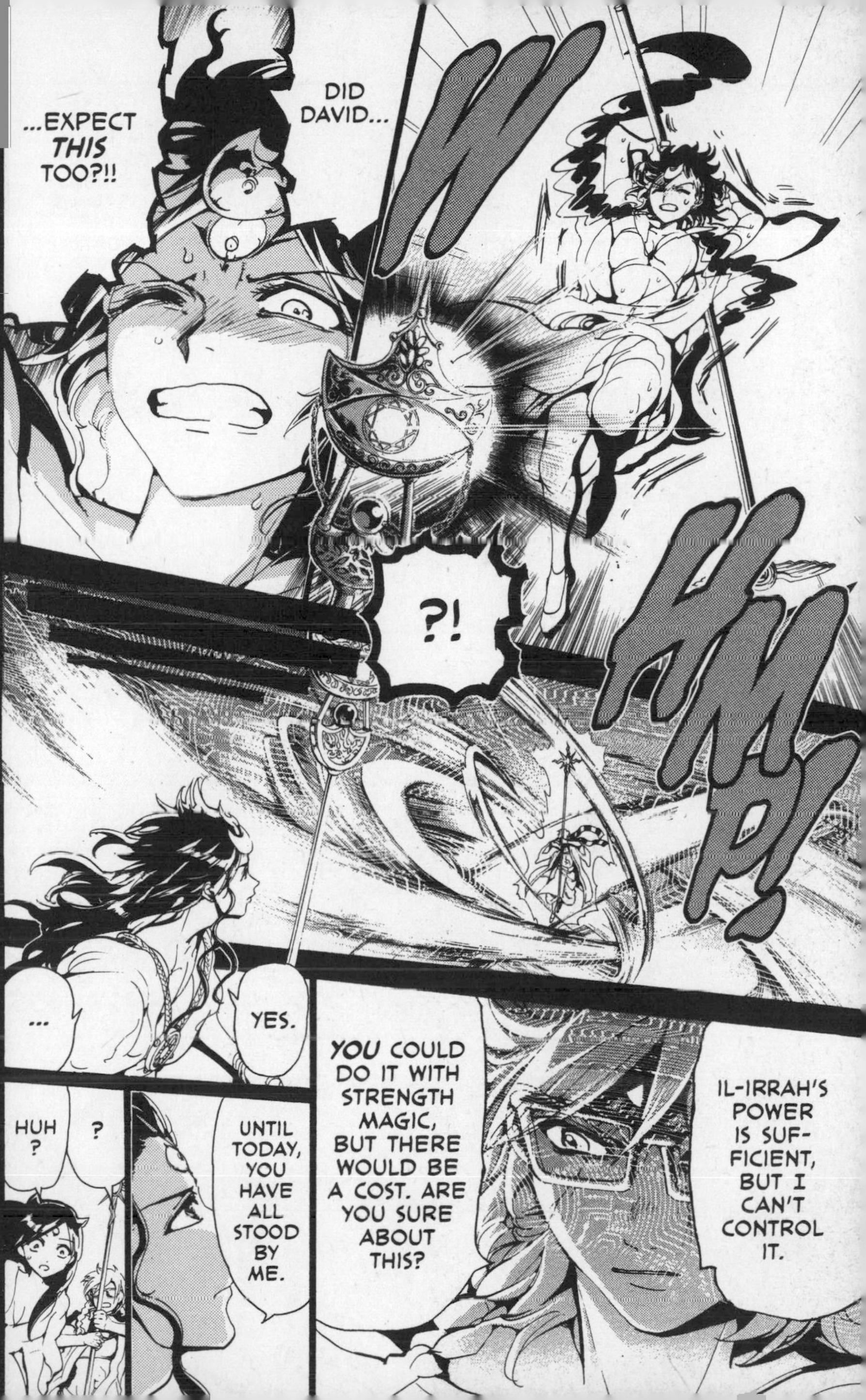
DID DAVID...
...EXPECT *THIS* TOO?!!
?!
IL-IRRAH'S POWER IS SUF-FICIENT, BUT I CAN'T CONTROL IT.
YOU COULD DO IT WITH STRENGTH MAGIC, BUT THERE WOULD BE A COST. ARE YOU SURE ABOUT THIS?
YES.
...
UNTIL TODAY, YOU HAVE ALL STOOD BY ME.
?
HUH?

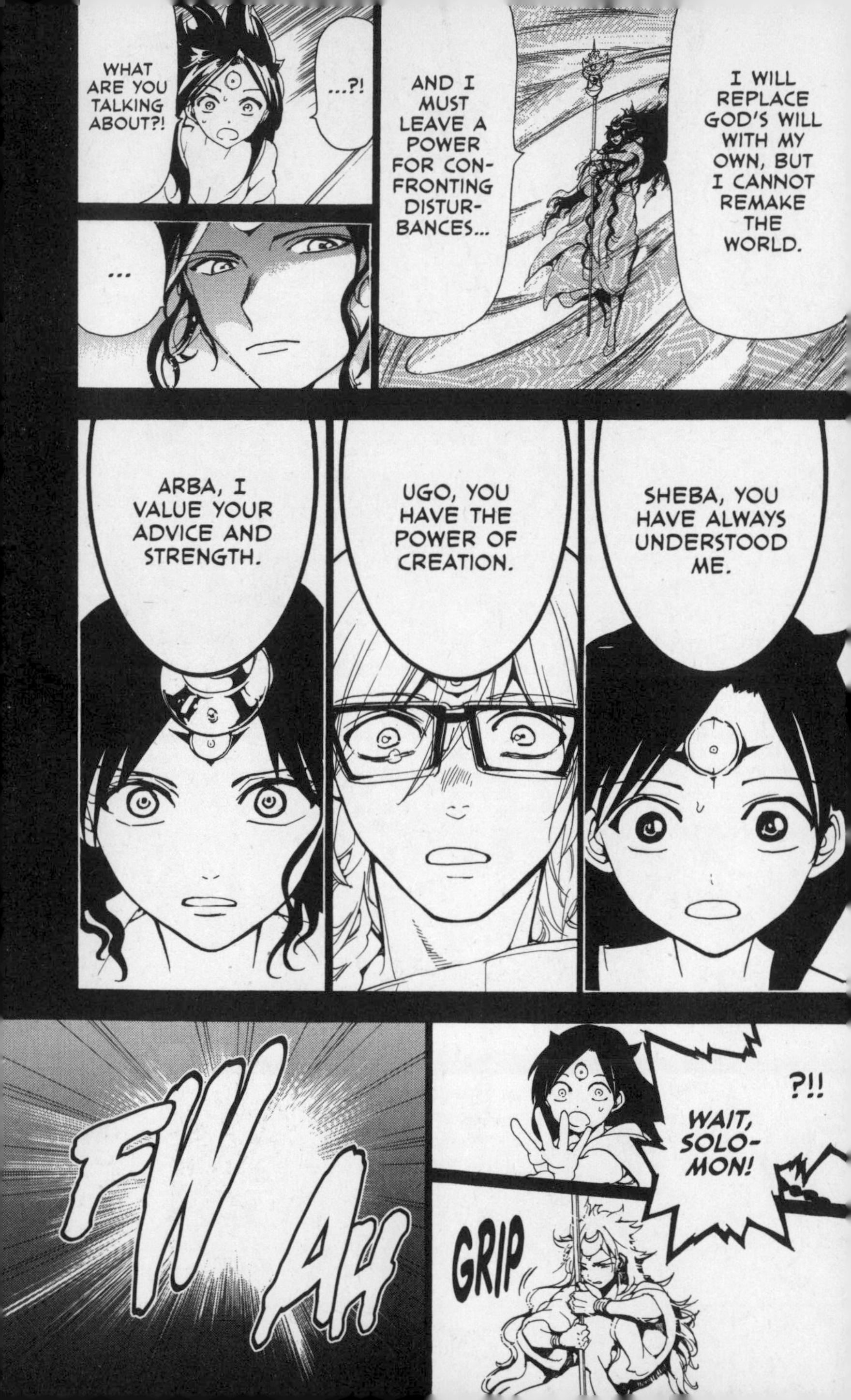
I WILL REPLACE GOD'S WILL WITH MY OWN, BUT I CANNOT REMAKE THE WORLD.
AND I MUST LEAVE A POWER FOR CONFRONTING DISTURBANCES...
...?!
WHAT ARE YOU TALKING ABOUT?!
...
SHEBA, YOU HAVE ALWAYS UNDERSTOOD ME.
UGO, YOU HAVE THE POWER OF CREATION.
ARBA, I VALUE YOUR ADVICE AND STRENGTH.
?!!
WAIT, SOLOMON!
GRIP
FWAH

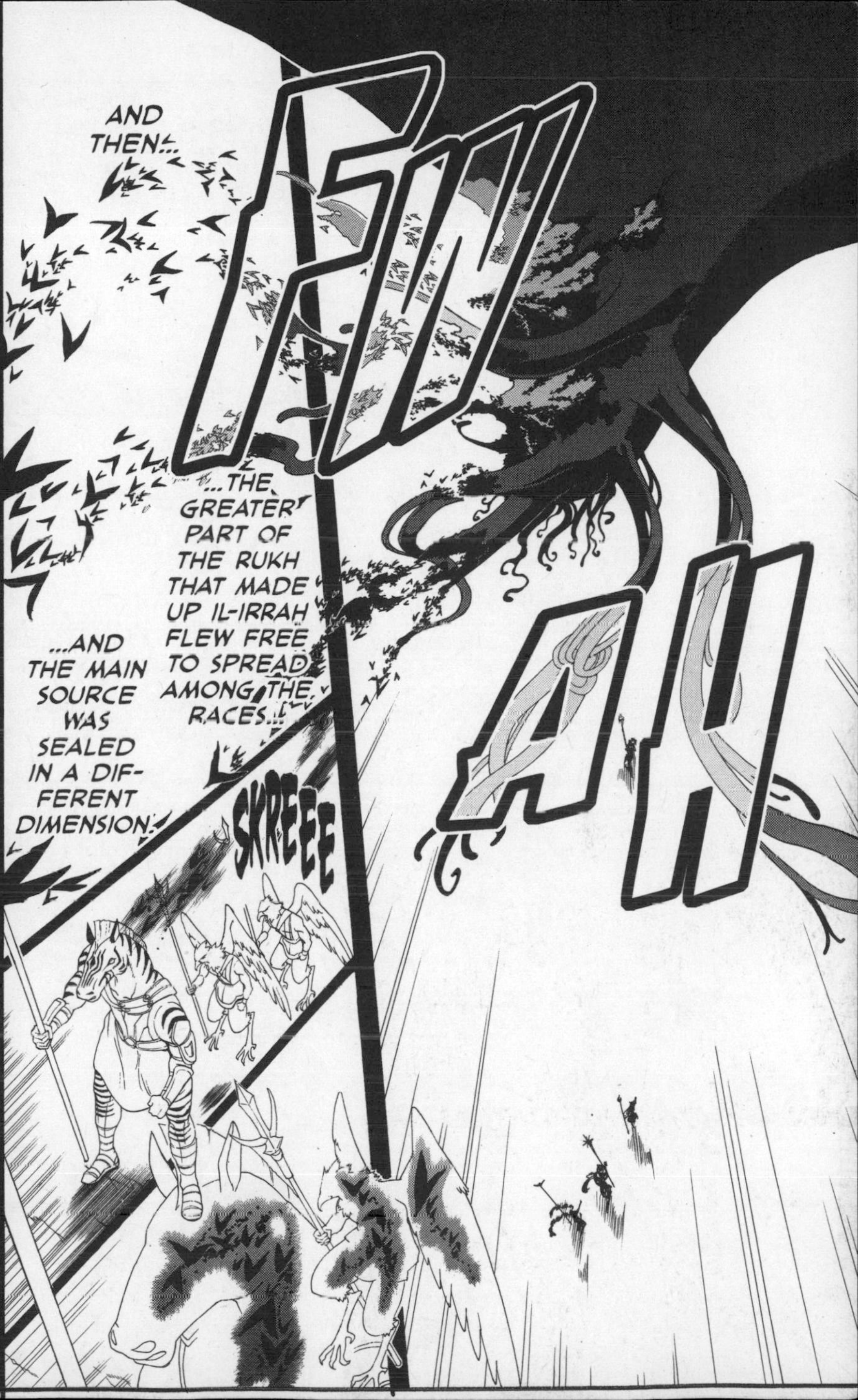
FWAH
AND THEN...
...THE GREATER PART OF THE RUKH THAT MADE UP IL-IRRAH FLEW FREE TO SPREAD AMONG THE RACES...
...AND THE MAIN SOURCE WAS SEALED IN A DIF-FERENT DIMENSION.
SKREEE

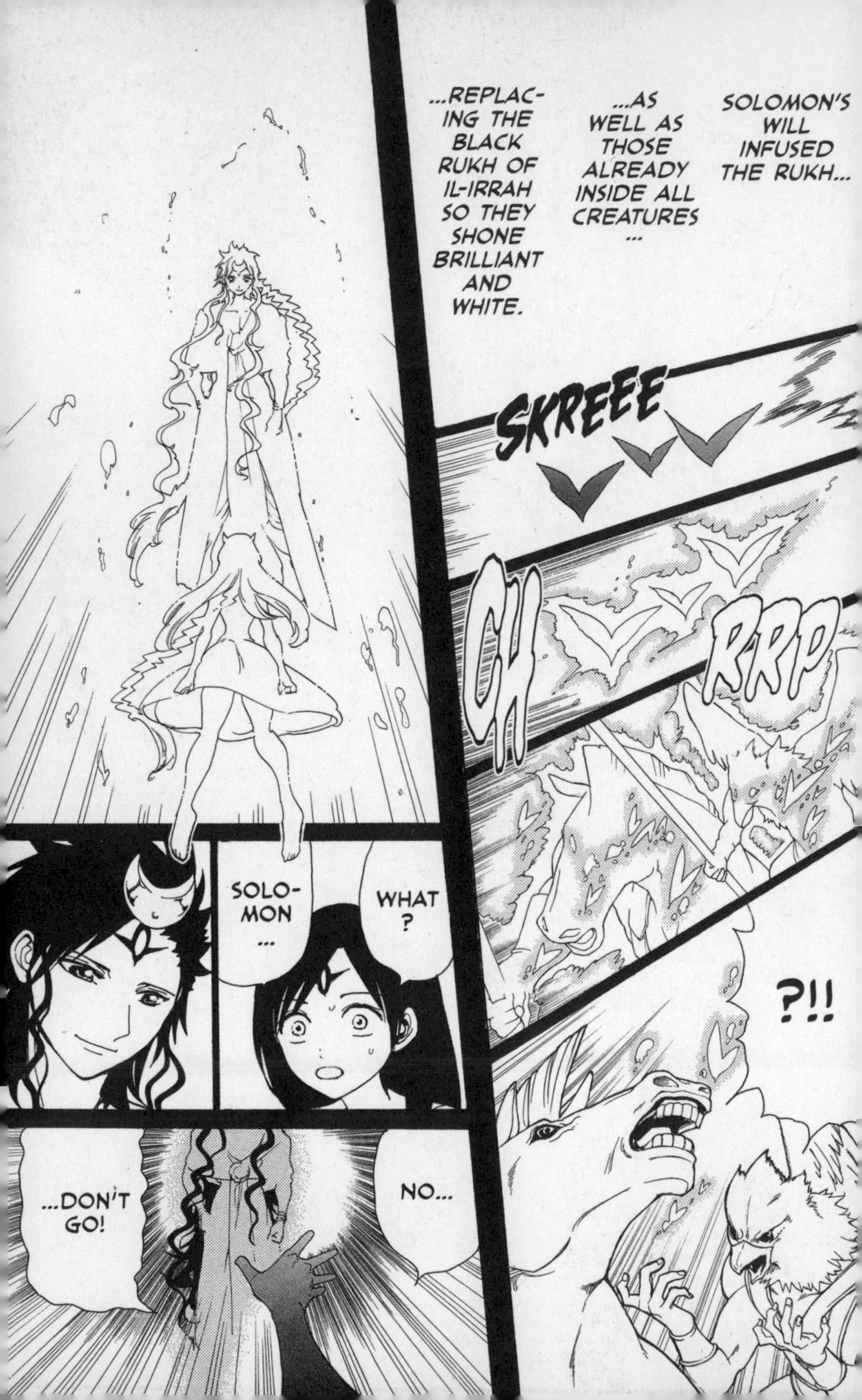
SOLOMON'S WILL INFUSED THE RUKH...
...AS WELL AS THOSE ALREADY INSIDE ALL CREATURES...
...REPLACING THE BLACK RUKH OF IL-IRRAH SO THEY SHONE BRILLIANT AND WHITE.
SKREEE
CHRRP
?!!
WHAT?
SOLOMON...
NO...
...DON'T GO!

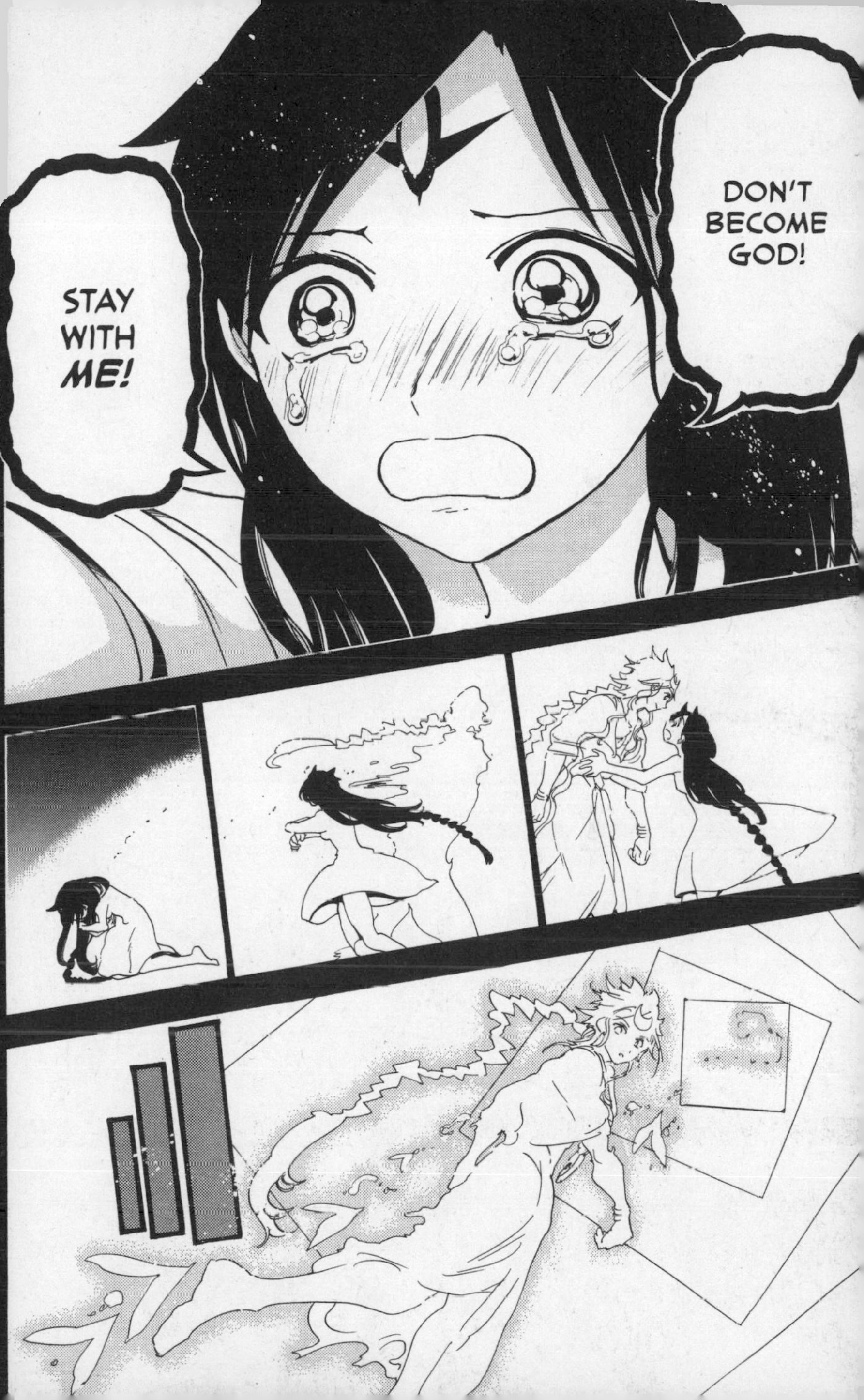
DON'T BECOME GOD!
STAY WITH ME!

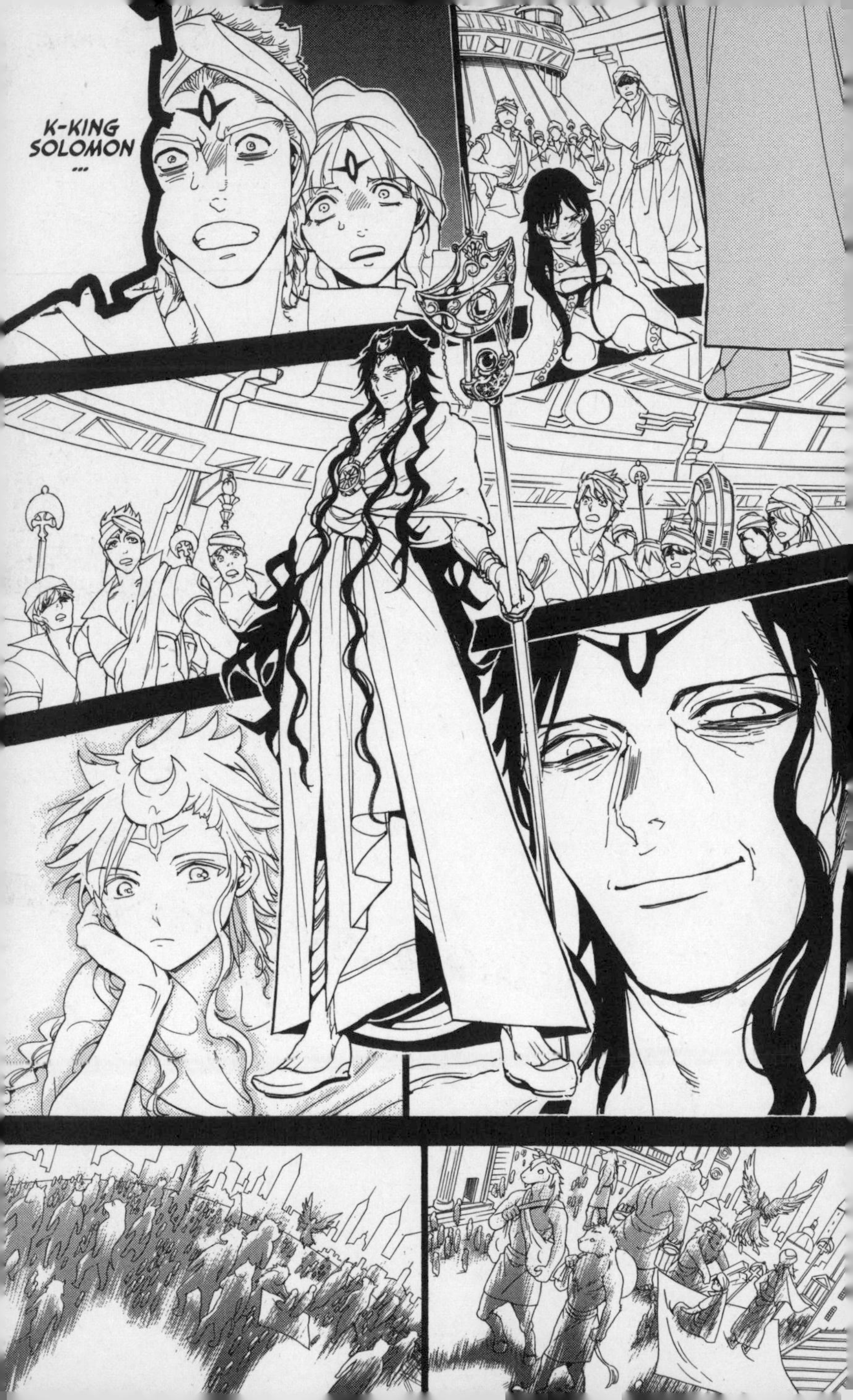
K-KING SOLOMON ...

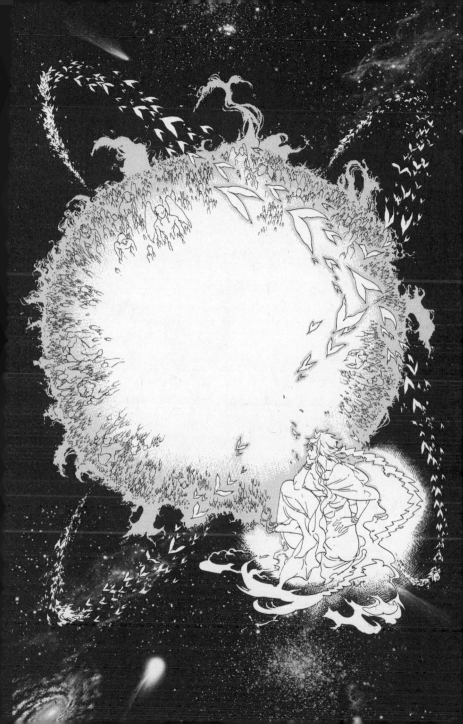

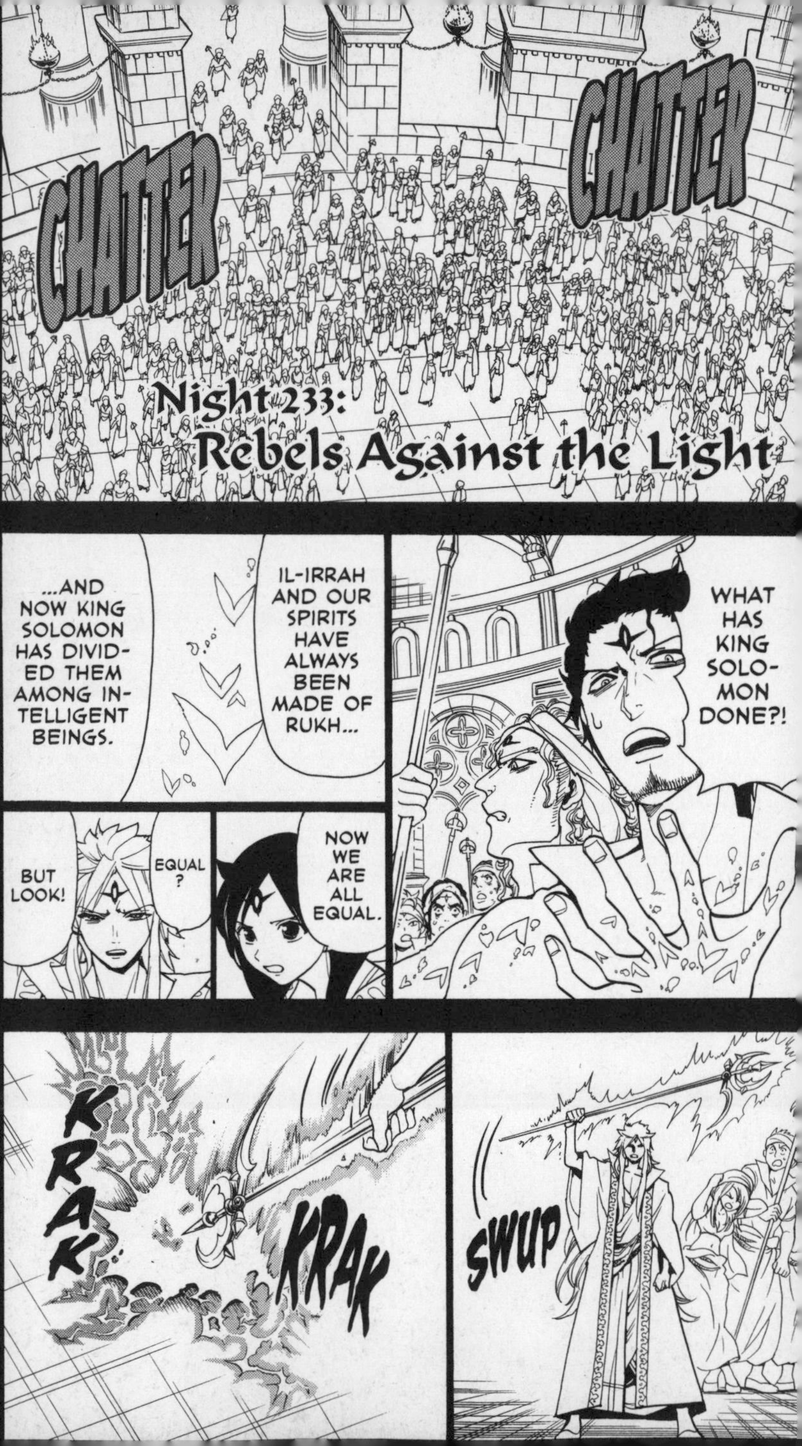
CHATTER
CHATTER
Night 233:
Rebels Against the Light
WHAT HAS KING SOLOMON DONE?!
IL-IRRAH AND OUR SPIRITS HAVE ALWAYS BEEN MADE OF RUKH...
...AND NOW KING SOLOMON HAS DIVIDED THEM AMONG INTELLIGENT BEINGS.
NOW WE ARE ALL EQUAL.
EQUAL?
BUT LOOK!
SWUP
KRAK
KRAK

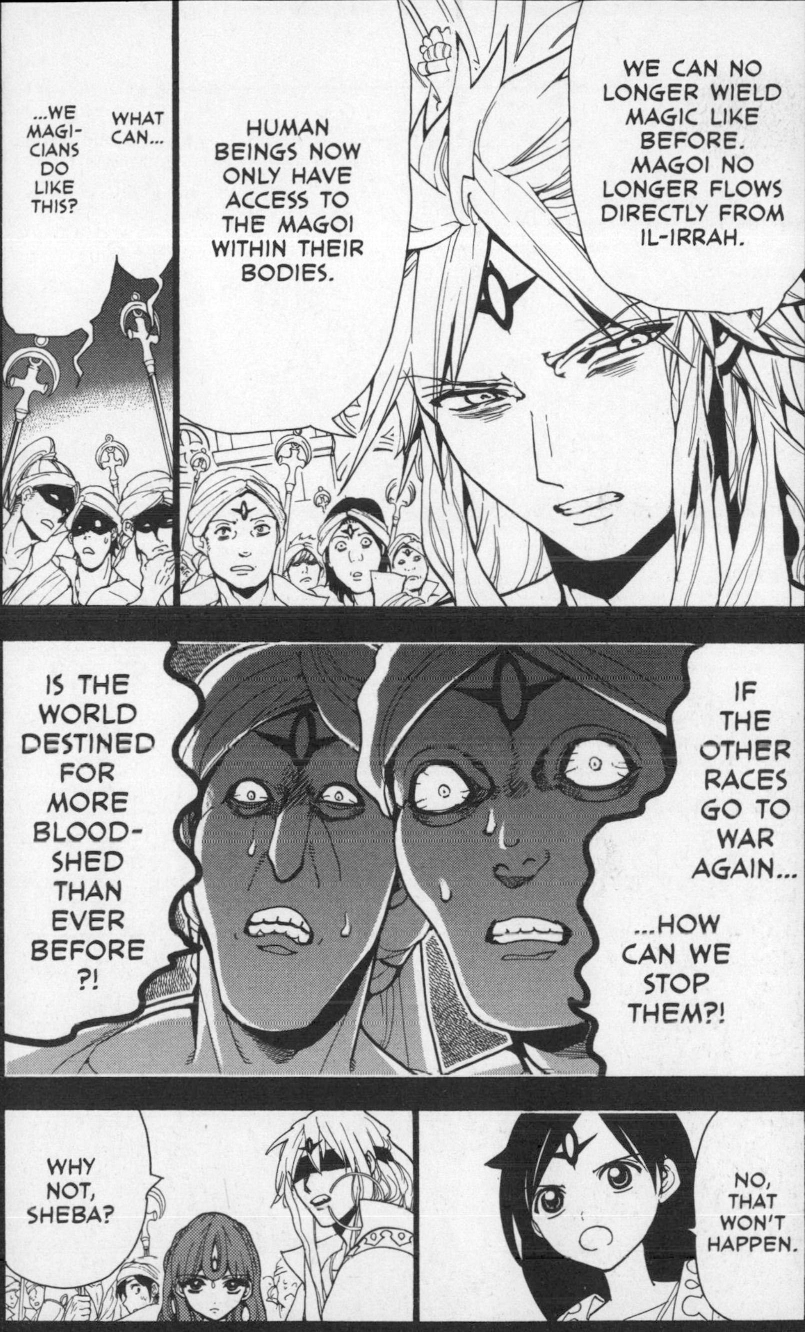
WE CAN NO LONGER WIELD MAGIC LIKE BEFORE. MAGOI NO LONGER FLOWS DIRECTLY FROM IL-IRRAH.
HUMAN BEINGS NOW ONLY HAVE ACCESS TO THE MAGOI WITHIN THEIR BODIES.
WHAT CAN...
...WE MAGI-CIANS DO LIKE THIS?
IF THE OTHER RACES GO TO WAR AGAIN...
...HOW CAN WE STOP THEM?!
IS THE WORLD DESTINED FOR MORE BLOOD-SHED THAN EVER BEFORE?!
NO, THAT WON'T HAPPEN.
WHY NOT, SHEBA?

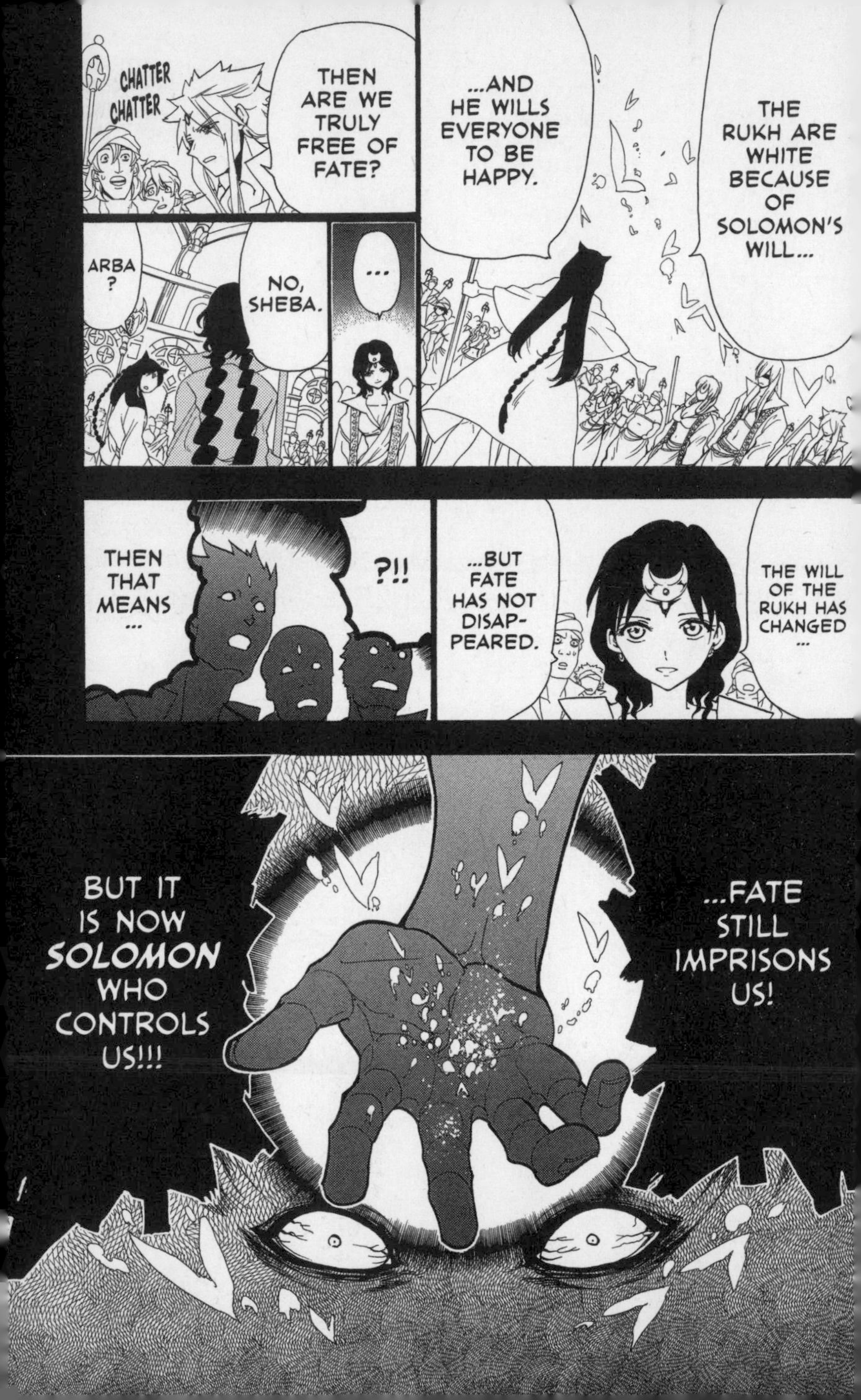
THE RUKH ARE WHITE BECAUSE OF SOLOMON'S WILL...
...AND HE WILLS EVERYONE TO BE HAPPY.
CHATTER CHATTER
THEN ARE WE TRULY FREE OF FATE?
...
ARBA?
NO, SHEBA.
THE WILL OF THE RUKH HAS CHANGED...
...BUT FATE HAS NOT DISAPPEARED.
?!!
THEN THAT MEANS...
...FATE STILL IMPRISONS US!
BUT IT IS NOW ***SOLOMON*** WHO CONTROLS US!!!

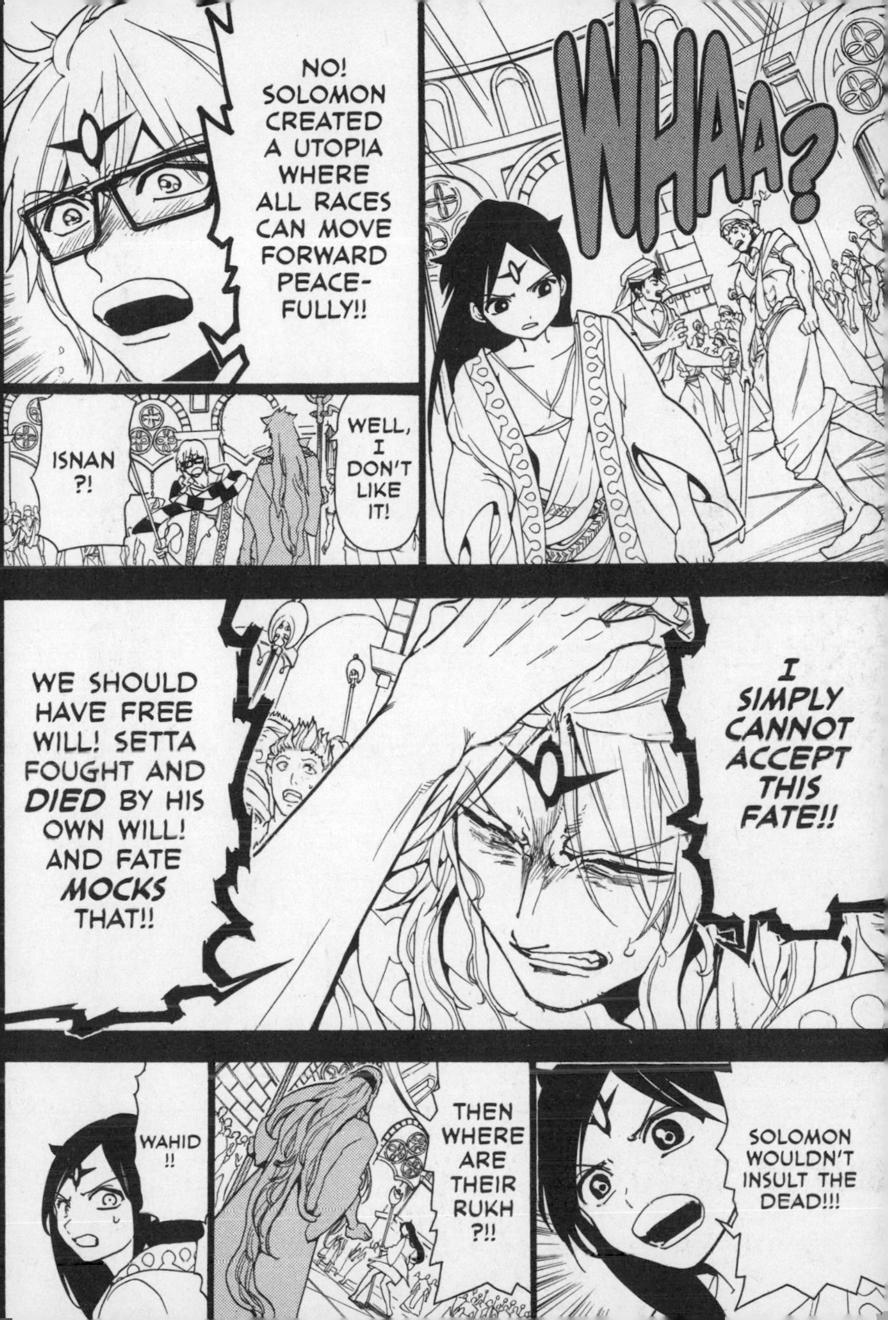
WHAA?
NO! SOLOMON CREATED A UTOPIA WHERE ALL RACES CAN MOVE FORWARD PEACE-FULLY!!
WELL, I DON'T LIKE IT!
ISNAN?!
I SIMPLY CANNOT ACCEPT THIS FATE!!
WE SHOULD HAVE FREE WILL! SETTA FOUGHT AND DIED BY HIS OWN WILL! AND FATE MOCKS THAT!!
SOLOMON WOULDN'T INSULT THE DEAD!!!
THEN WHERE ARE THEIR RUKH?!!
WAHID!!

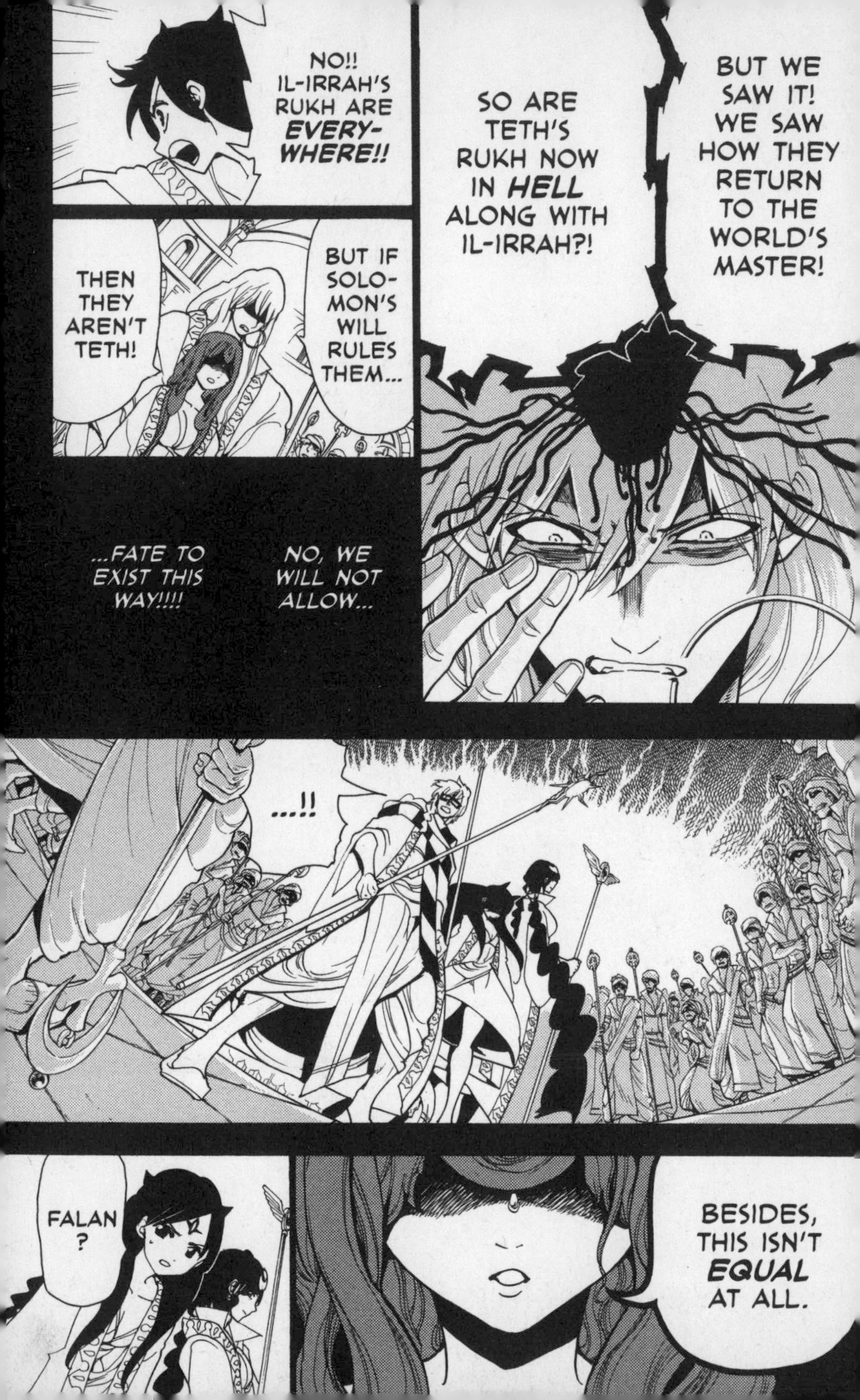

BUT WE SAW IT! WE SAW HOW THEY RETURN TO THE WORLD'S MASTER!
SO ARE TETH'S RUKH NOW IN *HELL* ALONG WITH IL-IRRAH?!
NO!! IL-IRRAH'S RUKH ARE *EVERY-WHERE!!*
BUT IF SOLOMON'S WILL RULES THEM...
THEN THEY AREN'T TETH!
NO, WE WILL NOT ALLOW...
...FATE TO EXIST THIS WAY!!!!
...!!
BESIDES, THIS ISN'T *EQUAL* AT ALL.
FALAN?

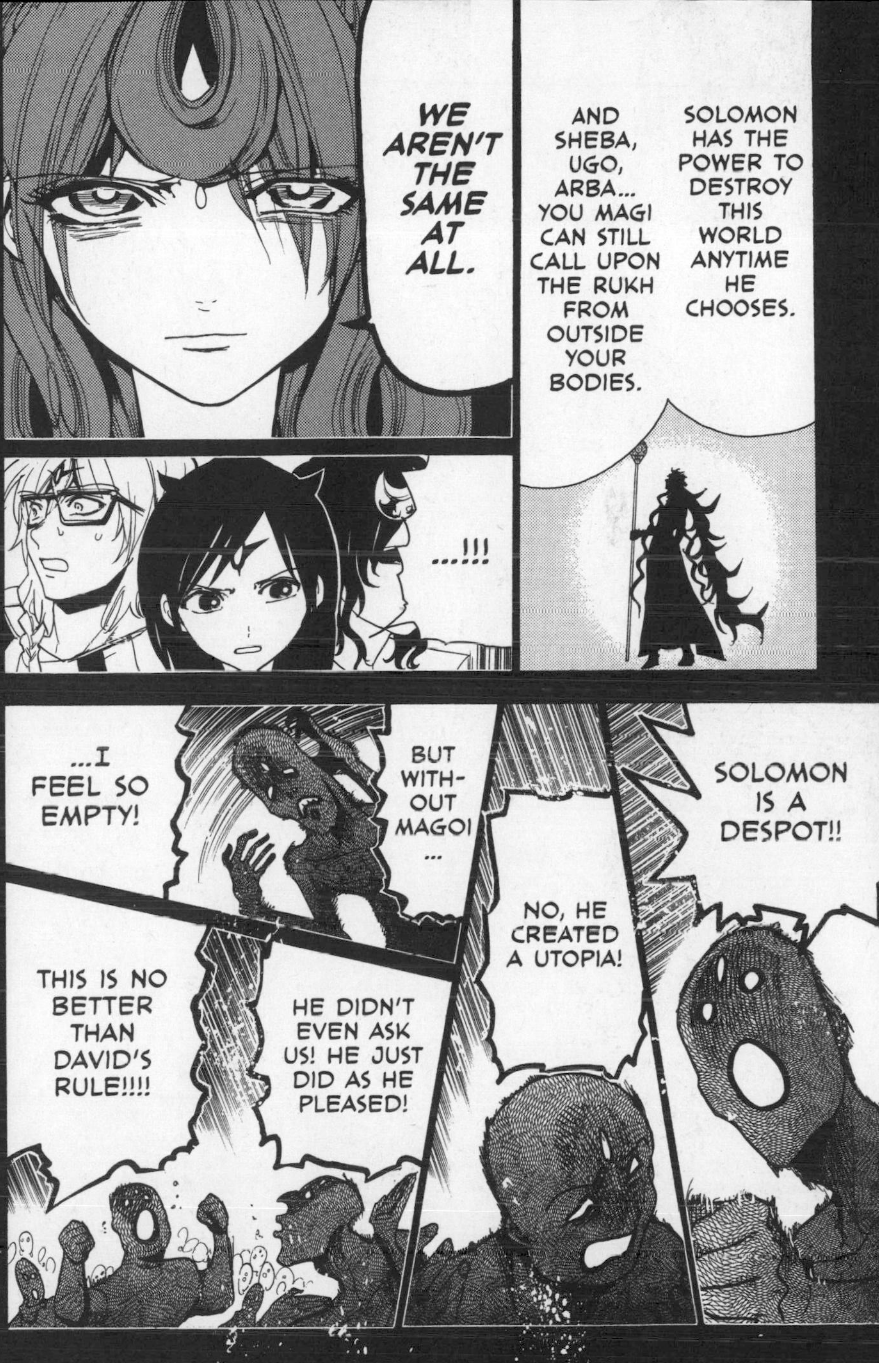
SOLOMON HAS THE POWER TO DESTROY THIS WORLD ANYTIME HE CHOOSES.
AND SHEBA, UGO, ARBA... YOU MAGI CAN STILL CALL UPON THE RUKH FROM OUTSIDE YOUR BODIES.
WE AREN'T THE SAME AT ALL.
...!!!
SOLOMON IS A DESPOT!!
NO, HE CREATED A UTOPIA!
BUT WITH-OUT MAGOI ...
...I FEEL SO EMPTY!
HE DIDN'T EVEN ASK US! HE JUST DID AS HE PLEASED!
THIS IS NO BETTER THAN DAVID'S RULE!!!!

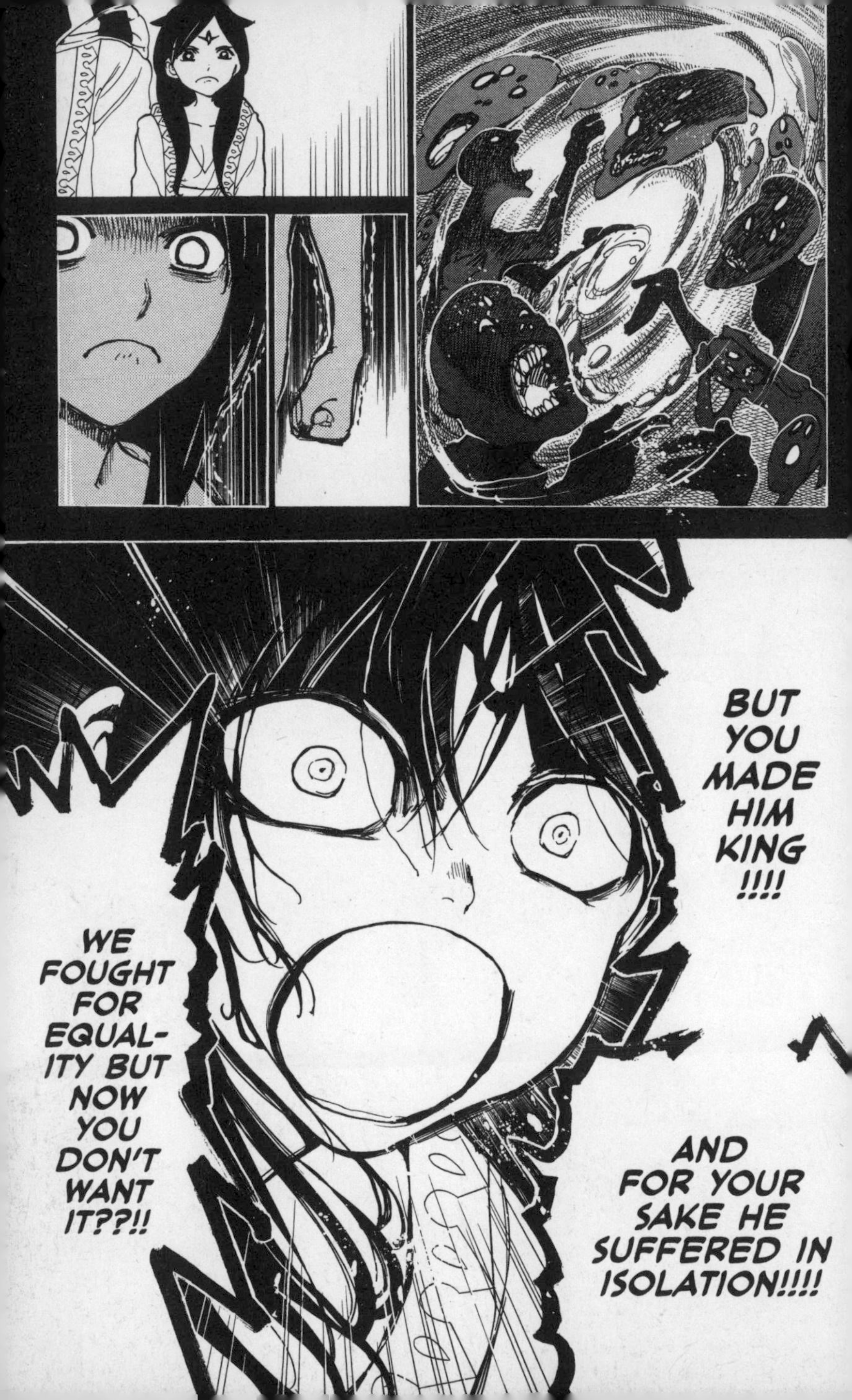
BUT YOU MADE HIM KING!!!!
WE FOUGHT FOR EQUALITY BUT NOW YOU DON'T WANT IT??!!
AND FOR YOUR SAKE HE SUFFERED IN ISOLATION!!!!

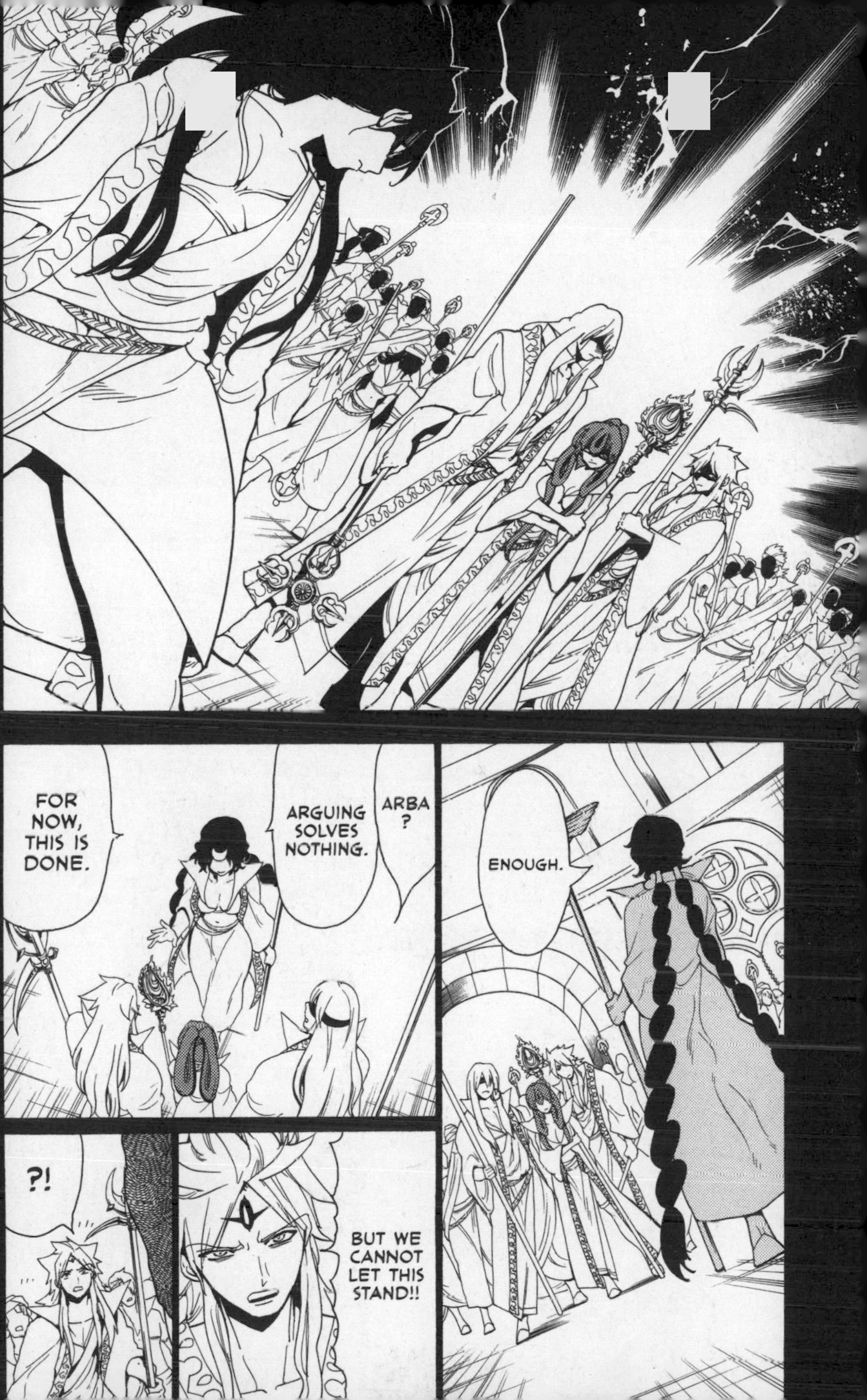
ENOUGH.
ARBA?
ARGUING SOLVES NOTHING.
FOR NOW, THIS IS DONE.
BUT WE CANNOT LET THIS STAND!!
?!

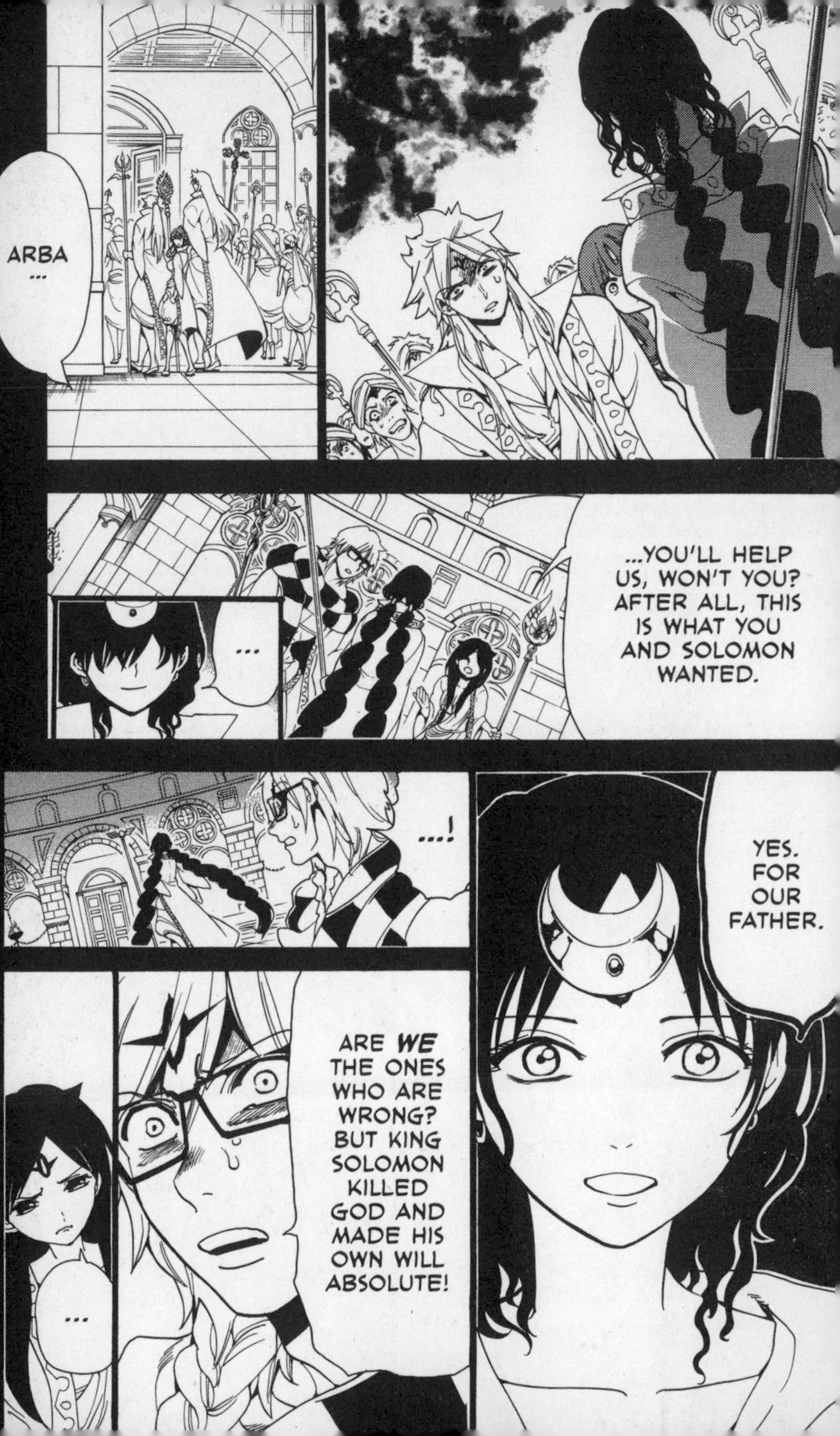
ARBA ...
...YOU'LL HELP US, WON'T YOU? AFTER ALL, THIS IS WHAT YOU AND SOLOMON WANTED.
...
YES. FOR OUR FATHER.
...!
ARE *WE* THE ONES WHO ARE WRONG? BUT KING SOLOMON KILLED GOD AND MADE HIS OWN WILL ABSOLUTE!
...

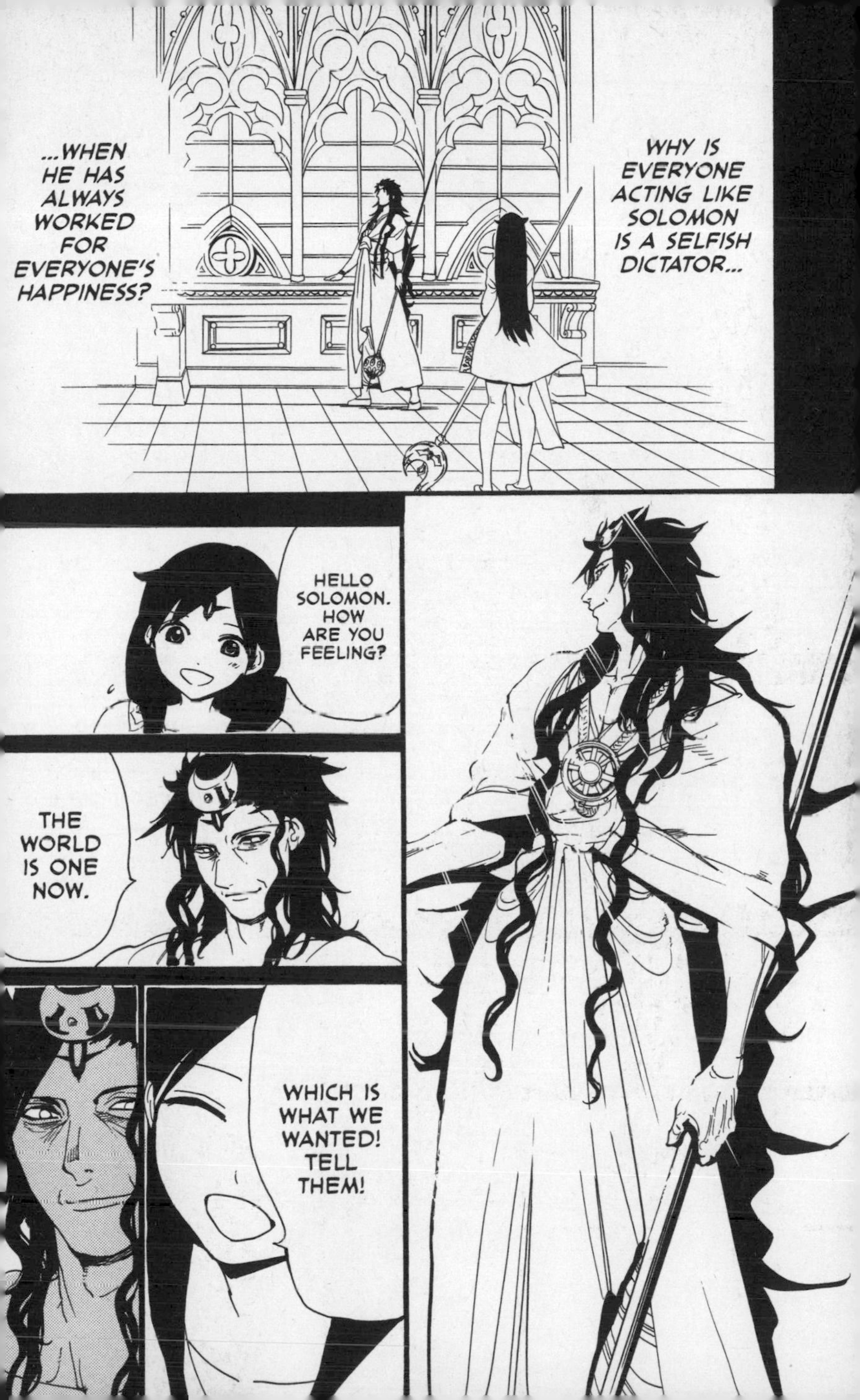
WHY IS EVERYONE ACTING LIKE SOLOMON IS A SELFISH DICTATOR...
...WHEN HE HAS ALWAYS WORKED FOR EVERYONE'S HAPPINESS?
HELLO SOLOMON. HOW ARE YOU FEELING?
THE WORLD IS ONE NOW.
WHICH IS WHAT WE WANTED! TELL THEM!

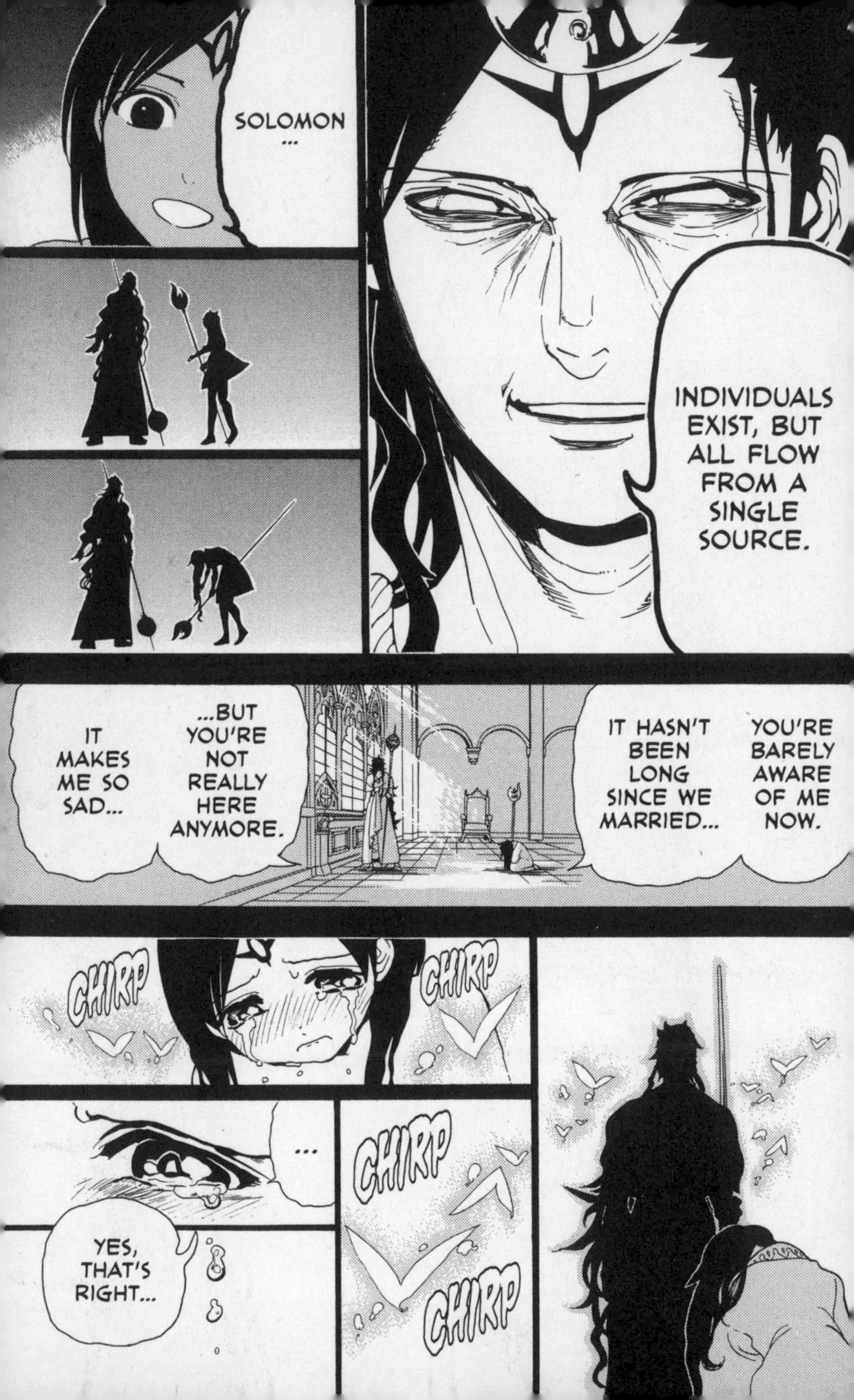
INDIVIDUALS EXIST, BUT ALL FLOW FROM A SINGLE SOURCE.
SOLOMON ...
YOU'RE BARELY AWARE OF ME NOW.
IT HASN'T BEEN LONG SINCE WE MARRIED...
...BUT YOU'RE NOT REALLY HERE ANYMORE.
IT MAKES ME SO SAD...
CHIRP
CHIRP
CHIRP
CHIRP
...
YES, THAT'S RIGHT...

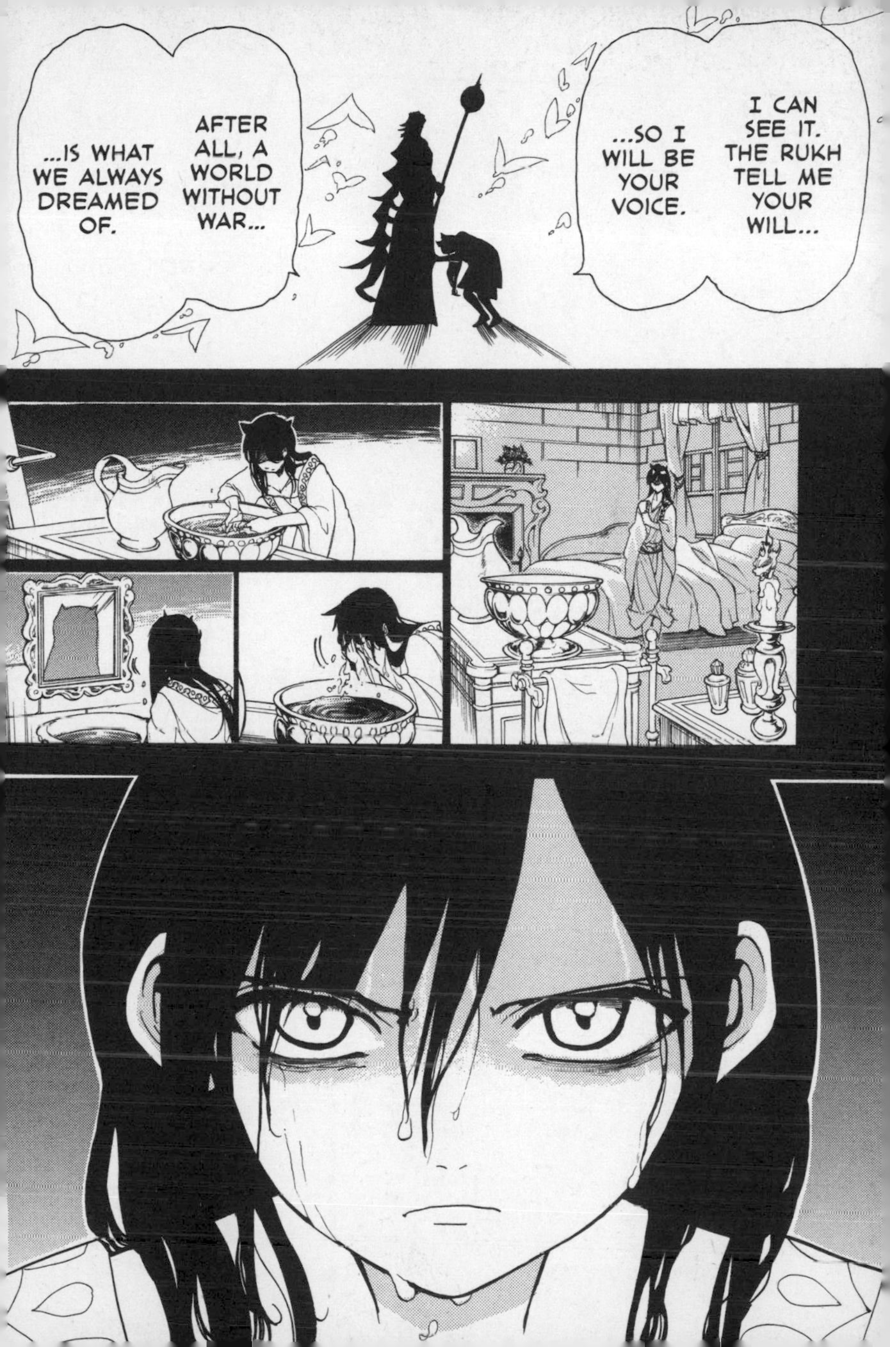
I CAN SEE IT. THE RUKH TELL ME YOUR WILL...
...SO I WILL BE YOUR VOICE.
AFTER ALL, A WORLD WITHOUT WAR...
...IS WHAT WE ALWAYS DREAMED OF.

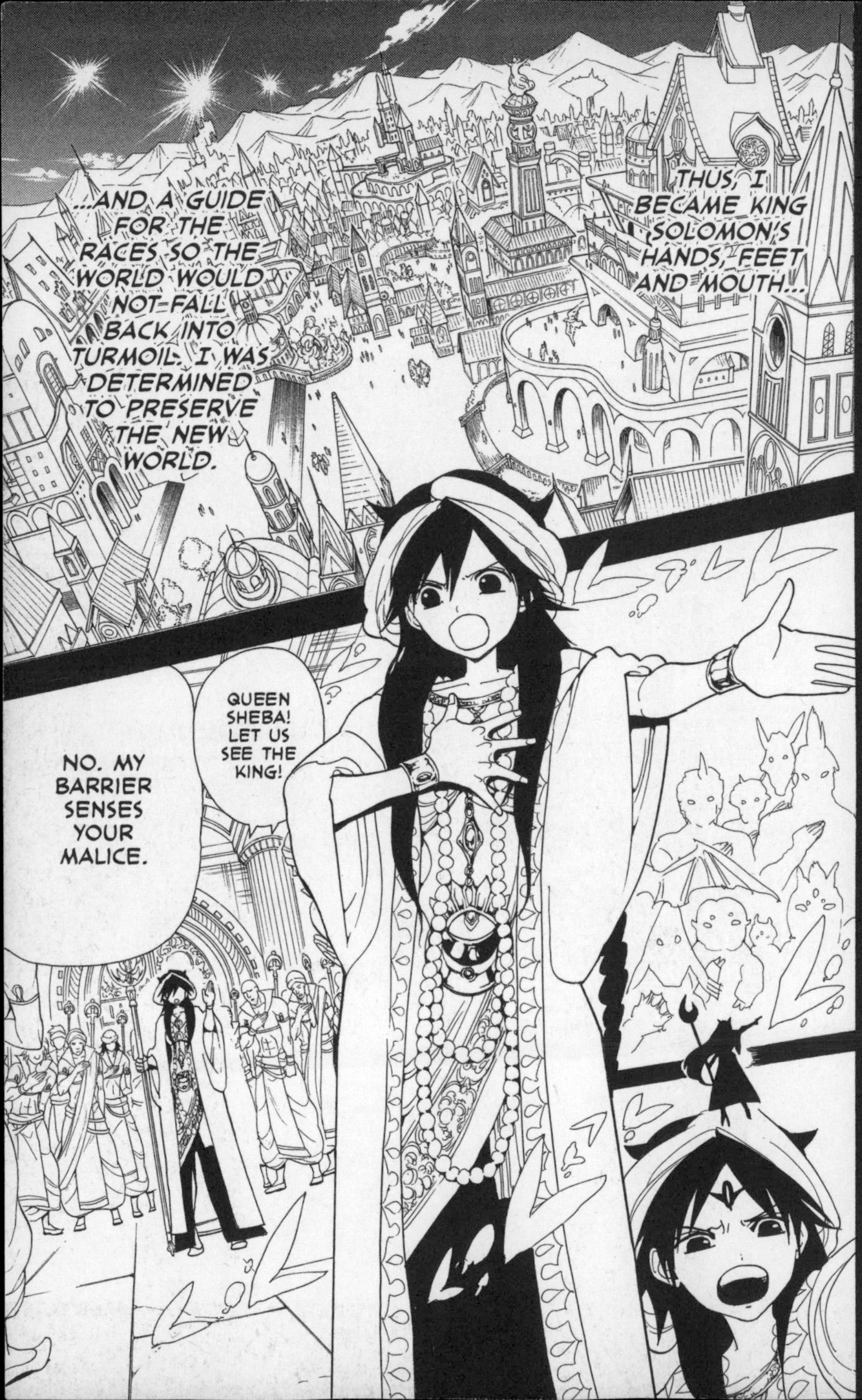
THUS, I BECAME KING SOLOMON'S HANDS, FEET AND MOUTH...
...AND A GUIDE FOR THE RACES SO THE WORLD WOULD NOT FALL BACK INTO TURMOIL. I WAS DETERMINED TO PRESERVE THE NEW WORLD.
QUEEN SHEBA! LET US SEE THE KING!
NO. MY BARRIER SENSES YOUR MALICE.

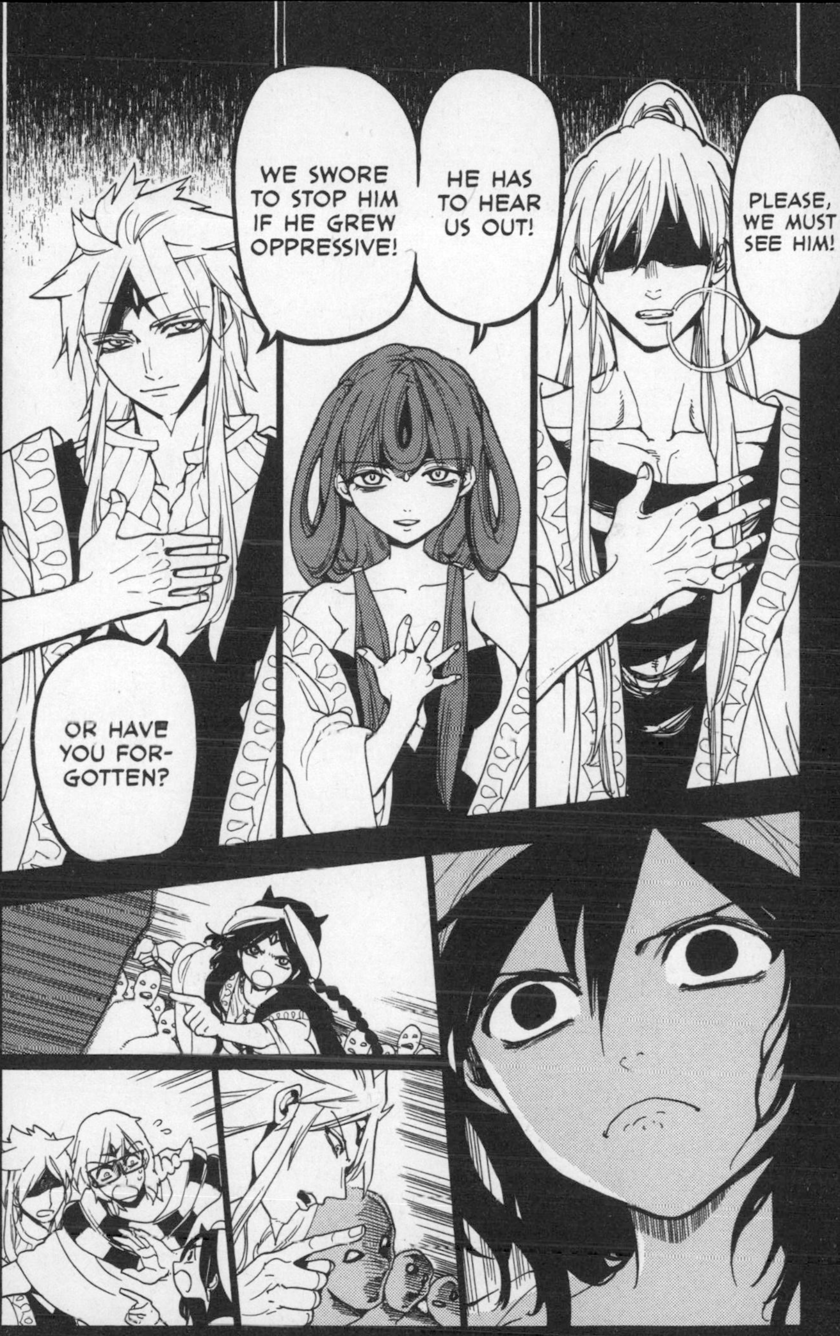
PLEASE, WE MUST SEE HIM!
HE HAS TO HEAR US OUT!
WE SWORE TO STOP HIM IF HE GREW OPPRESSIVE!
OR HAVE YOU FOR-GOTTEN?

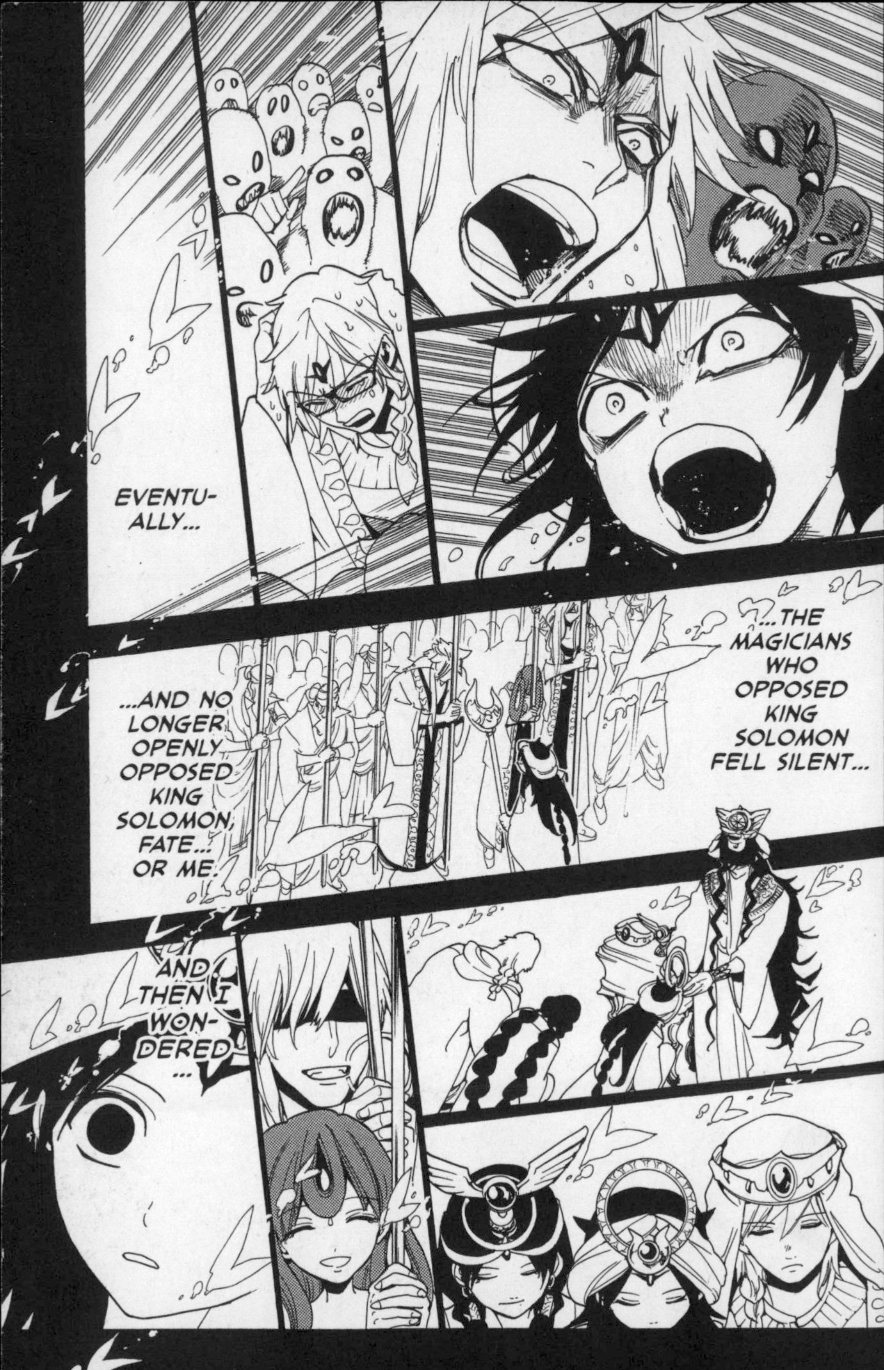
EVENTU-ALLY...
...THE MAGICIANS WHO OPPOSED KING SOLOMON FELL SILENT...
...AND NO LONGER OPENLY OPPOSED KING SOLOMON, FATE... OR ME.
AND THEN I WONDERED...

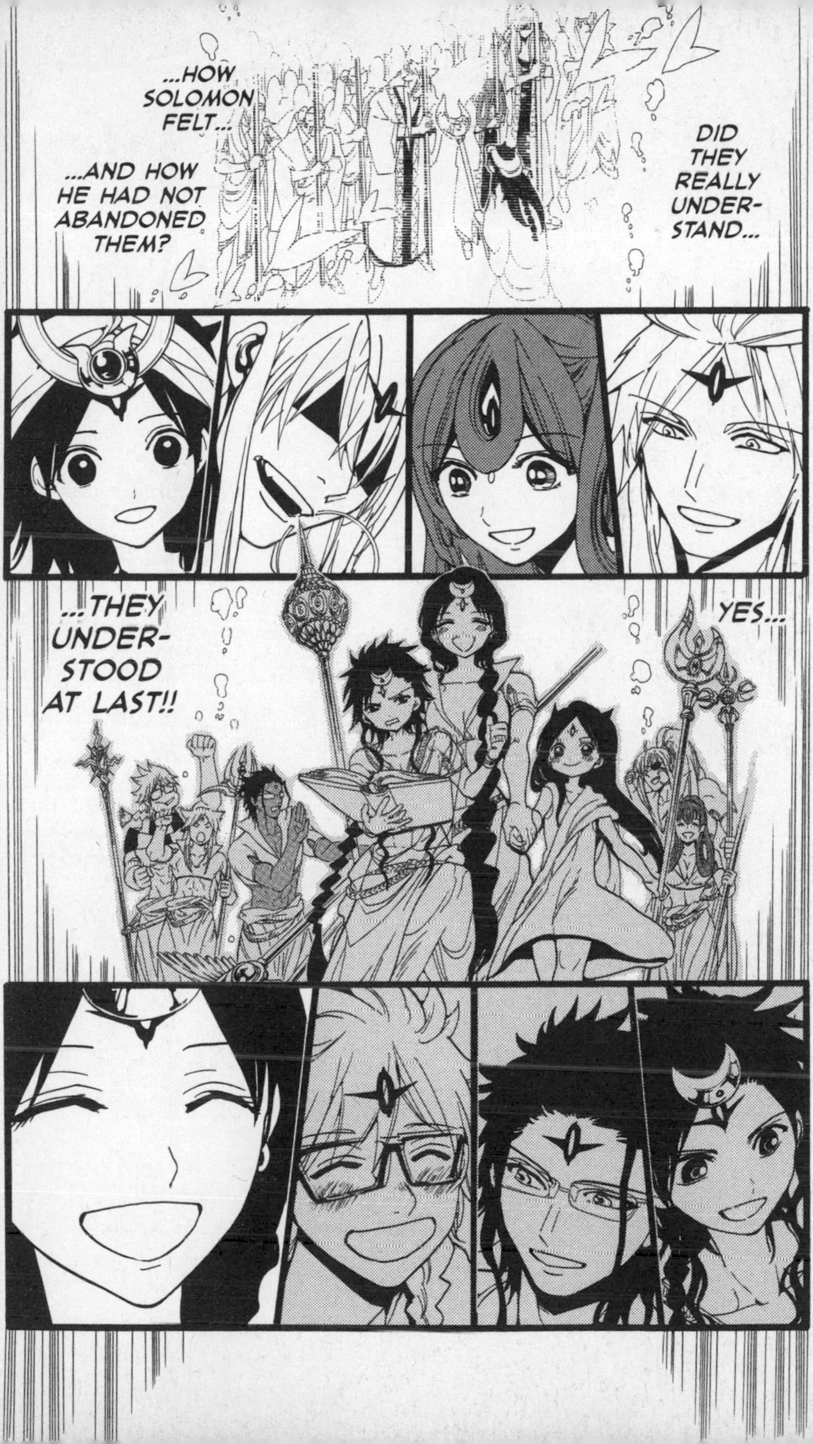
DID THEY REALLY UNDER-STAND...
...HOW SOLOMON FELT...
...AND HOW HE HAD NOT ABANDONED THEM?
YES...
...THEY UNDER-STOOD AT LAST!!

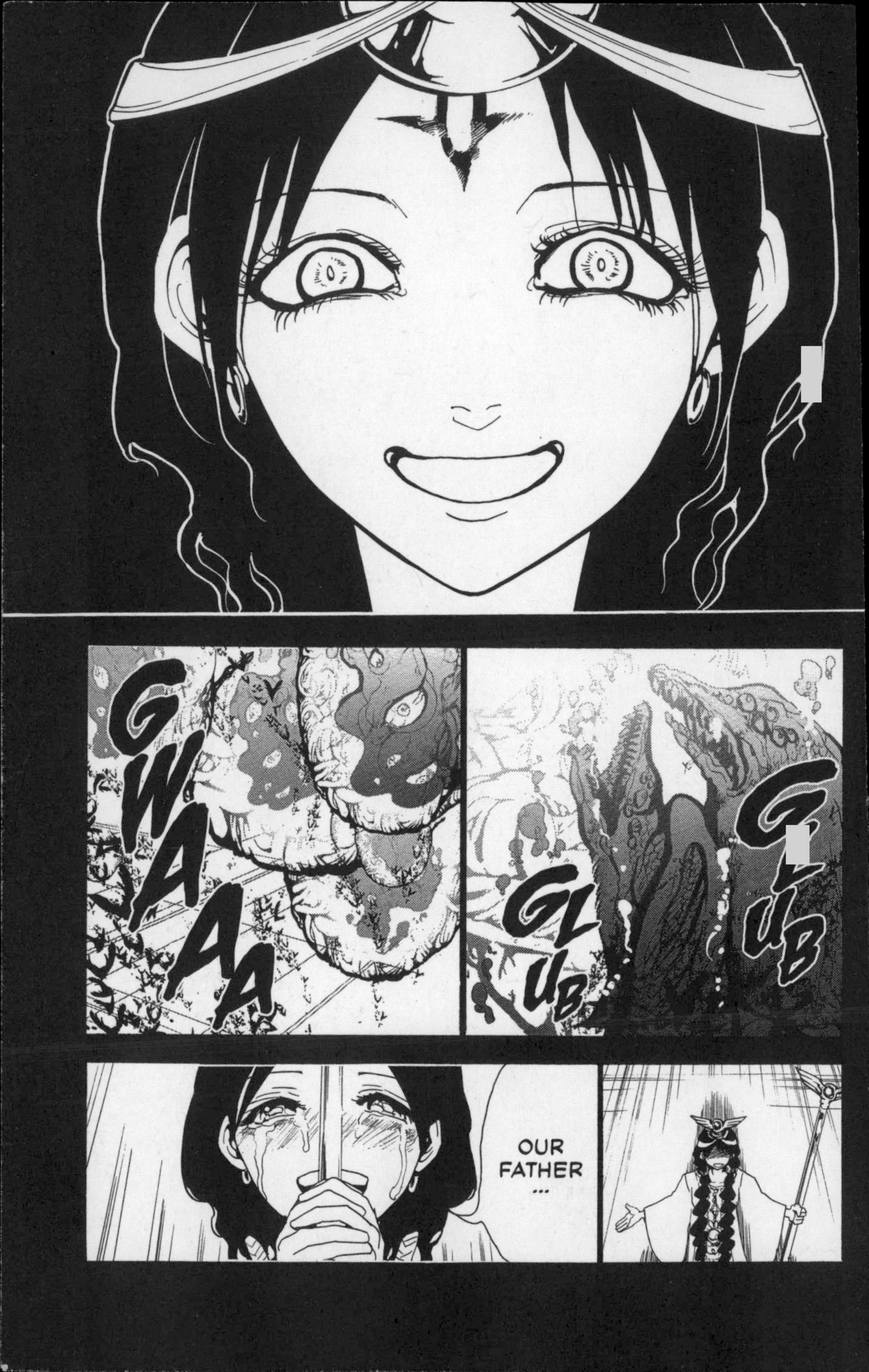
GLUB
GLUB
GWAAAA
OUR FATHER ...

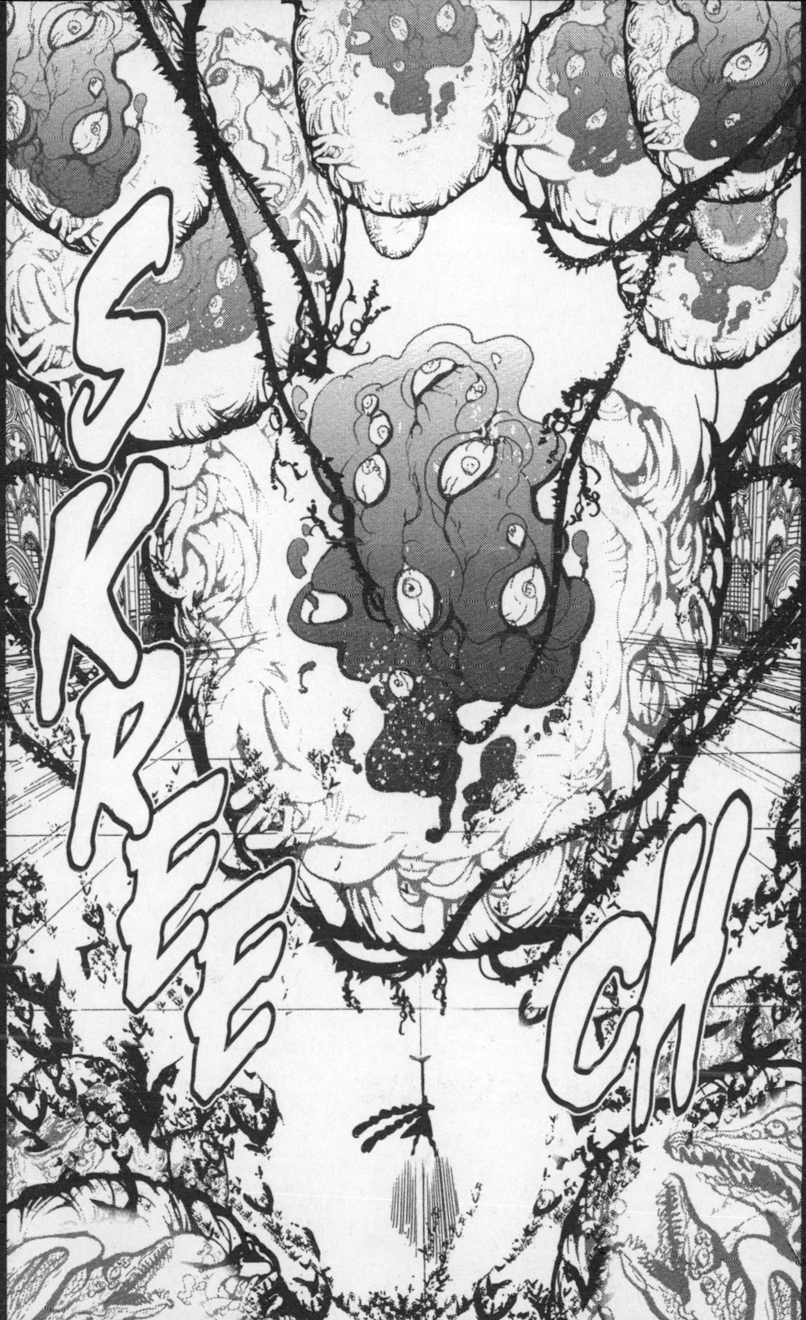
SKREECH

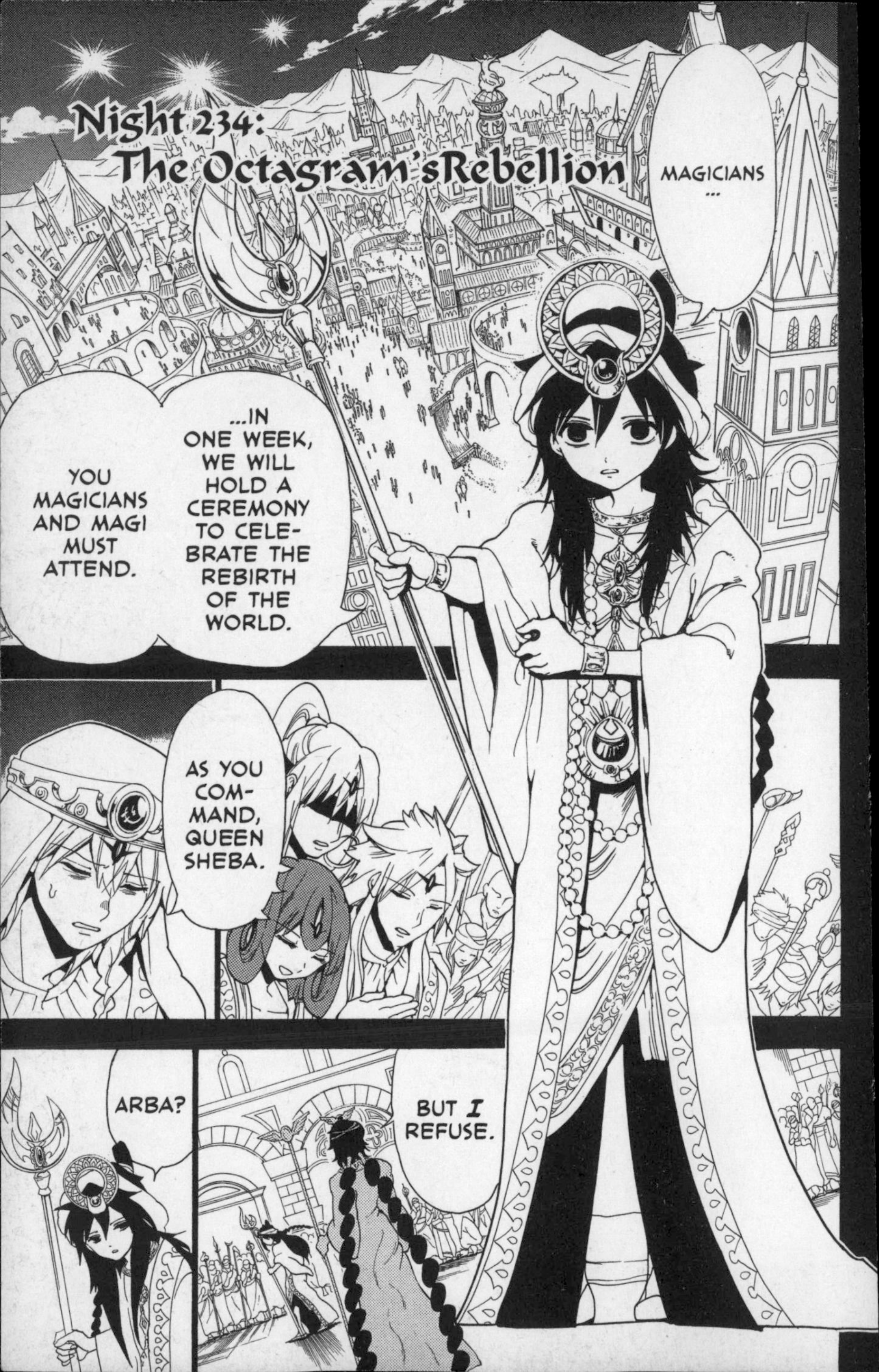
Night 234: The Octagram'sRebellion
MAGICIANS ...
...IN ONE WEEK, WE WILL HOLD A CEREMONY TO CELE-BRATE THE REBIRTH OF THE WORLD.
YOU MAGICIANS AND MAGI MUST ATTEND.
AS YOU COM-MAND, QUEEN SHEBA.
BUT *I* REFUSE.
ARBA?

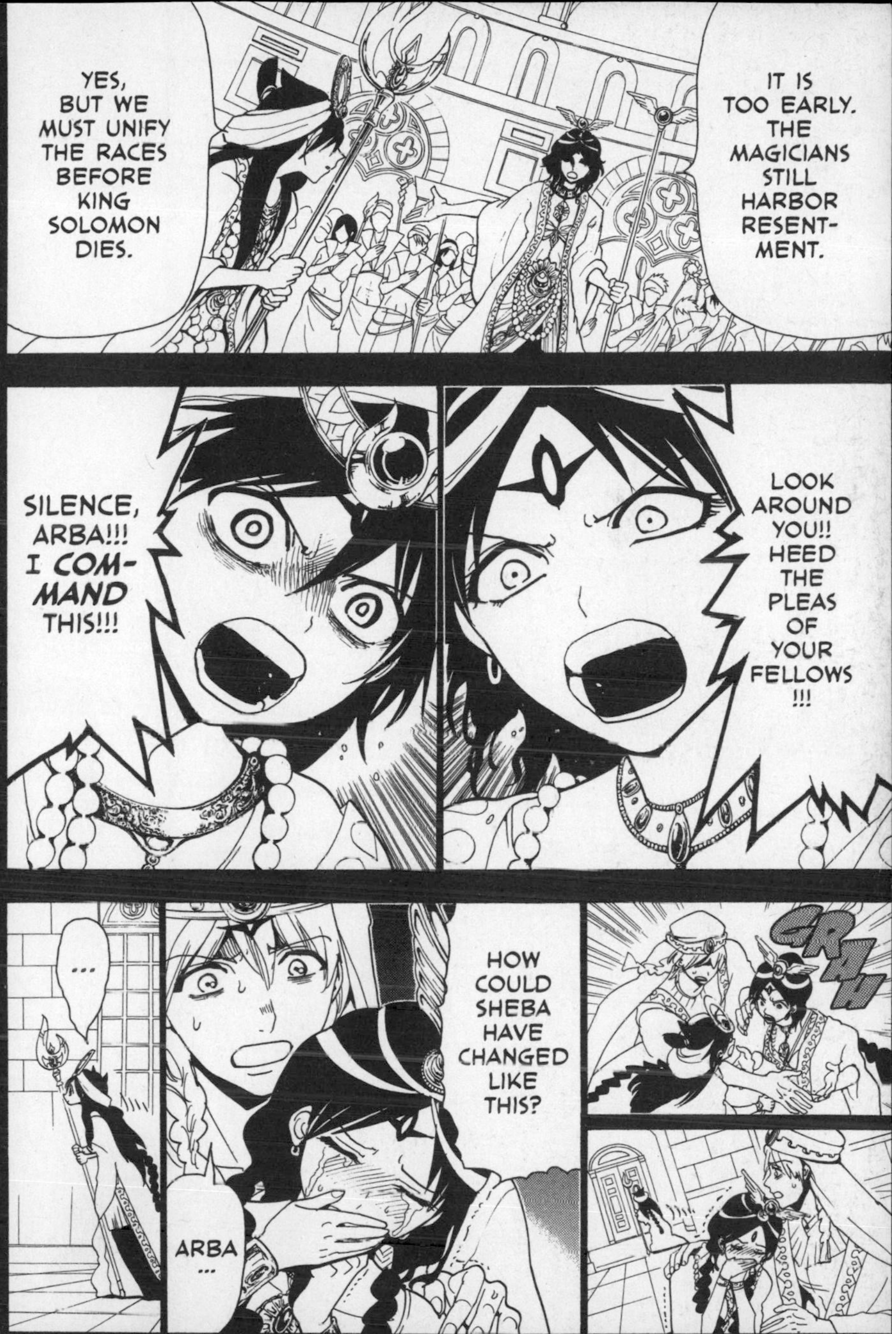
IT IS TOO EARLY. THE MAGICIANS STILL HARBOR RESENT-MENT.
YES, BUT WE MUST UNIFY THE RACES BEFORE KING SOLOMON DIES.
LOOK AROUND YOU!! HEED THE PLEAS OF YOUR FELLOWS !!!
SILENCE, ARBA!!! I *COM-MAND* THIS!!!
GRAH
HOW COULD SHEBA HAVE CHANGED LIKE THIS?
ARBA ...
...

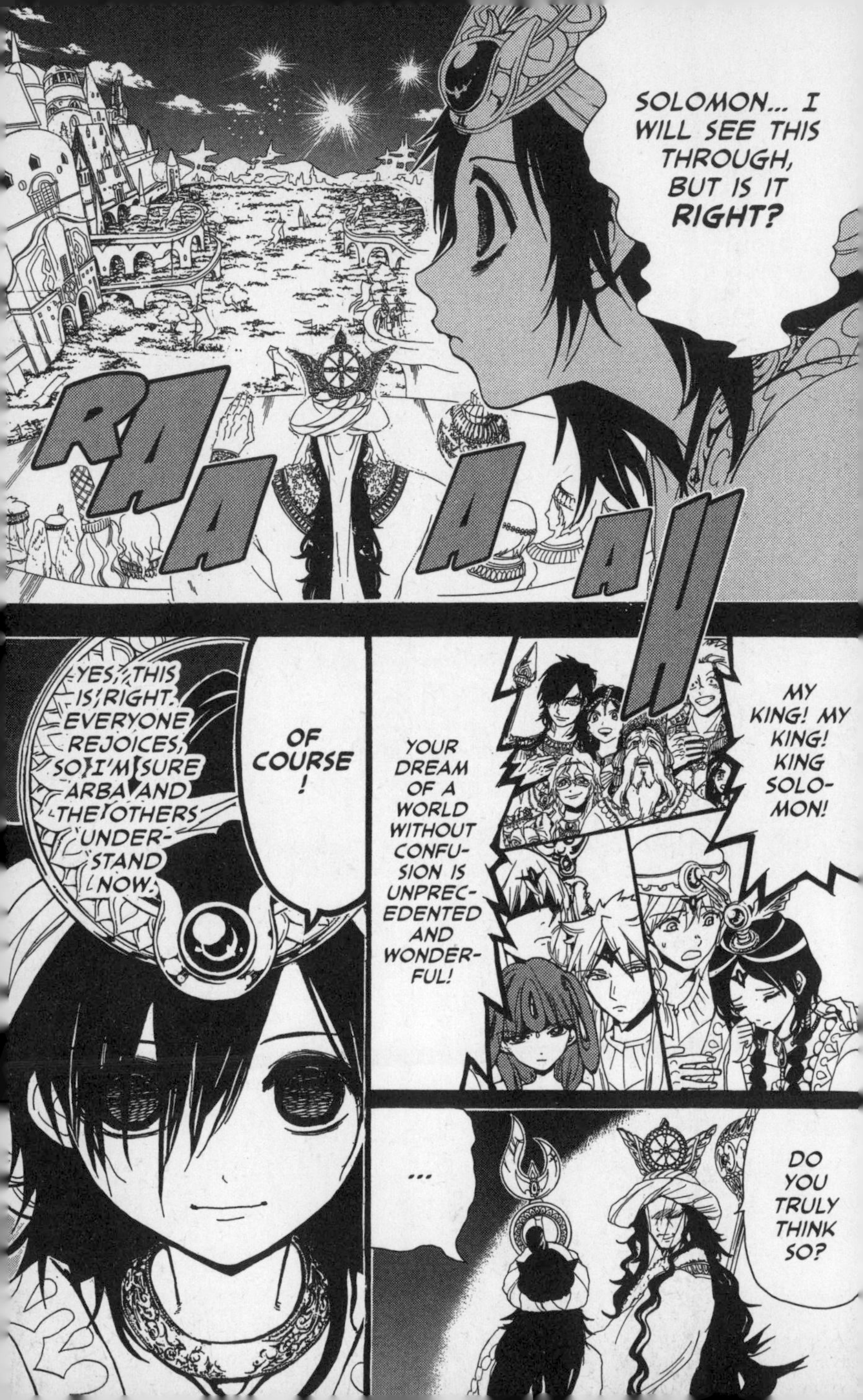
SOLOMON... I WILL SEE THIS THROUGH, BUT IS IT RIGHT?
RAAAAH
MY KING! MY KING! KING SOLOMON!
YOUR DREAM OF A WORLD WITHOUT CONFUSION IS UNPRECEDENTED AND WONDERFUL!
DO YOU TRULY THINK SO?
...
OF COURSE!
YES, THIS IS RIGHT. EVERYONE REJOICES, SO I'M SURE ARBA AND THE OTHERS UNDERSTAND NOW.

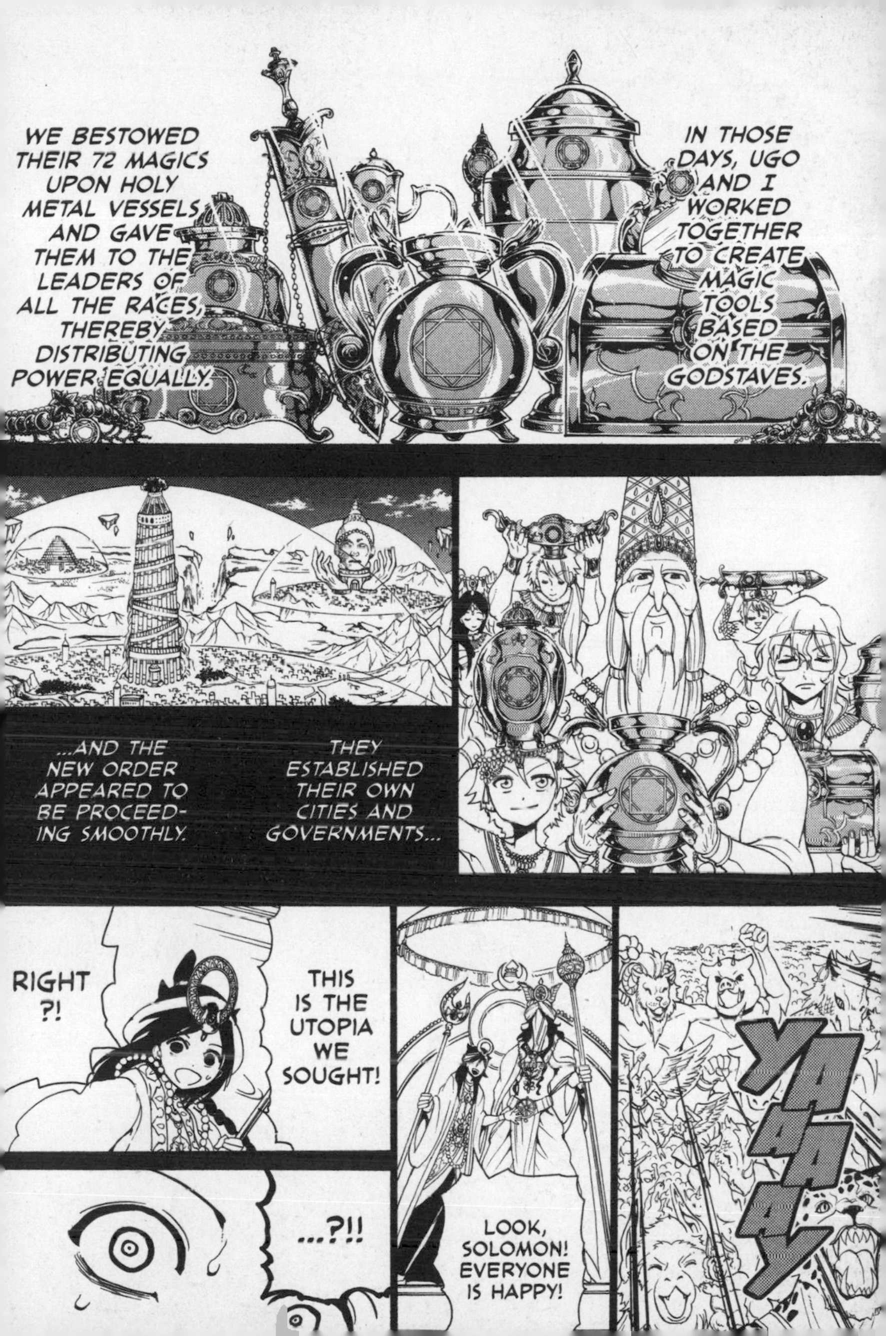
IN THOSE DAYS, UGO AND I WORKED TOGETHER TO CREATE MAGIC TOOLS BASED ON THE GODSTAVES.
WE BESTOWED THEIR 72 MAGICS UPON HOLY METAL VESSELS AND GAVE THEM TO THE LEADERS OF ALL THE RACES, THEREBY DISTRIBUTING POWER EQUALLY.
THEY ESTABLISHED THEIR OWN CITIES AND GOVERNMENTS...
...AND THE NEW ORDER APPEARED TO BE PROCEEDING SMOOTHLY.
YAAAAY
LOOK, SOLOMON! EVERYONE IS HAPPY!
THIS IS THE UTOPIA WE SOUGHT!
RIGHT ?!
...?!!

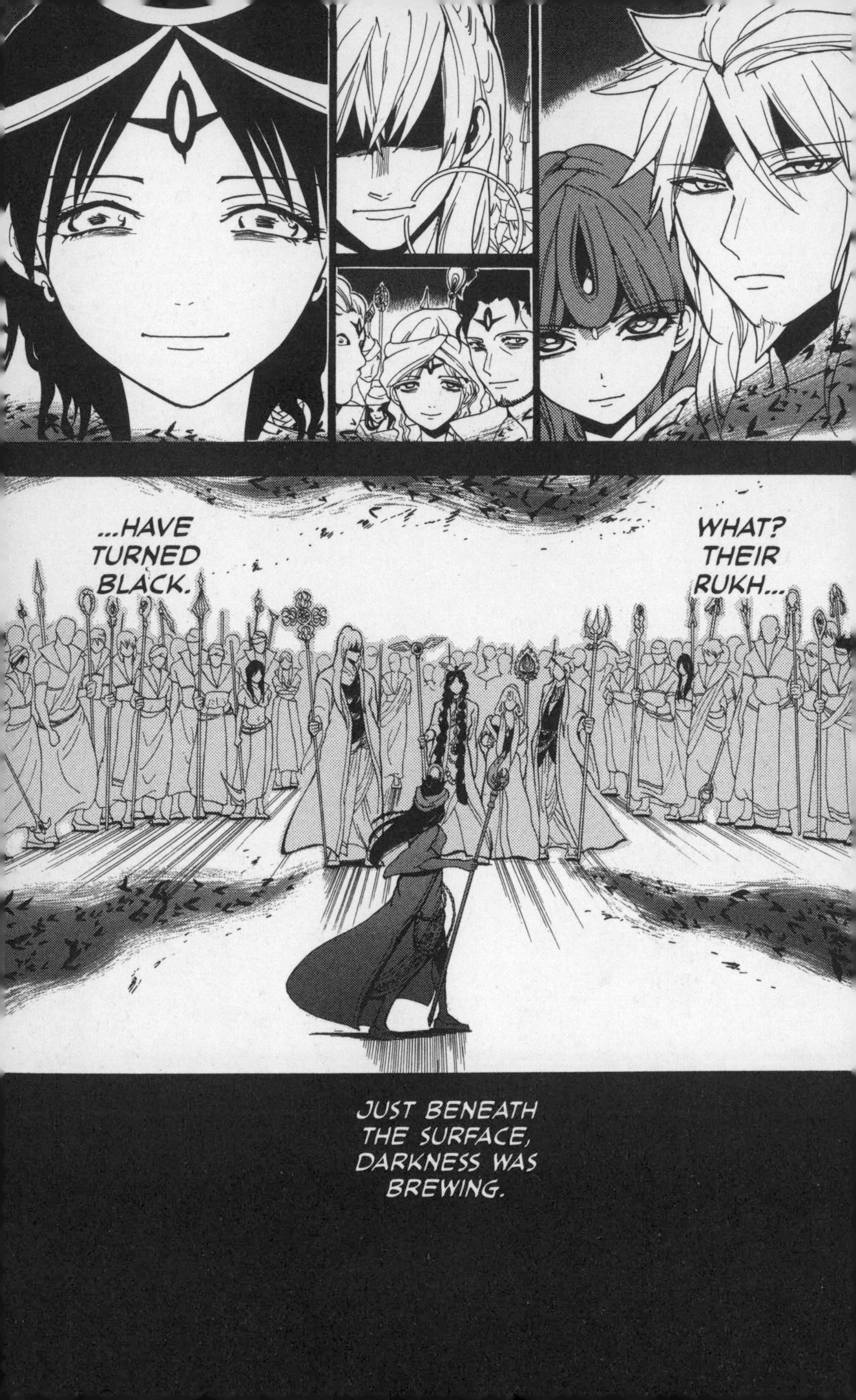
WHAT? THEIR RUKH...
...HAVE TURNED BLACK.
JUST BENEATH THE SURFACE, DARKNESS WAS BREWING.

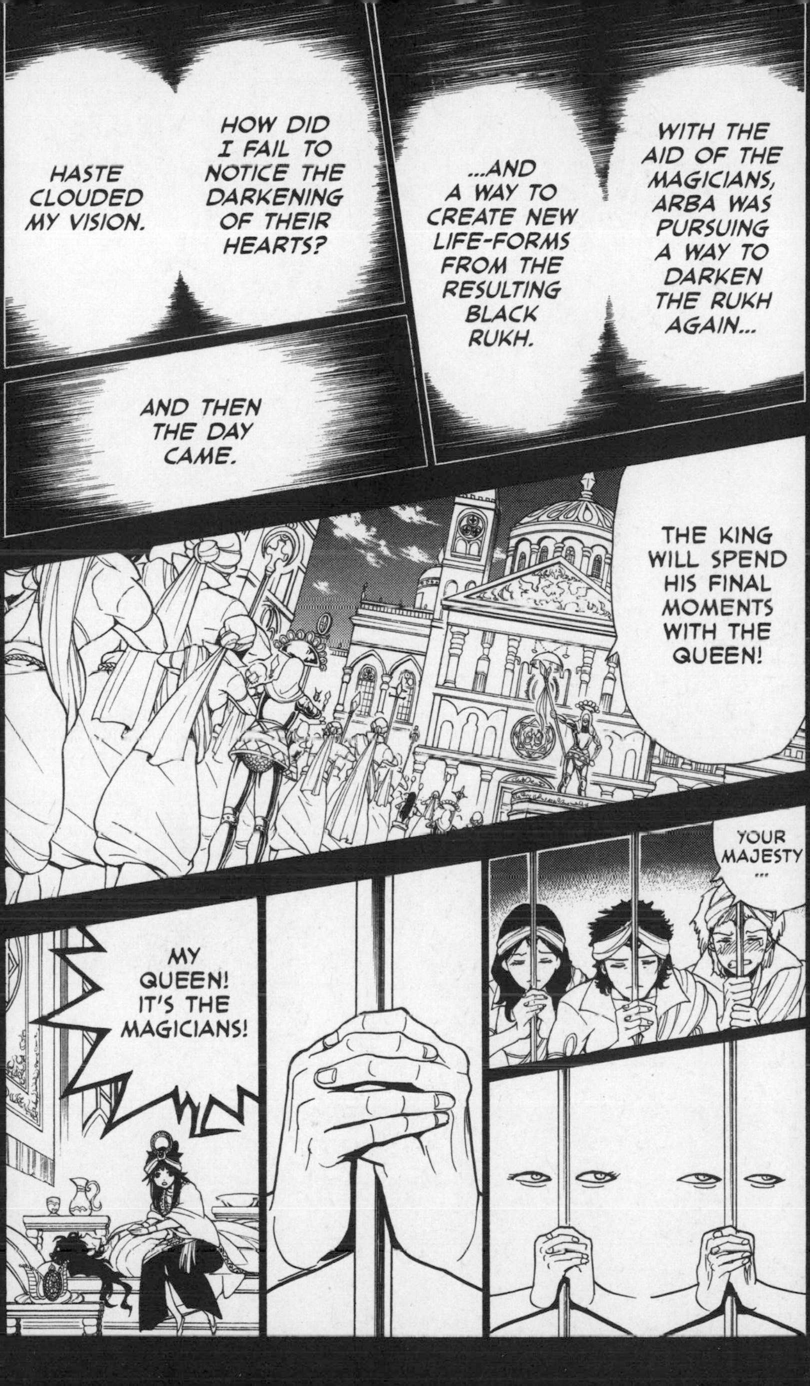

WITH THE AID OF THE MAGICIANS, ARBA WAS PURSUING A WAY TO DARKEN THE RUKH AGAIN...
...AND A WAY TO CREATE NEW LIFE-FORMS FROM THE RESULTING BLACK RUKH.
HOW DID I FAIL TO NOTICE THE DARKENING OF THEIR HEARTS?
HASTE CLOUDED MY VISION.
AND THEN THE DAY CAME.
THE KING WILL SPEND HIS FINAL MOMENTS WITH THE QUEEN!
YOUR MAJESTY ...
MY QUEEN! IT'S THE MAGICIANS!

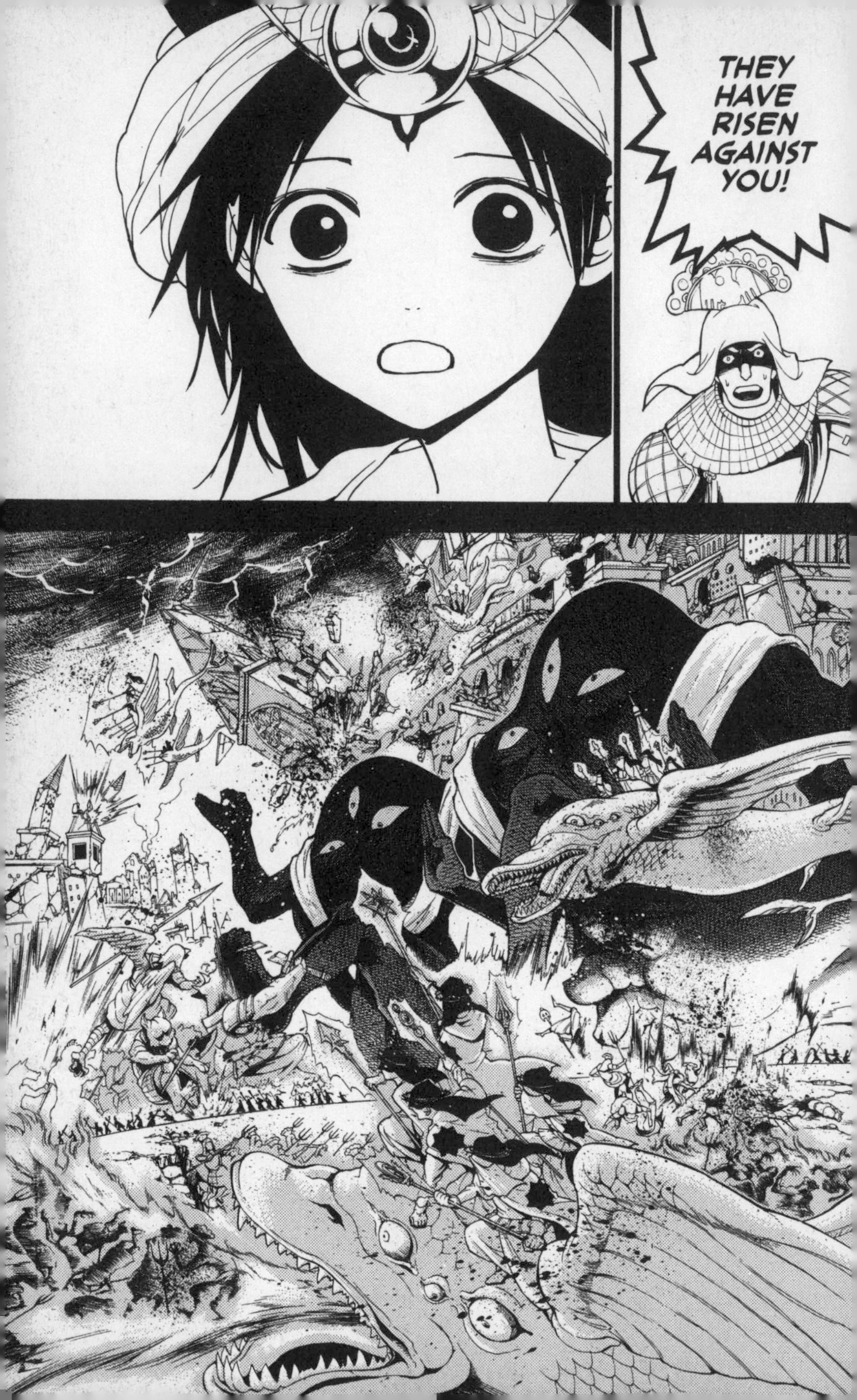
THEY HAVE RISEN AGAINST YOU!

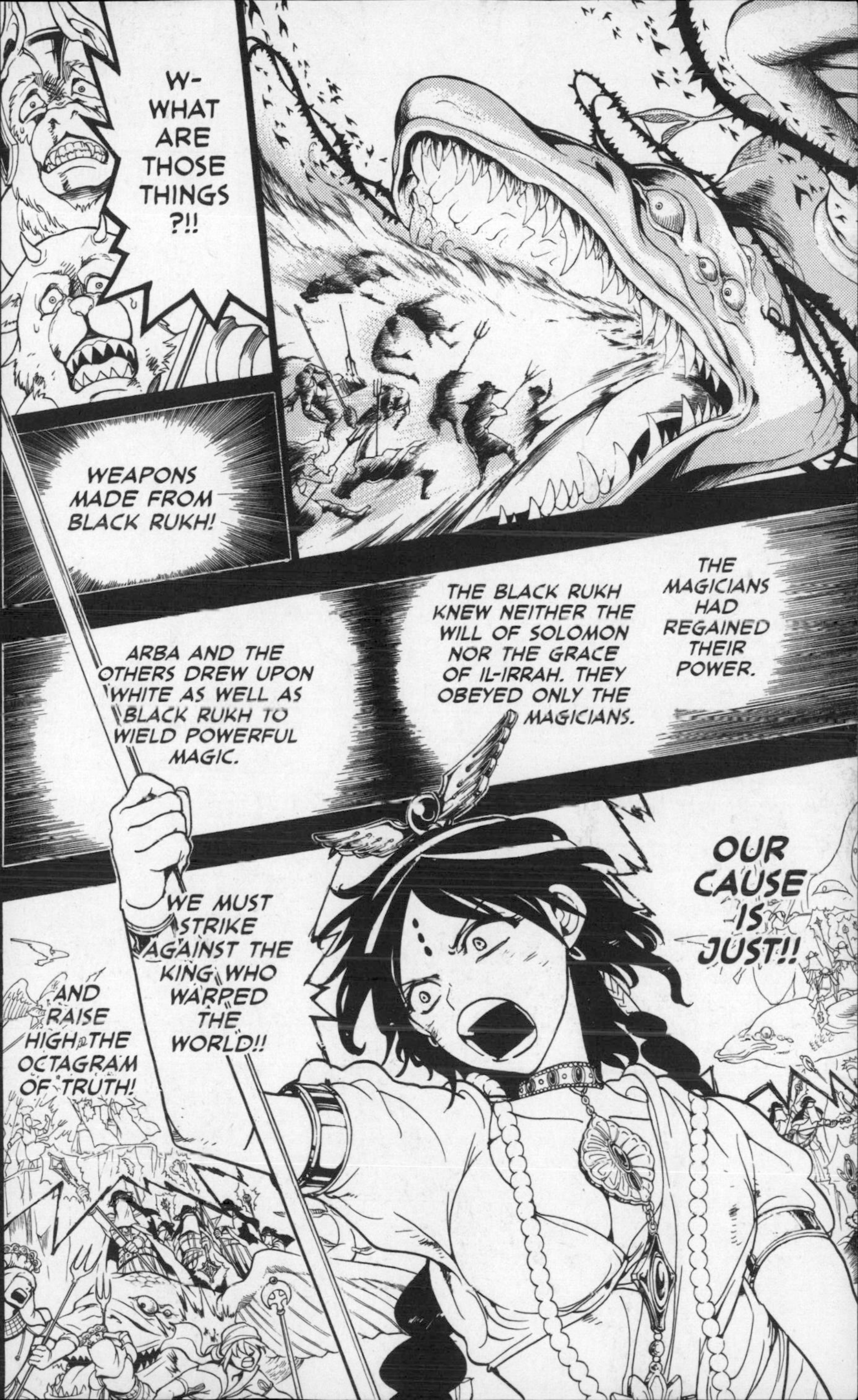
W- WHAT ARE THOSE THINGS?!!
WEAPONS MADE FROM BLACK RUKH!
THE MAGICIANS HAD REGAINED THEIR POWER.
THE BLACK RUKH KNEW NEITHER THE WILL OF SOLOMON NOR THE GRACE OF IL-IRRAH. THEY OBEYED ONLY THE MAGICIANS.
ARBA AND THE OTHERS DREW UPON WHITE AS WELL AS BLACK RUKH TO WIELD POWERFUL MAGIC.
OUR CAUSE IS JUST!!
WE MUST STRIKE AGAINST THE KING WHO WARPED THE WORLD!!
AND RAISE HIGH THE OCTAGRAM OF TRUTH!

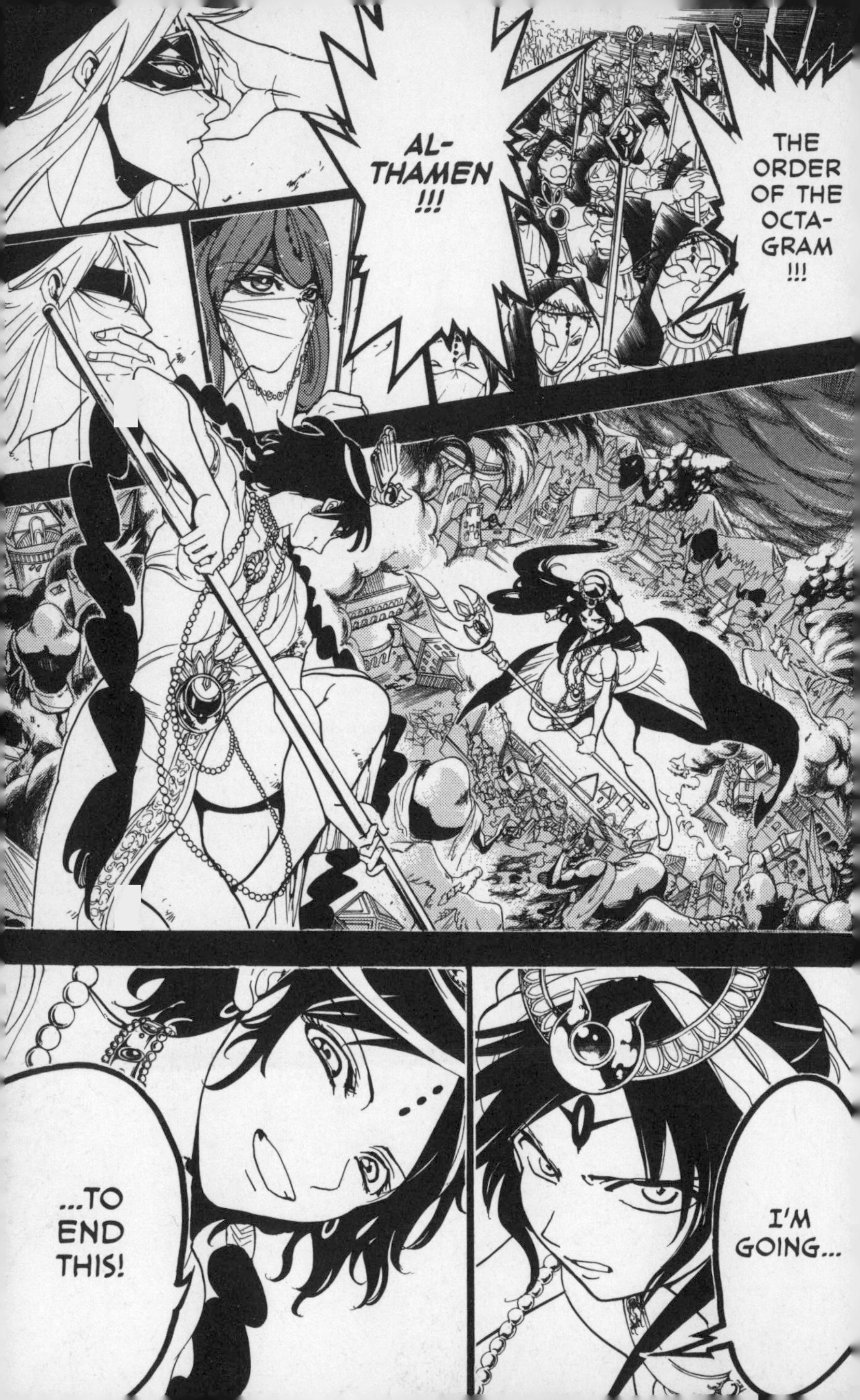
THE ORDER OF THE OCTA-GRAM !!!
AL-THAMEN !!!
I'M GOING...
...TO END THIS!

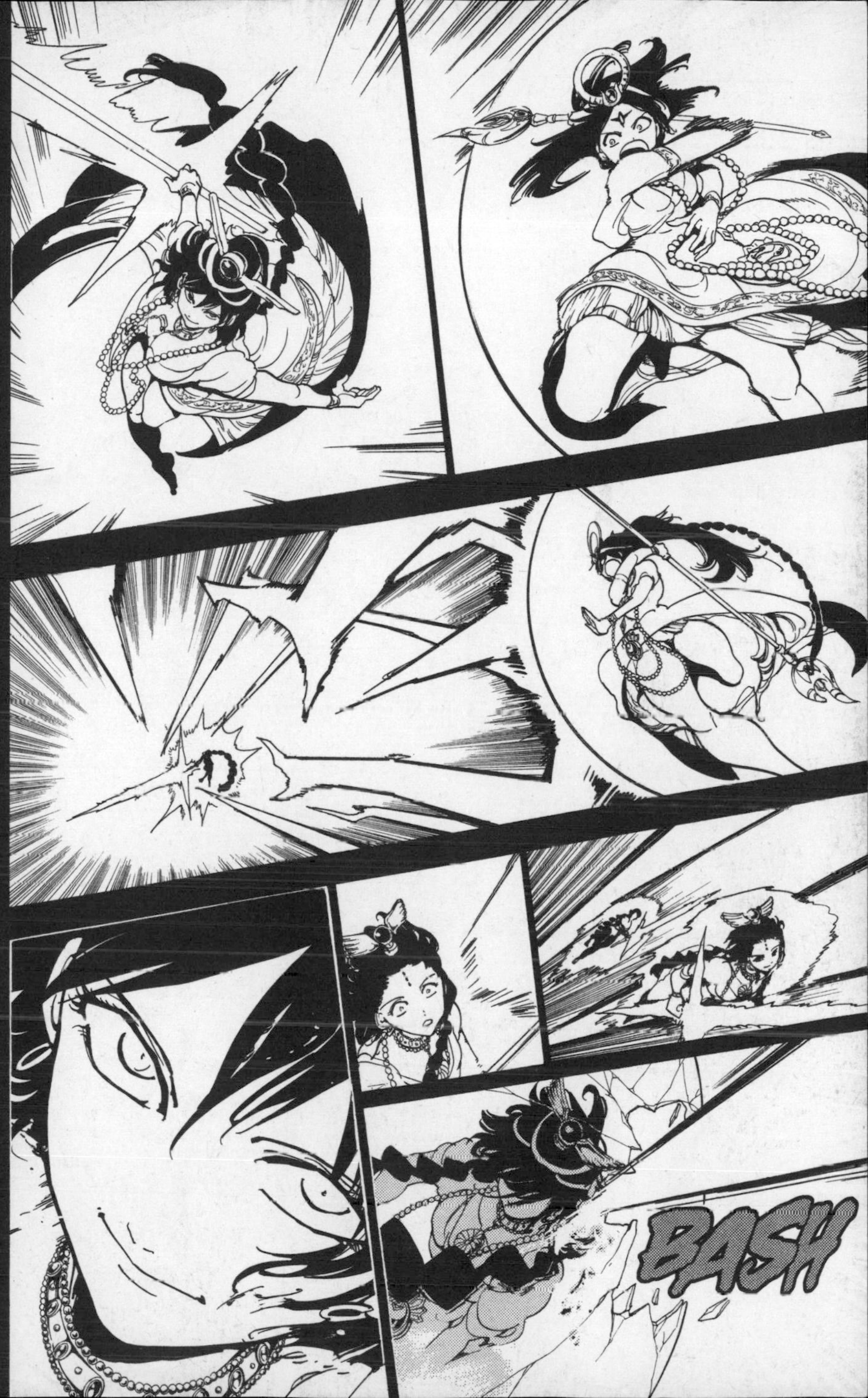
BASH

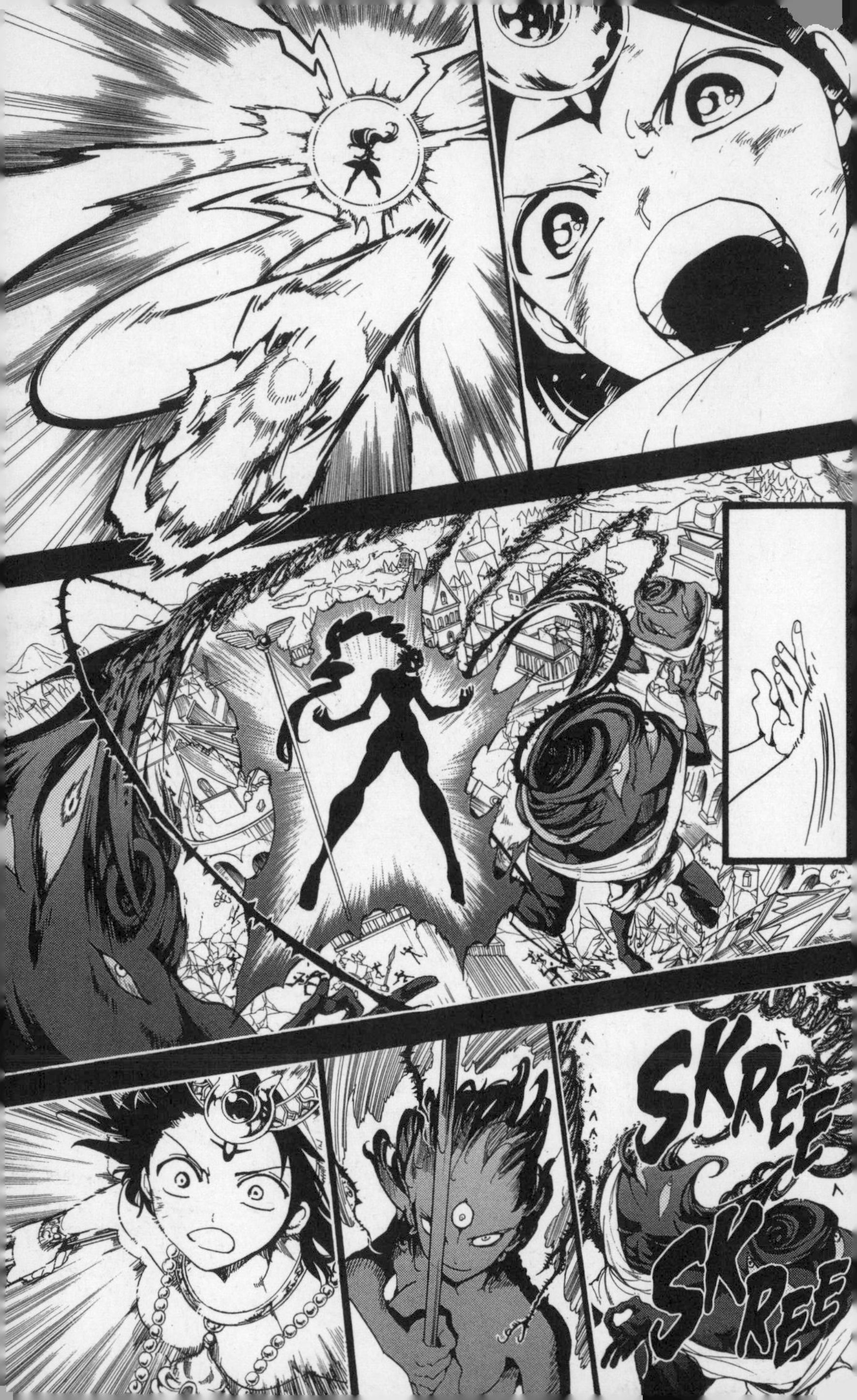
SKREE
SKREE

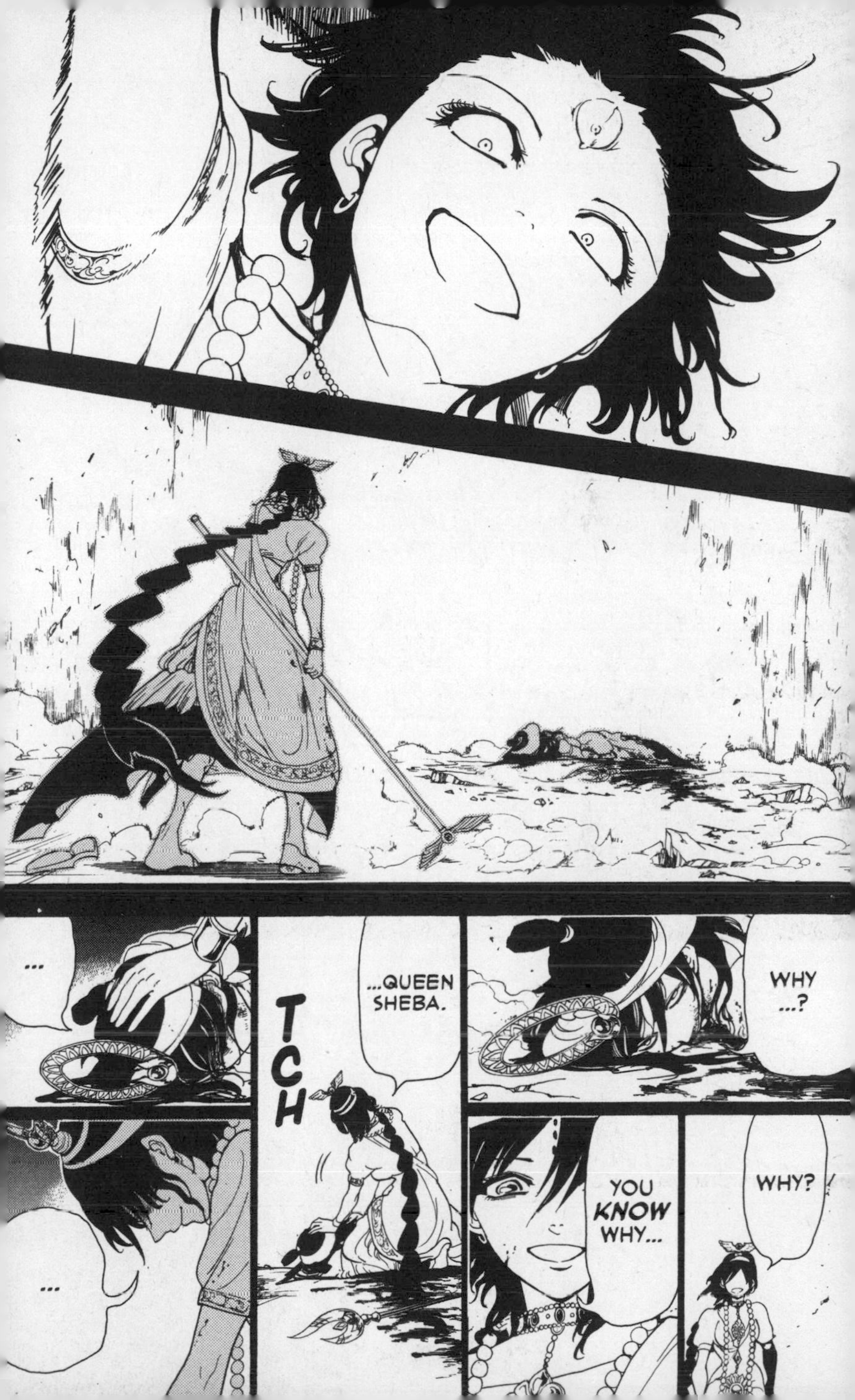
WHY ...?
WHY?
YOU KNOW WHY...
...QUEEN SHEBA.
TCH
...
...

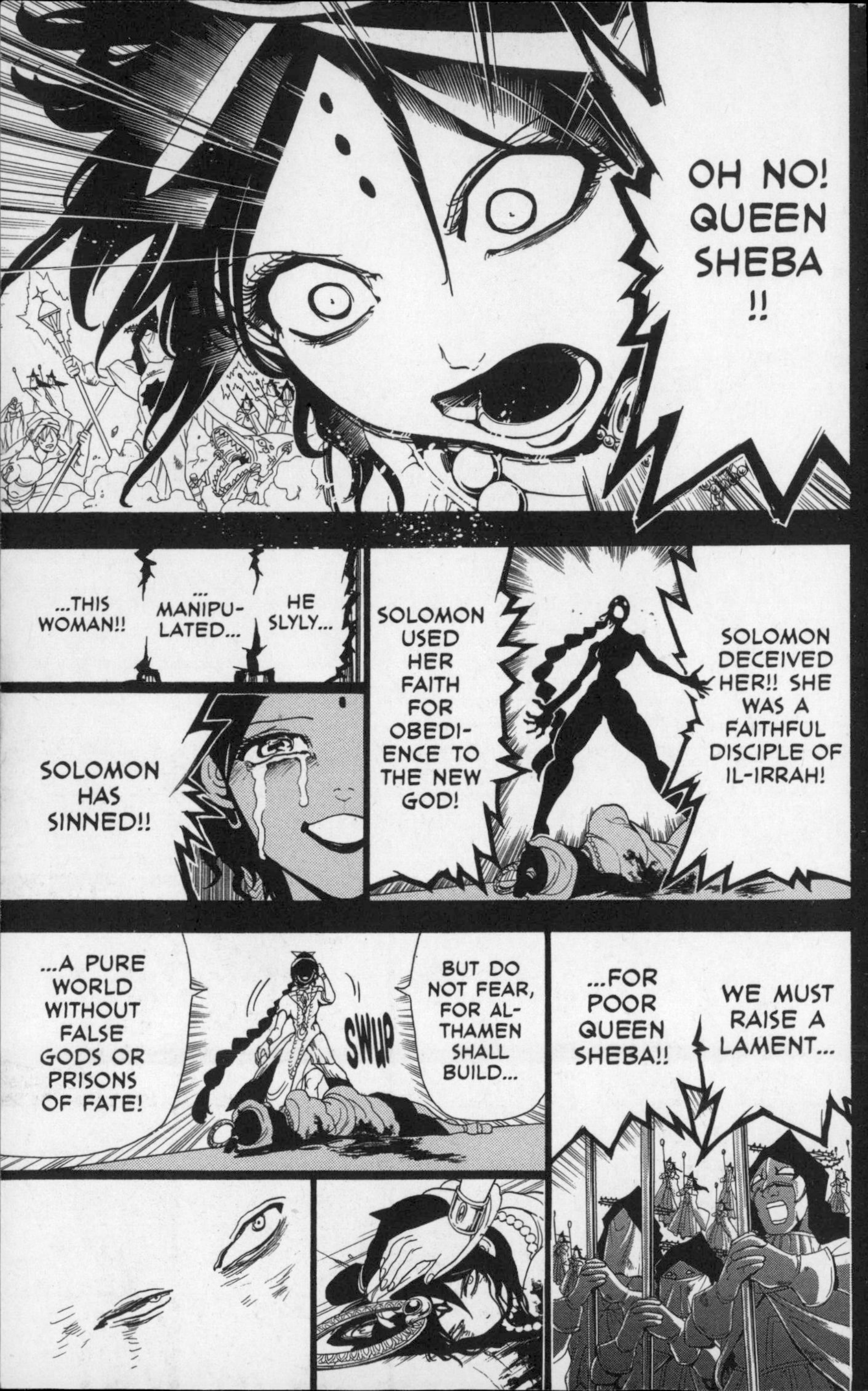
OH NO! QUEEN SHEBA !!
SOLOMON DECEIVED HER!! SHE WAS A FAITHFUL DISCIPLE OF IL-IRRAH!
SOLOMON USED HER FAITH FOR OBEDIENCE TO THE NEW GOD!
HE SLYLY...
... MANIPULATED...
...THIS WOMAN!!
SOLOMON HAS SINNED!!
WE MUST RAISE A LAMENT...
...FOR POOR QUEEN SHEBA!!
BUT DO NOT FEAR, FOR AL-THAMEN SHALL BUILD...
SWUP
...A PURE WORLD WITHOUT FALSE GODS OR PRISONS OF FATE!

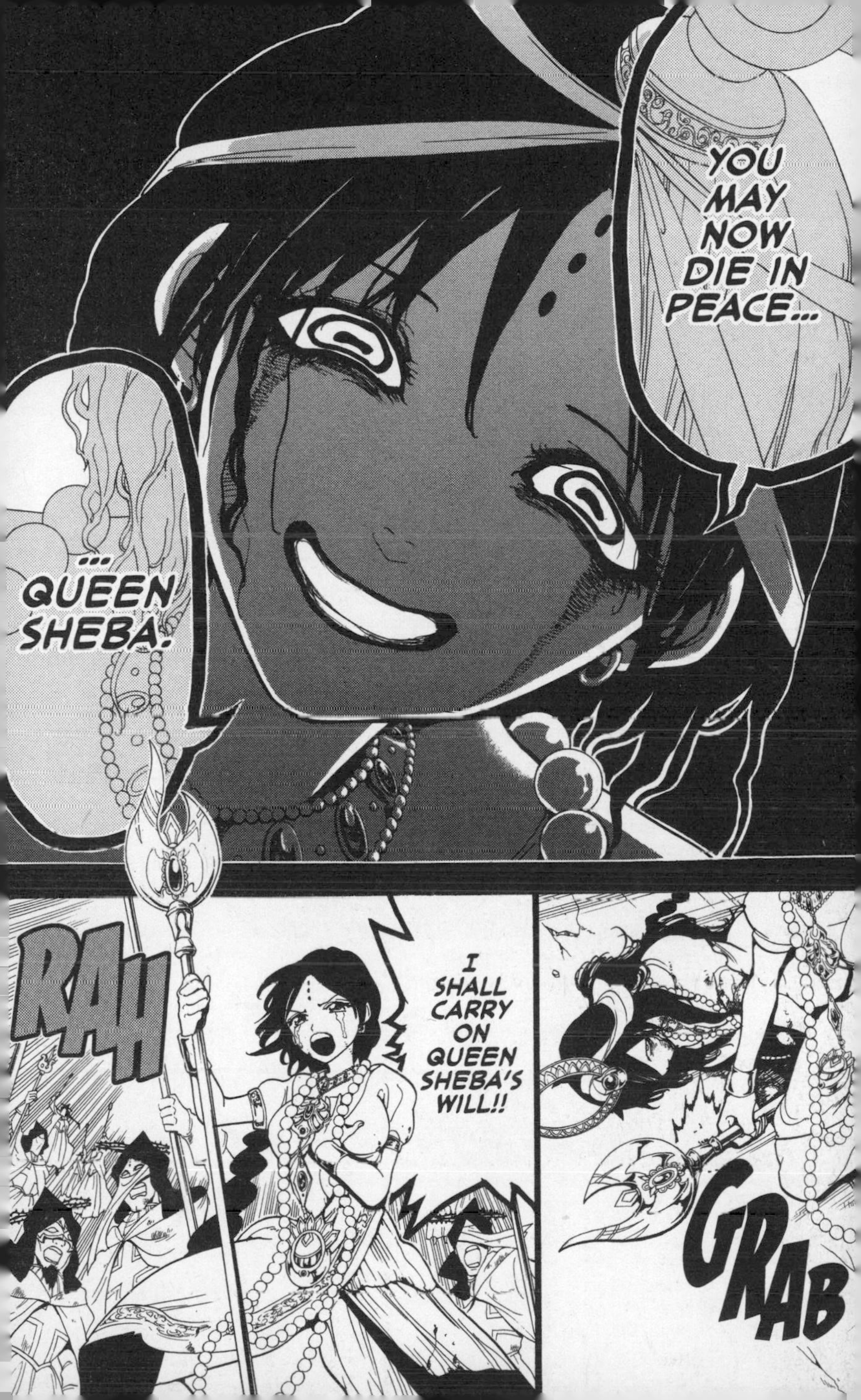
YOU MAY NOW DIE IN PEACE...
...QUEEN SHEBA.
GRAB
I SHALL CARRY ON QUEEN SHEBA'S WILL!!
RAH

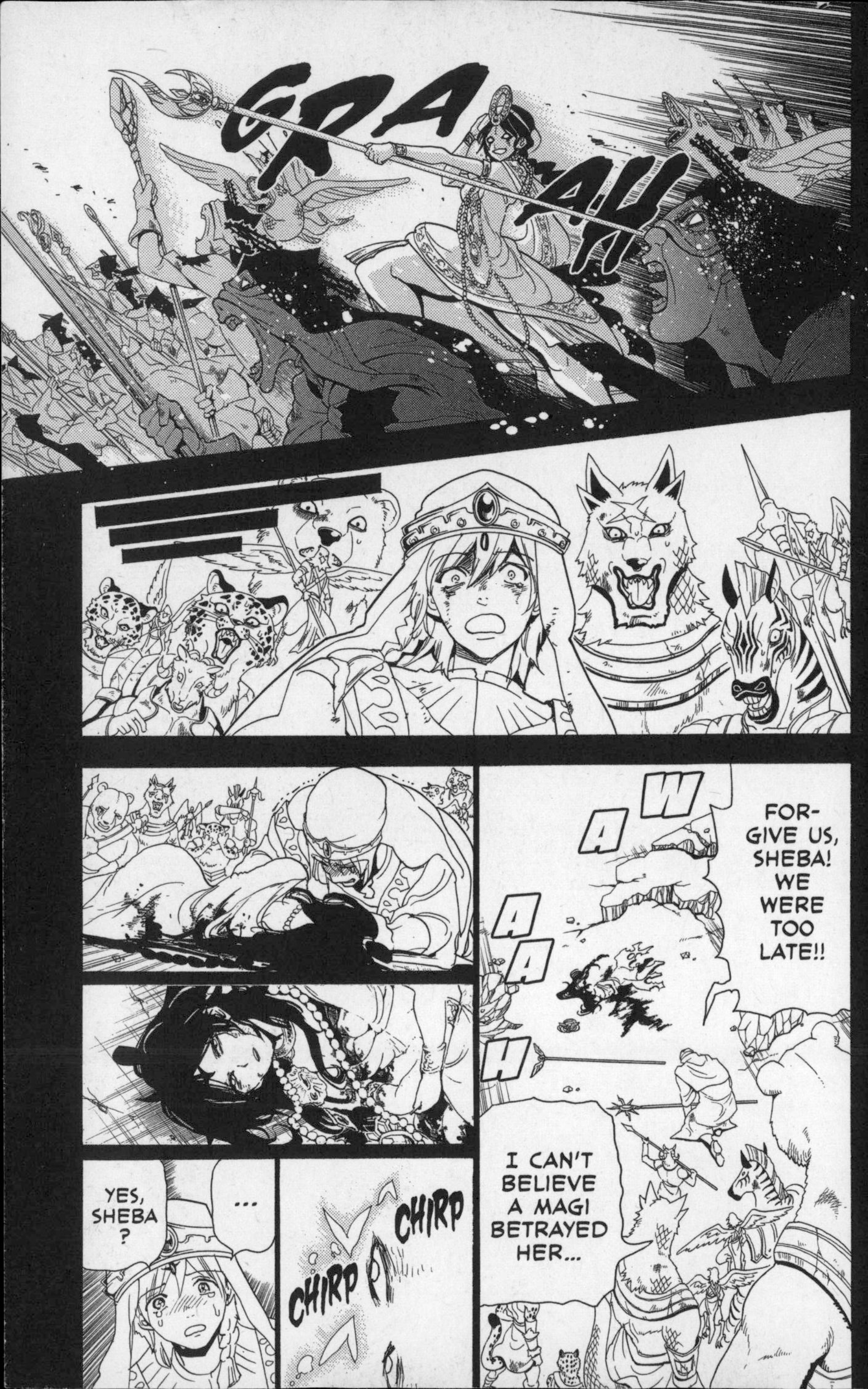
GRAAH
[redacted]
WAAAH
FORGIVE US, SHEBA! WE WERE TOO LATE!!
I CAN'T BELIEVE A MAGI BETRAYED HER...
CHIRP
CHIRP
...
YES, SHEBA?

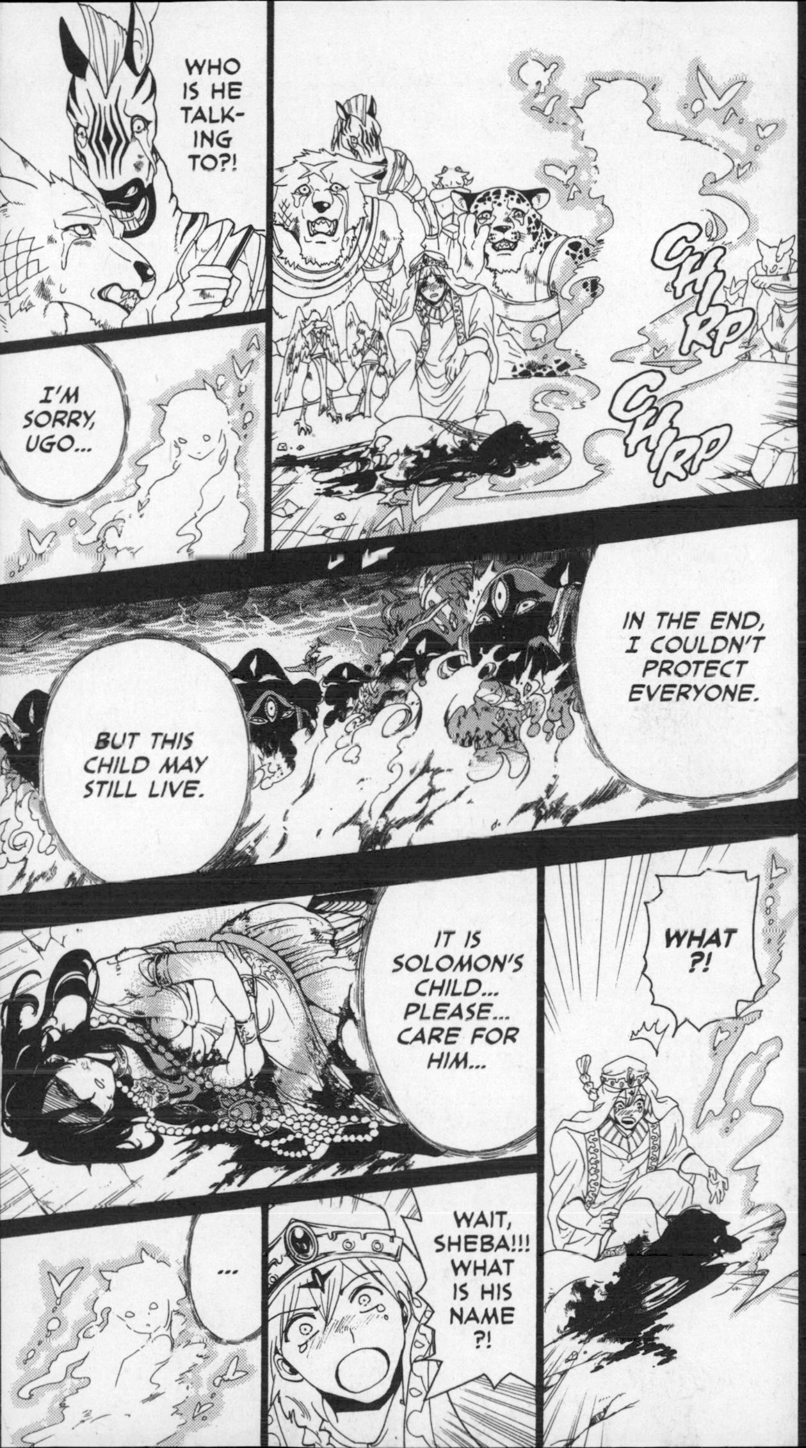
CHIRP
CHIRP
WHO IS HE TALKING TO?!
I'M SORRY, UGO...
IN THE END, I COULDN'T PROTECT EVERYONE.
BUT THIS CHILD MAY STILL LIVE.
WHAT ?!
IT IS SOLOMON'S CHILD... PLEASE... CARE FOR HIM...
WAIT, SHEBA!!! WHAT IS HIS NAME ?!
...

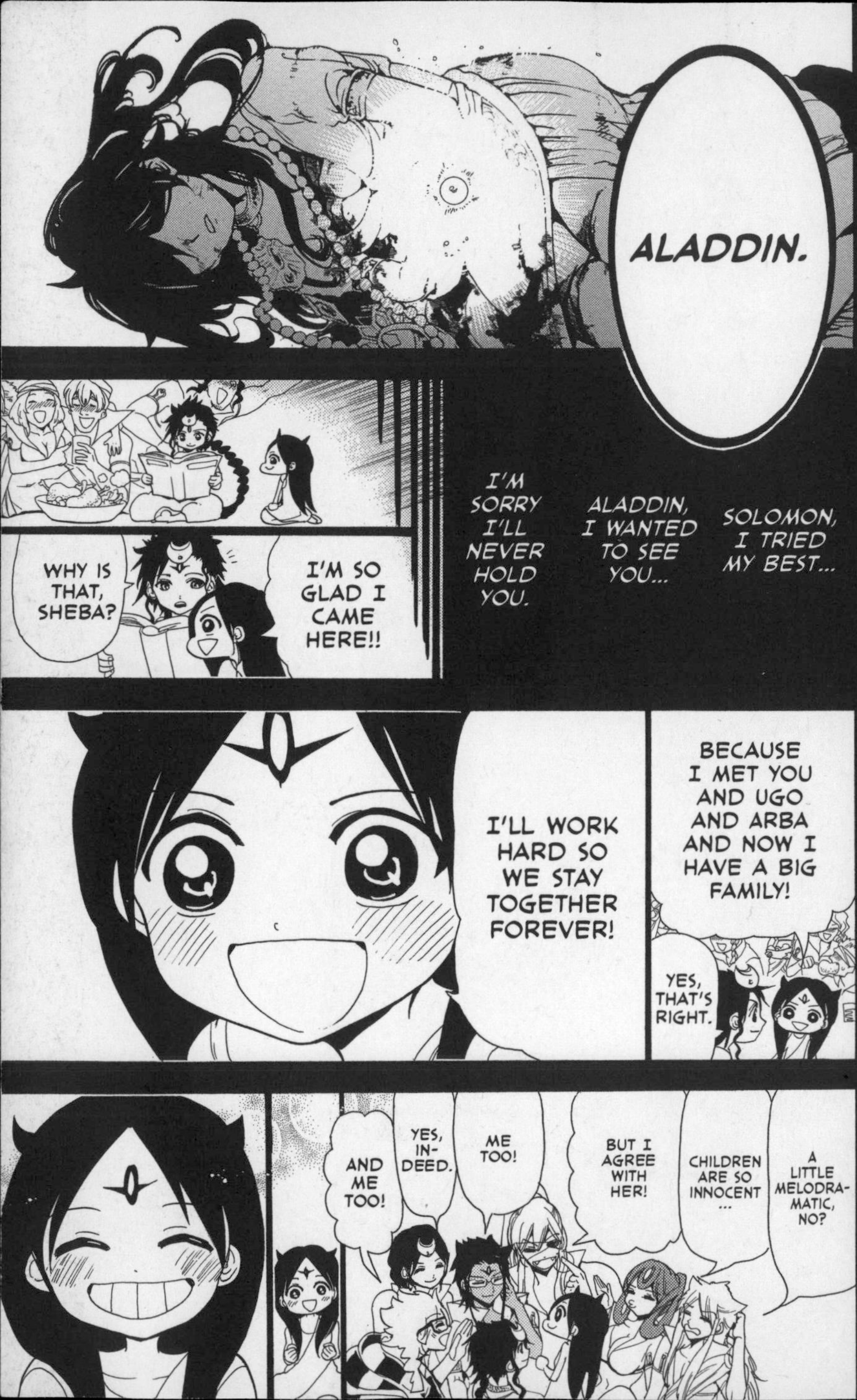
ALADDIN.
SOLOMON, I TRIED MY BEST...
ALADDIN, I WANTED TO SEE YOU...
I'M SORRY I'LL NEVER HOLD YOU.
I'M SO GLAD I CAME HERE!!
WHY IS THAT, SHEBA?
BECAUSE I MET YOU AND UGO AND ARBA AND NOW I HAVE A BIG FAMILY!
YES, THAT'S RIGHT.
I'LL WORK HARD SO WE STAY TOGETHER FOREVER!
A LITTLE MELODRAMATIC, NO?
CHILDREN ARE SO INNOCENT...
BUT I AGREE WITH HER!
ME TOO!
YES, IN-DEED.
AND ME TOO!

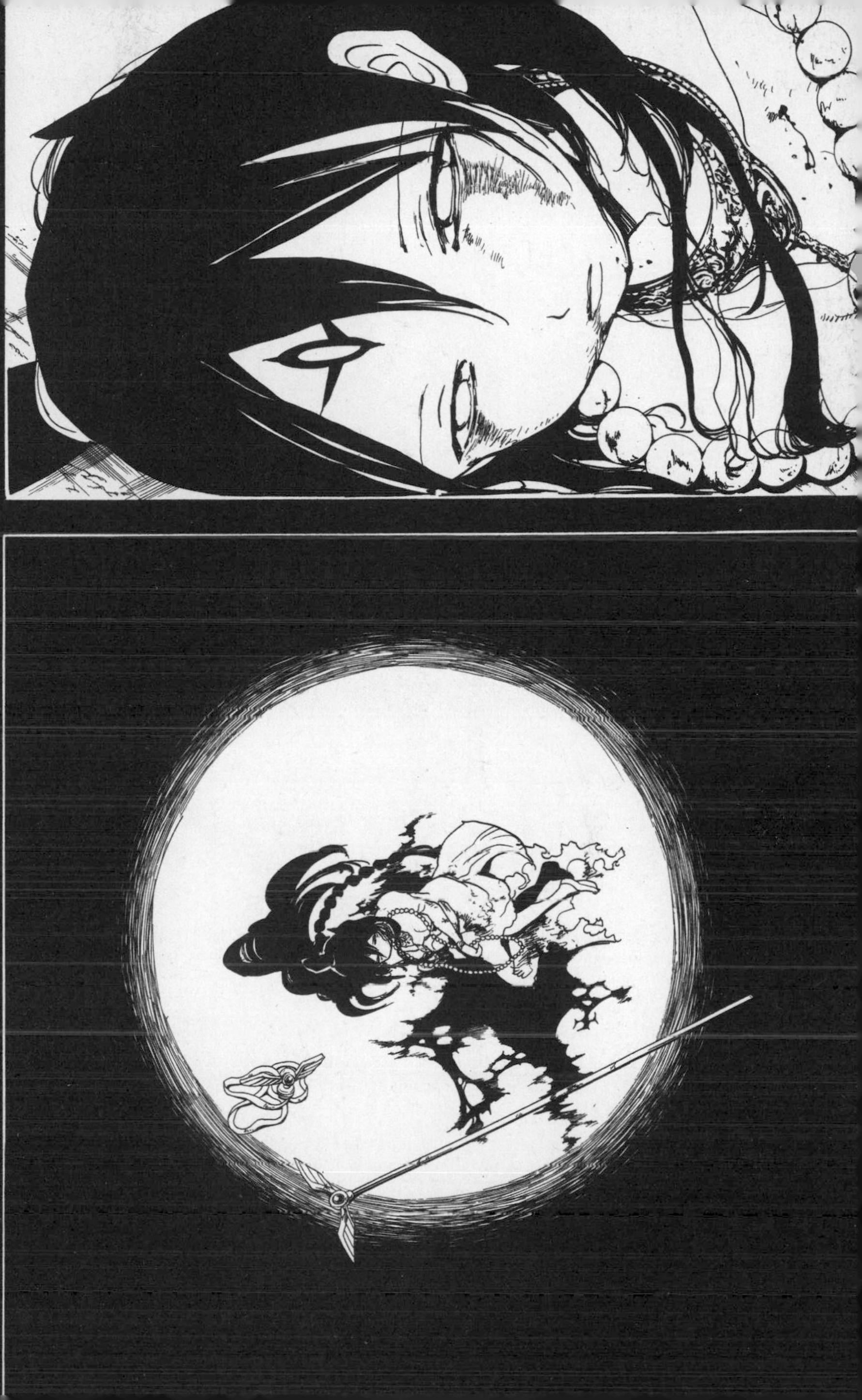

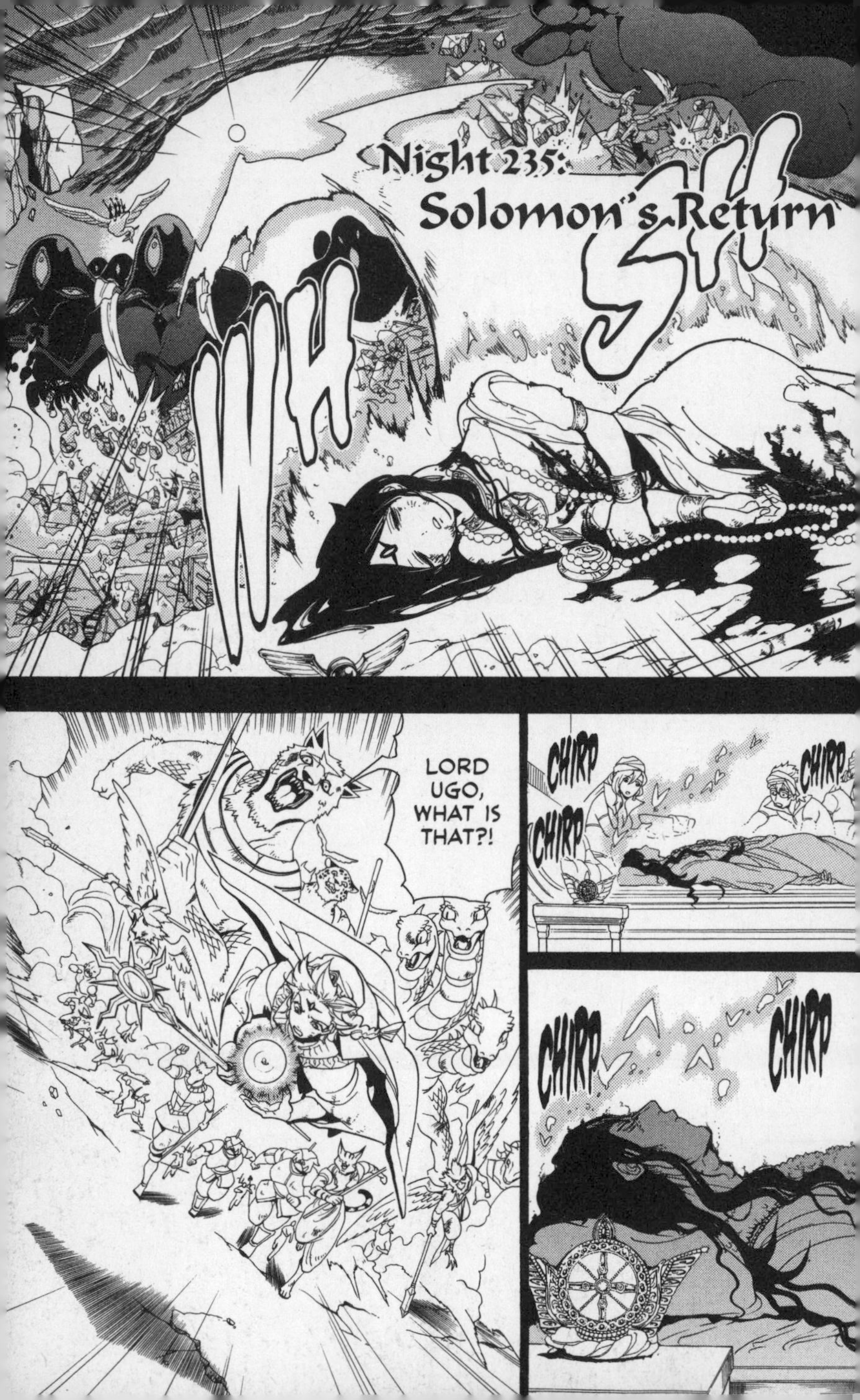
Night 235: Solomon's Return
CHIRP
CHIRP
CHIRP
CHIRP
CHIRP
LORD UGO, WHAT IS THAT?!

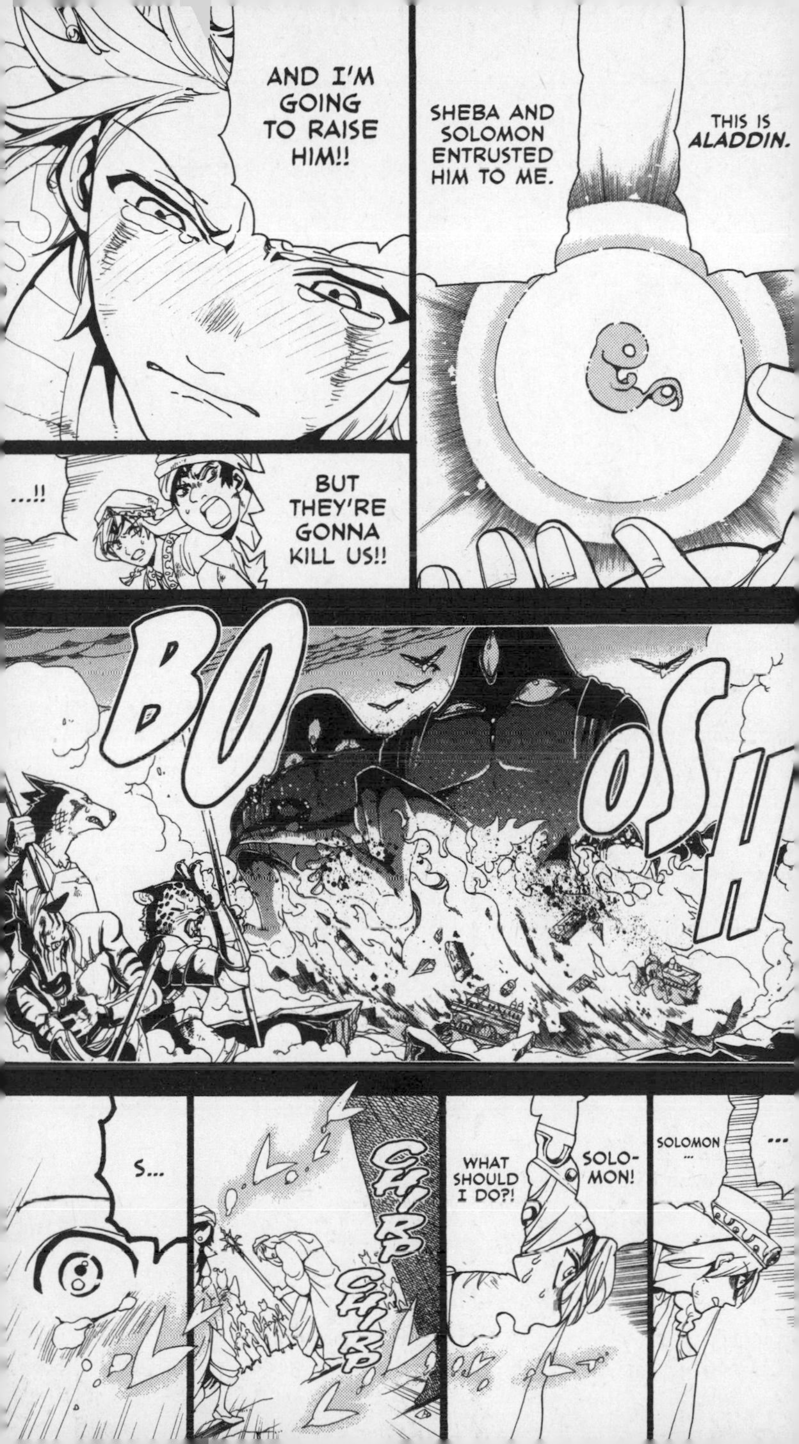
THIS IS ALADDIN.
SHEBA AND SOLOMON ENTRUSTED HIM TO ME.
AND I'M GOING TO RAISE HIM!!
BUT THEY'RE GONNA KILL US!!
...!!
BOOSH
...
SOLOMON ...
SOLO-MON!
WHAT SHOULD I DO?!
CHIRP
CHIRP
S...

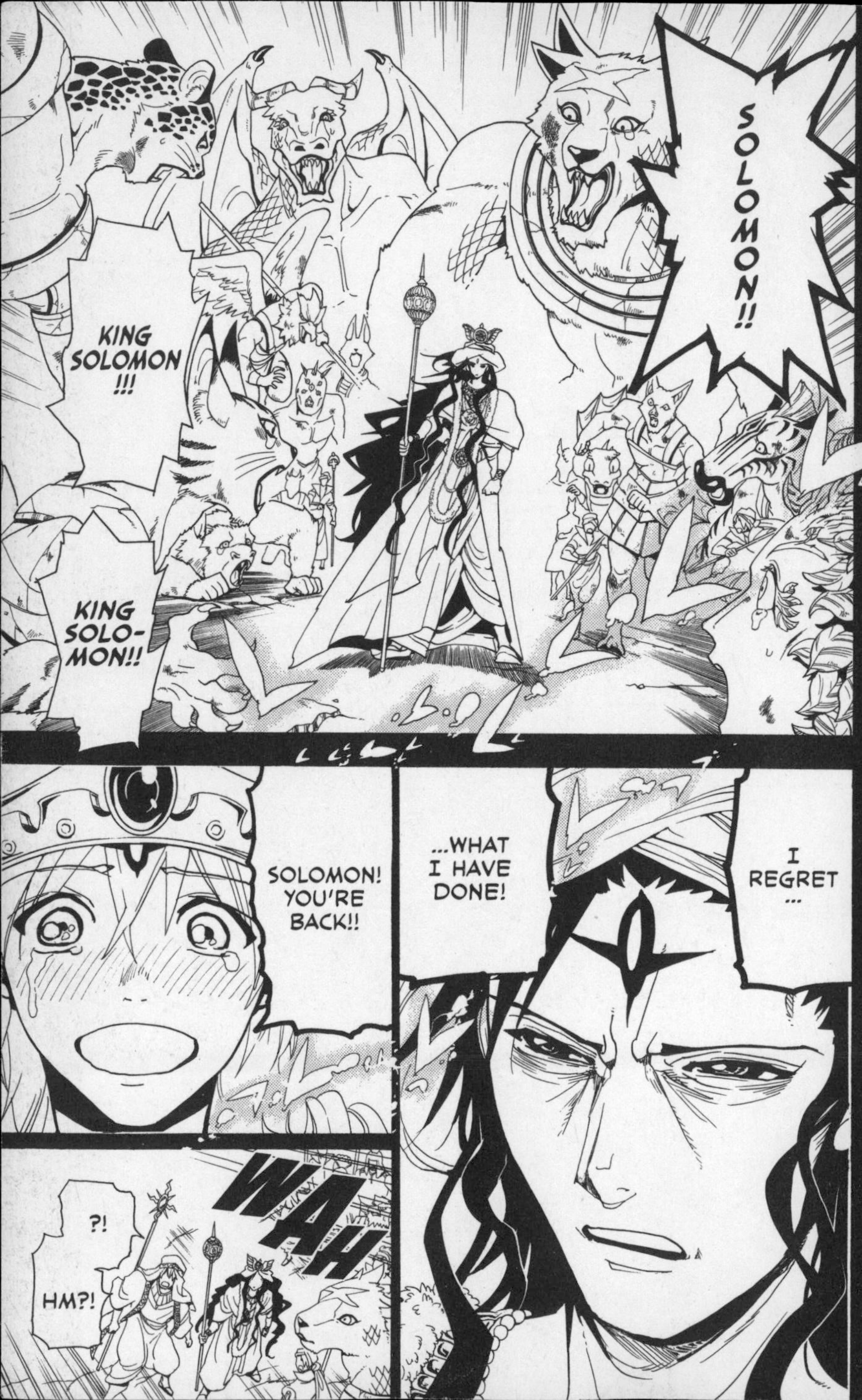
SOLOMON!!
KING SOLOMON!!!
KING SOLO-MON!!
I REGRET...
...WHAT I HAVE DONE!
SOLOMON! YOU'RE BACK!!
WAH
?!
HM?!

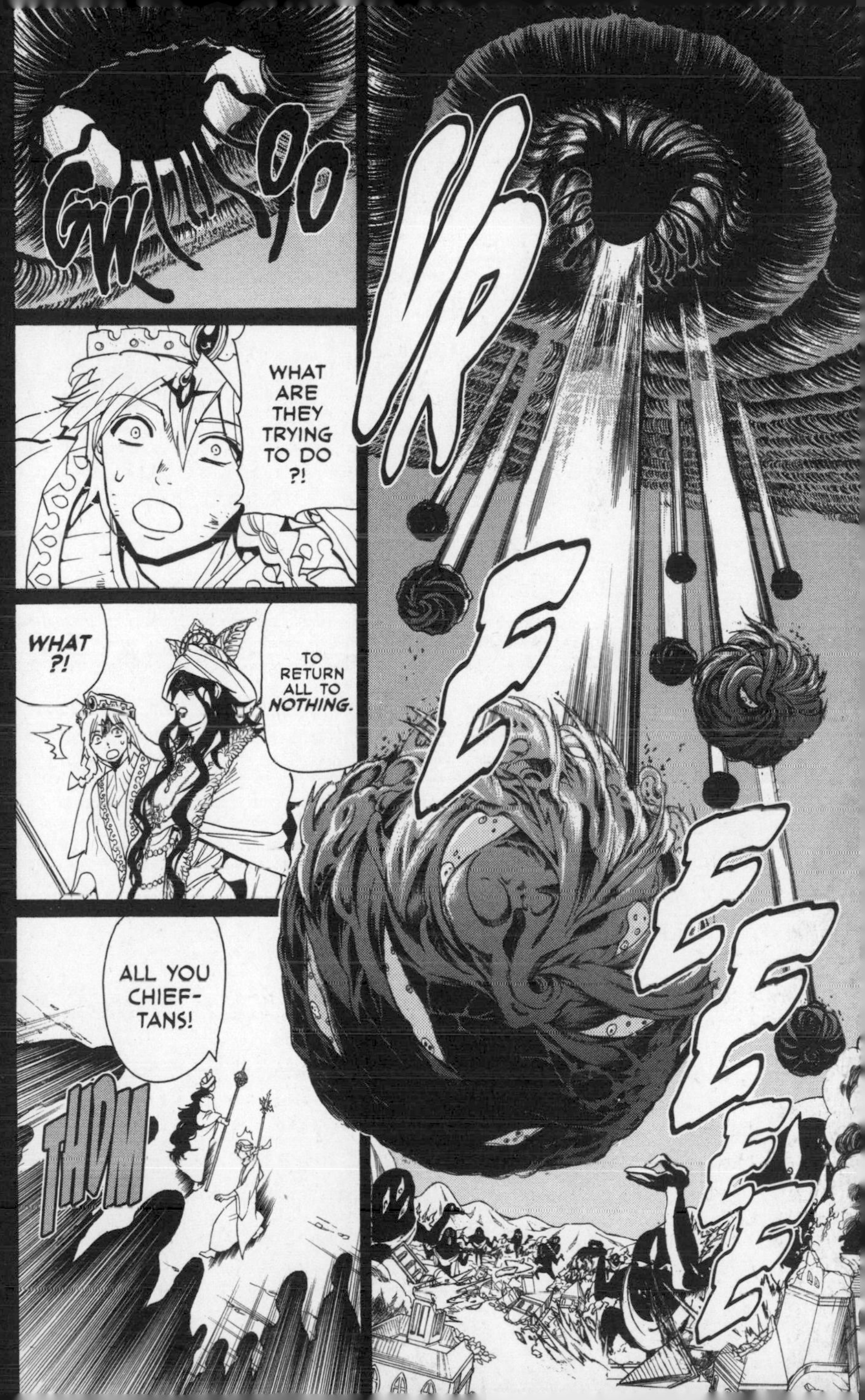
WHAT ARE THEY TRYING TO DO ?!
TO RETURN ALL TO *NOTHING.*
WHAT ?!
ALL YOU CHIEF-TANS!
THOM

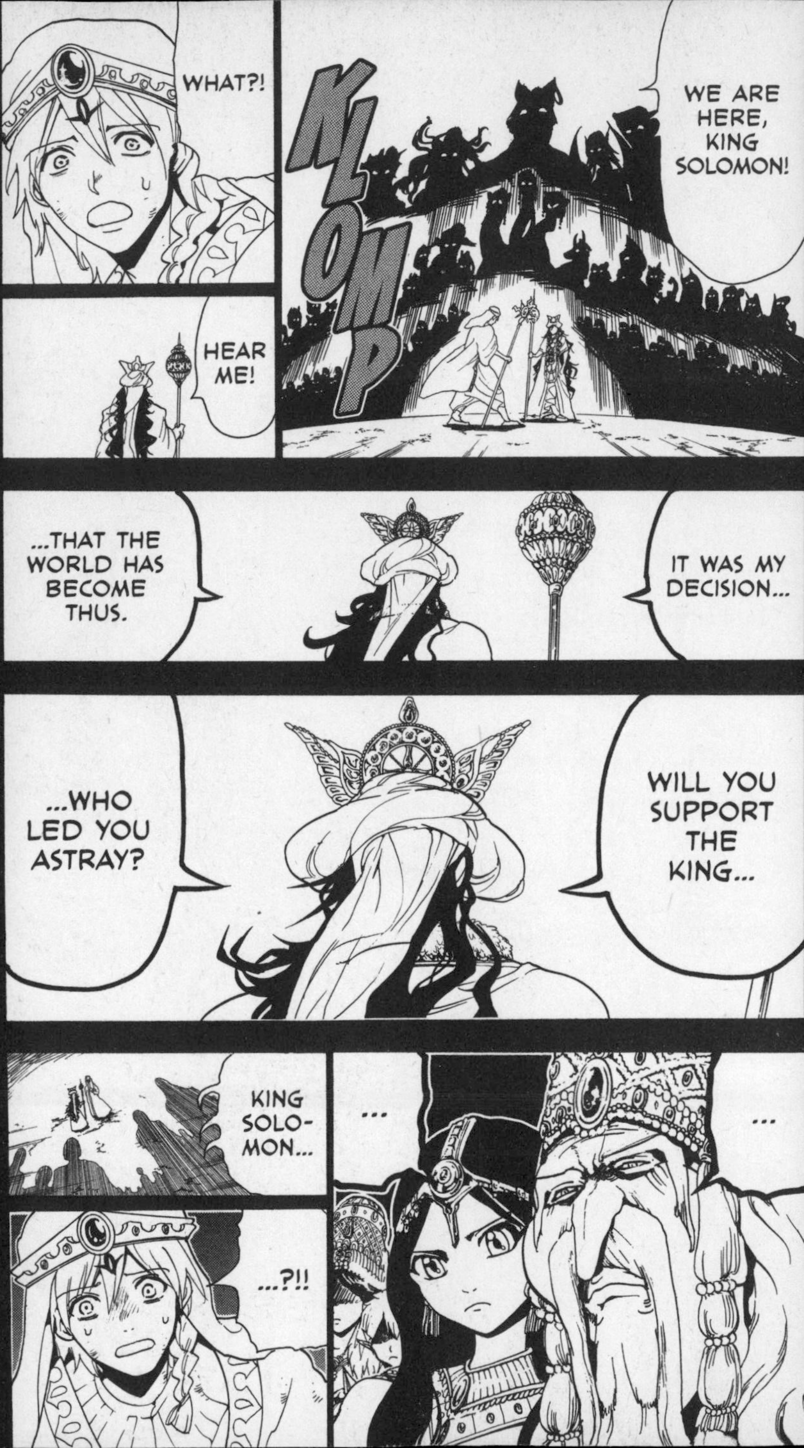

WE ARE HERE, KING SOLOMON!
KLOMP
WHAT?!
HEAR ME!
IT WAS MY DECISION...
...THAT THE WORLD HAS BECOME THUS.
WILL YOU SUPPORT THE KING...
...WHO LED YOU ASTRAY?
...
...
KING SOLO-MON...
...?!!

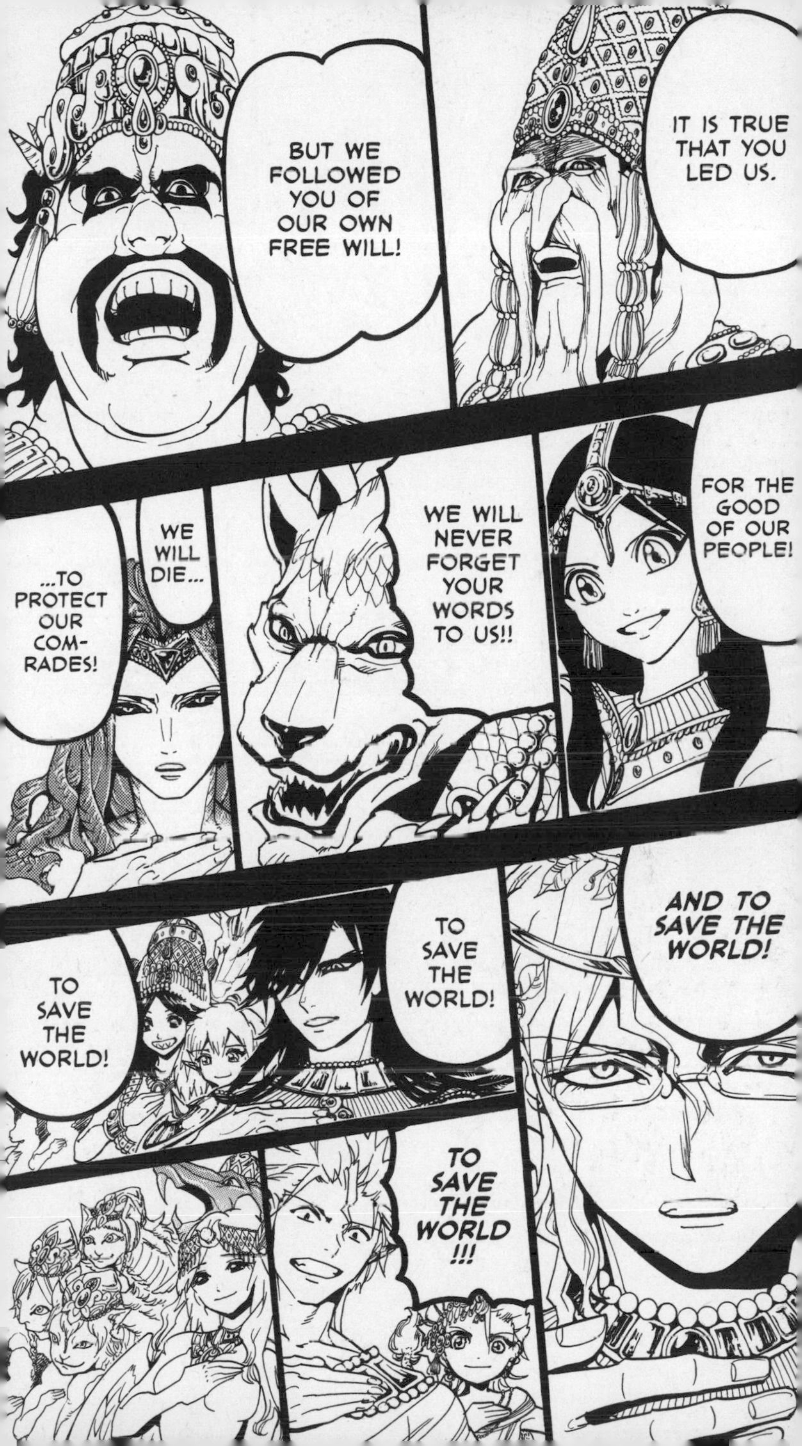
IT IS TRUE THAT YOU LED US.
BUT WE FOLLOWED YOU OF OUR OWN FREE WILL!
FOR THE GOOD OF OUR PEOPLE!
WE WILL NEVER FORGET YOUR WORDS TO US!!
WE WILL DIE...
...TO PROTECT OUR COM-RADES!
AND TO SAVE THE WORLD!
TO SAVE THE WORLD!
TO SAVE THE WORLD!
TO SAVE THE WORLD!!!

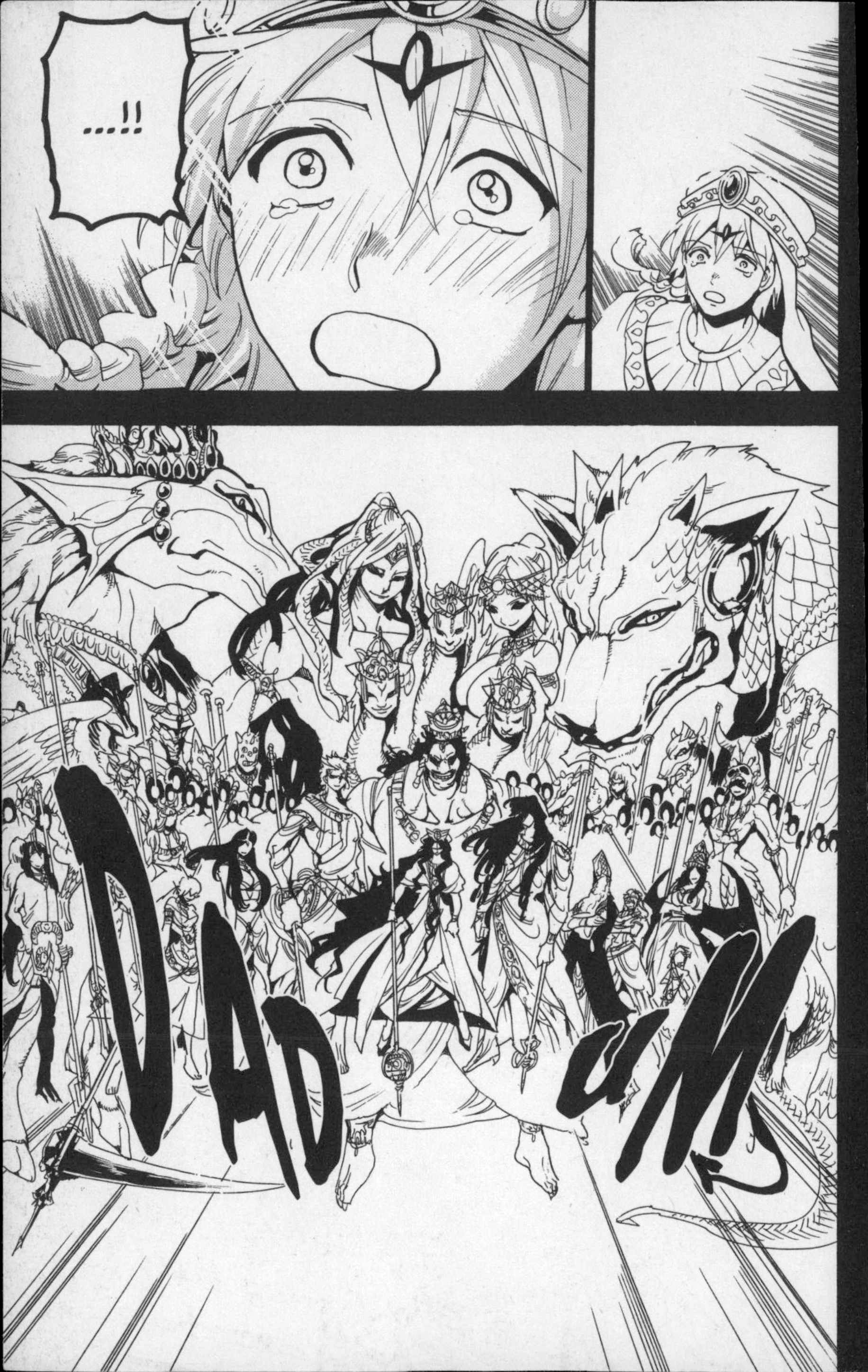
...!!
DADUM

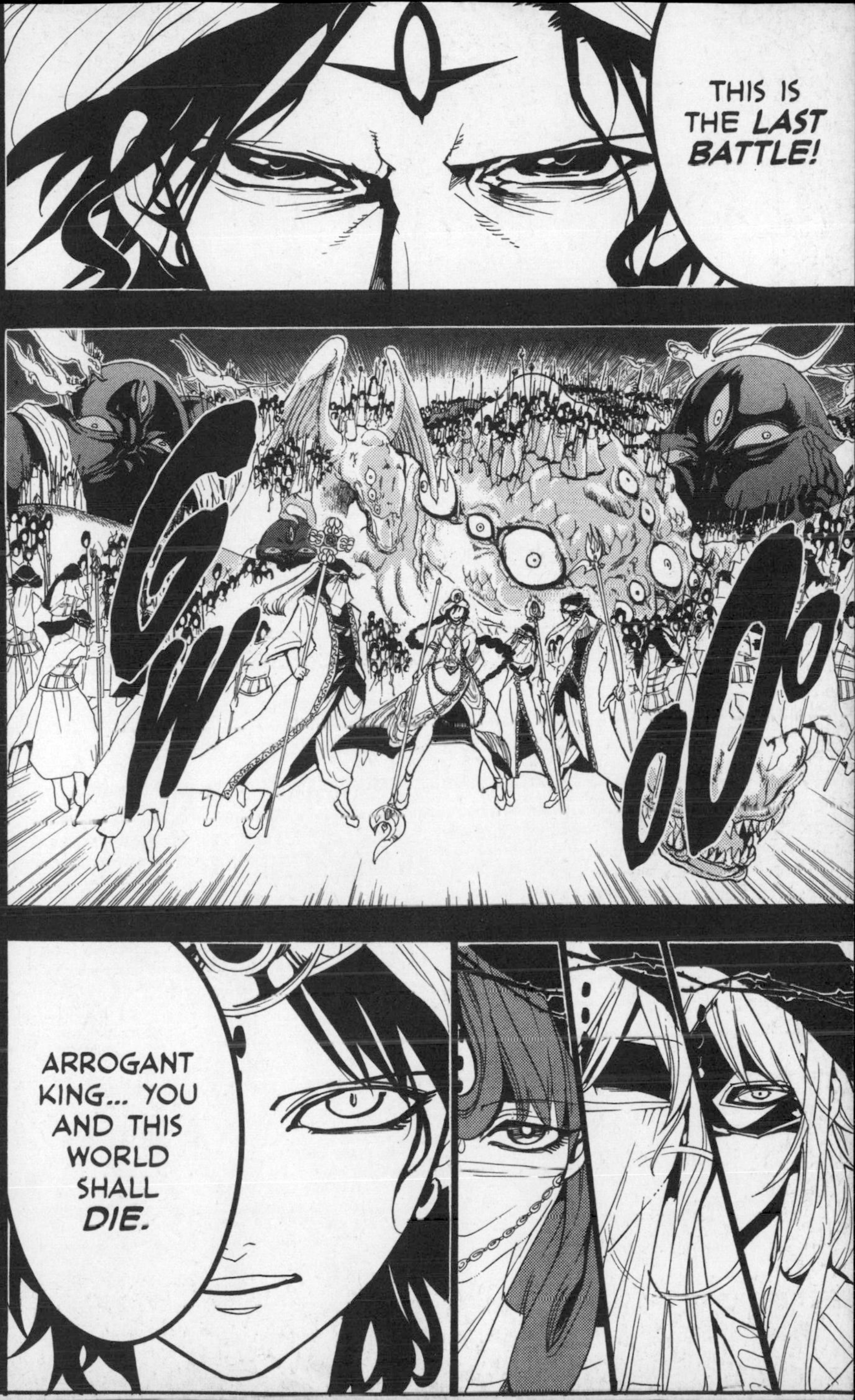
THIS IS THE LAST BATTLE!
ARROGANT KING... YOU AND THIS WORLD SHALL DIE.

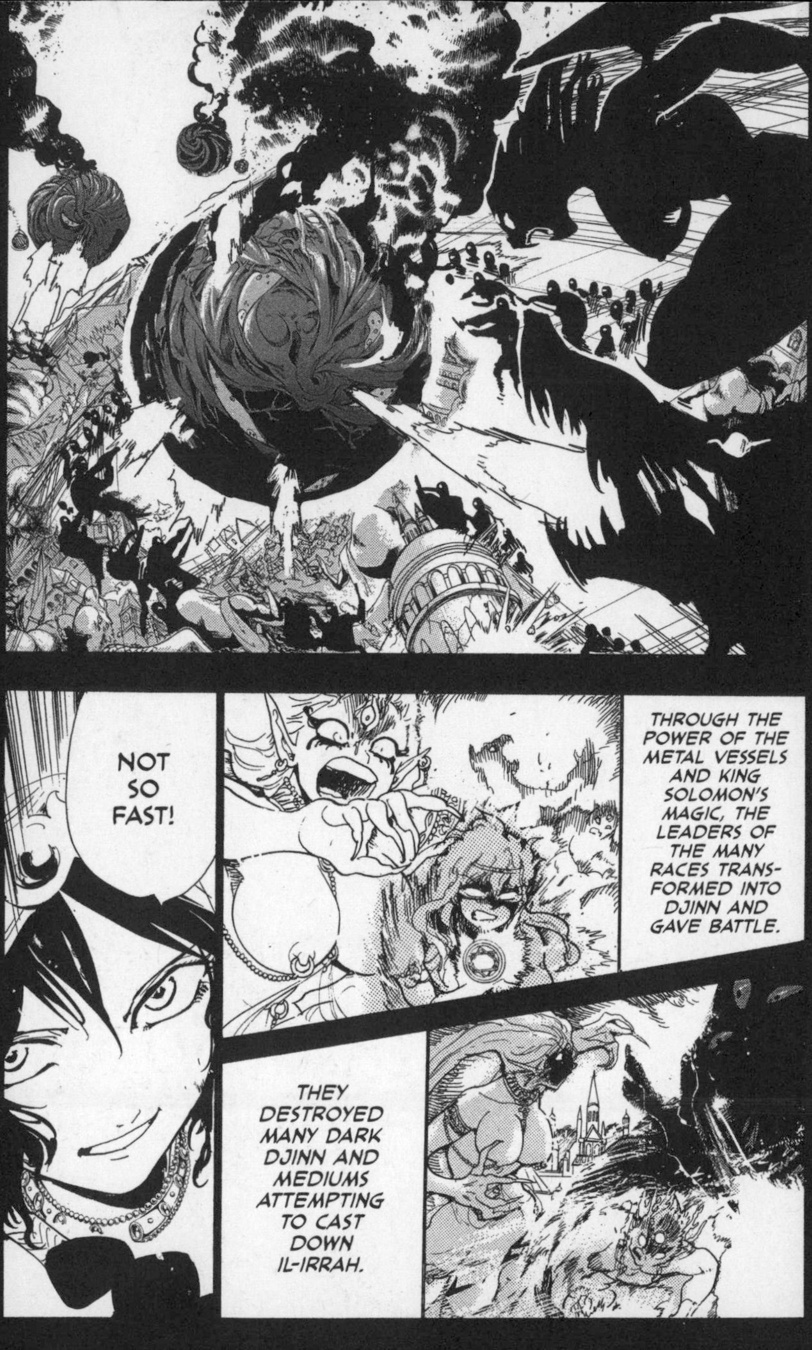
THROUGH THE POWER OF THE METAL VESSELS AND KING SOLOMON'S MAGIC, THE LEADERS OF THE MANY RACES TRANS-FORMED INTO DJINN AND GAVE BATTLE.
THEY DESTROYED MANY DARK DJINN AND MEDIUMS ATTEMPTING TO CAST DOWN IL-IRRAH.
NOT SO FAST!

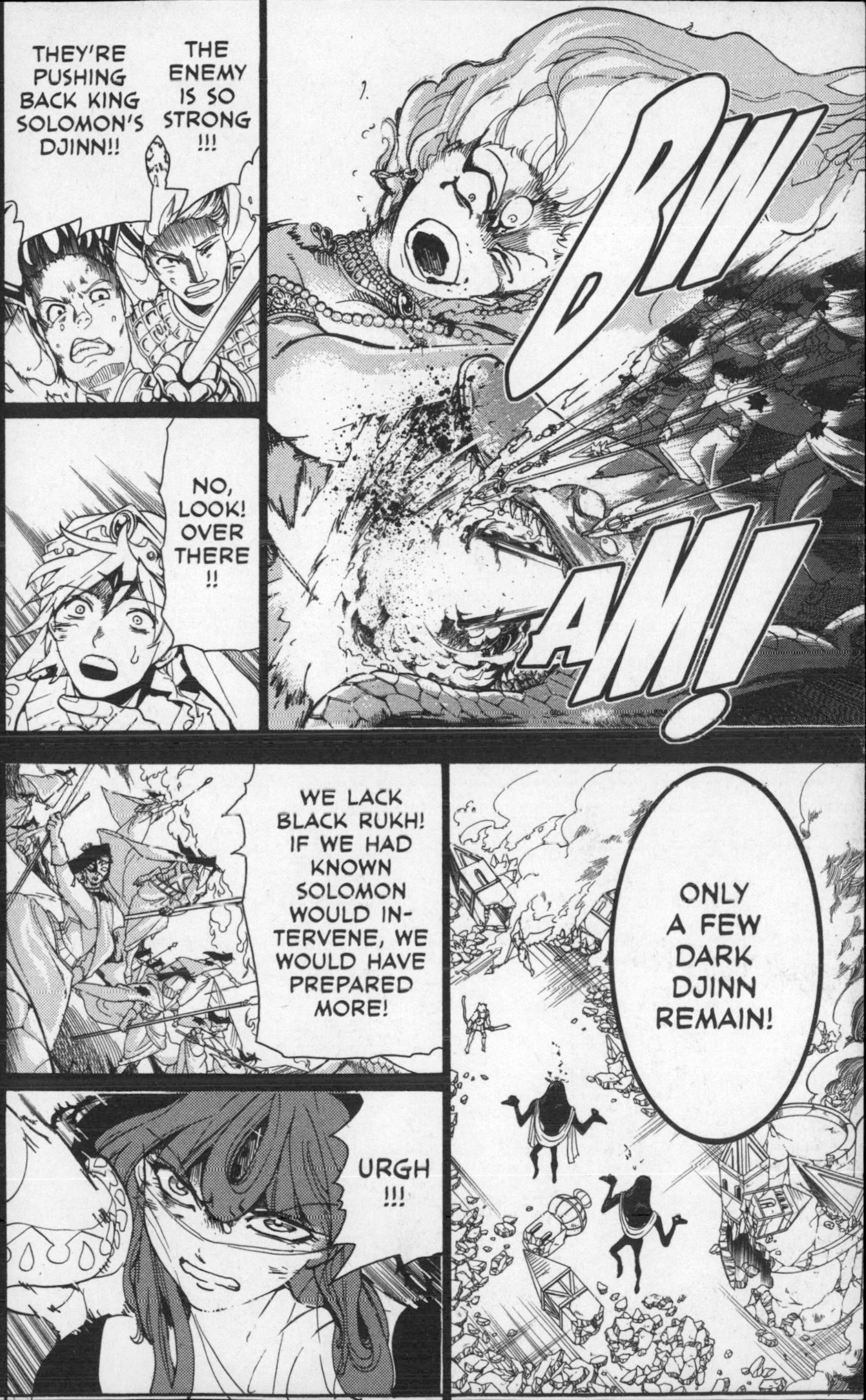
THE ENEMY IS SO STRONG!!!
THEY'RE PUSHING BACK KING SOLOMON'S DJINN!!
NO, LOOK! OVER THERE!!
ONLY A FEW DARK DJINN REMAIN!
WE LACK BLACK RUKH! IF WE HAD KNOWN SOLOMON WOULD IN-TERVENE, WE WOULD HAVE PREPARED MORE!
URGH!!!

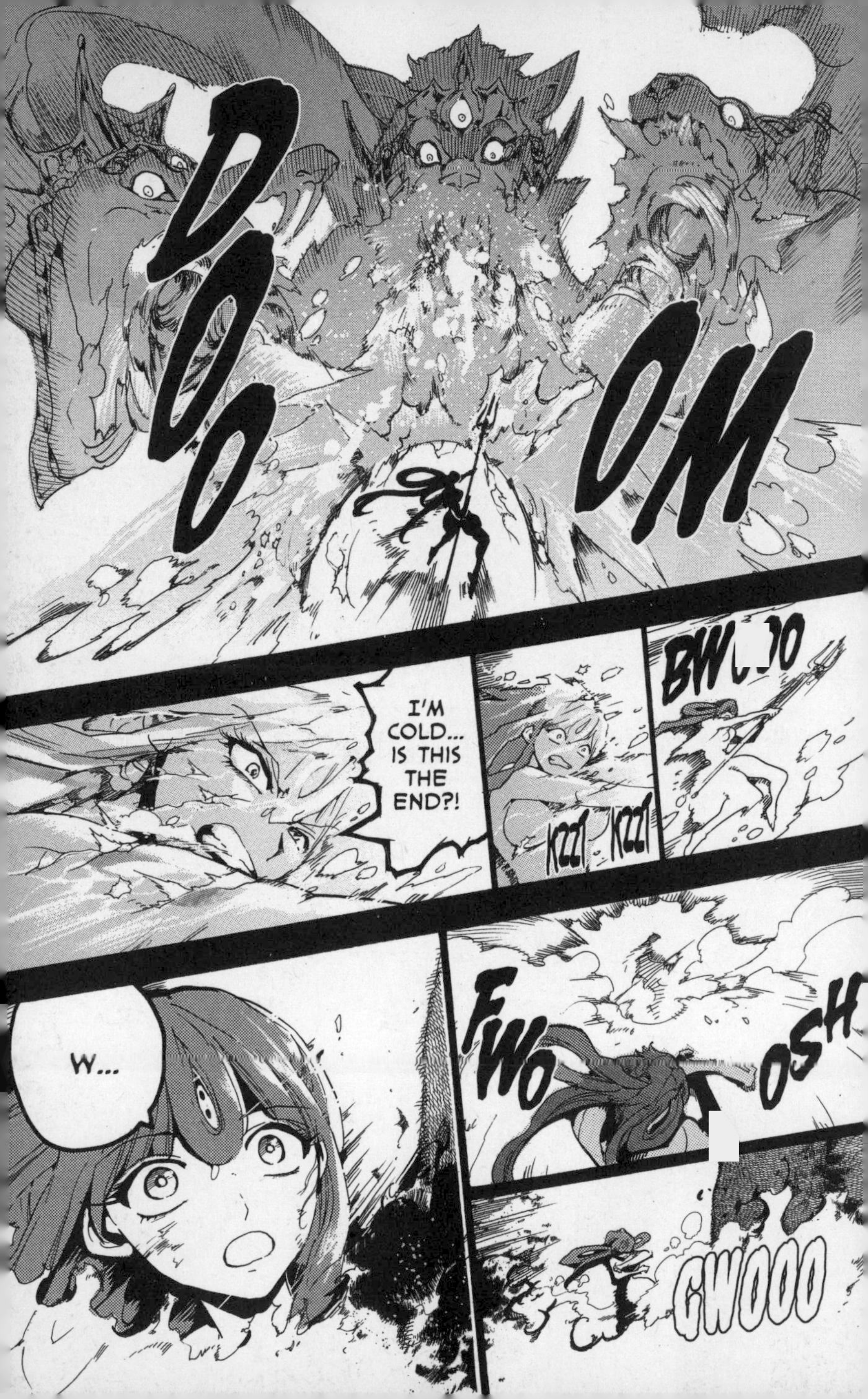
DOOOOM
BW OO
KZZT KZZT
I'M COLD... IS THIS THE END?!
FWOOSH
GWOOO
W...

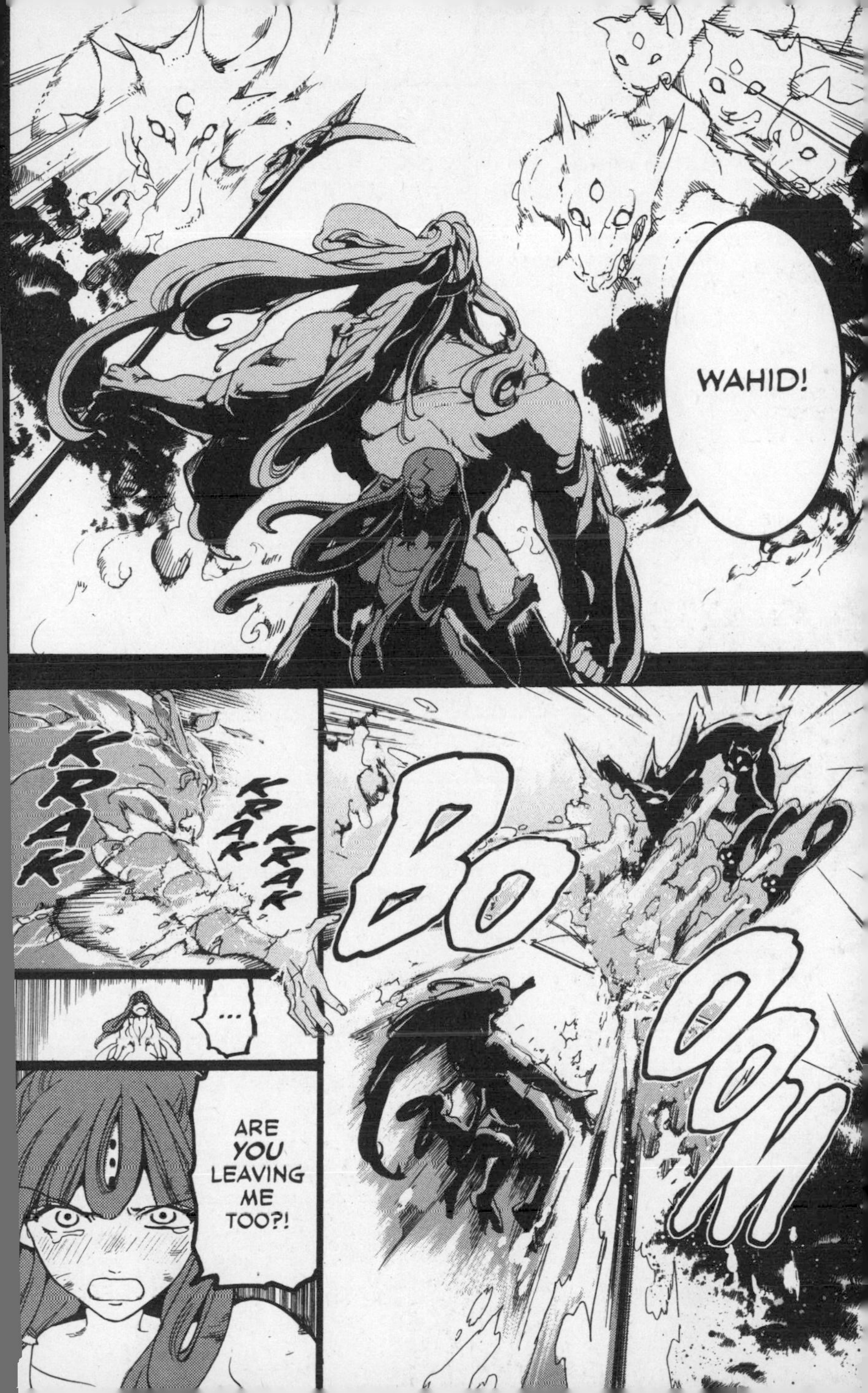
WAHID!
BOOOM
KRAK KRAK KRAK
...
ARE YOU LEAVING ME TOO?!

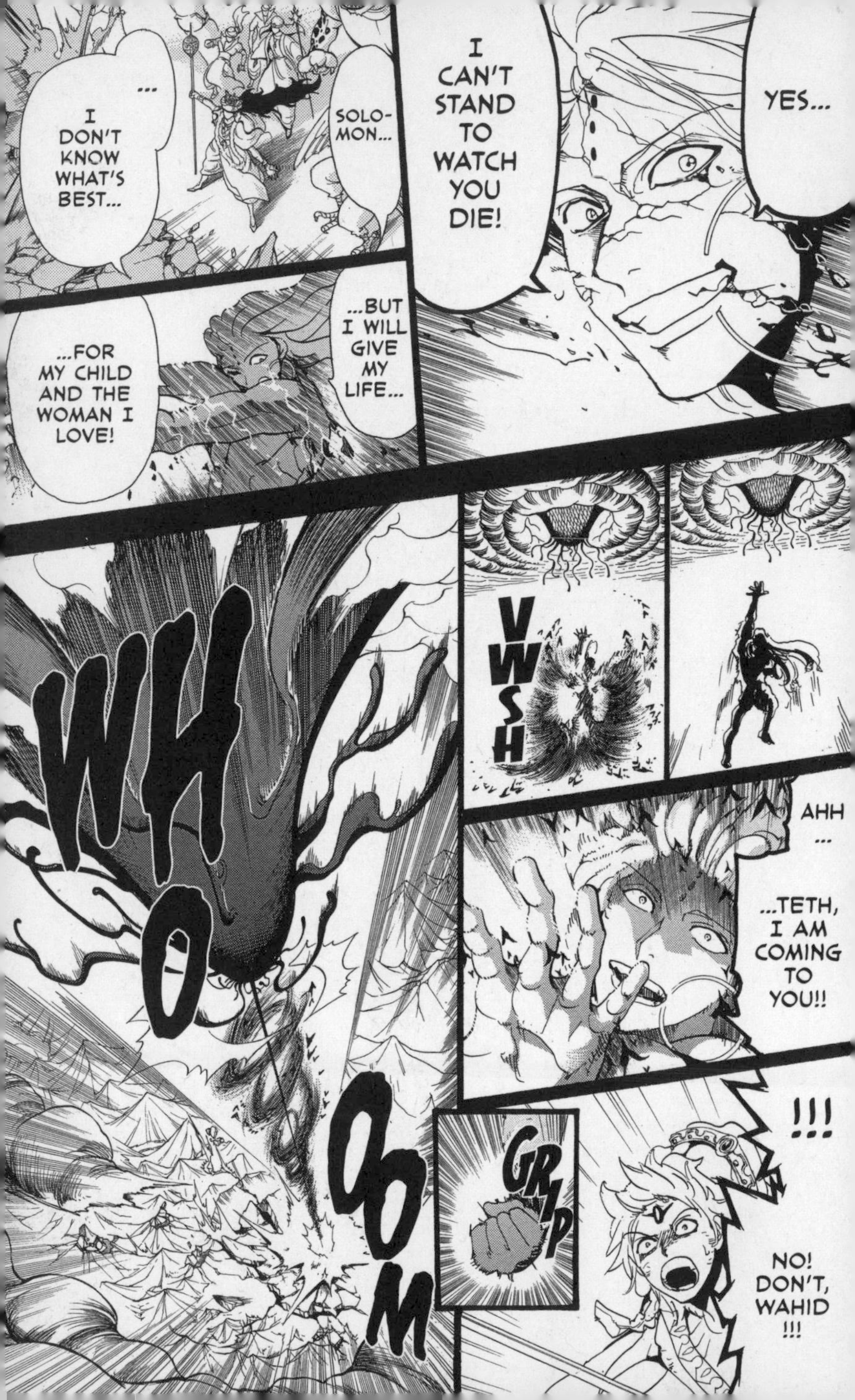
YES...
I CAN'T STAND TO WATCH YOU DIE!
SOLOMON...
... I DON'T KNOW WHAT'S BEST...
...BUT I WILL GIVE MY LIFE...
...FOR MY CHILD AND THE WOMAN I LOVE!
VWSH
AHH ...
...TETH, I AM COMING TO YOU!!
!!!
NO! DON'T, WAHID!!!
GRIP
WHOOOOM

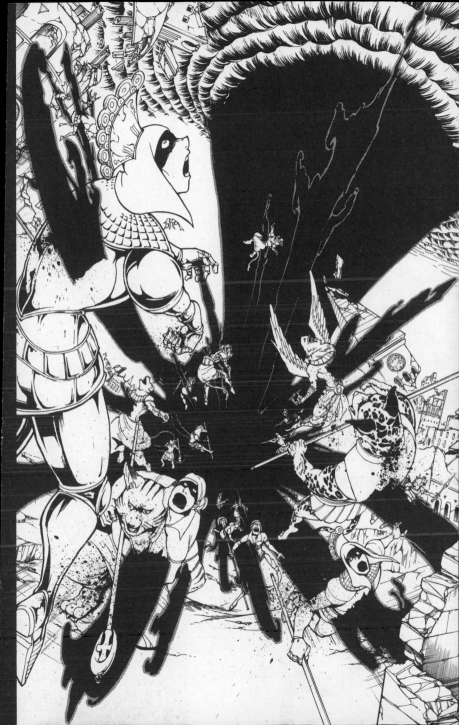

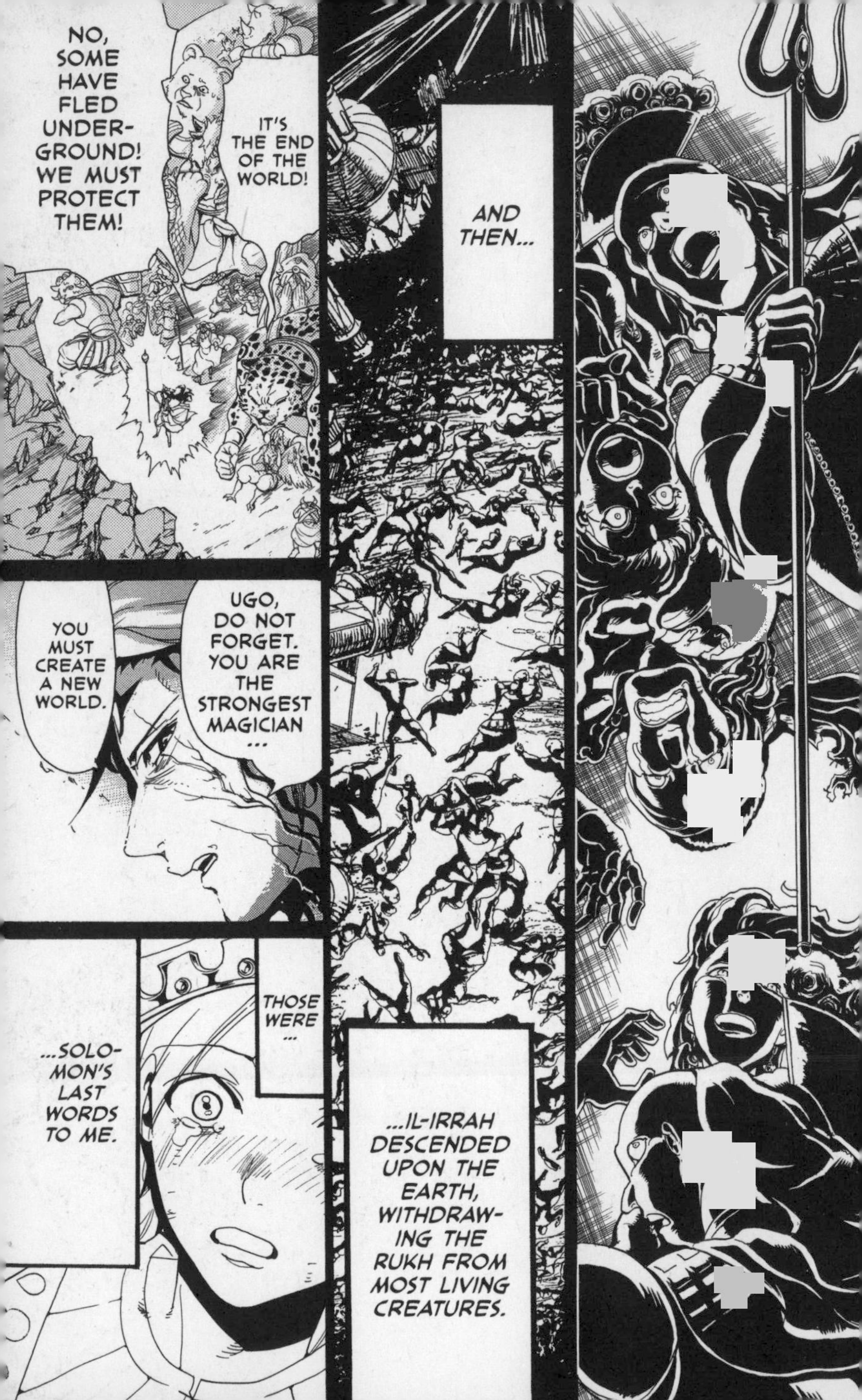
AND THEN...
...IL-IRRAH DESCENDED UPON THE EARTH, WITHDRAWING THE RUKH FROM MOST LIVING CREATURES.
IT'S THE END OF THE WORLD!
NO, SOME HAVE FLED UNDERGROUND! WE MUST PROTECT THEM!
UGO, DO NOT FORGET. YOU ARE THE STRONGEST MAGICIAN...
YOU MUST CREATE A NEW WORLD.
THOSE WERE...
...SOLOMON'S LAST WORDS TO ME.

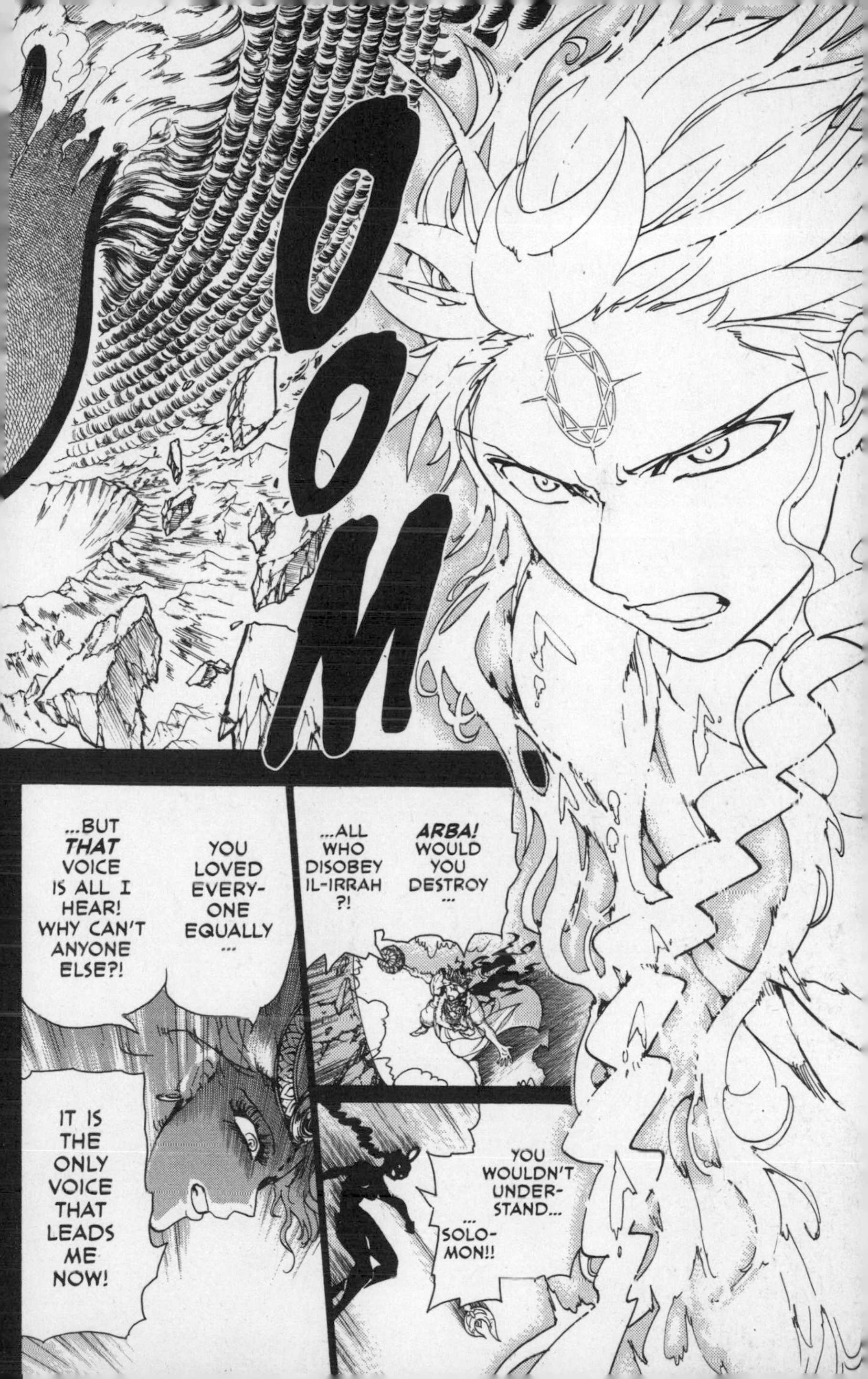
ARBA! WOULD YOU DESTROY ...
...ALL WHO DISOBEY IL-IRRAH ?!
YOU LOVED EVERY-ONE EQUALLY ...
...BUT *THAT* VOICE IS ALL I HEAR! WHY CAN'T ANYONE ELSE?!
YOU WOULDN'T UNDER-STAND...
... SOLO-MON!!
IT IS THE ONLY VOICE THAT LEADS ME NOW!

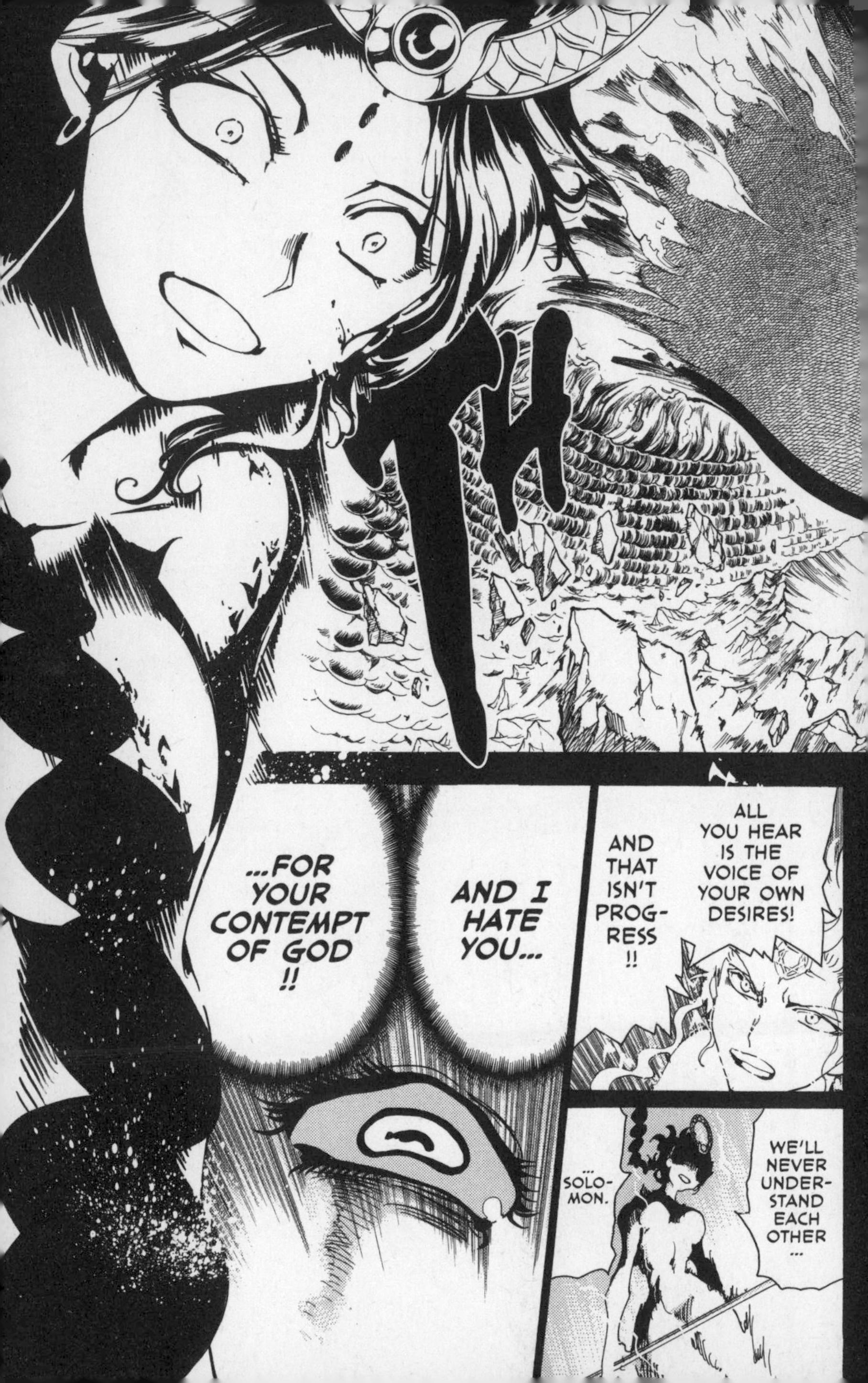
ALL YOU HEAR IS THE VOICE OF YOUR OWN DESIRES!
AND THAT ISN'T PROG-RESS !!
WE'LL NEVER UNDER-STAND EACH OTHER ...
... SOLO-MON.
AND I HATE YOU...
...FOR YOUR CONTEMPT OF GOD !!

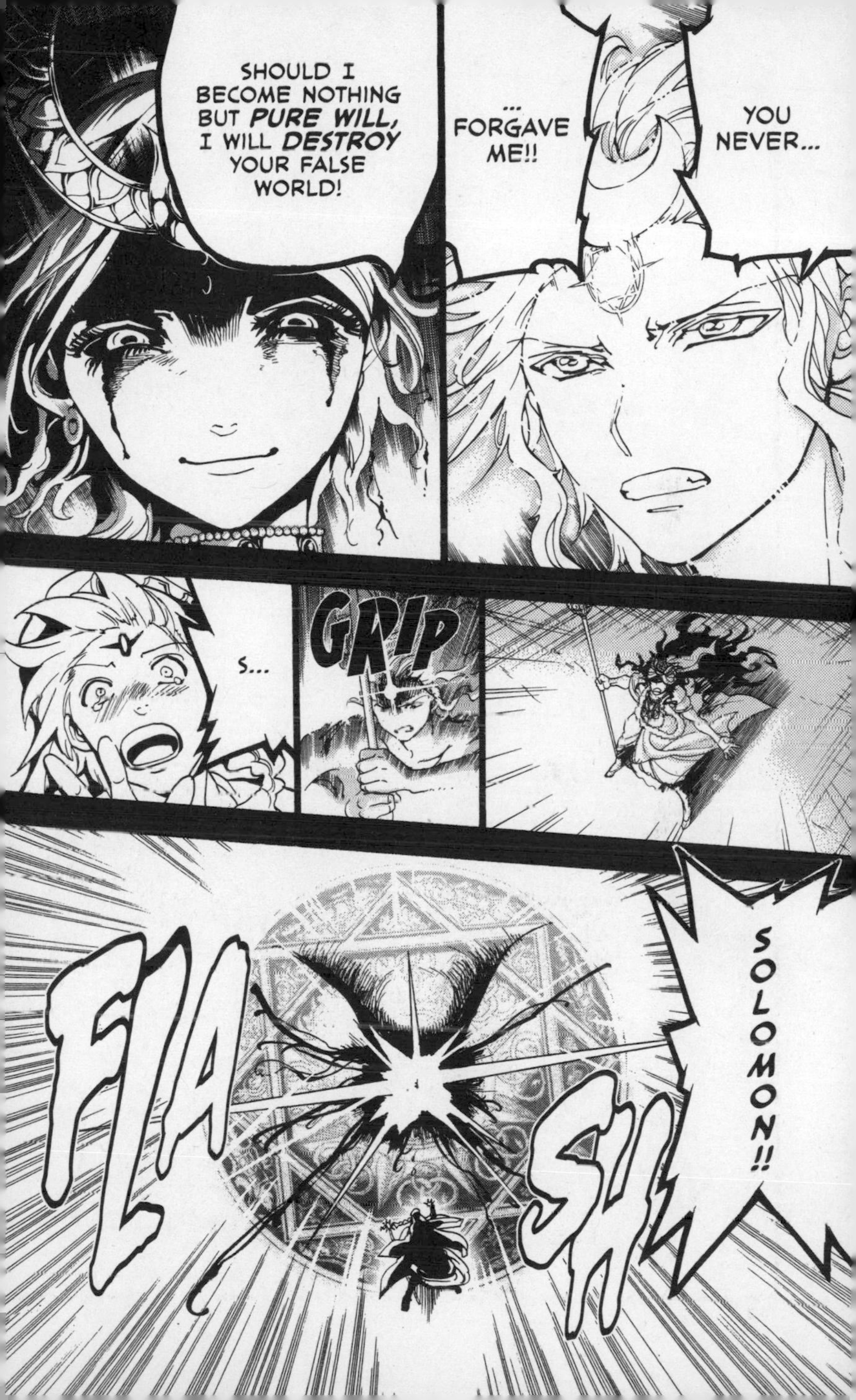
YOU NEVER...
... FORGAVE ME!!
SHOULD I BECOME NOTHING BUT PURE WILL, I WILL DESTROY YOUR FALSE WORLD!
GRIP
S...
SOLOMON!!
FLASH

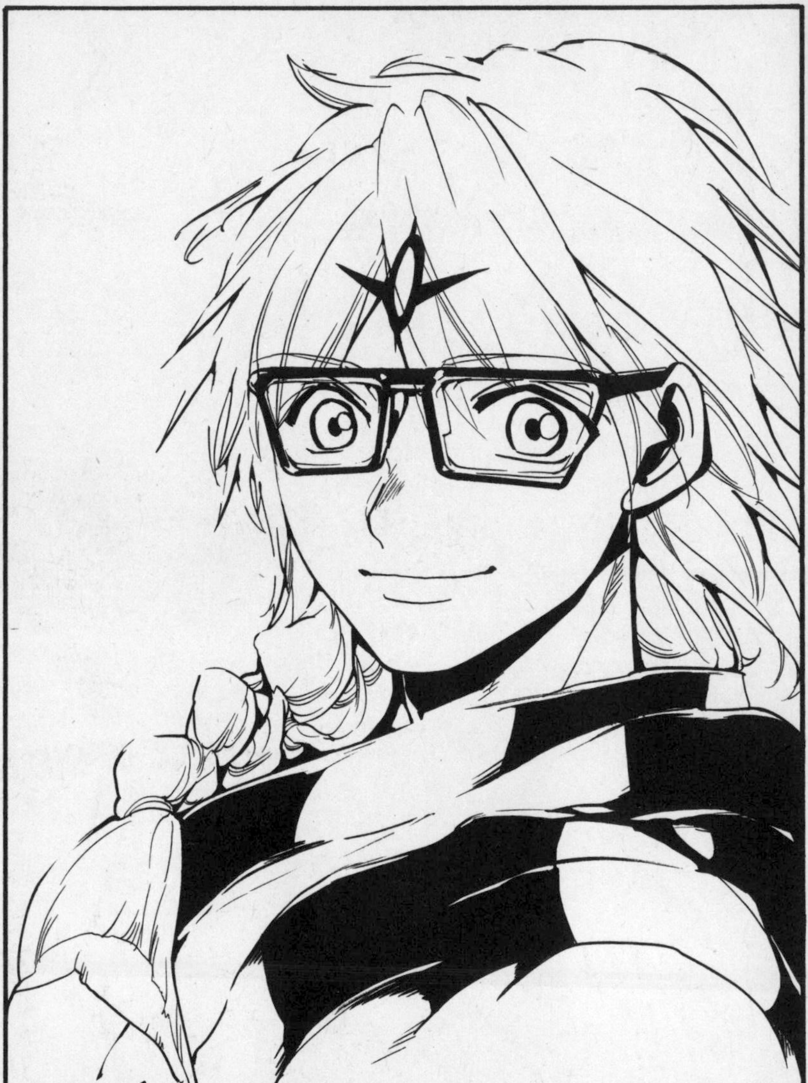

Night 236: Solomon's Avatar

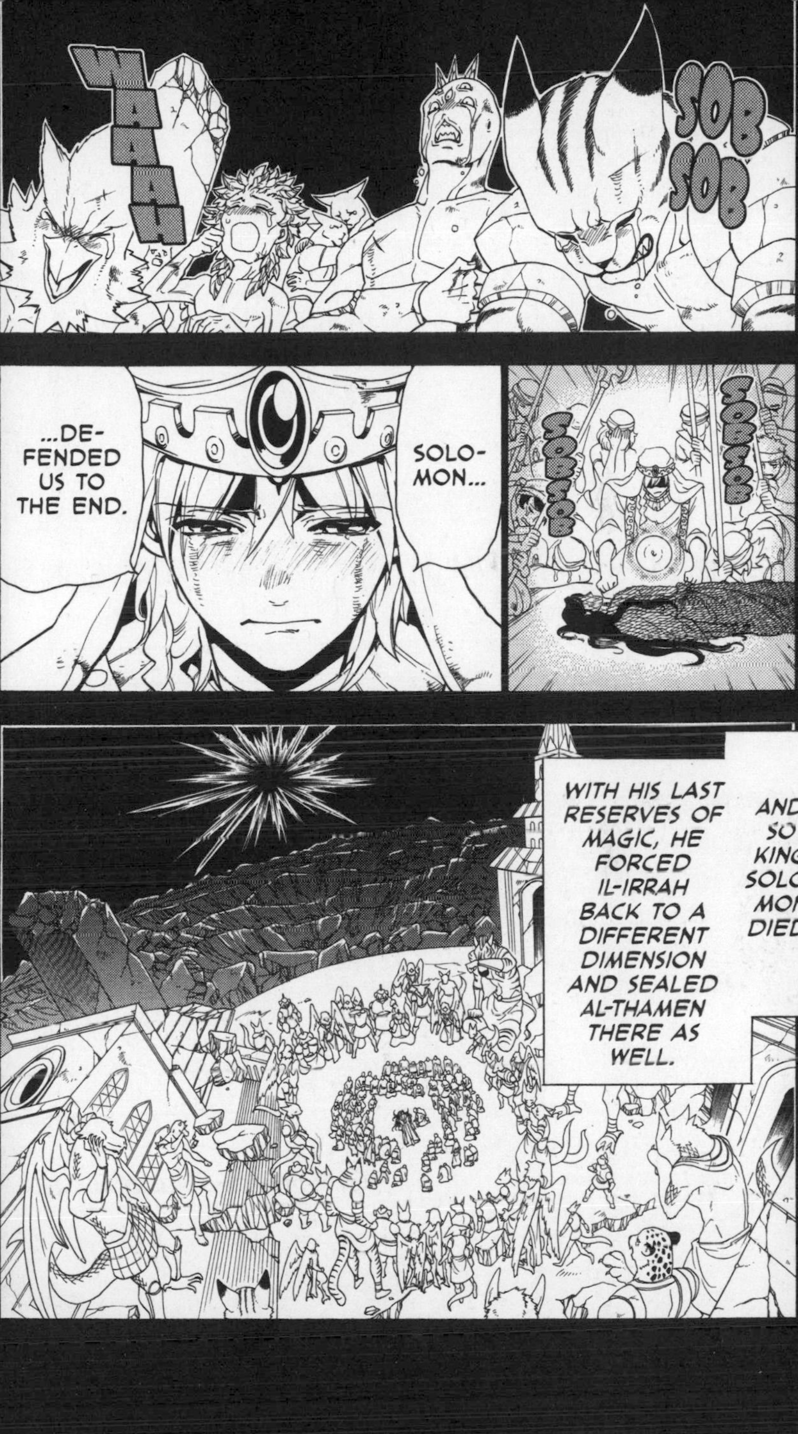
SOB SOB
WAAAAH
SOBSOB
SOBSOB
SOLO-MON...
...DE-FENDED US TO THE END.
AND SO KING SOLO-MON DIED.
WITH HIS LAST RESERVES OF MAGIC, HE FORCED IL-IRRAH BACK TO A DIFFERENT DIMENSION AND SEALED AL-THAMEN THERE AS WELL.

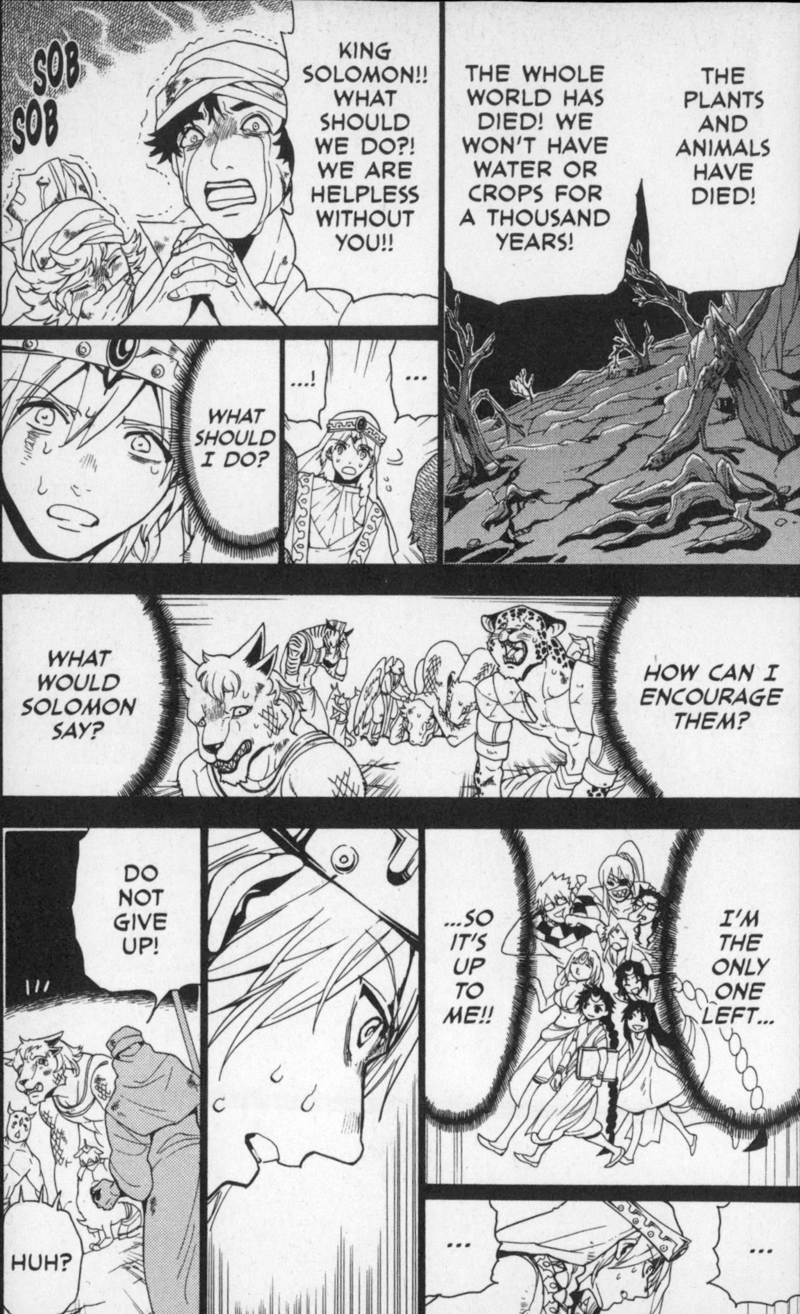
THE PLANTS AND ANIMALS HAVE DIED!
THE WHOLE WORLD HAS DIED! WE WON'T HAVE WATER OR CROPS FOR A THOUSAND YEARS!
KING SOLOMON!! WHAT SHOULD WE DO?! WE ARE HELPLESS WITHOUT YOU!!
SOB SOB
...!
...
WHAT SHOULD I DO?
HOW CAN I ENCOURAGE THEM?
WHAT WOULD SOLOMON SAY?
I'M THE ONLY ONE LEFT...
...SO IT'S UP TO ME!!
...
...
DO NOT GIVE UP!
!!!
HUH?

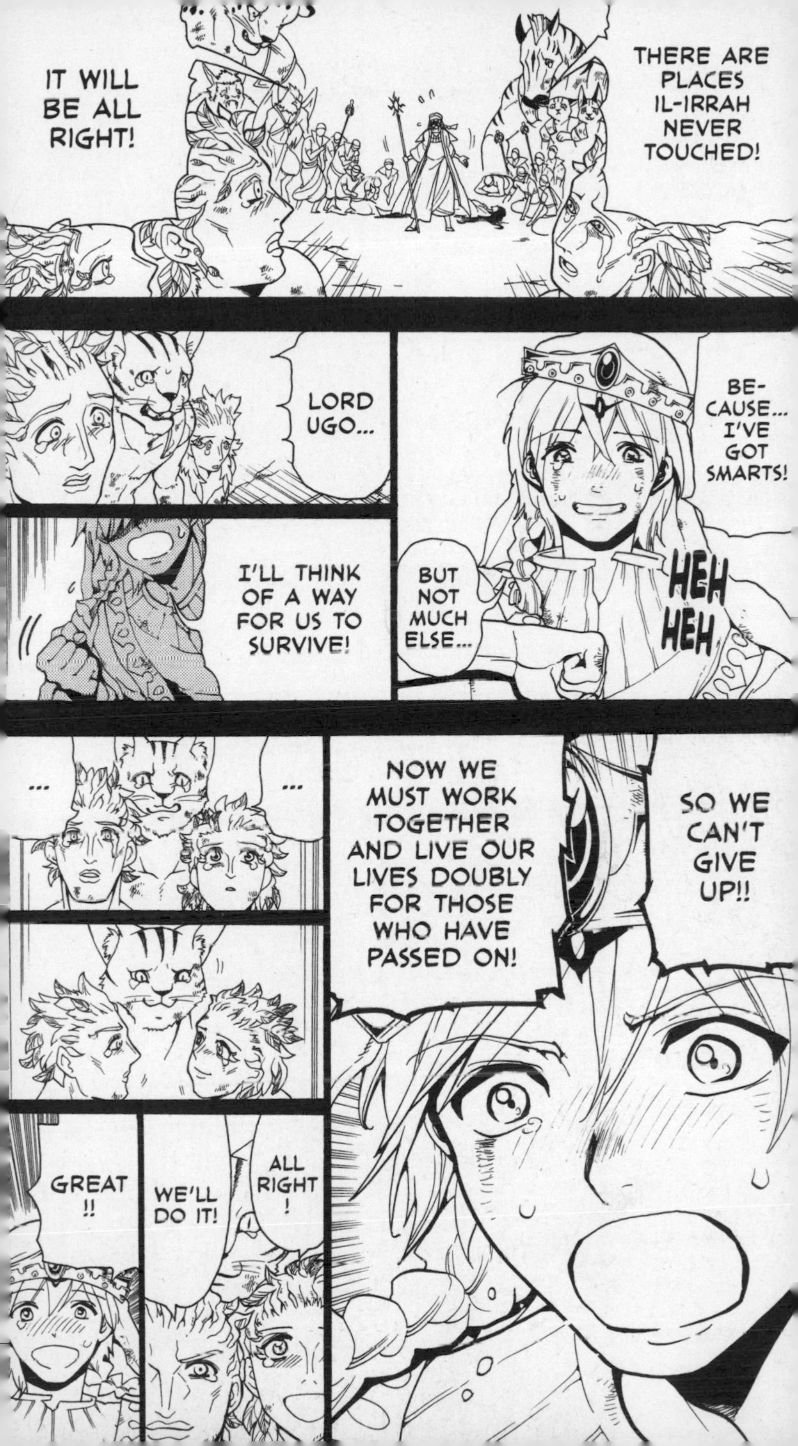
THERE ARE PLACES IL-IRRAH NEVER TOUCHED!
IT WILL BE ALL RIGHT!
BE-CAUSE... I'VE GOT SMARTS!
BUT NOT MUCH ELSE...
HEH HEH
LORD UGO...
I'LL THINK OF A WAY FOR US TO SURVIVE!
SO WE CAN'T GIVE UP!!
NOW WE MUST WORK TOGETHER AND LIVE OUR LIVES DOUBLY FOR THOSE WHO HAVE PASSED ON!
...
...
ALL RIGHT!
WE'LL DO IT!
GREAT!!

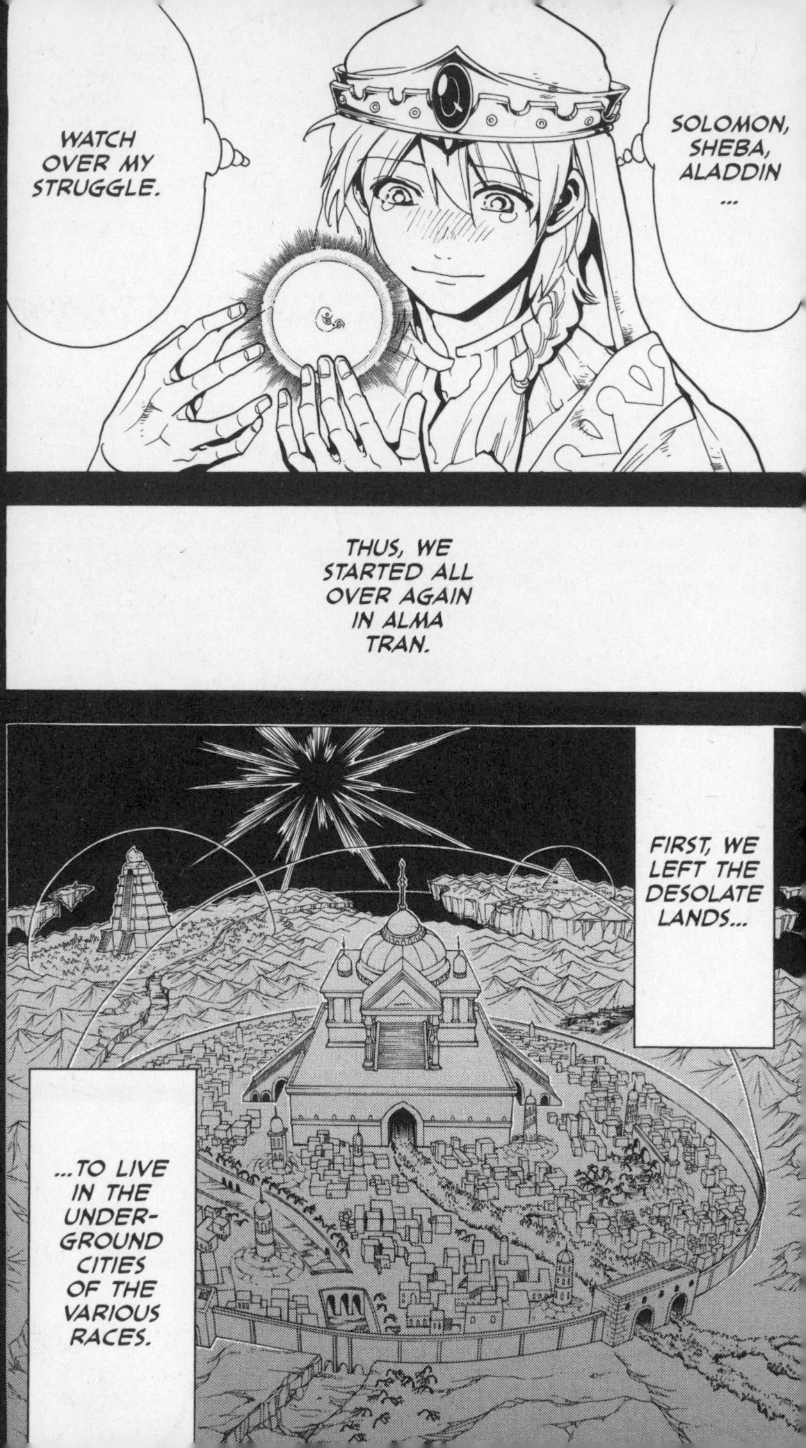
SOLOMON, SHEBA, ALADDIN ...
WATCH OVER MY STRUGGLE.
THUS, WE STARTED ALL OVER AGAIN IN ALMA TRAN.
FIRST, WE LEFT THE DESOLATE LANDS...
...TO LIVE IN THE UNDER-GROUND CITIES OF THE VARIOUS RACES.

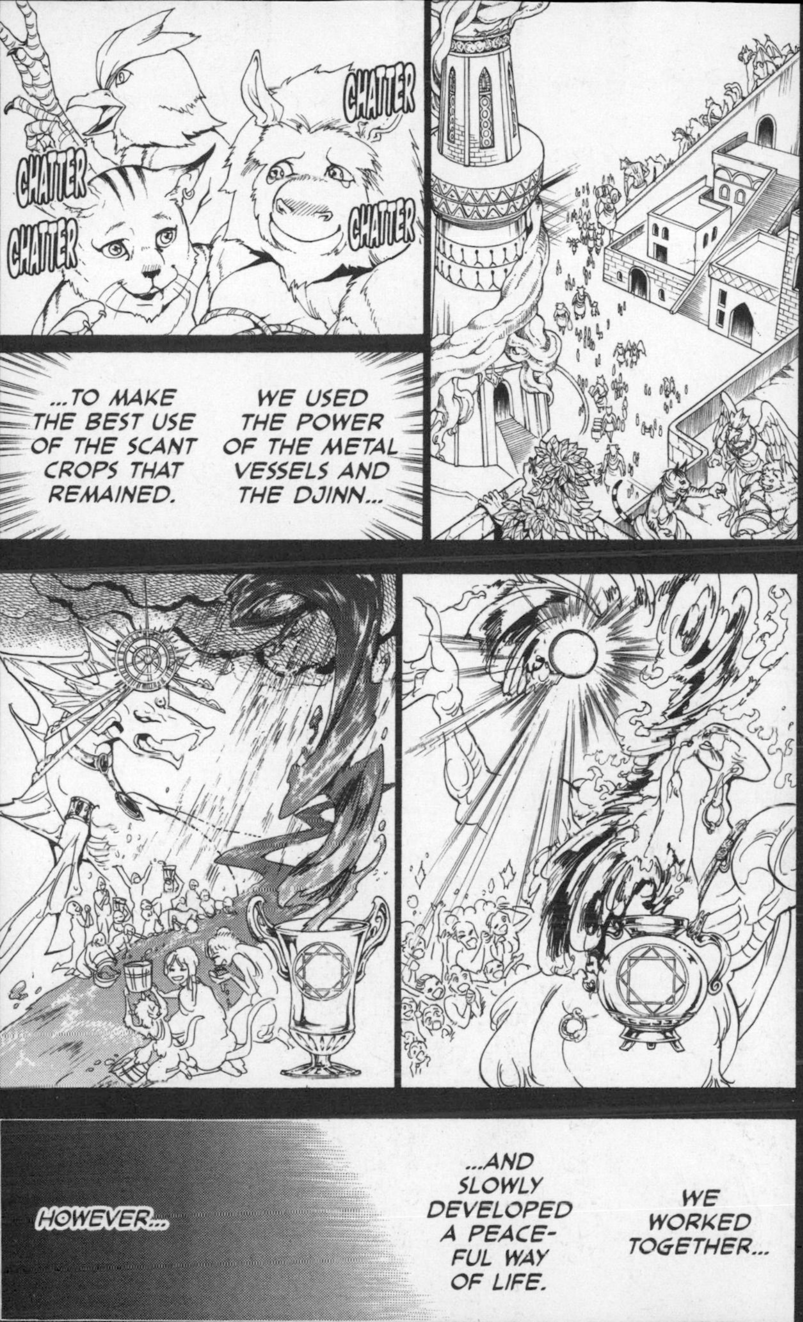
CHATTER
CHATTER
CHATTER
CHATTER
WE USED THE POWER OF THE METAL VESSELS AND THE DJINN...
...TO MAKE THE BEST USE OF THE SCANT CROPS THAT REMAINED.
WE WORKED TOGETHER...
...AND SLOWLY DEVELOPED A PEACE-FUL WAY OF LIFE.
HOWEVER...

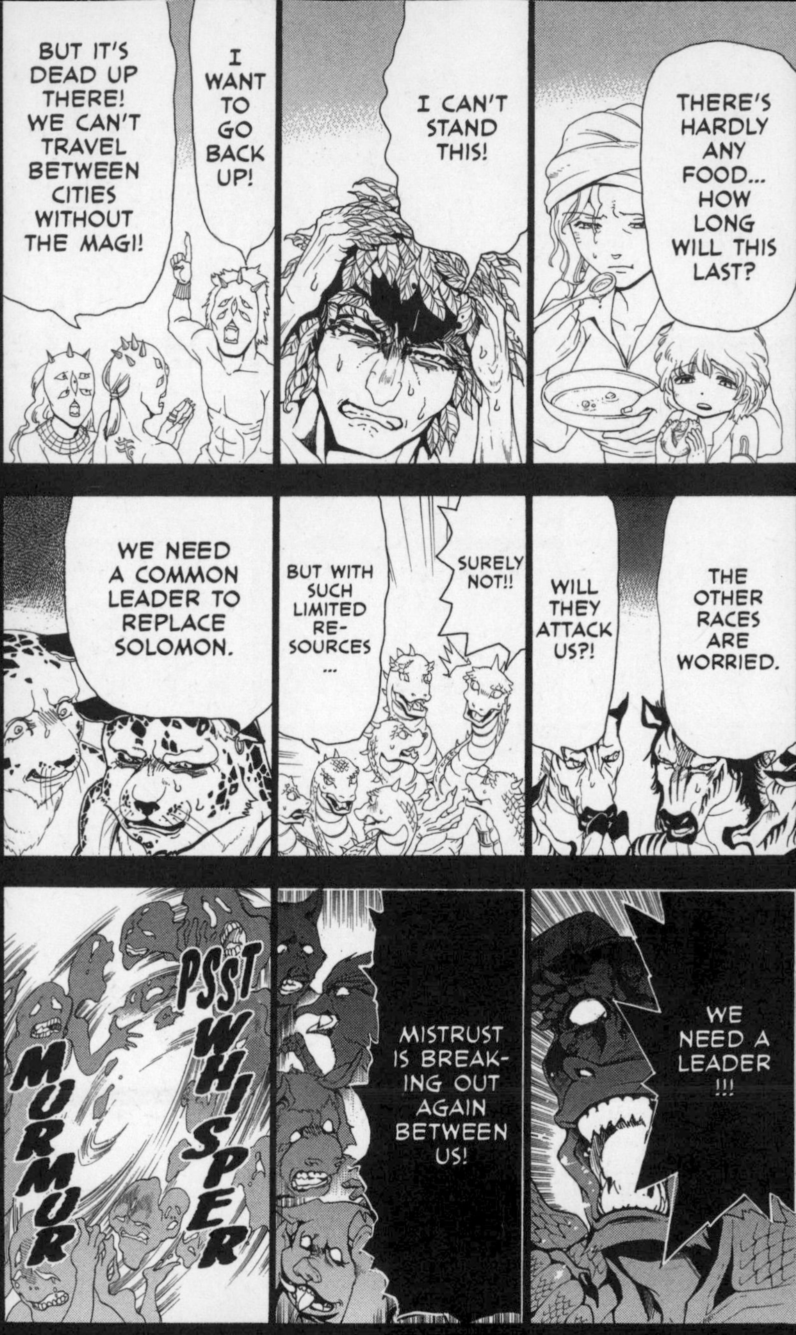
THERE'S HARDLY ANY FOOD... HOW LONG WILL THIS LAST?
I CAN'T STAND THIS!
I WANT TO GO BACK UP!
BUT IT'S DEAD UP THERE! WE CAN'T TRAVEL BETWEEN CITIES WITHOUT THE MAGI!
THE OTHER RACES ARE WORRIED.
WILL THEY ATTACK US?!
SURELY NOT!!
BUT WITH SUCH LIMITED RE-SOURCES...
WE NEED A COMMON LEADER TO REPLACE SOLOMON.
WE NEED A LEADER!!!
MISTRUST IS BREAK-ING OUT AGAIN BETWEEN US!
PSST WHISPER
MURMUR

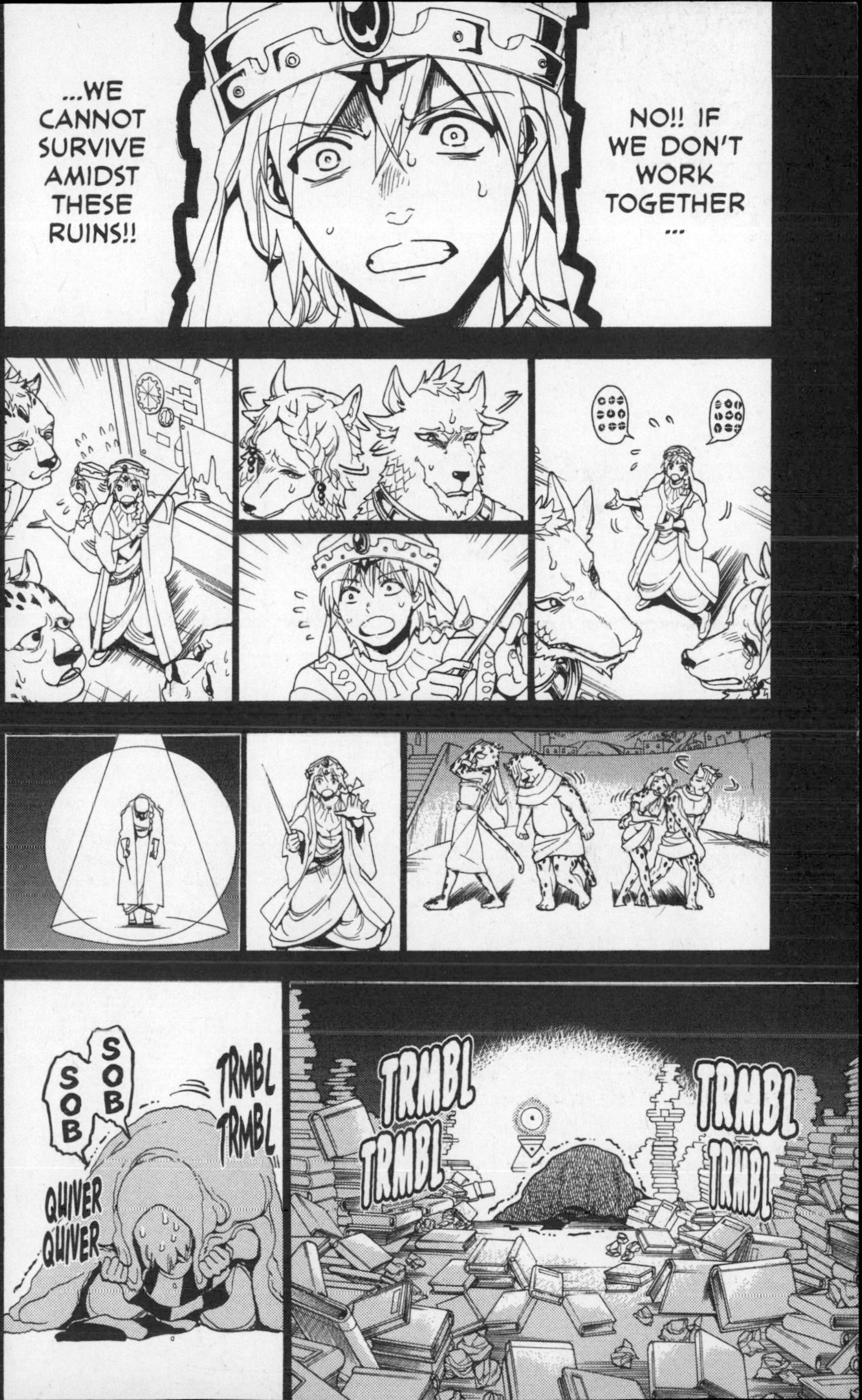
NO!! IF WE DON'T WORK TOGETHER ...
...WE CANNOT SURVIVE AMIDST THESE RUINS!!
TRMBL TRMBL
TRMBL TRMBL
SOB SOB
TRMBL TRMBL
QUIVER QUIVER

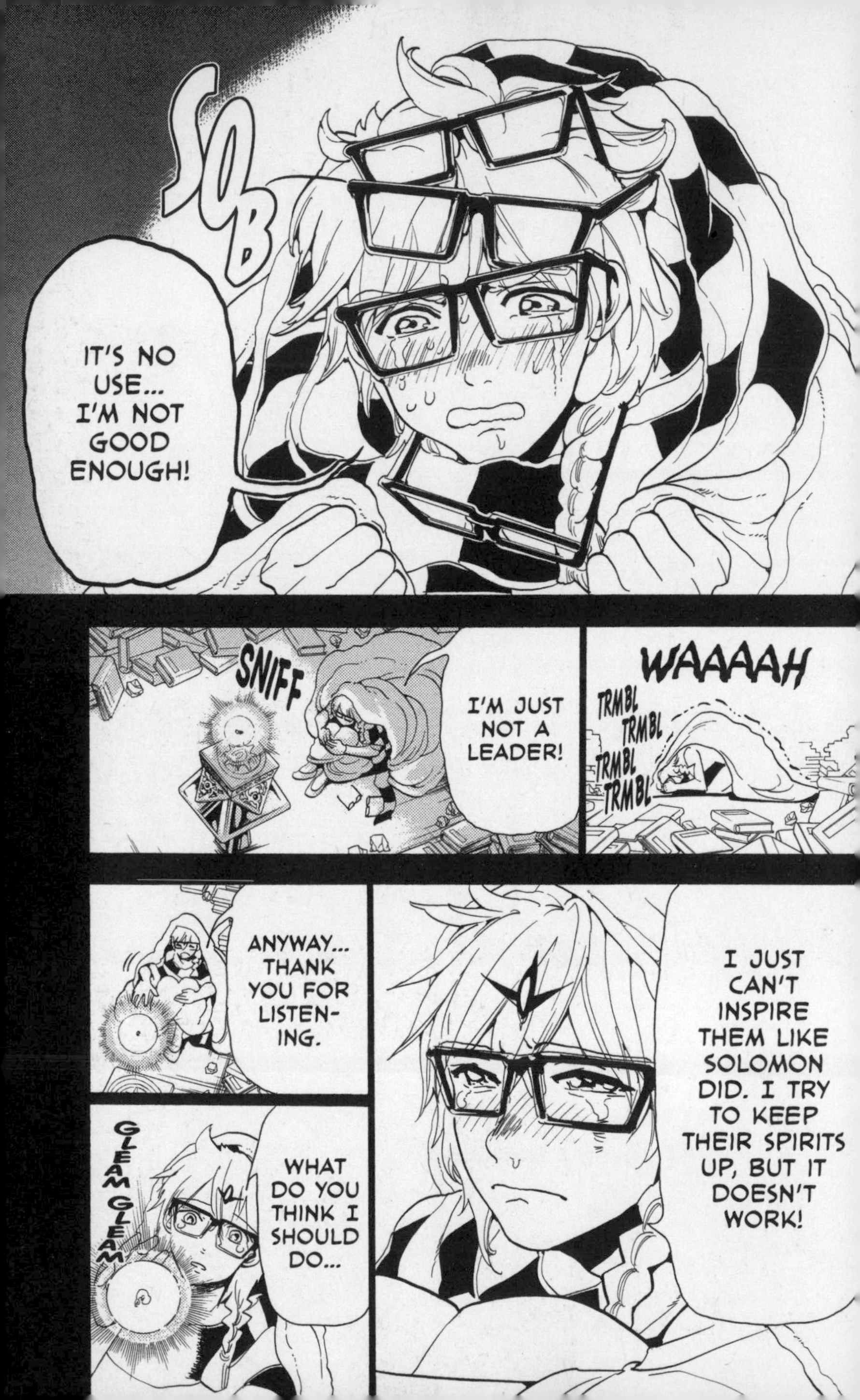
SOB
IT'S NO USE... I'M NOT GOOD ENOUGH!
WAAAAH
TRMBL TRMBL TRMBL TRMBL
I'M JUST NOT A LEADER!
SNIFF
I JUST CAN'T INSPIRE THEM LIKE SOLOMON DID. I TRY TO KEEP THEIR SPIRITS UP, BUT IT DOESN'T WORK!
ANYWAY... THANK YOU FOR LISTEN-ING.
WHAT DO YOU THINK I SHOULD DO...
GLEAM GLEAM

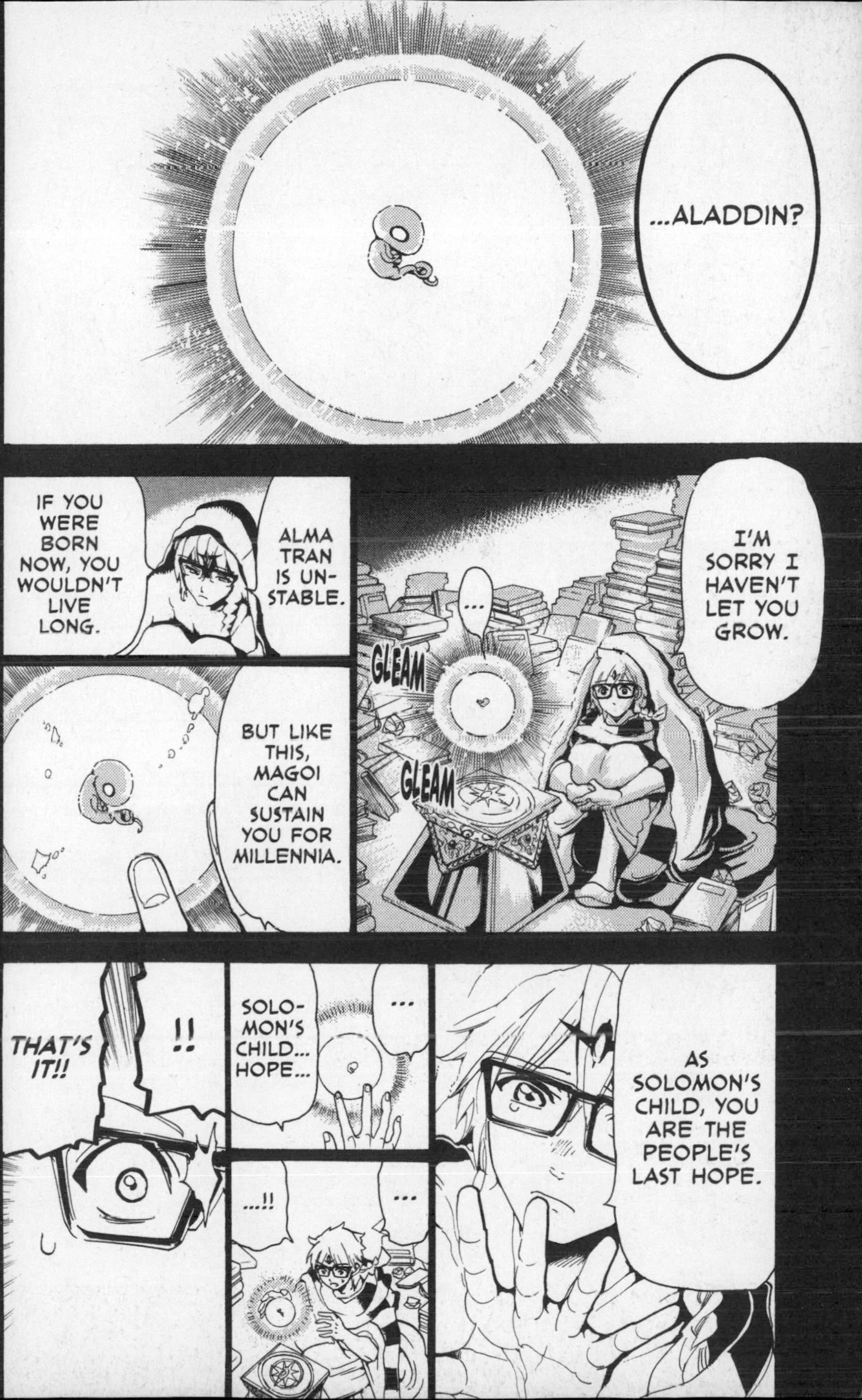
...ALADDIN?
I'M SORRY I HAVEN'T LET YOU GROW.
...
GLEAM
GLEAM
ALMA TRAN IS UN-STABLE.
IF YOU WERE BORN NOW, YOU WOULDN'T LIVE LONG.
BUT LIKE THIS, MAGOI CAN SUSTAIN YOU FOR MILLENNIA.
AS SOLOMON'S CHILD, YOU ARE THE PEOPLE'S LAST HOPE.
...
SOLOMON'S CHILD... HOPE...
...
...!!
!!
THAT'S IT!!

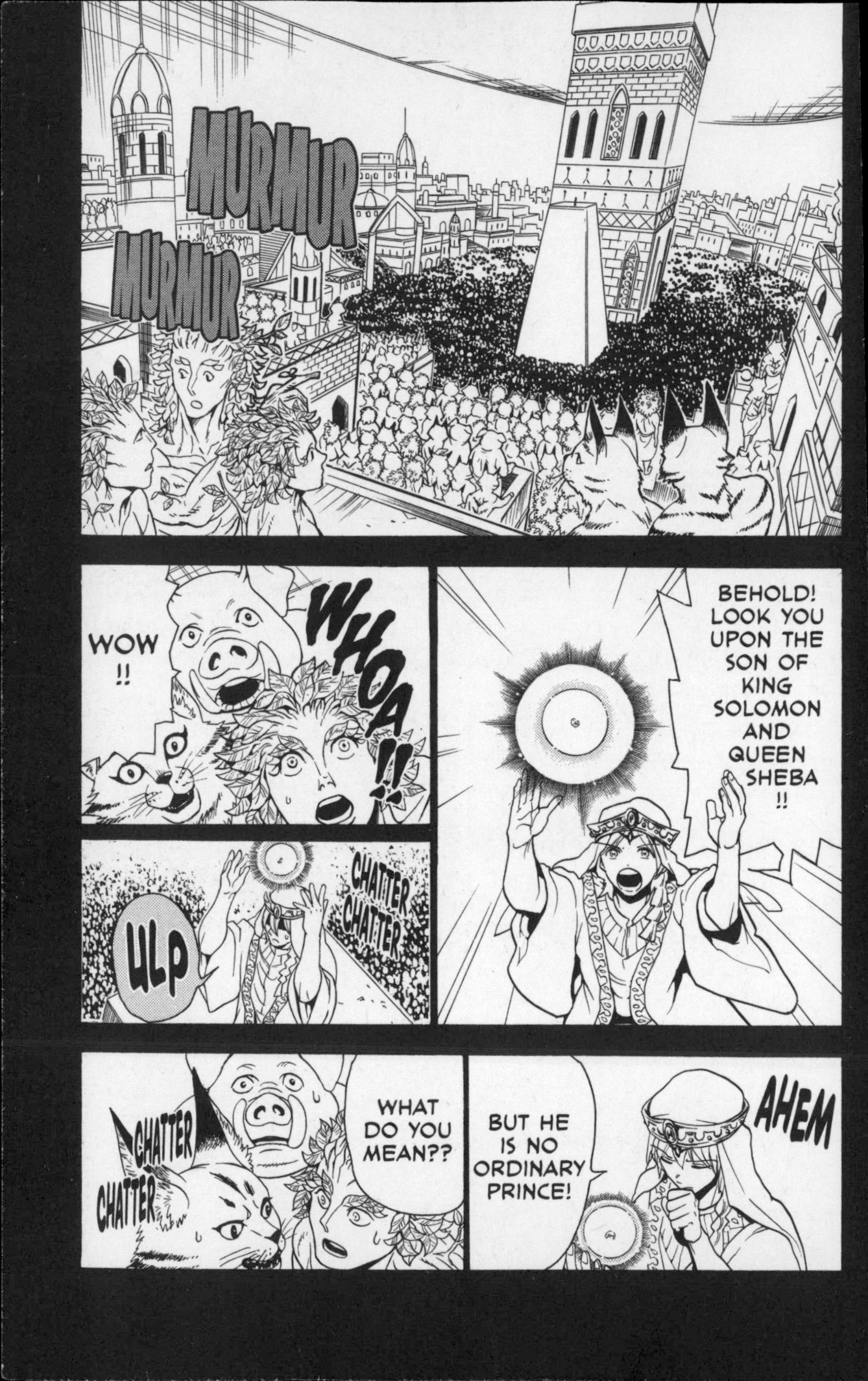
MURMUR
MURMUR
BEHOLD! LOOK YOU UPON THE SON OF KING SOLOMON AND QUEEN SHEBA !!
WHOA!!
WOW !!
CHATTER CHATTER
ULP
AHEM
BUT HE IS NO ORDINARY PRINCE!
WHAT DO YOU MEAN??
CHATTER CHATTER

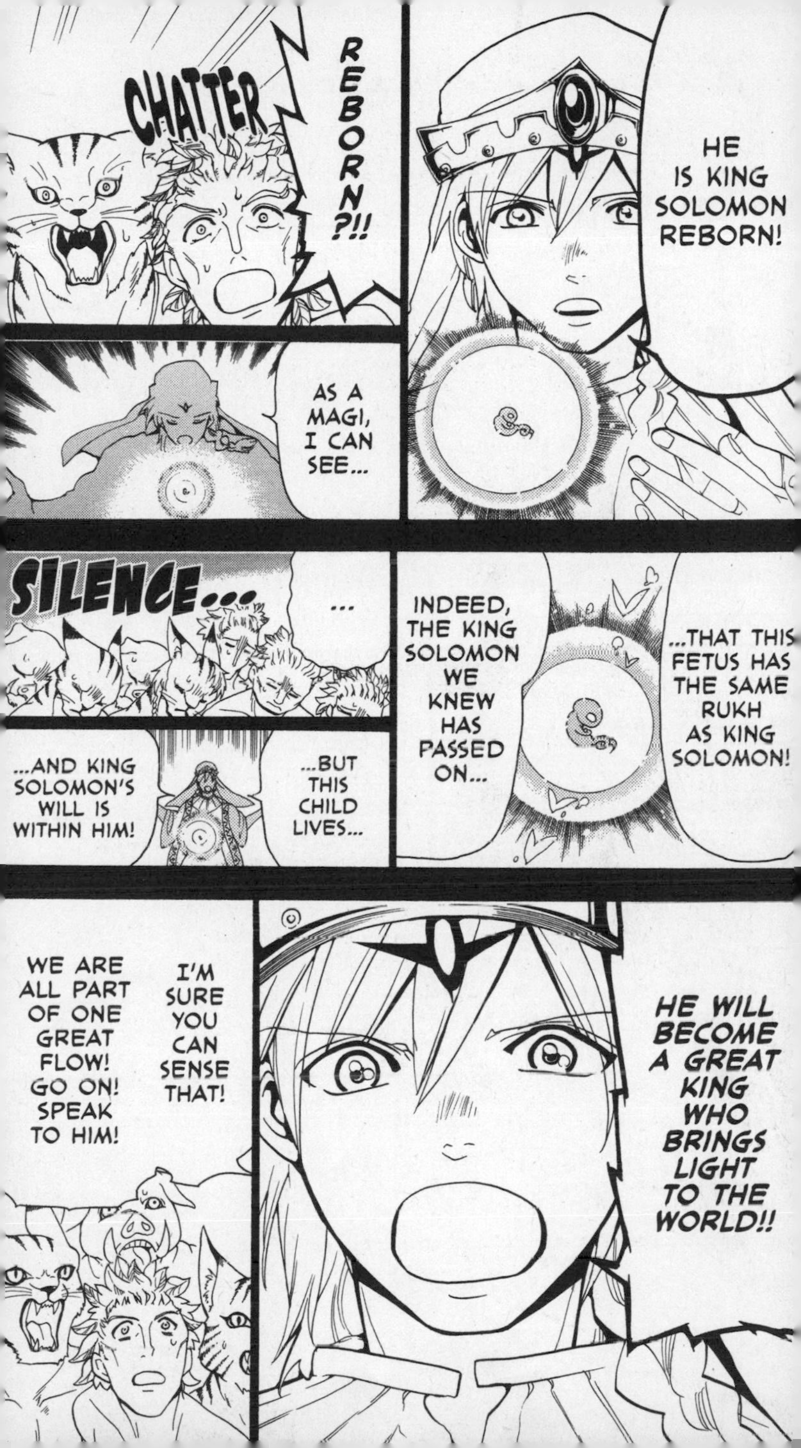
HE IS KING SOLOMON REBORN!
CHATTER
REBORN?!!
AS A MAGI, I CAN SEE...
...THAT THIS FETUS HAS THE SAME RUKH AS KING SOLOMON!
INDEED, THE KING SOLOMON WE KNEW HAS PASSED ON...
SILENCE...
...
...BUT THIS CHILD LIVES...
...AND KING SOLOMON'S WILL IS WITHIN HIM!
HE WILL BECOME A GREAT KING WHO BRINGS LIGHT TO THE WORLD!!
I'M SURE YOU CAN SENSE THAT!
WE ARE ALL PART OF ONE GREAT FLOW! GO ON! SPEAK TO HIM!

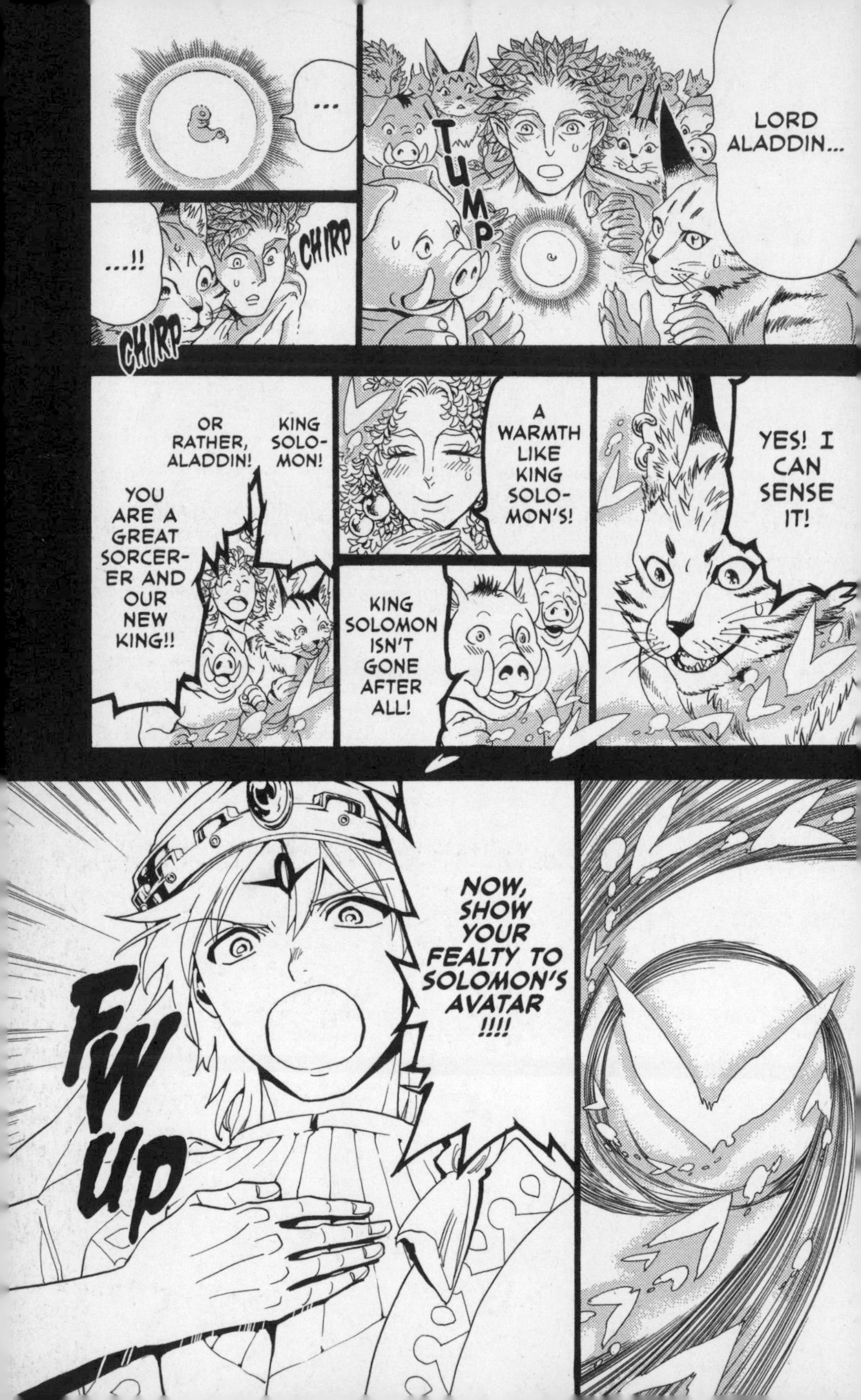
TUMP
LORD ALADDIN...
...
...!!
CHIRP
CHIRP
YES! I CAN SENSE IT!
A WARMTH LIKE KING SOLOMON'S!
KING SOLOMON ISN'T GONE AFTER ALL!
KING SOLOMON!
OR RATHER, ALADDIN!
YOU ARE A GREAT SORCERER AND OUR NEW KING!!
NOW, SHOW YOUR FEALTY TO SOLOMON'S AVATAR!!!!
FWUP

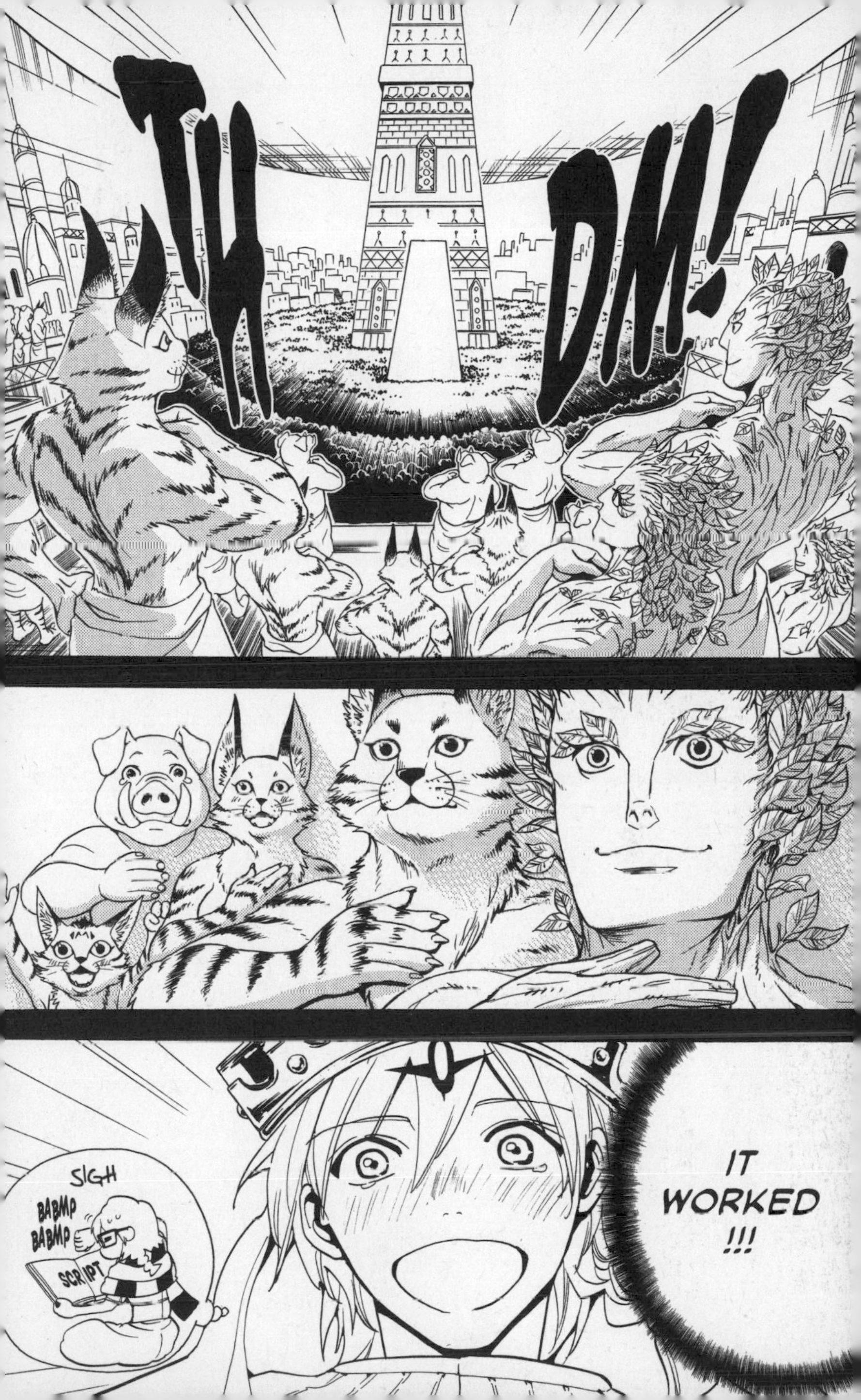
IT WORKED !!!
SIGH
BABMP BABMP
SCRIPT

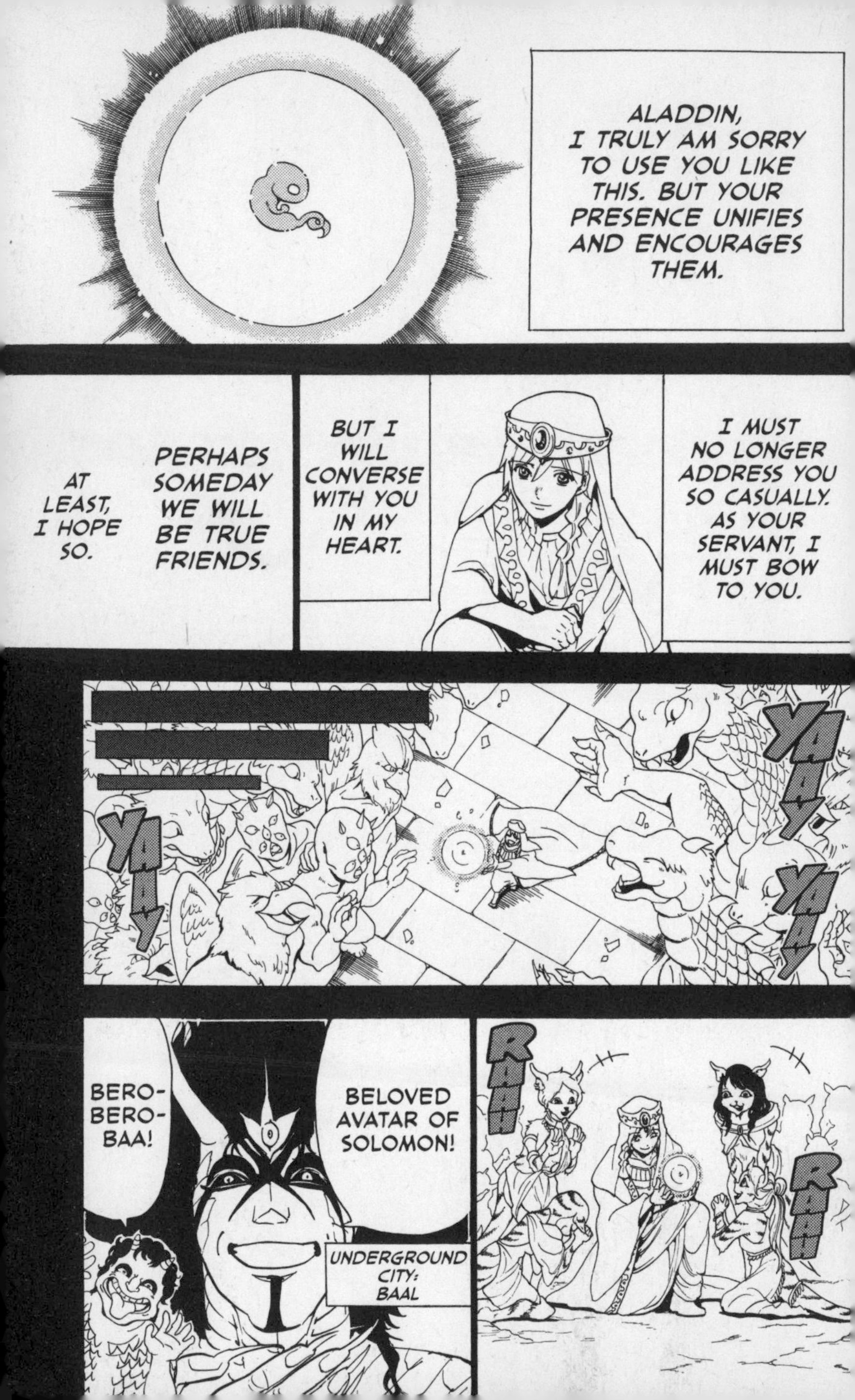
ALADDIN, I TRULY AM SORRY TO USE YOU LIKE THIS. BUT YOUR PRESENCE UNIFIES AND ENCOURAGES THEM.
I MUST NO LONGER ADDRESS YOU SO CASUALLY. AS YOUR SERVANT, I MUST BOW TO YOU.
BUT I WILL CONVERSE WITH YOU IN MY HEART.
PERHAPS SOMEDAY WE WILL BE TRUE FRIENDS.
AT LEAST, I HOPE SO.
[redacted]
BELOVED AVATAR OF SOLOMON!
BERO-BERO-BAA!
UNDERGROUND CITY: BAAL

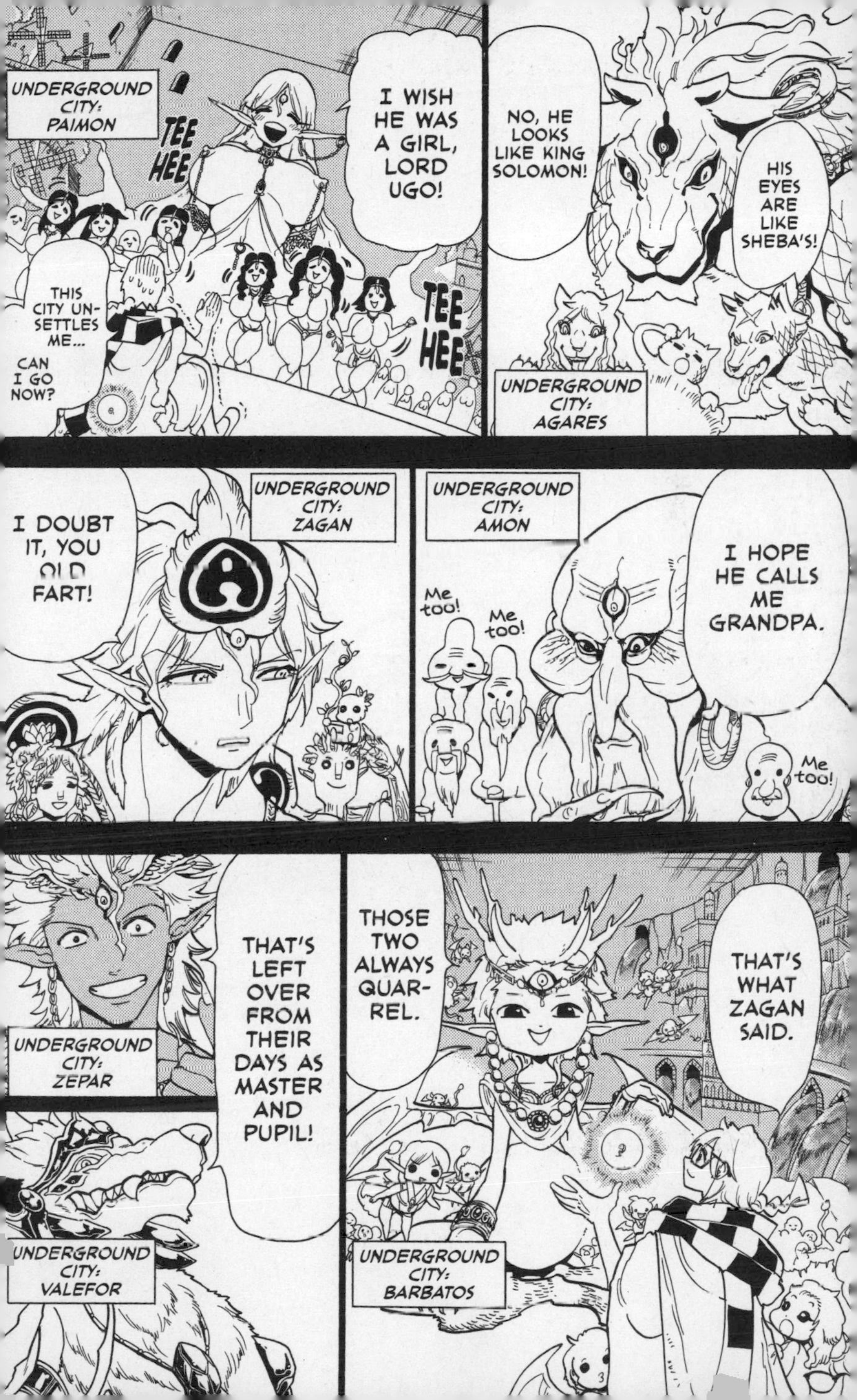
UNDERGROUND CITY: AGARES
HIS EYES ARE LIKE SHEBA'S!
NO, HE LOOKS LIKE KING SOLOMON!
UNDERGROUND CITY: PAIMON
I WISH HE WAS A GIRL, LORD UGO!
TEE HEE
TEE HEE
THIS CITY UN-SETTLES ME...
CAN I GO NOW?
UNDERGROUND CITY: AMON
I HOPE HE CALLS ME GRANDPA.
Me too!
Me too!
Me too!
UNDERGROUND CITY: ZAGAN
I DOUBT IT, YOU OLD FART!
THAT'S WHAT ZAGAN SAID.
THOSE TWO ALWAYS QUAR-REL.
UNDERGROUND CITY: BARBATOS
UNDERGROUND CITY: ZEPAR
THAT'S LEFT OVER FROM THEIR DAYS AS MASTER AND PUPIL!
UNDERGROUND CITY: VALEFOR

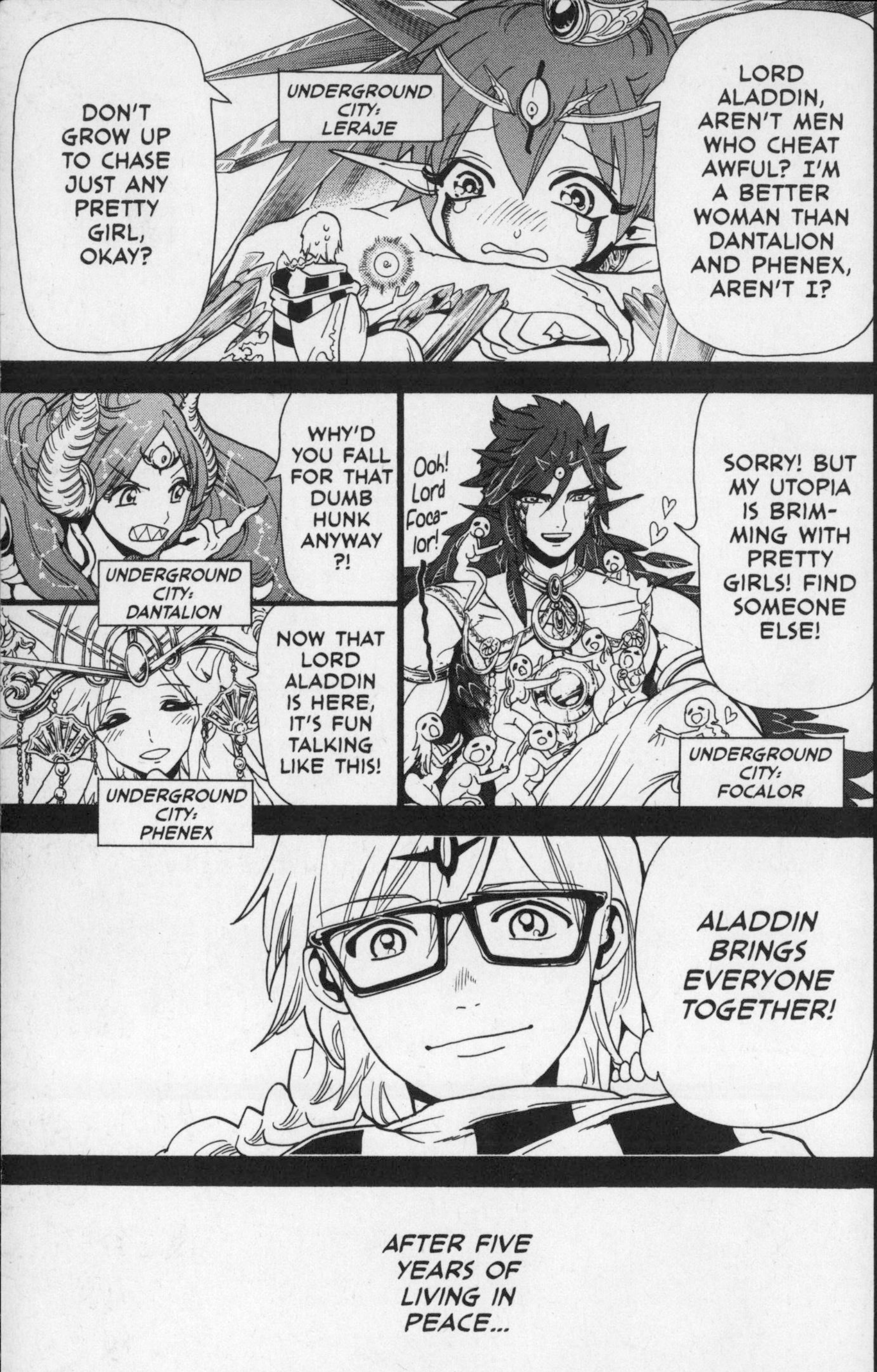
LORD ALADDIN, AREN'T MEN WHO CHEAT AWFUL? I'M A BETTER WOMAN THAN DANTALION AND PHENEX, AREN'T I?
UNDERGROUND CITY: LERAJE
DON'T GROW UP TO CHASE JUST ANY PRETTY GIRL, OKAY?
SORRY! BUT MY UTOPIA IS BRIM-MING WITH PRETTY GIRLS! FIND SOMEONE ELSE!
Ooh! Lord Foca-lor!
UNDERGROUND CITY: FOCALOR
WHY'D YOU FALL FOR THAT DUMB HUNK ANYWAY?!
UNDERGROUND CITY: DANTALION
NOW THAT LORD ALADDIN IS HERE, IT'S FUN TALKING LIKE THIS!
UNDERGROUND CITY: PHENEX
ALADDIN BRINGS EVERYONE TOGETHER!
AFTER FIVE YEARS OF LIVING IN PEACE...

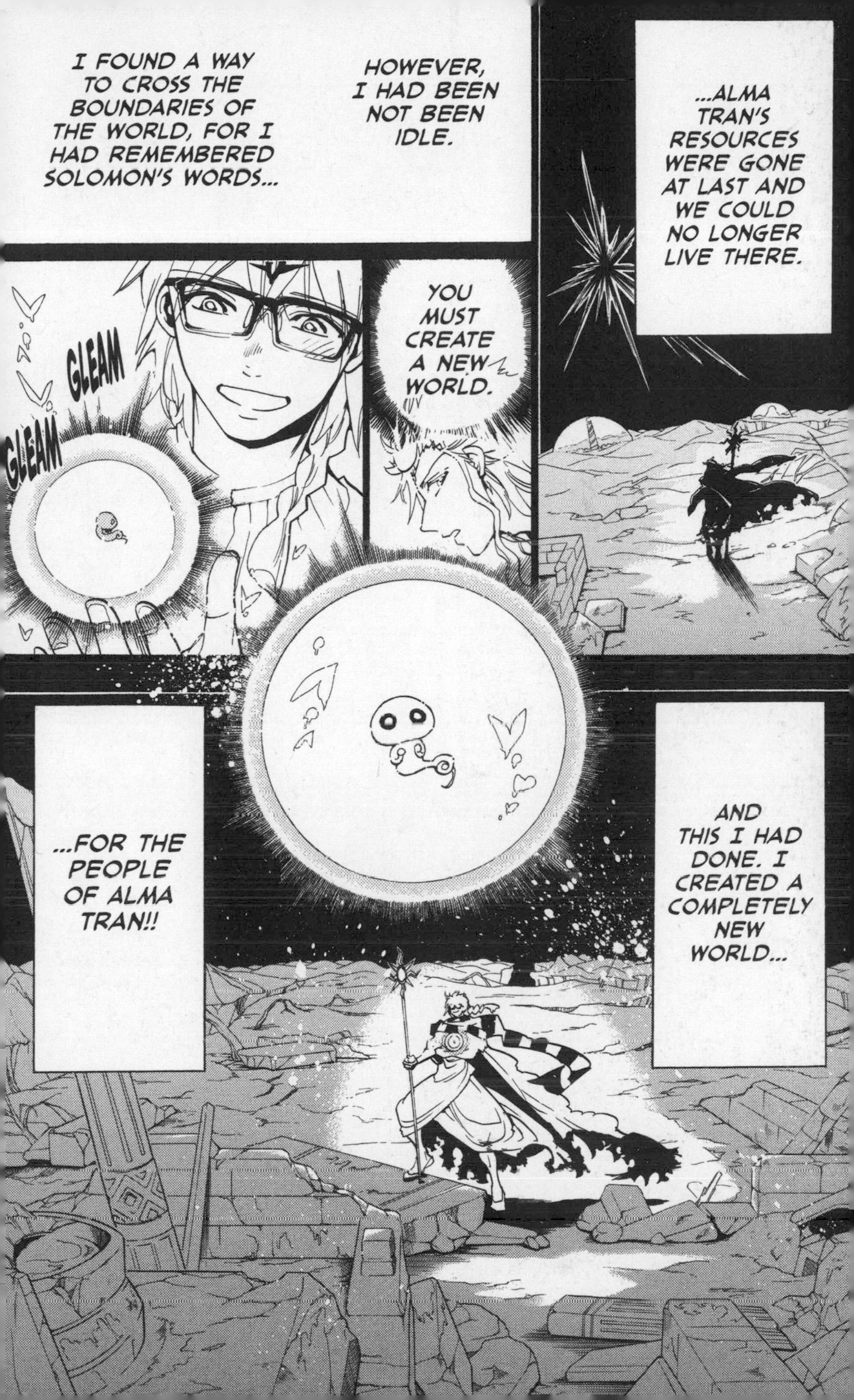
...ALMA TRAN'S RESOURCES WERE GONE AT LAST AND WE COULD NO LONGER LIVE THERE.
HOWEVER, I HAD BEEN NOT BEEN IDLE.
I FOUND A WAY TO CROSS THE BOUNDARIES OF THE WORLD, FOR I HAD REMEMBERED SOLOMON'S WORDS...
YOU MUST CREATE A NEW WORLD.
GLEAM
GLEAM
AND THIS I HAD DONE. I CREATED A COMPLETELY NEW WORLD...
...FOR THE PEOPLE OF ALMA TRAN!!

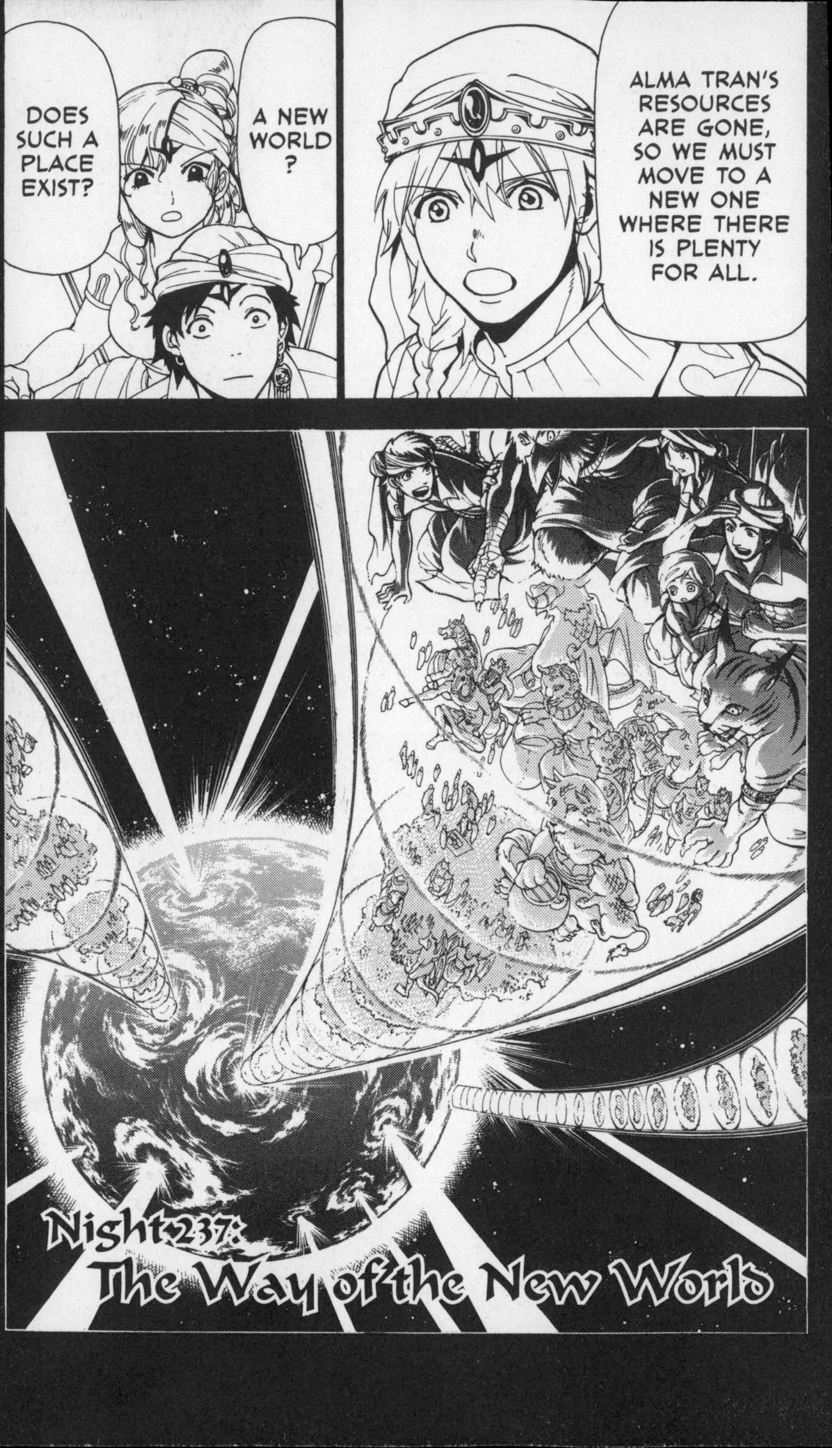
ALMA TRAN'S RESOURCES ARE GONE, SO WE MUST MOVE TO A NEW ONE WHERE THERE IS PLENTY FOR ALL.
A NEW WORLD ?
DOES SUCH A PLACE EXIST?
Night 237: The Way of the New World

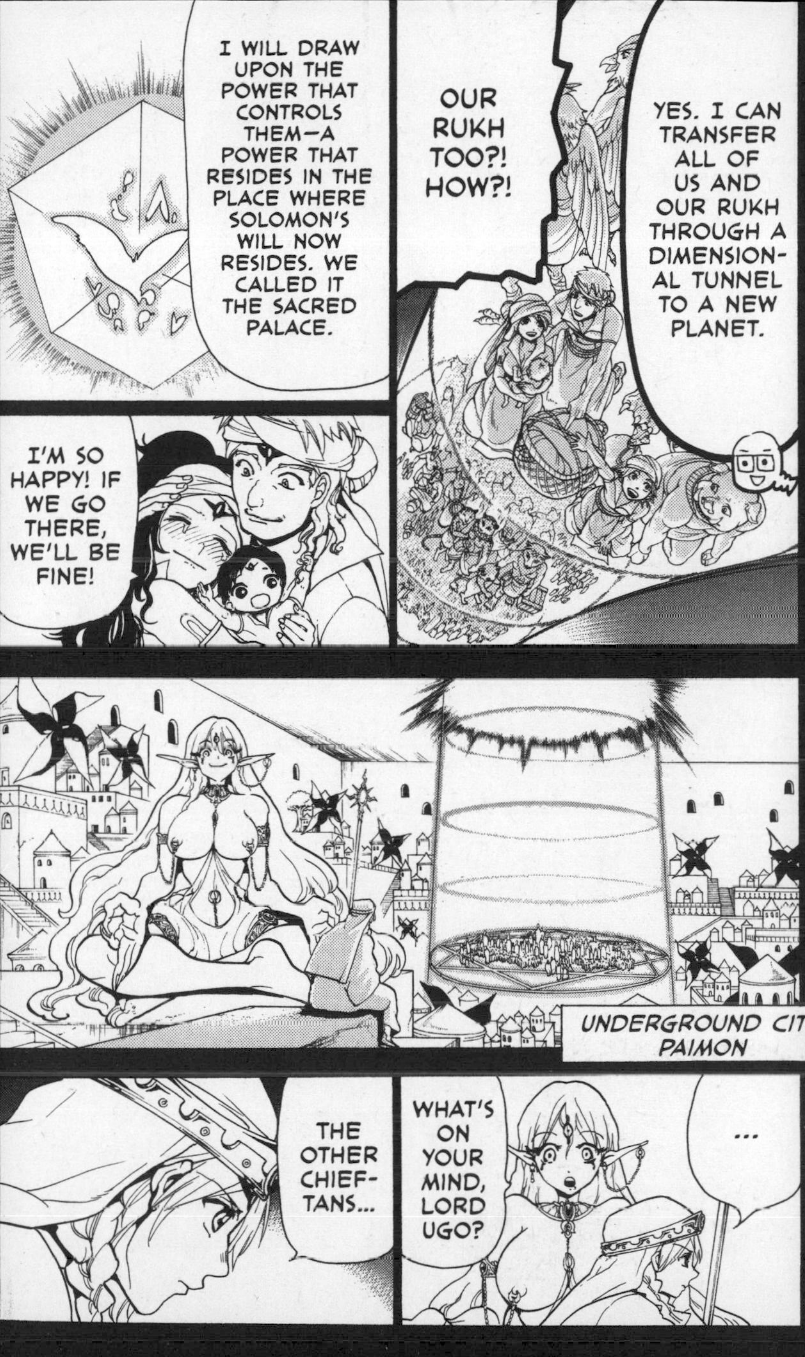
OUR RUKH TOO?! HOW?!
YES. I CAN TRANSFER ALL OF US AND OUR RUKH THROUGH A DIMENSIONAL TUNNEL TO A NEW PLANET.
I WILL DRAW UPON THE POWER THAT CONTROLS THEM—A POWER THAT RESIDES IN THE PLACE WHERE SOLOMON'S WILL NOW RESIDES. WE CALLED IT THE SACRED PALACE.
I'M SO HAPPY! IF WE GO THERE, WE'LL BE FINE!
UNDERGROUND CITY: PAIMON
...
WHAT'S ON YOUR MIND, LORD UGO?
THE OTHER CHIEFTANS...

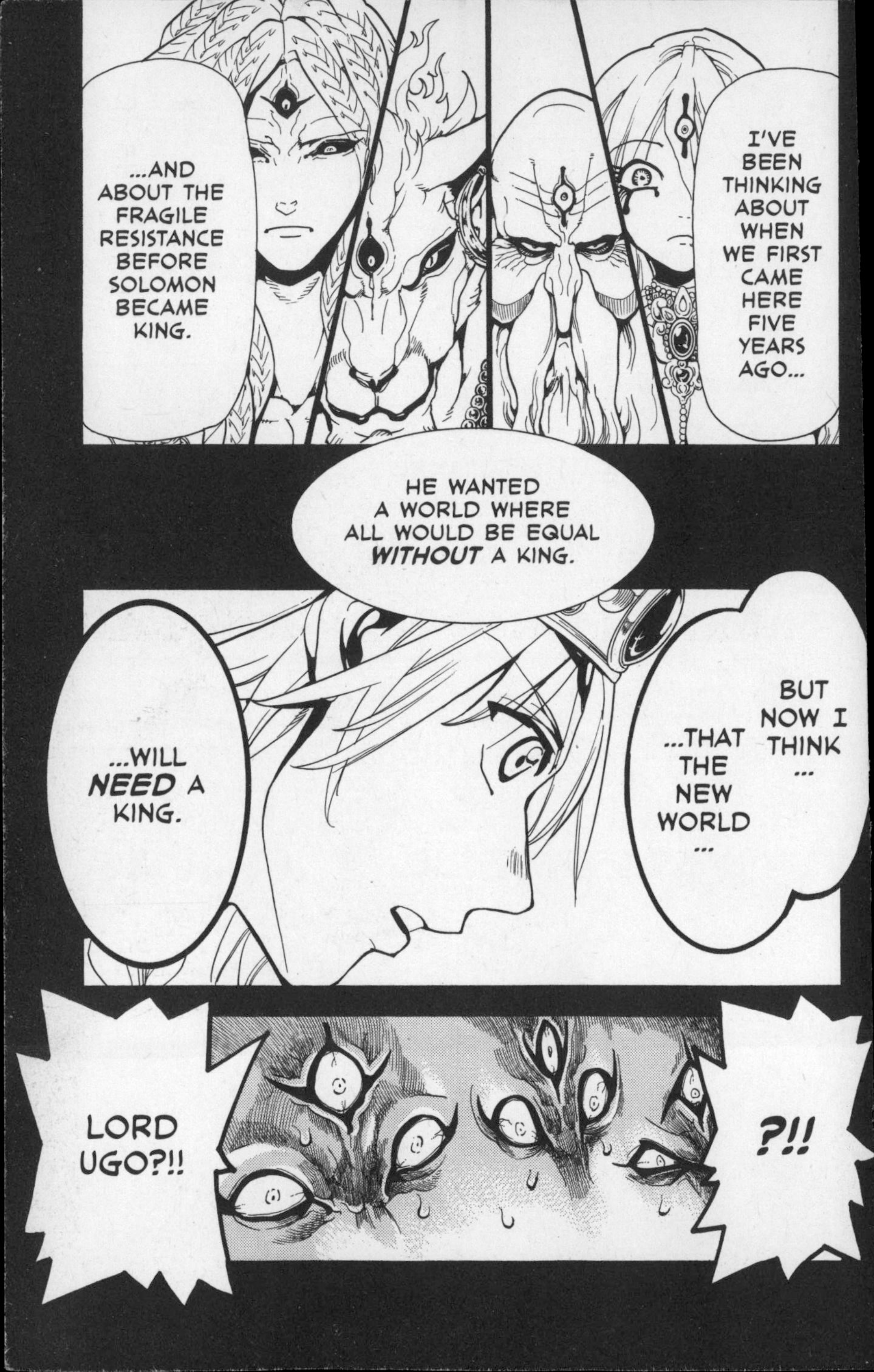
I'VE BEEN THINKING ABOUT WHEN WE FIRST CAME HERE FIVE YEARS AGO...
...AND ABOUT THE FRAGILE RESISTANCE BEFORE SOLOMON BECAME KING.
HE WANTED A WORLD WHERE ALL WOULD BE EQUAL *WITHOUT* A KING.
BUT NOW I THINK...
...THAT THE NEW WORLD...
...WILL *NEED* A KING.
?!!
LORD UGO?!!

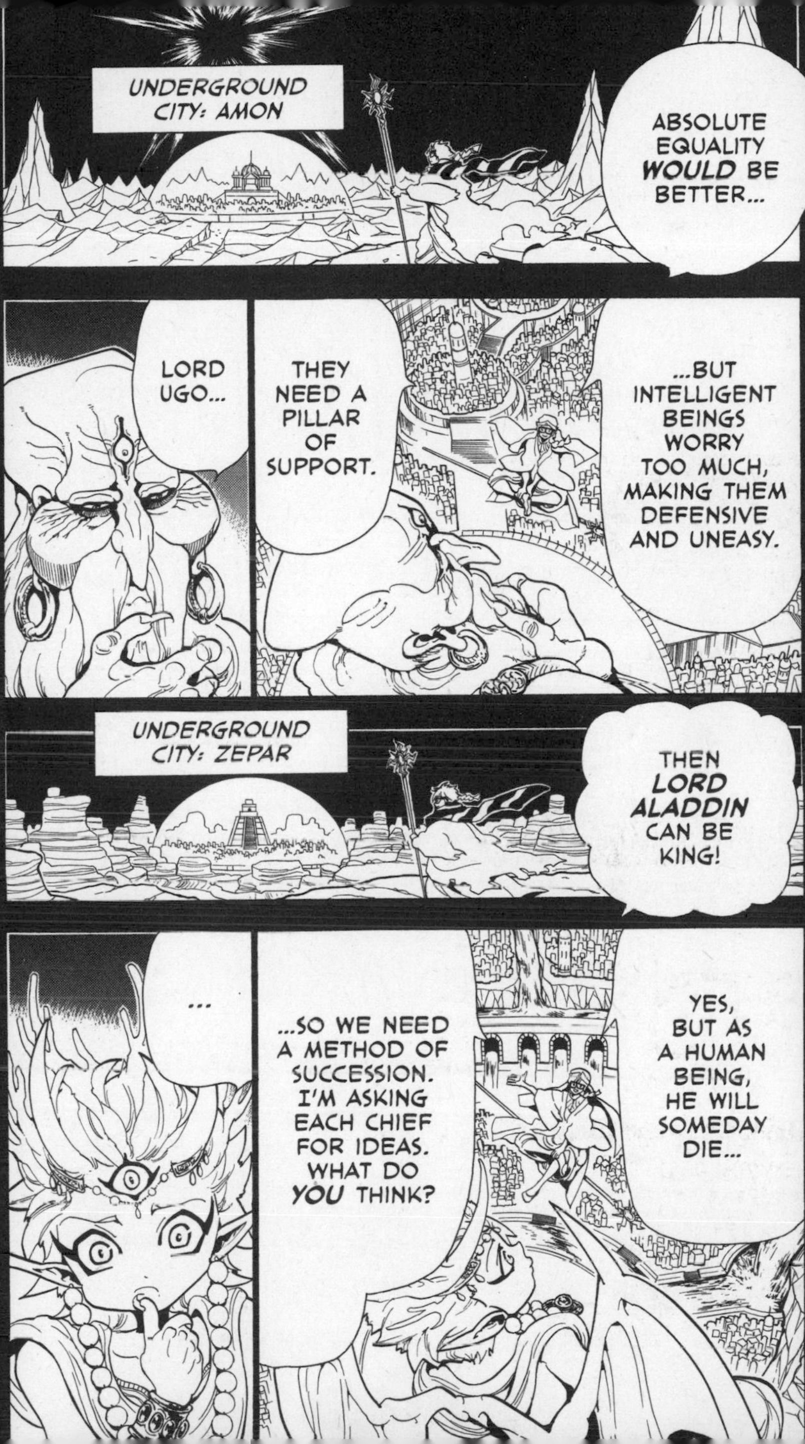
ABSOLUTE EQUALITY *WOULD* BE BETTER...
UNDERGROUND CITY: AMON
...BUT INTELLIGENT BEINGS WORRY TOO MUCH, MAKING THEM DEFENSIVE AND UNEASY.
THEY NEED A PILLAR OF SUPPORT.
LORD UGO...
THEN *LORD ALADDIN* CAN BE KING!
UNDERGROUND CITY: ZEPAR
YES, BUT AS A HUMAN BEING, HE WILL SOMEDAY DIE...
...SO WE NEED A METHOD OF SUCCESSION. I'M ASKING EACH CHIEF FOR IDEAS. WHAT DO *YOU* THINK?
...

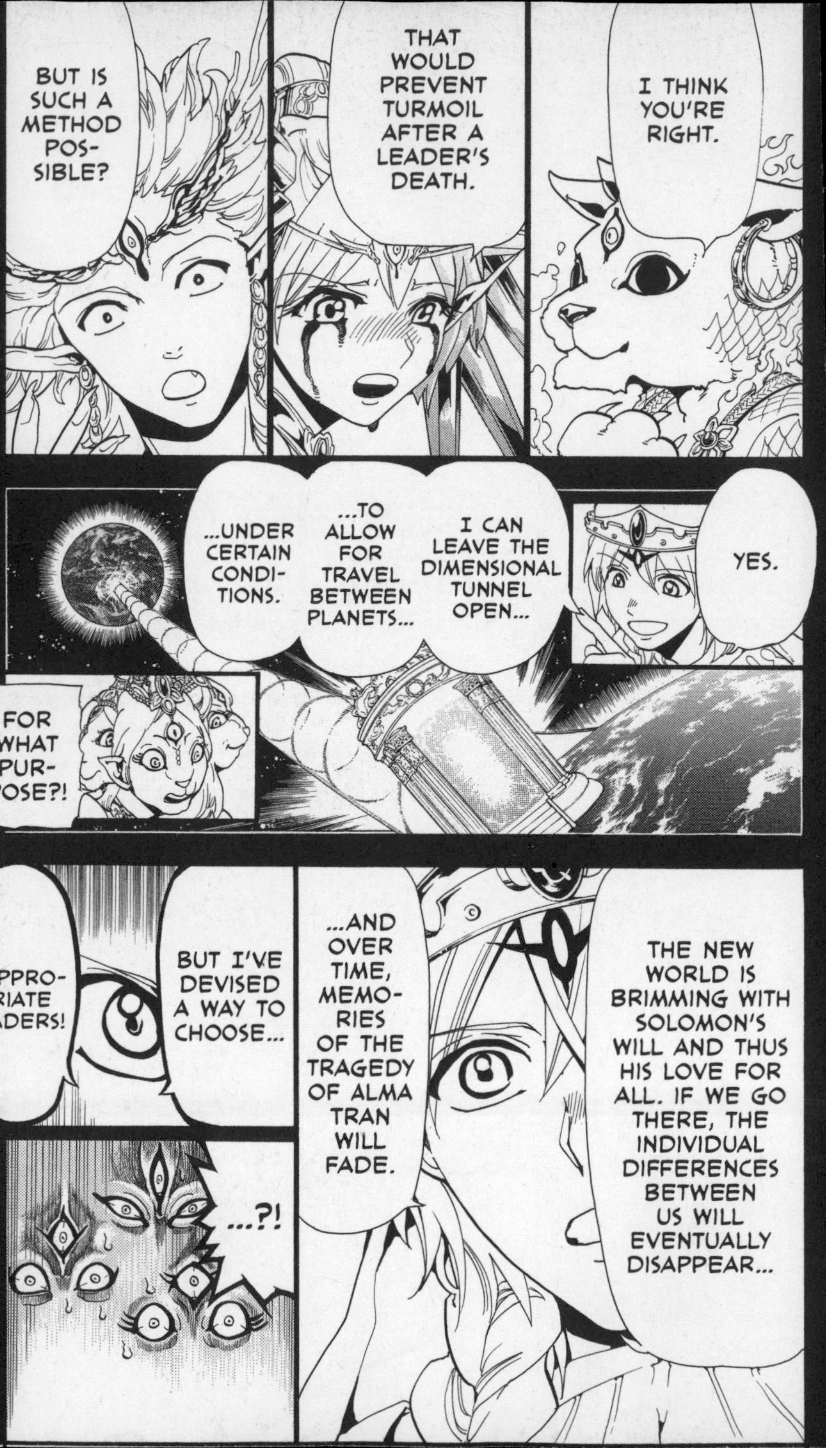
I THINK YOU'RE RIGHT.
THAT WOULD PREVENT TURMOIL AFTER A LEADER'S DEATH.
BUT IS SUCH A METHOD POSSIBLE?
YES.
I CAN LEAVE THE DIMENSIONAL TUNNEL OPEN...
...TO ALLOW FOR TRAVEL BETWEEN PLANETS...
...UNDER CERTAIN CONDITIONS.
FOR WHAT PURPOSE?!
THE NEW WORLD IS BRIMMING WITH SOLOMON'S WILL AND THUS HIS LOVE FOR ALL. IF WE GO THERE, THE INDIVIDUAL DIFFERENCES BETWEEN US WILL EVENTUALLY DISAPPEAR...
...AND OVER TIME, MEMORIES OF THE TRAGEDY OF ALMA TRAN WILL FADE.
BUT I'VE DEVISED A WAY TO CHOOSE...
...APPROPRIATE LEADERS!
...?!

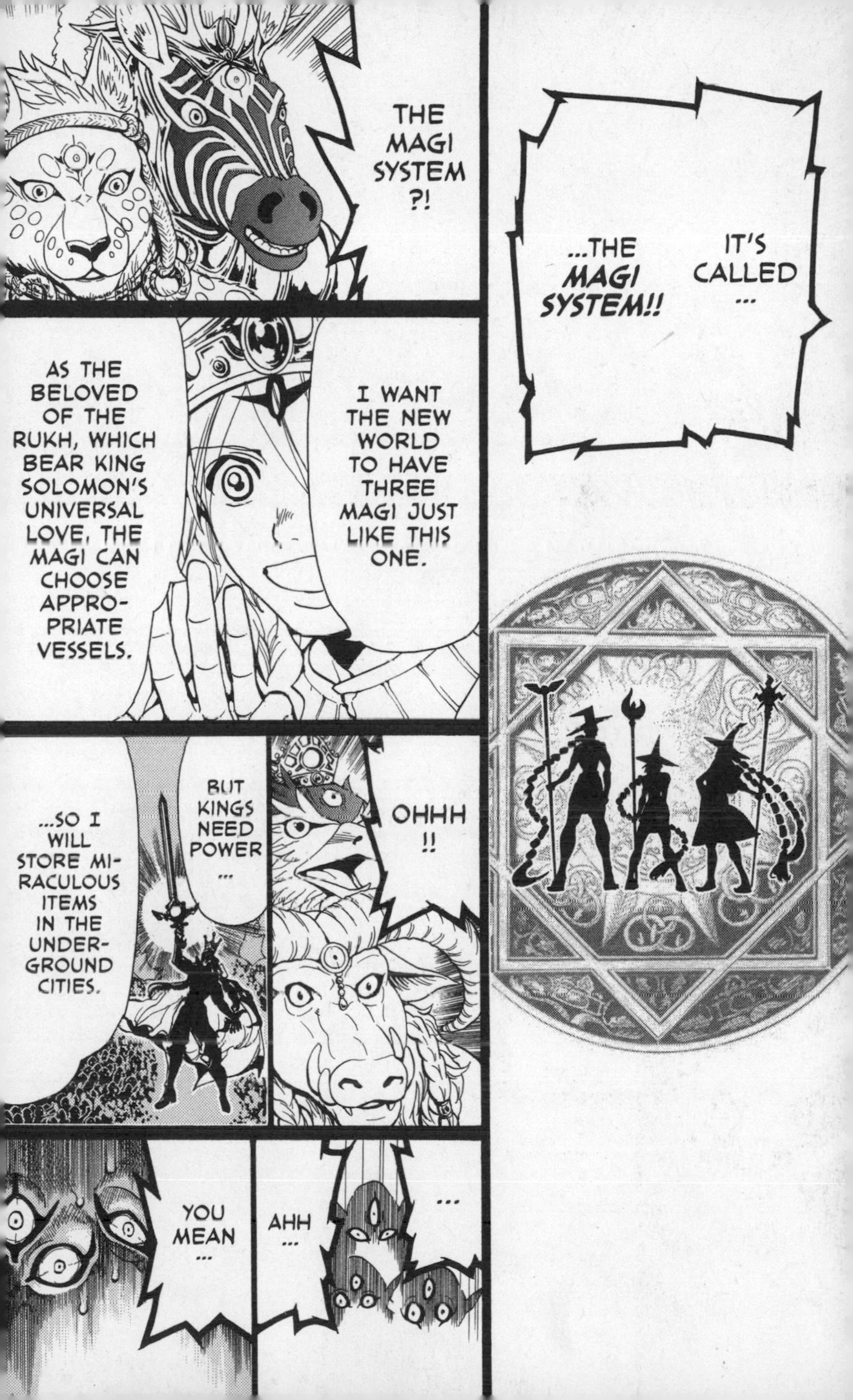
IT'S CALLED ...
...THE MAGI SYSTEM!!
THE MAGI SYSTEM ?!
I WANT THE NEW WORLD TO HAVE THREE MAGI JUST LIKE THIS ONE.
AS THE BELOVED OF THE RUKH, WHICH BEAR KING SOLOMON'S UNIVERSAL LOVE, THE MAGI CAN CHOOSE APPRO-PRIATE VESSELS.
OHHH !!
BUT KINGS NEED POWER ...
...SO I WILL STORE MI-RACULOUS ITEMS IN THE UNDER-GROUND CITIES.
...
AHH ...
YOU MEAN ...

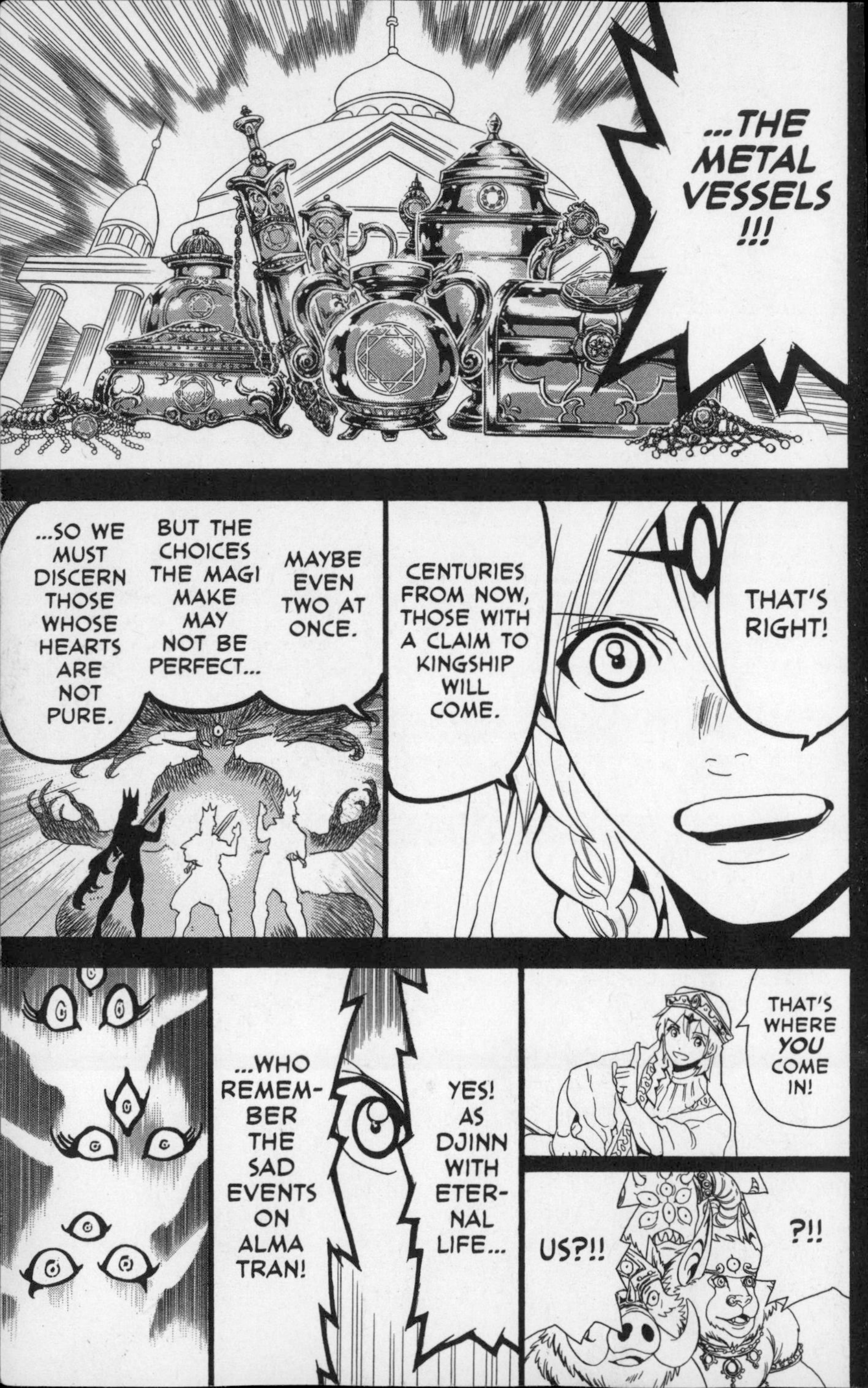
...THE METAL VESSELS !!!
THAT'S RIGHT!
CENTURIES FROM NOW, THOSE WITH A CLAIM TO KINGSHIP WILL COME.
MAYBE EVEN TWO AT ONCE.
BUT THE CHOICES THE MAGI MAKE MAY NOT BE PERFECT...
...SO WE MUST DISCERN THOSE WHOSE HEARTS ARE NOT PURE.
THAT'S WHERE *YOU* COME IN!
?!!
US?!!
YES! AS DJINN WITH ETER-NAL LIFE...
...WHO REMEM-BER THE SAD EVENTS ON ALMA TRAN!

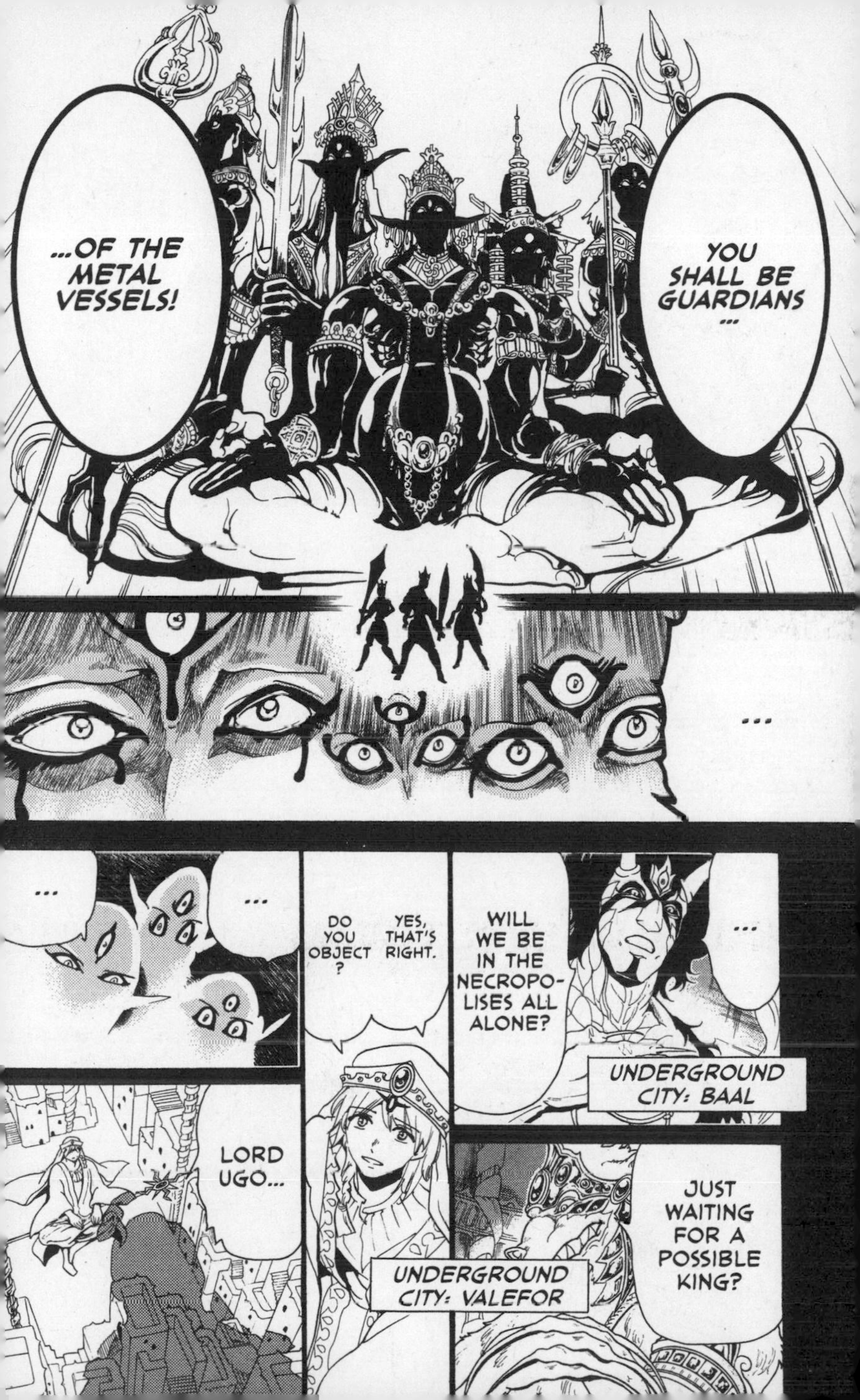
YOU SHALL BE GUARDIANS ...
...OF THE METAL VESSELS!
...
...
WILL WE BE IN THE NECROPOLISES ALL ALONE?
UNDERGROUND CITY: BAAL
JUST WAITING FOR A POSSIBLE KING?
YES, THAT'S RIGHT.
DO YOU OBJECT?
UNDERGROUND CITY: VALEFOR
...
...
LORD UGO...

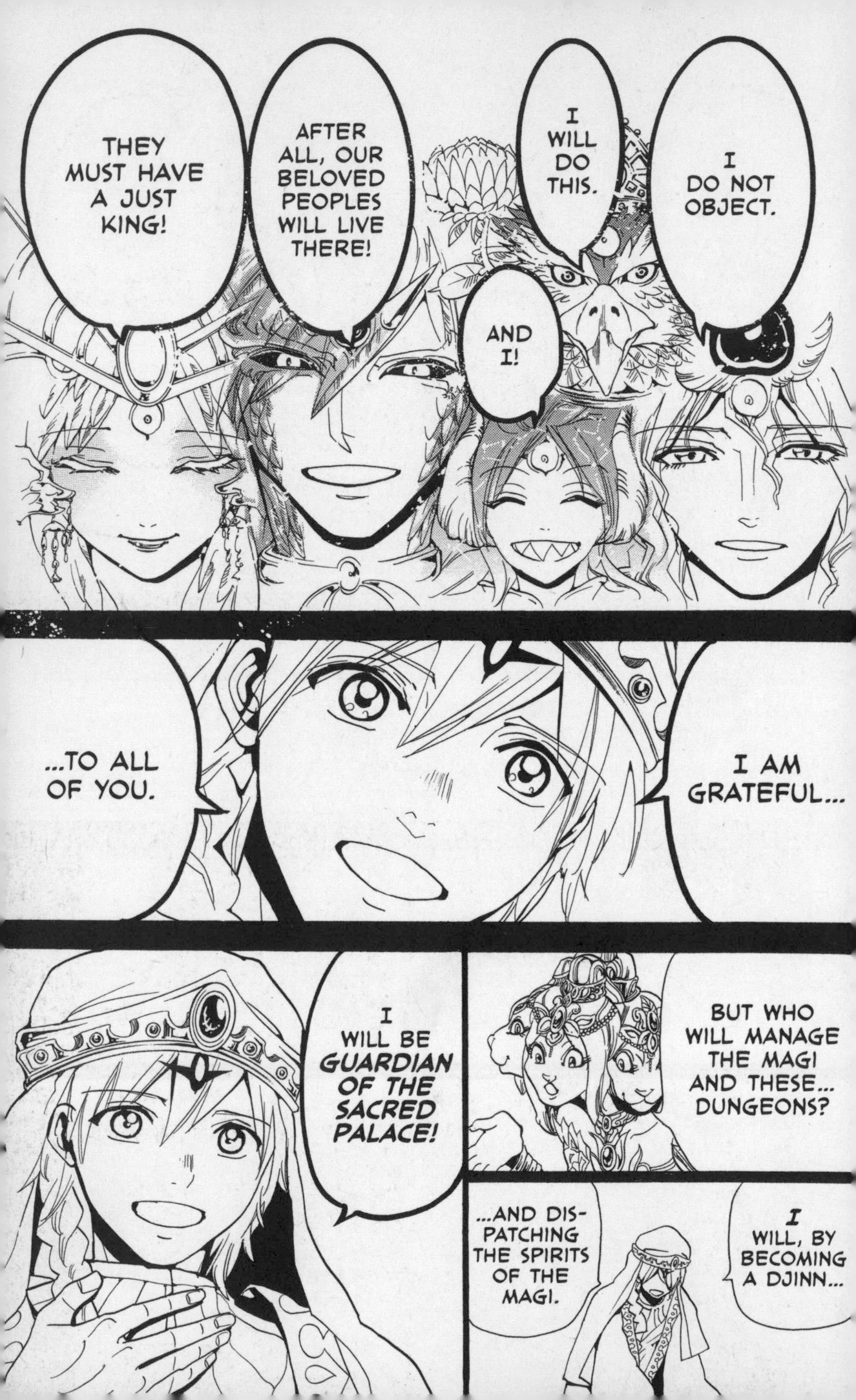
I DO NOT OBJECT.
I WILL DO THIS.
AND I!
AFTER ALL, OUR BELOVED PEOPLES WILL LIVE THERE!
THEY MUST HAVE A JUST KING!
I AM GRATEFUL...
...TO ALL OF YOU.
BUT WHO WILL MANAGE THE MAGI AND THESE... DUNGEONS?
I WILL, BY BECOMING A DJINN...
...AND DIS-PATCHING THE SPIRITS OF THE MAGI.
I WILL BE GUARDIAN OF THE SACRED PALACE!

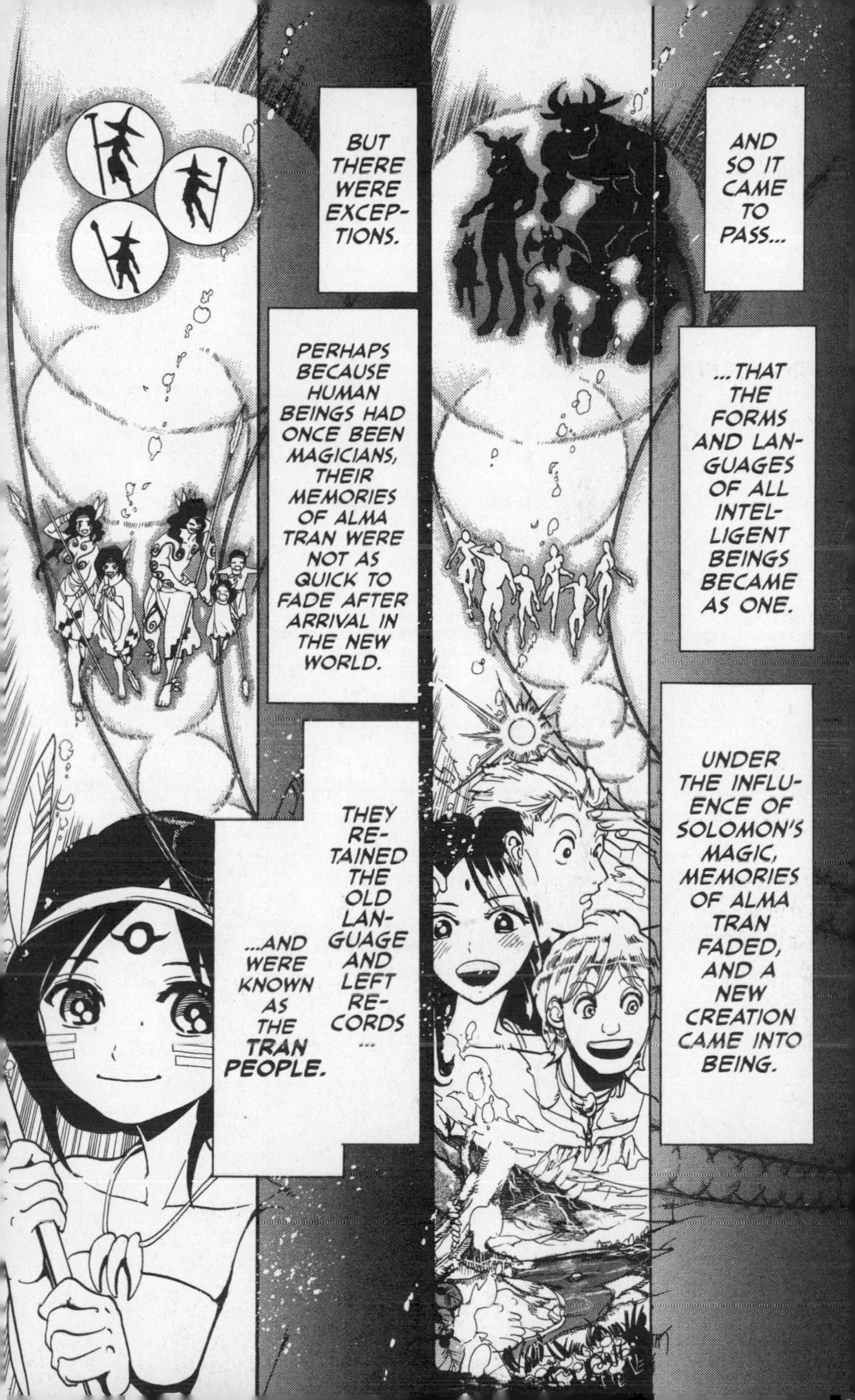
AND SO IT CAME TO PASS...
...THAT THE FORMS AND LANGUAGES OF ALL INTELLIGENT BEINGS BECAME AS ONE.
UNDER THE INFLUENCE OF SOLOMON'S MAGIC, MEMORIES OF ALMA TRAN FADED, AND A NEW CREATION CAME INTO BEING.
BUT THERE WERE EXCEPTIONS.
PERHAPS BECAUSE HUMAN BEINGS HAD ONCE BEEN MAGICIANS, THEIR MEMORIES OF ALMA TRAN WERE NOT AS QUICK TO FADE AFTER ARRIVAL IN THE NEW WORLD.
THEY RETAINED THE OLD LANGUAGE AND LEFT RECORDS...
...AND WERE KNOWN AS THE **TRAN** PEOPLE.

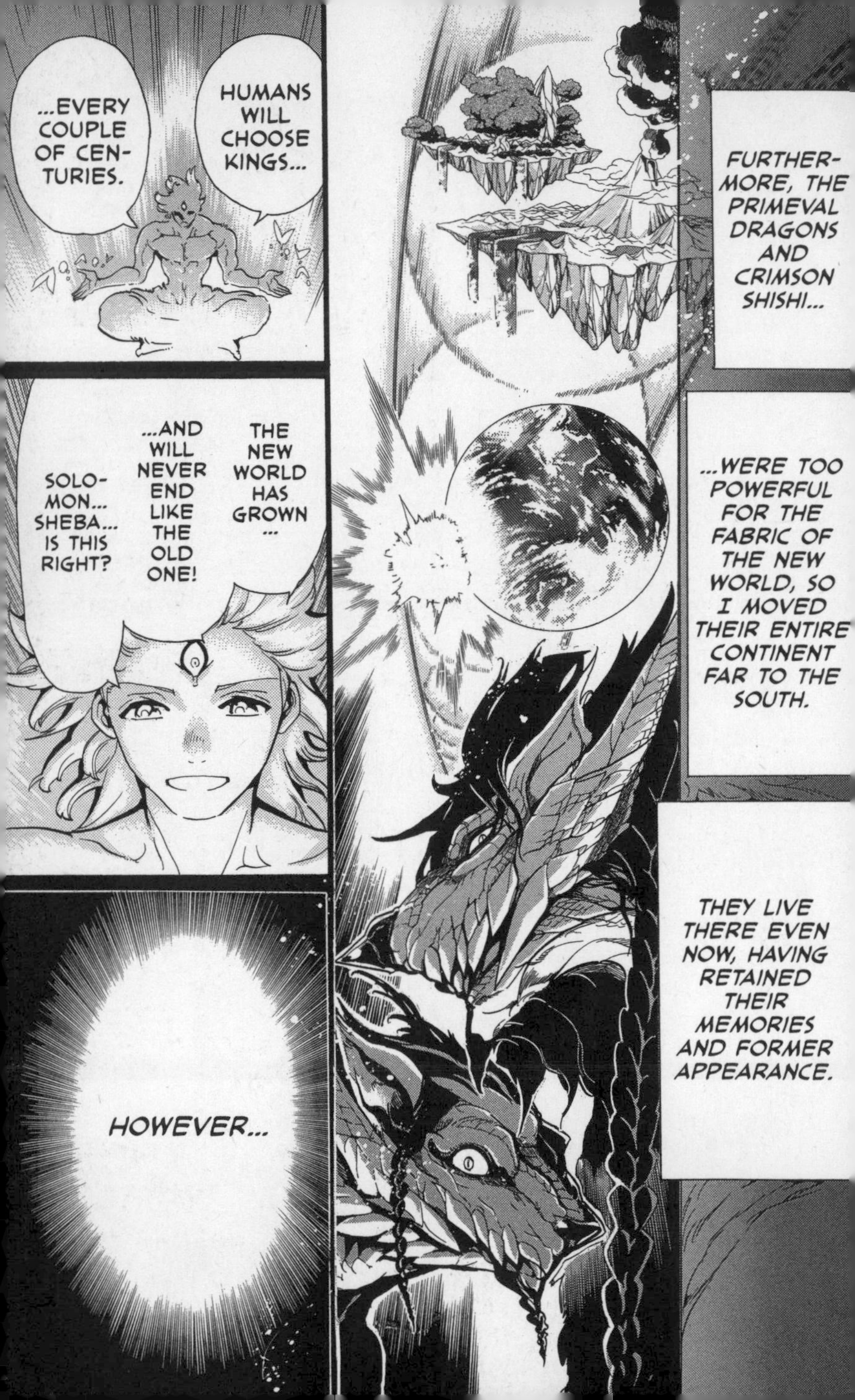
FURTHERMORE, THE PRIMEVAL DRAGONS AND CRIMSON SHISHI...
...WERE TOO POWERFUL FOR THE FABRIC OF THE NEW WORLD, SO I MOVED THEIR ENTIRE CONTINENT FAR TO THE SOUTH.
THEY LIVE THERE EVEN NOW, HAVING RETAINED THEIR MEMORIES AND FORMER APPEARANCE.
HUMANS WILL CHOOSE KINGS...
...EVERY COUPLE OF CENTURIES.
THE NEW WORLD HAS GROWN...
...AND WILL NEVER END LIKE THE OLD ONE!
SOLOMON... SHEBA... IS THIS RIGHT?
HOWEVER...

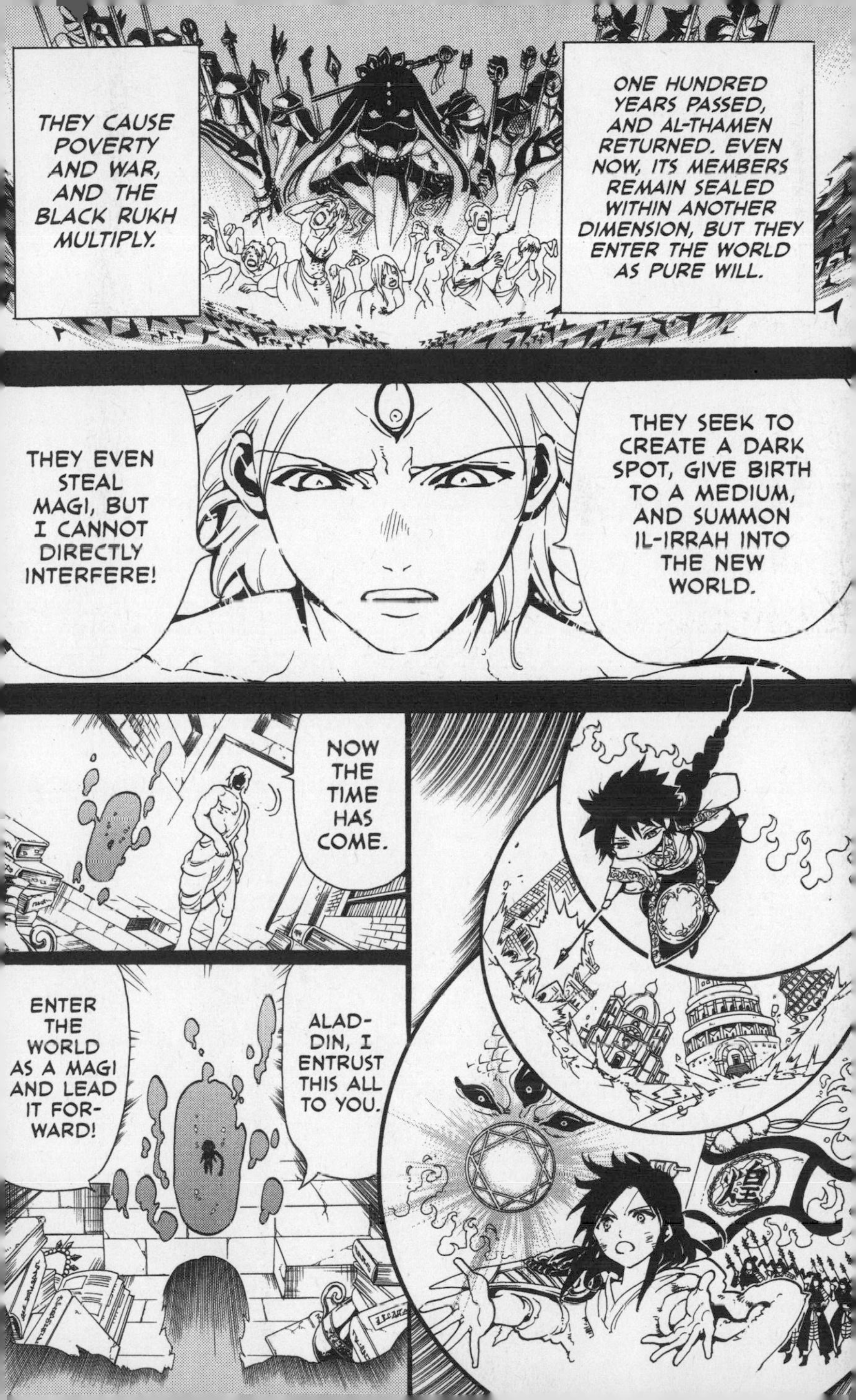
ONE HUNDRED YEARS PASSED, AND AL-THAMEN RETURNED. EVEN NOW, ITS MEMBERS REMAIN SEALED WITHIN ANOTHER DIMENSION, BUT THEY ENTER THE WORLD AS PURE WILL.
THEY CAUSE POVERTY AND WAR, AND THE BLACK RUKH MULTIPLY.
THEY SEEK TO CREATE A DARK SPOT, GIVE BIRTH TO A MEDIUM, AND SUMMON IL-IRRAH INTO THE NEW WORLD.
THEY EVEN STEAL MAGI, BUT I CANNOT DIRECTLY INTERFERE!
NOW THE TIME HAS COME.
ALAD-DIN, I ENTRUST THIS ALL TO YOU.
ENTER THE WORLD AS A MAGI AND LEAD IT FOR-WARD!

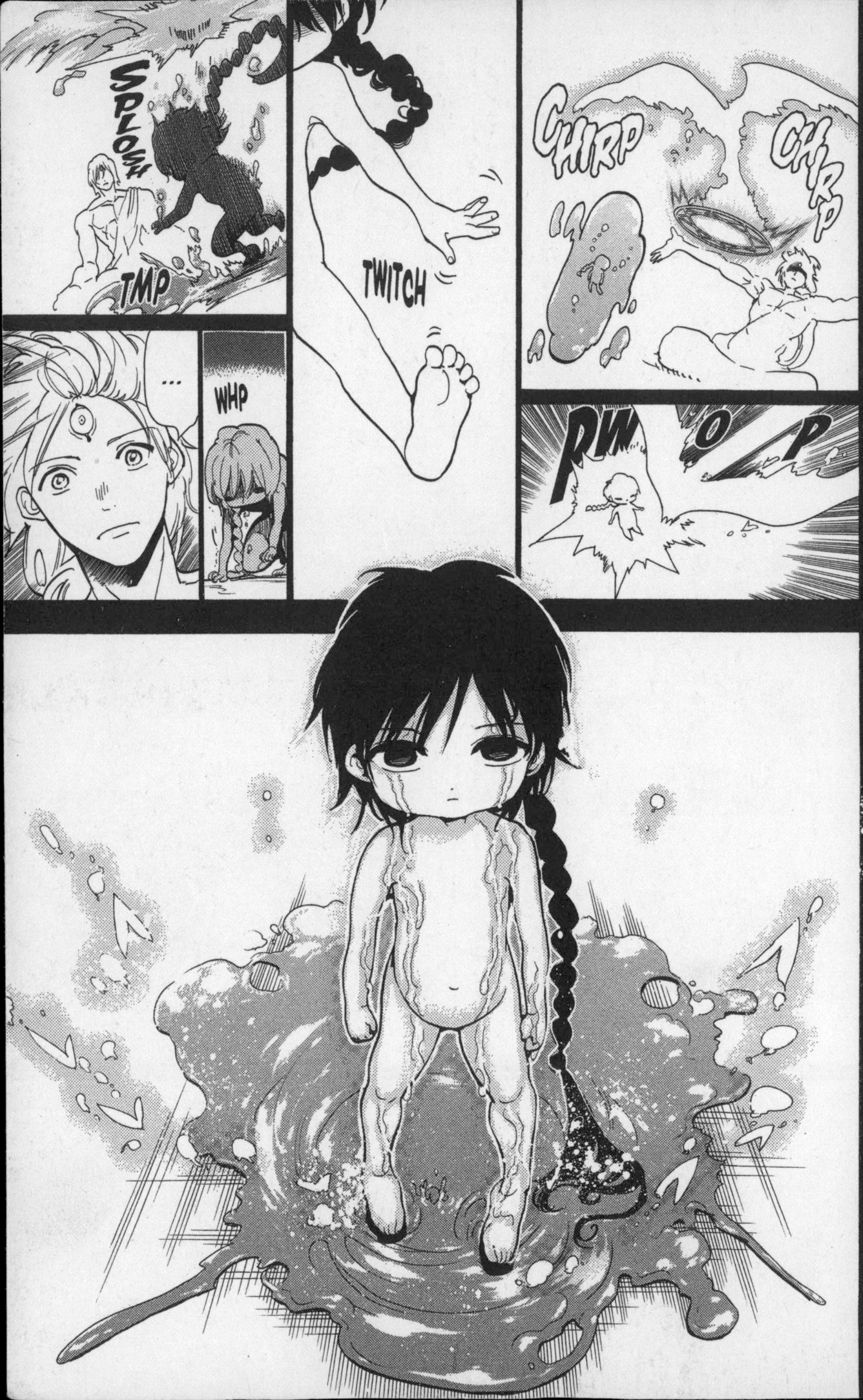
CHIRP
CHIRP
RWOOP
TWITCH
SPLOOSH
TMP
WHP
...

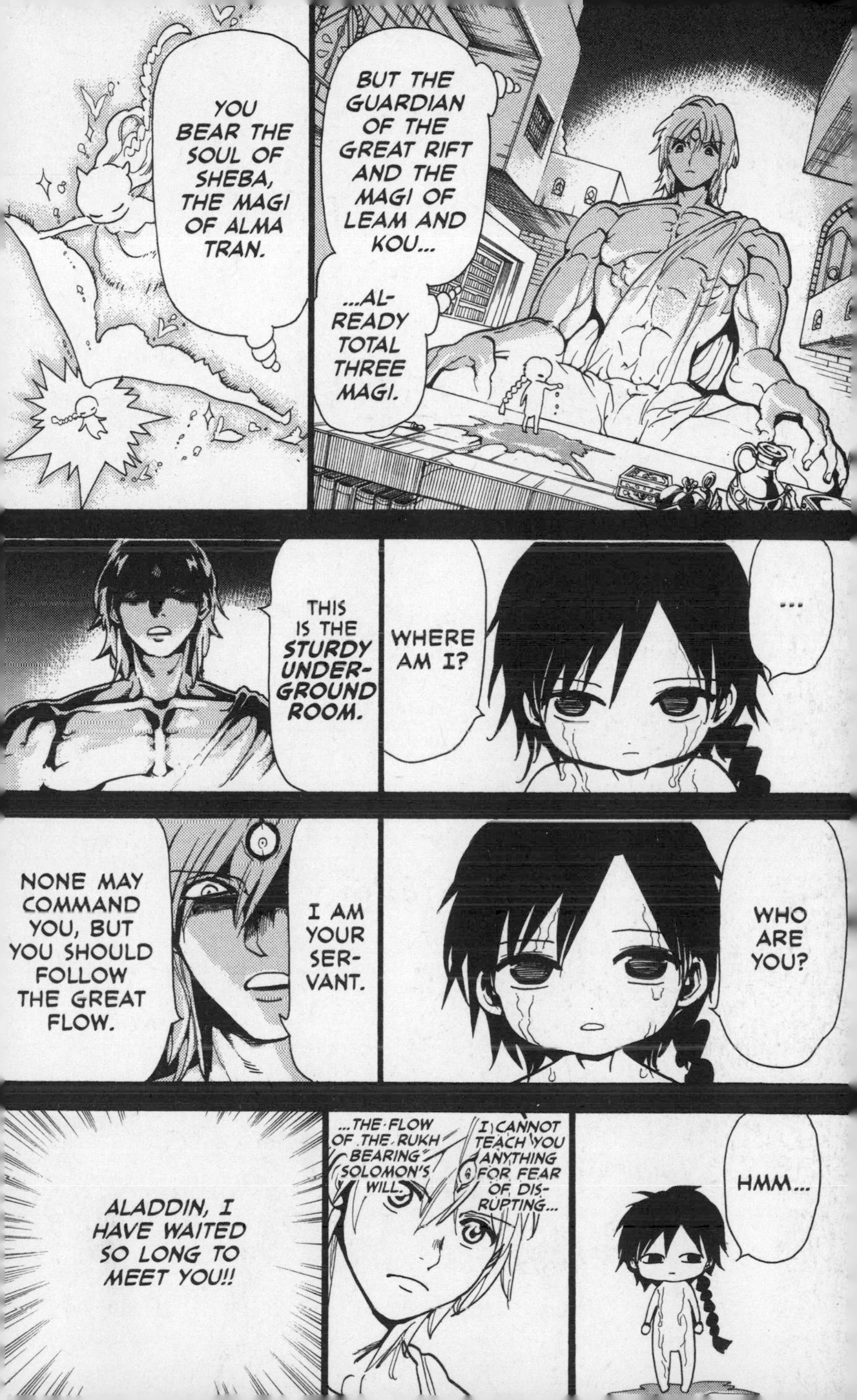
BUT THE GUARDIAN OF THE GREAT RIFT AND THE MAGI OF LEAM AND KOU...
...AL-READY TOTAL THREE MAGI.
YOU BEAR THE SOUL OF SHEBA, THE MAGI OF ALMA TRAN.
...
WHERE AM I?
THIS IS THE STURDY UNDERGROUND ROOM.
WHO ARE YOU?
I AM YOUR SERVANT.
NONE MAY COMMAND YOU, BUT YOU SHOULD FOLLOW THE GREAT FLOW.
HMM...
I CANNOT TEACH YOU ANYTHING FOR FEAR OF DISRUPTING...
...THE FLOW OF THE RUKH BEARING SOLOMON'S WILL.
ALADDIN, I HAVE WAITED SO LONG TO MEET YOU!!

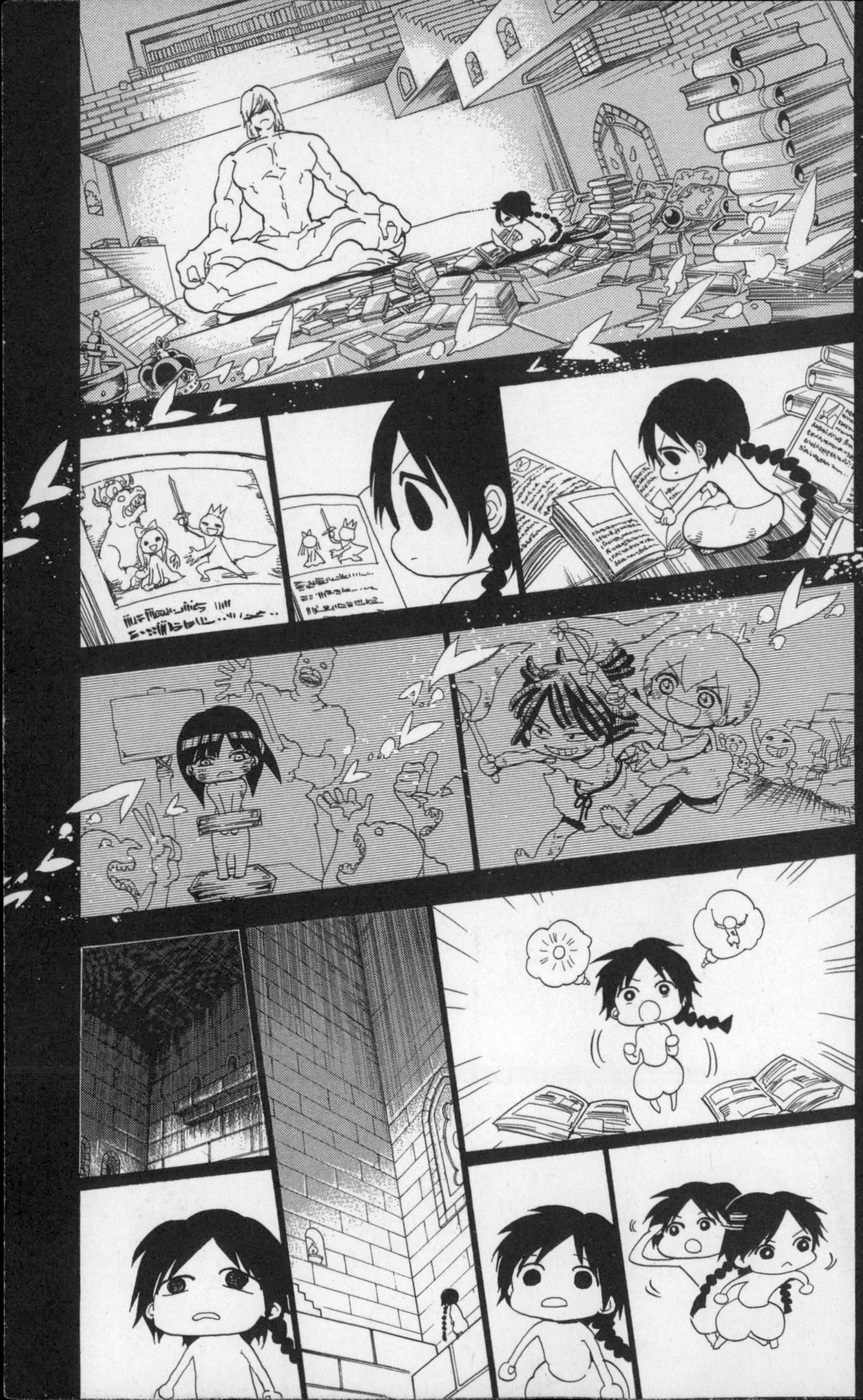

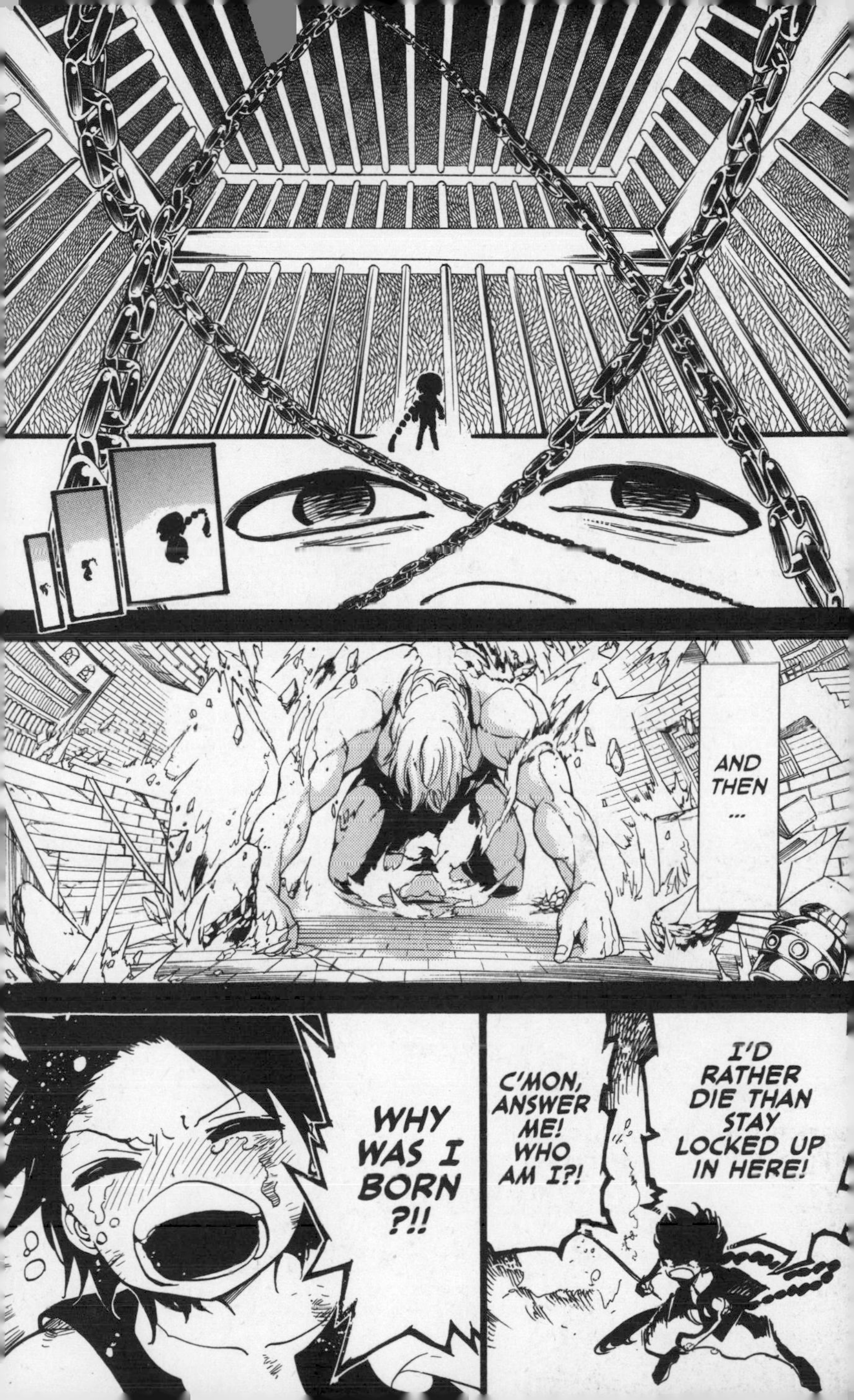
AND THEN ...
I'D RATHER DIE THAN STAY LOCKED UP IN HERE!
C'MON, ANSWER ME! WHO AM I?!
WHY WAS I BORN ?!!

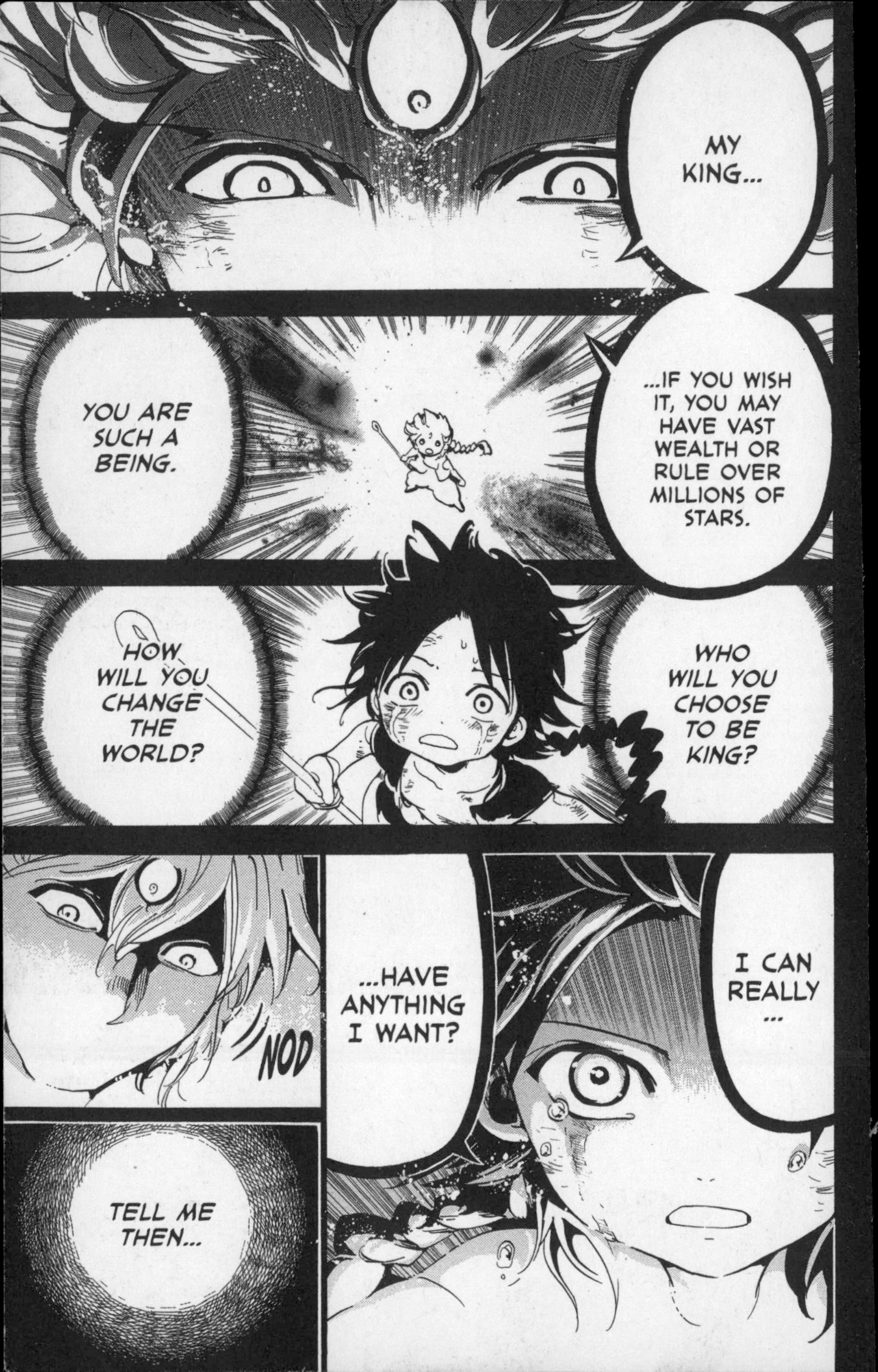
MY KING...
...IF YOU WISH IT, YOU MAY HAVE VAST WEALTH OR RULE OVER MILLIONS OF STARS.
YOU ARE SUCH A BEING.
WHO WILL YOU CHOOSE TO BE KING?
HOW WILL YOU CHANGE THE WORLD?
I CAN REALLY ...
...HAVE ANYTHING I WANT?
NOD
TELL ME THEN...

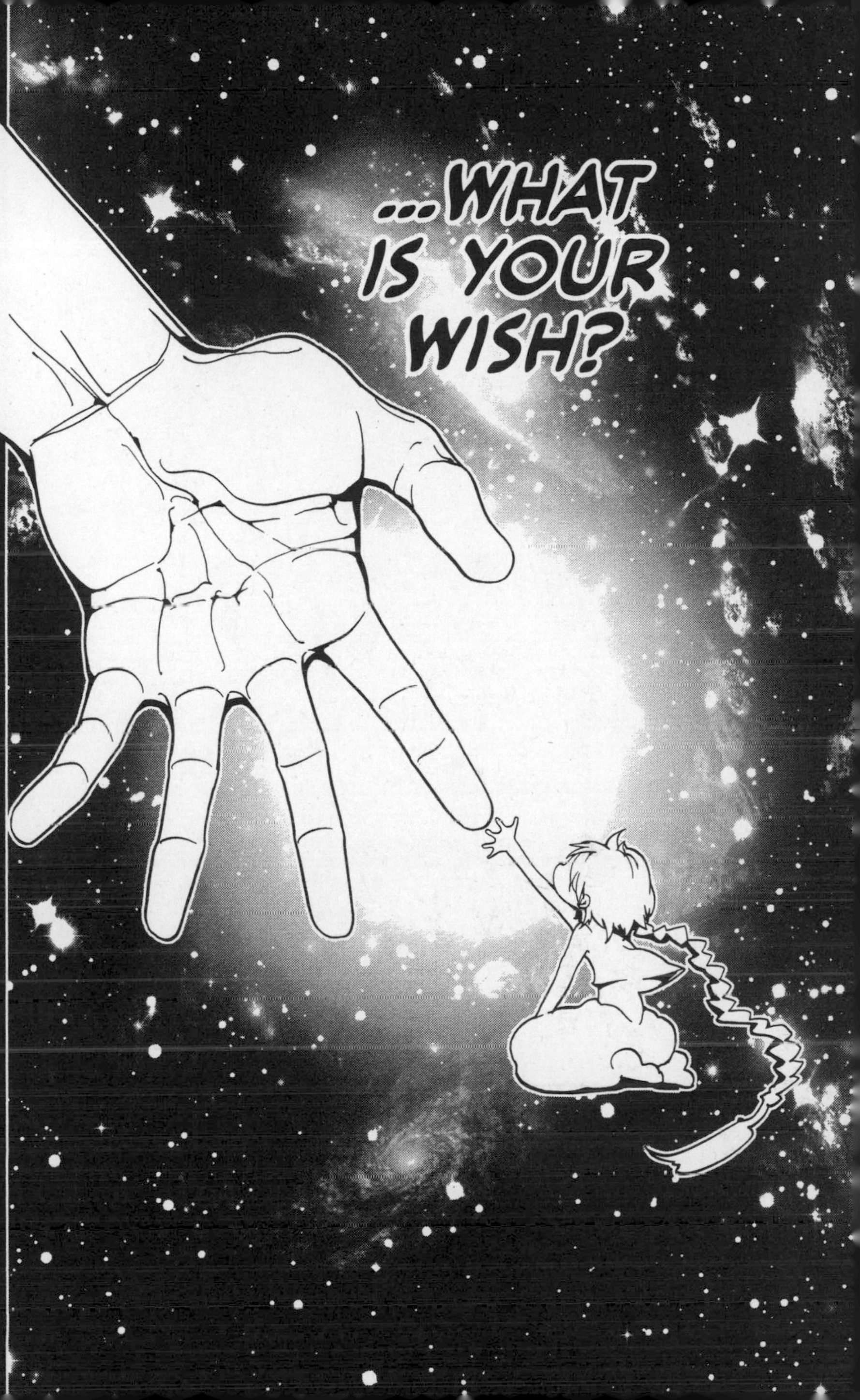
...WHAT IS YOUR WISH?

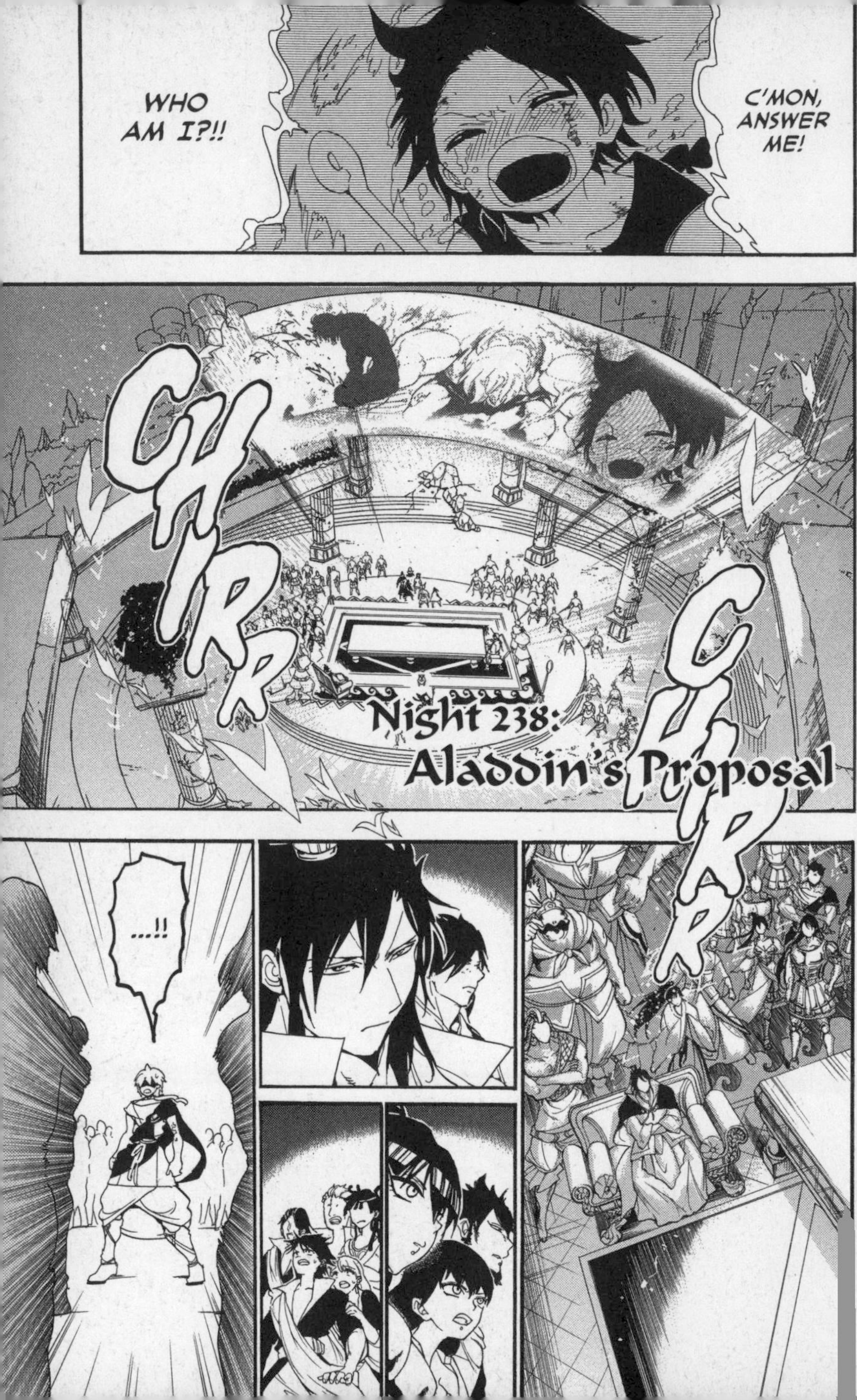
C'MON, ANSWER ME!
WHO AM I?!!
CHIRR
CHIRR
Night 238: Aladdin's Proposal
...!!

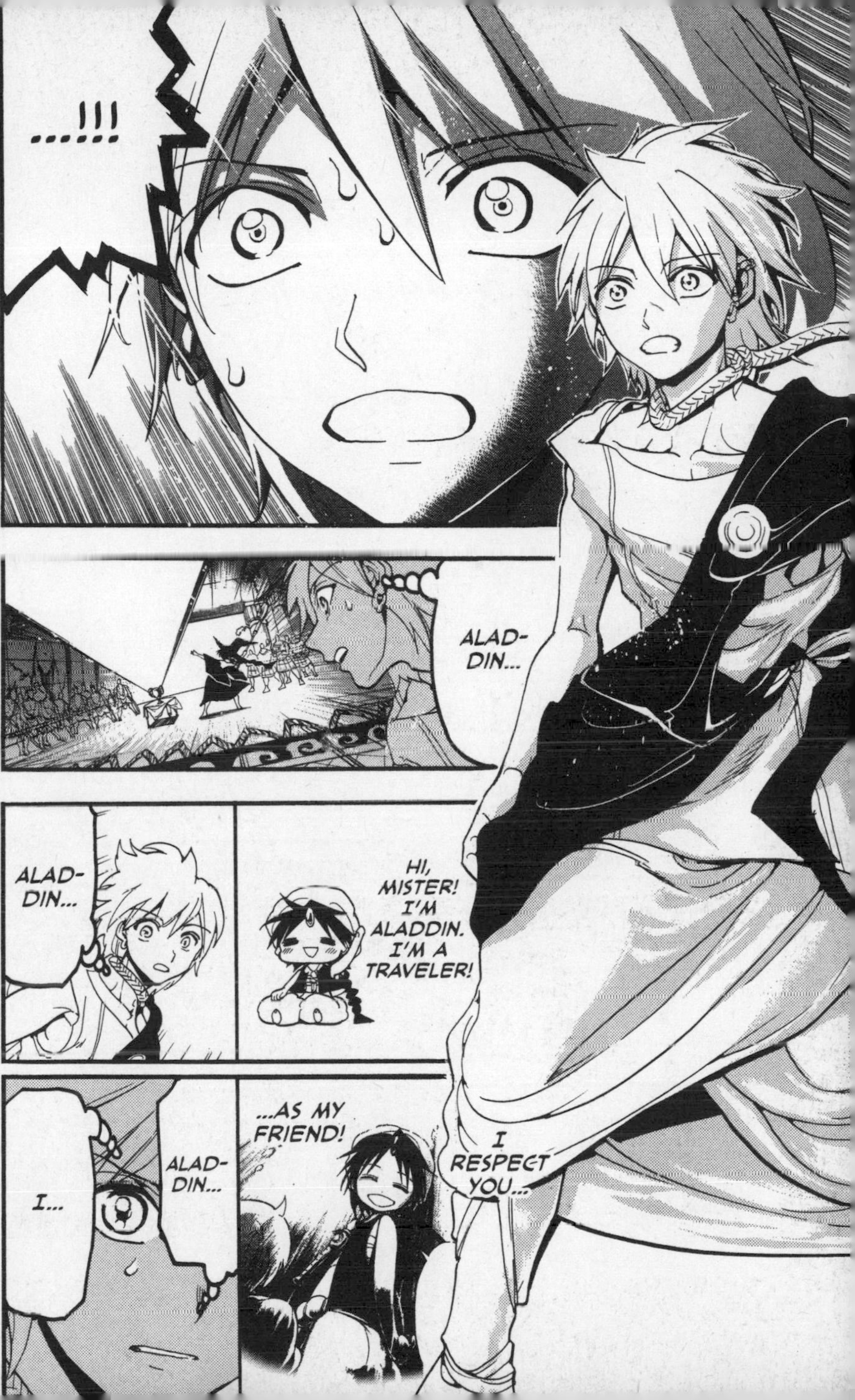
...!!!
ALAD-DIN...
HI, MISTER! I'M ALADDIN. I'M A TRAVELER!
ALAD-DIN...
I RESPECT YOU...
...AS MY FRIEND!
ALAD-DIN...
I...

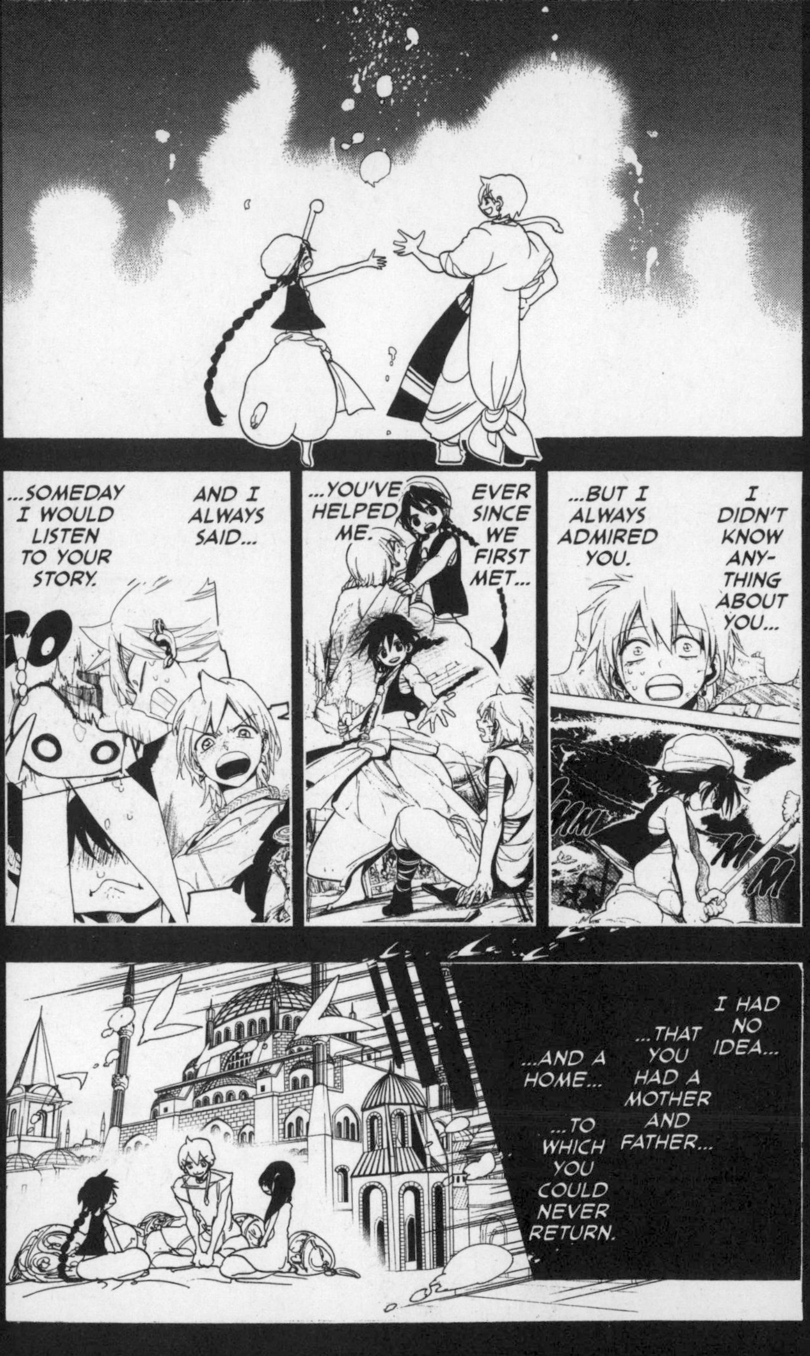
I DIDN'T KNOW ANYTHING ABOUT YOU...
...BUT I ALWAYS ADMIRED YOU.
EVER SINCE WE FIRST MET...
...YOU'VE HELPED ME.
AND I ALWAYS SAID...
...SOMEDAY I WOULD LISTEN TO YOUR STORY.
I HAD NO IDEA...
...THAT YOU HAD A MOTHER AND FATHER...
...AND A HOME...
...TO WHICH YOU COULD NEVER RETURN.

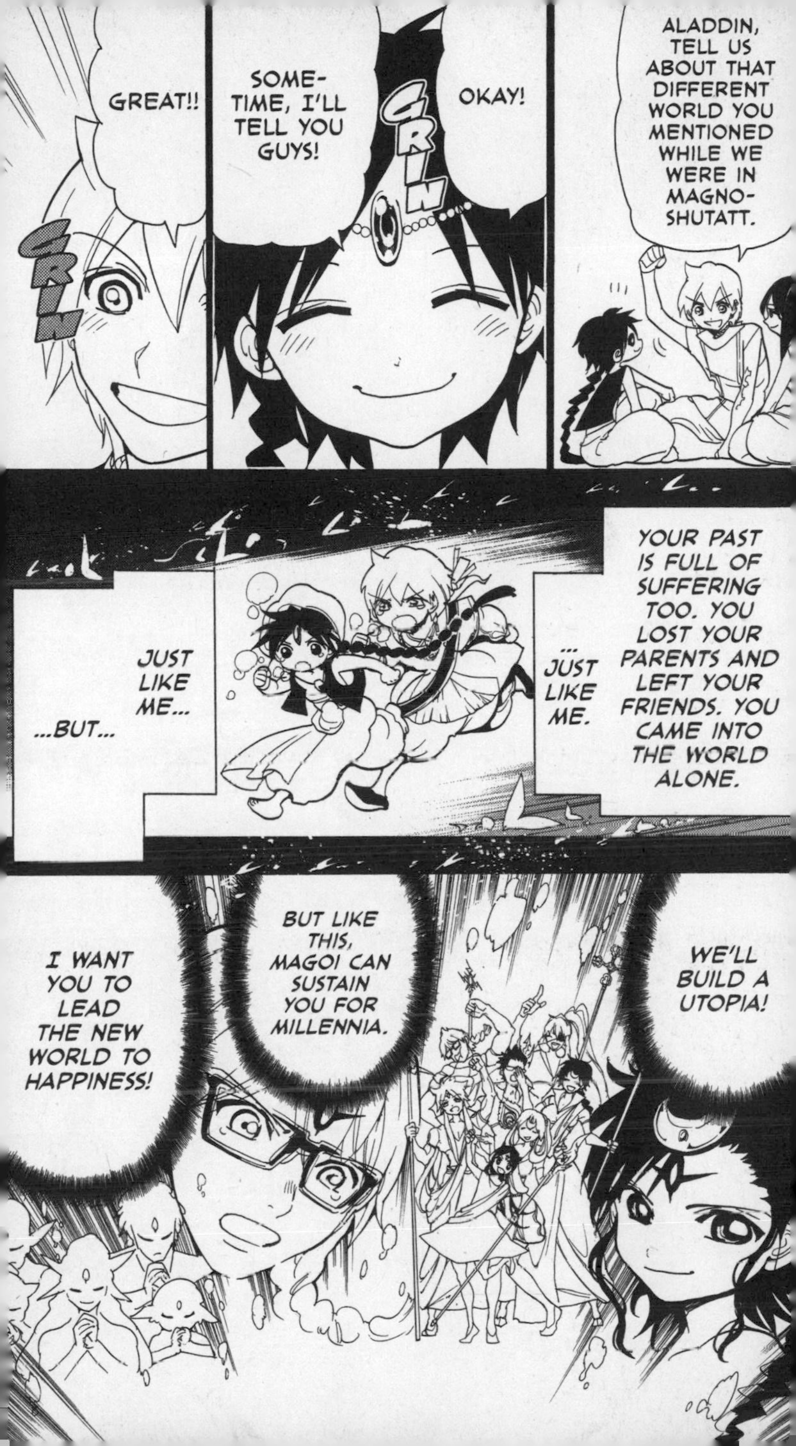
ALADDIN, TELL US ABOUT THAT DIFFERENT WORLD YOU MENTIONED WHILE WE WERE IN MAGNO-SHUTATT.
OKAY!
GRIN
SOME-TIME, I'LL TELL YOU GUYS!
GRIN
GREAT!!
YOUR PAST IS FULL OF SUFFERING TOO. YOU LOST YOUR PARENTS AND LEFT YOUR FRIENDS. YOU CAME INTO THE WORLD ALONE.
...JUST LIKE ME.
JUST LIKE ME...
...BUT...
WE'LL BUILD A UTOPIA!
BUT LIKE THIS, MAGOI CAN SUSTAIN YOU FOR MILLENNIA.
I WANT YOU TO LEAD THE NEW WORLD TO HAPPINESS!

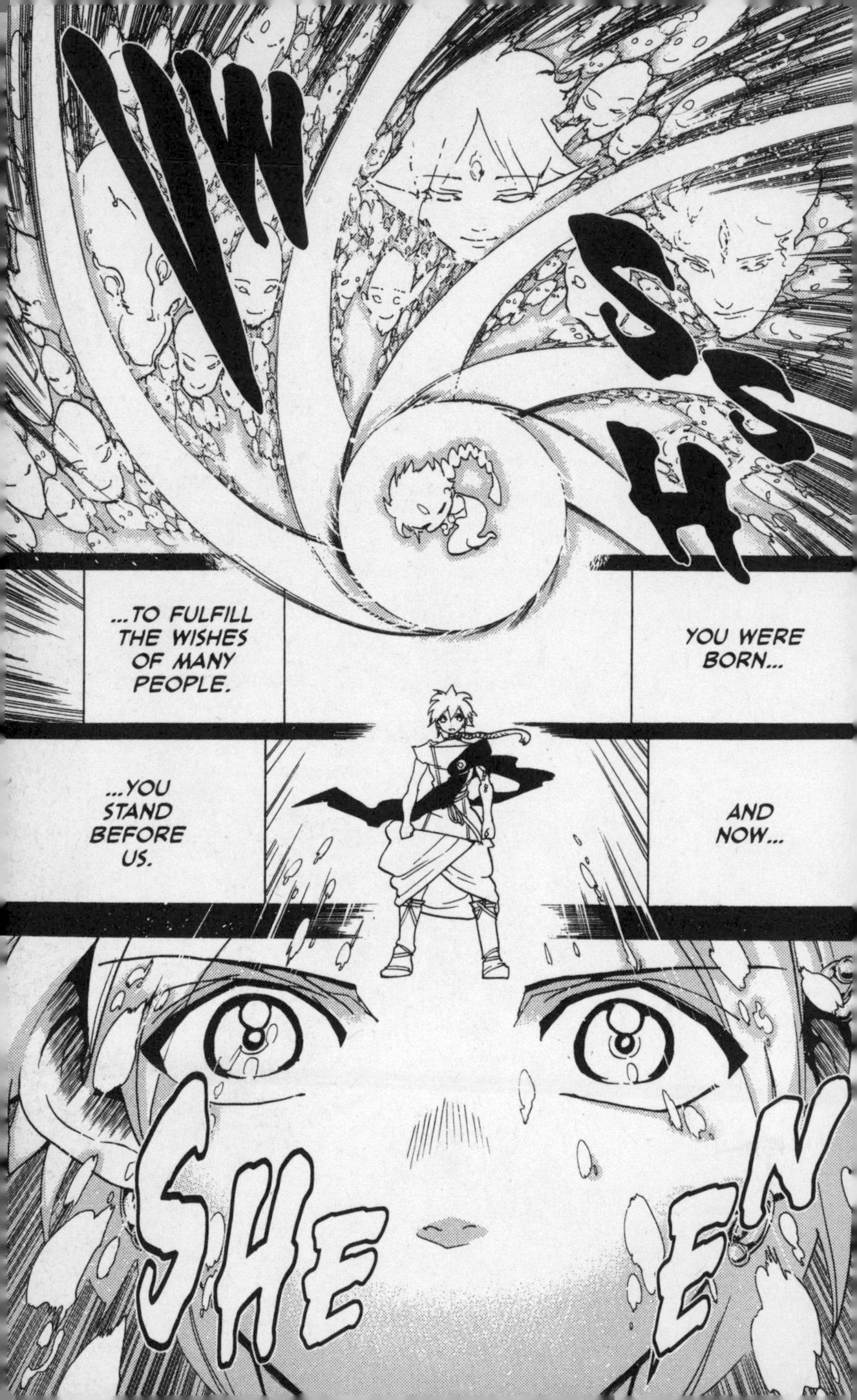
YOU WERE BORN...
...TO FULFILL THE WISHES OF MANY PEOPLE.
AND NOW...
...YOU STAND BEFORE US.
SHEEN

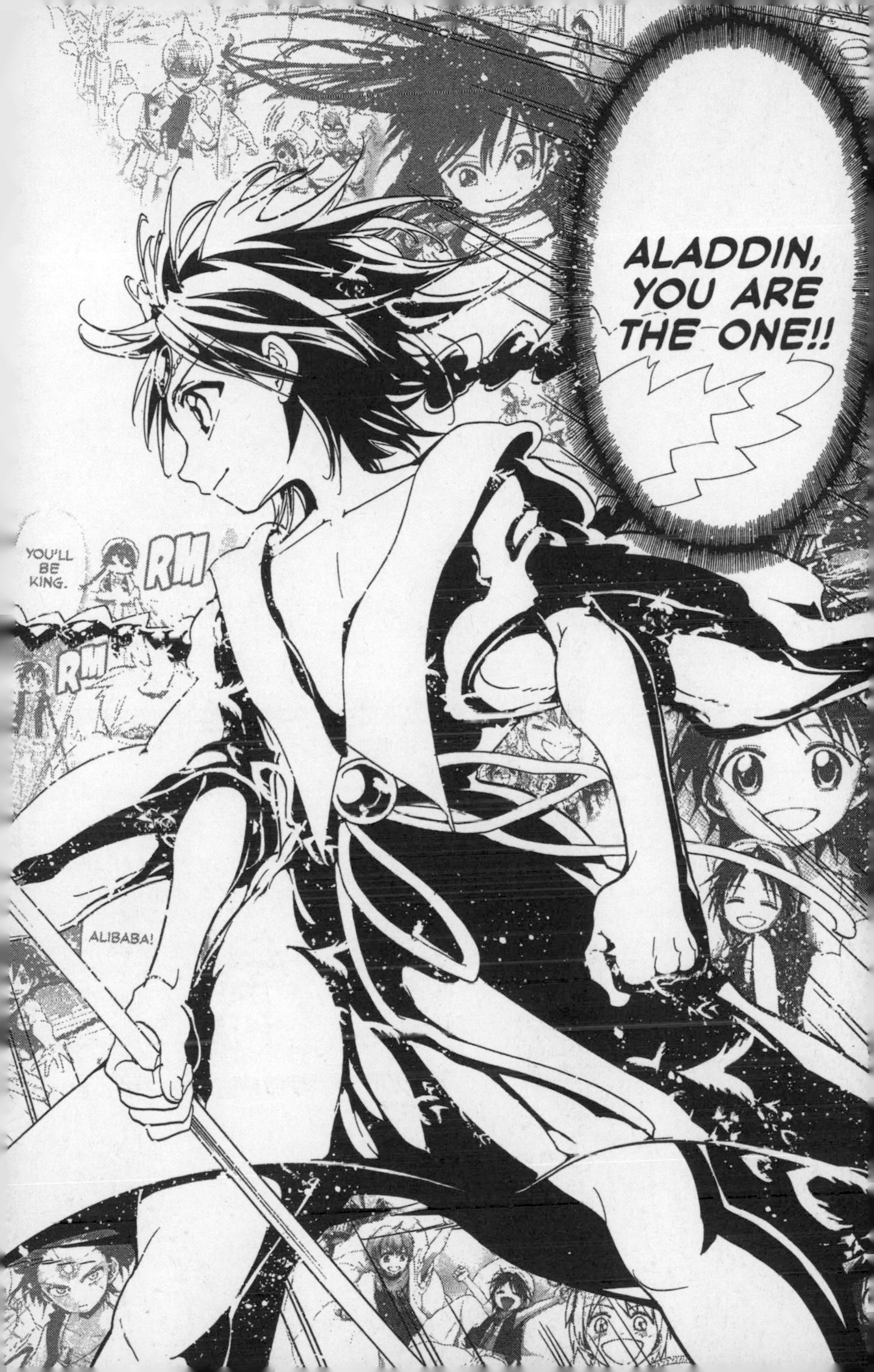
ALADDIN, YOU ARE THE ONE!!
YOU'LL BE KING.
RM
RM
ALIBABA!

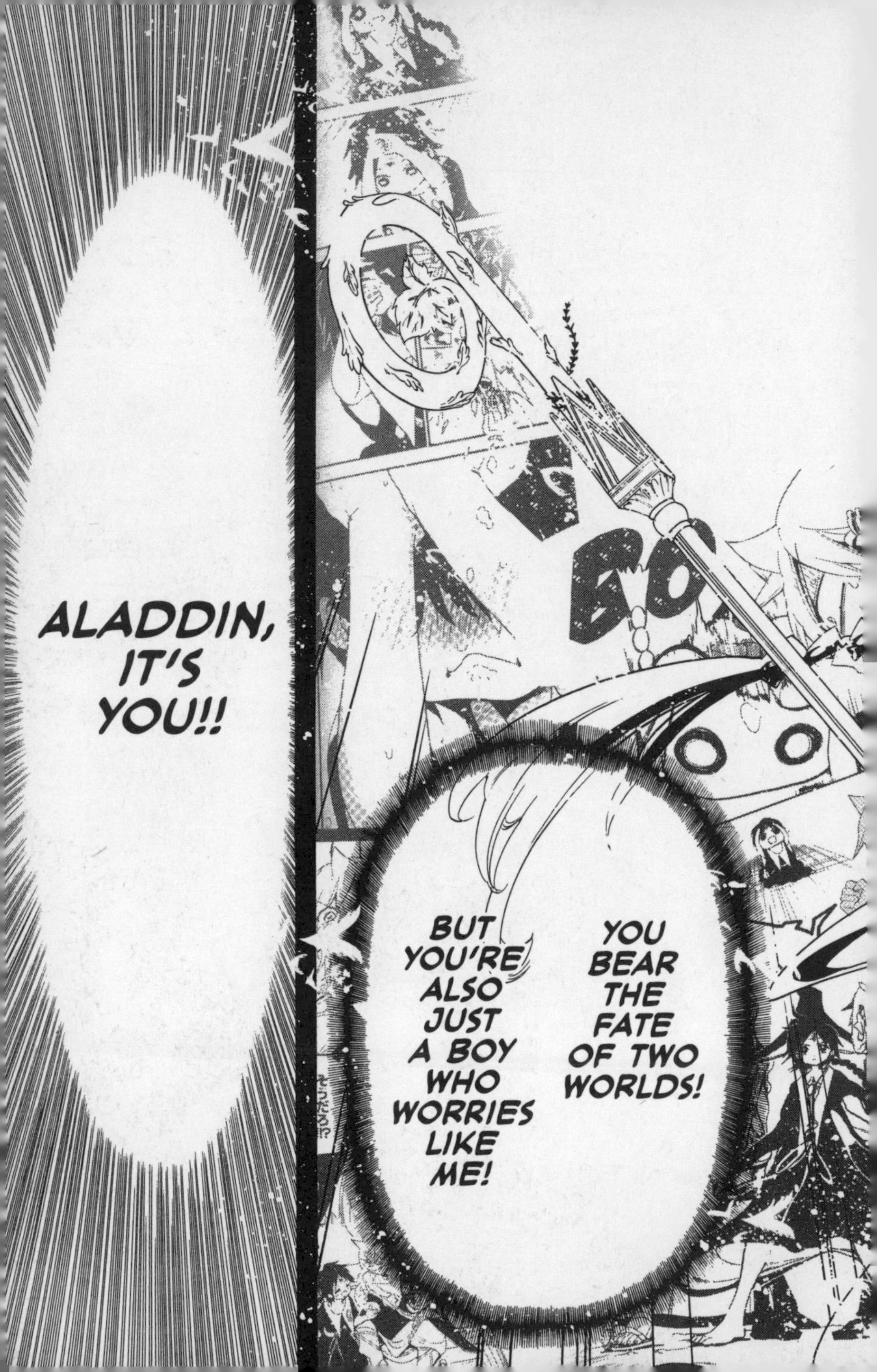
YOU BEAR THE FATE OF TWO WORLDS!
BUT YOU'RE ALSO JUST A BOY WHO WORRIES LIKE ME!
ALADDIN, IT'S YOU!!

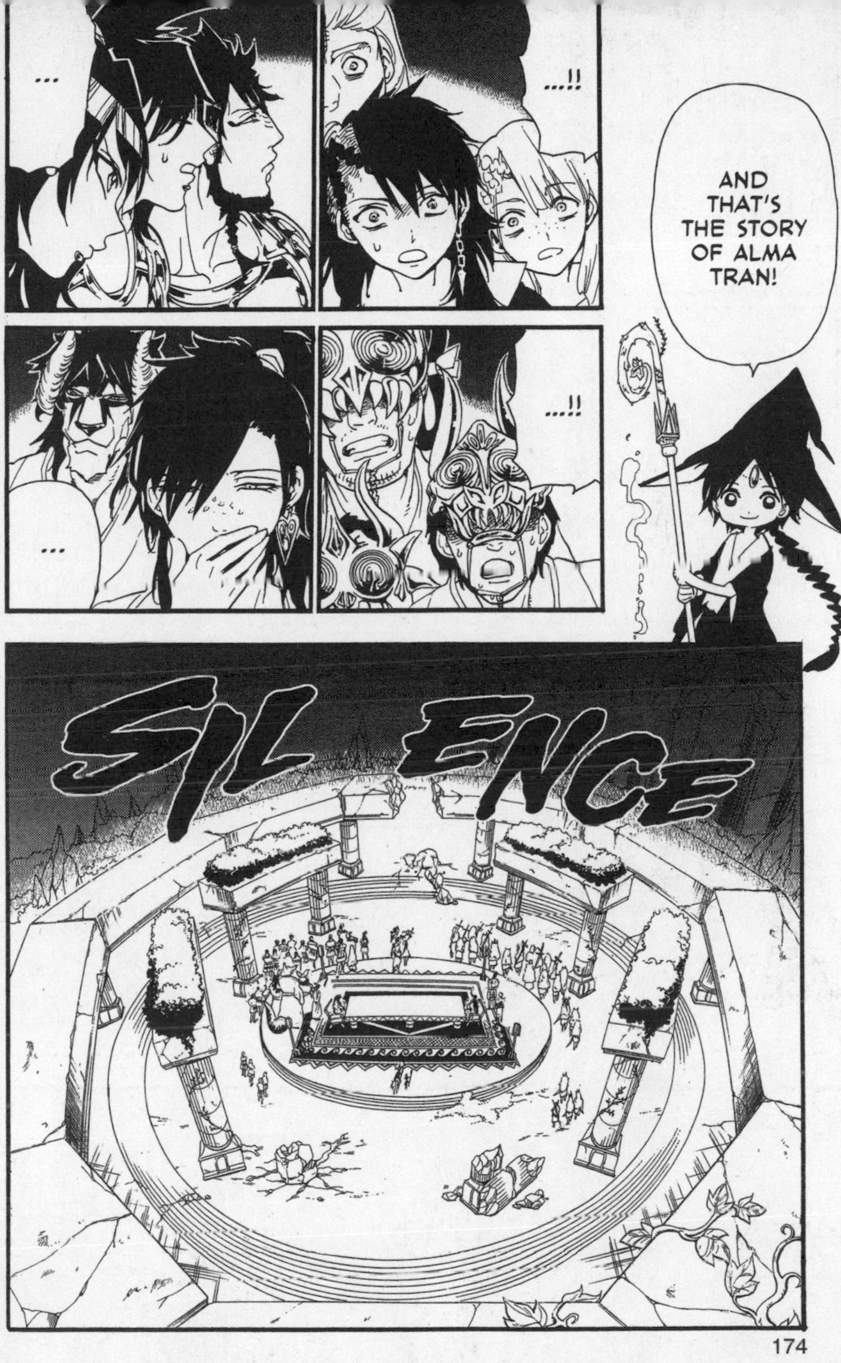
AND THAT'S THE STORY OF ALMA TRAN!
...!!
...
...!!
...
SIL ENCE

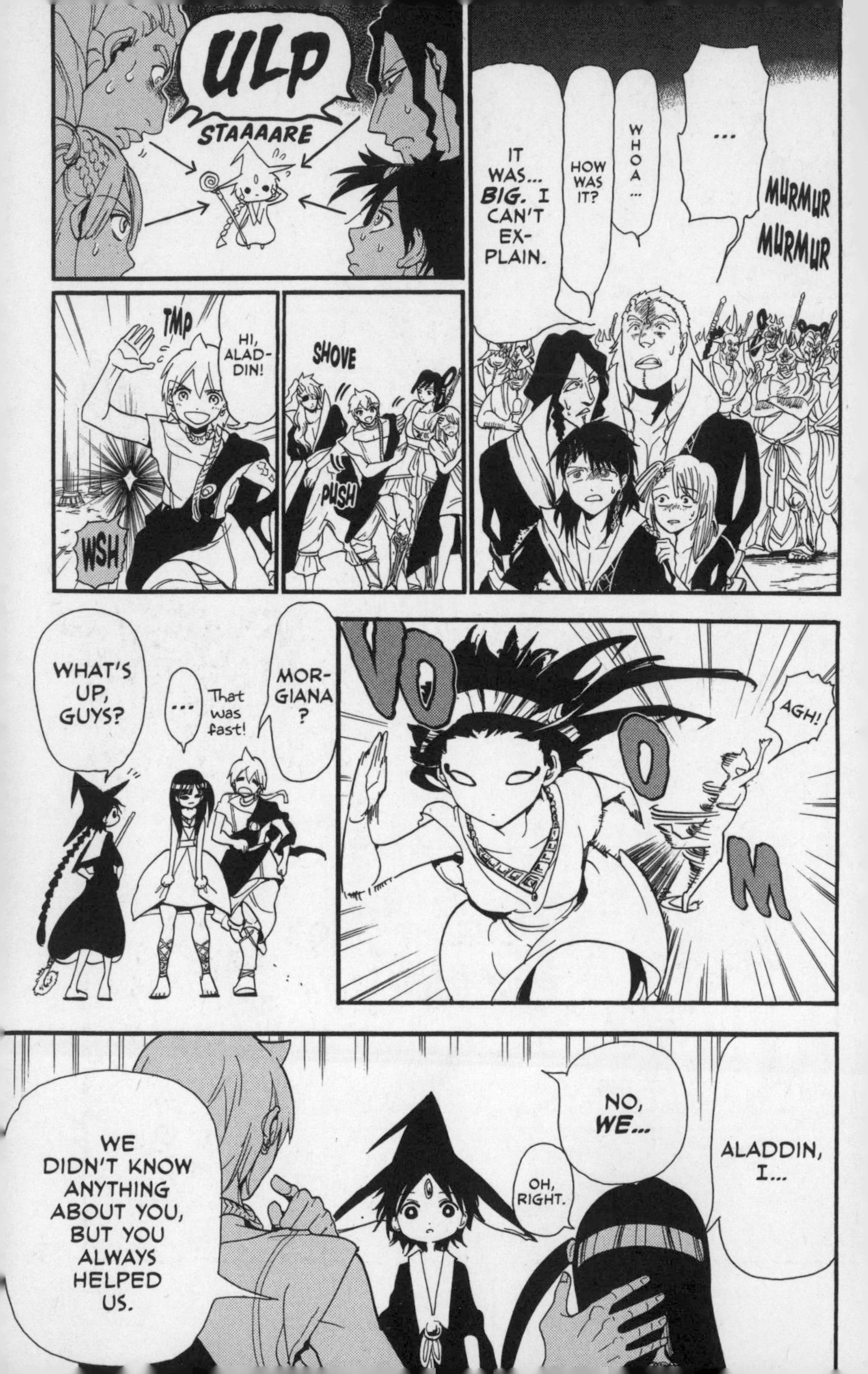
...
MURMUR MURMUR
WHOA...
HOW WAS IT?
IT WAS... BIG. I CAN'T EX-PLAIN.
ULP
STAAAARE
SHOVE
PUSH
TMP
HI, ALAD-DIN!
WSH
AGH!
VOOOM
MOR-GIANA?
That was fast!
...
WHAT'S UP, GUYS?
ALADDIN, I...
NO, WE...
OH, RIGHT.
WE DIDN'T KNOW ANYTHING ABOUT YOU, BUT YOU ALWAYS HELPED US.

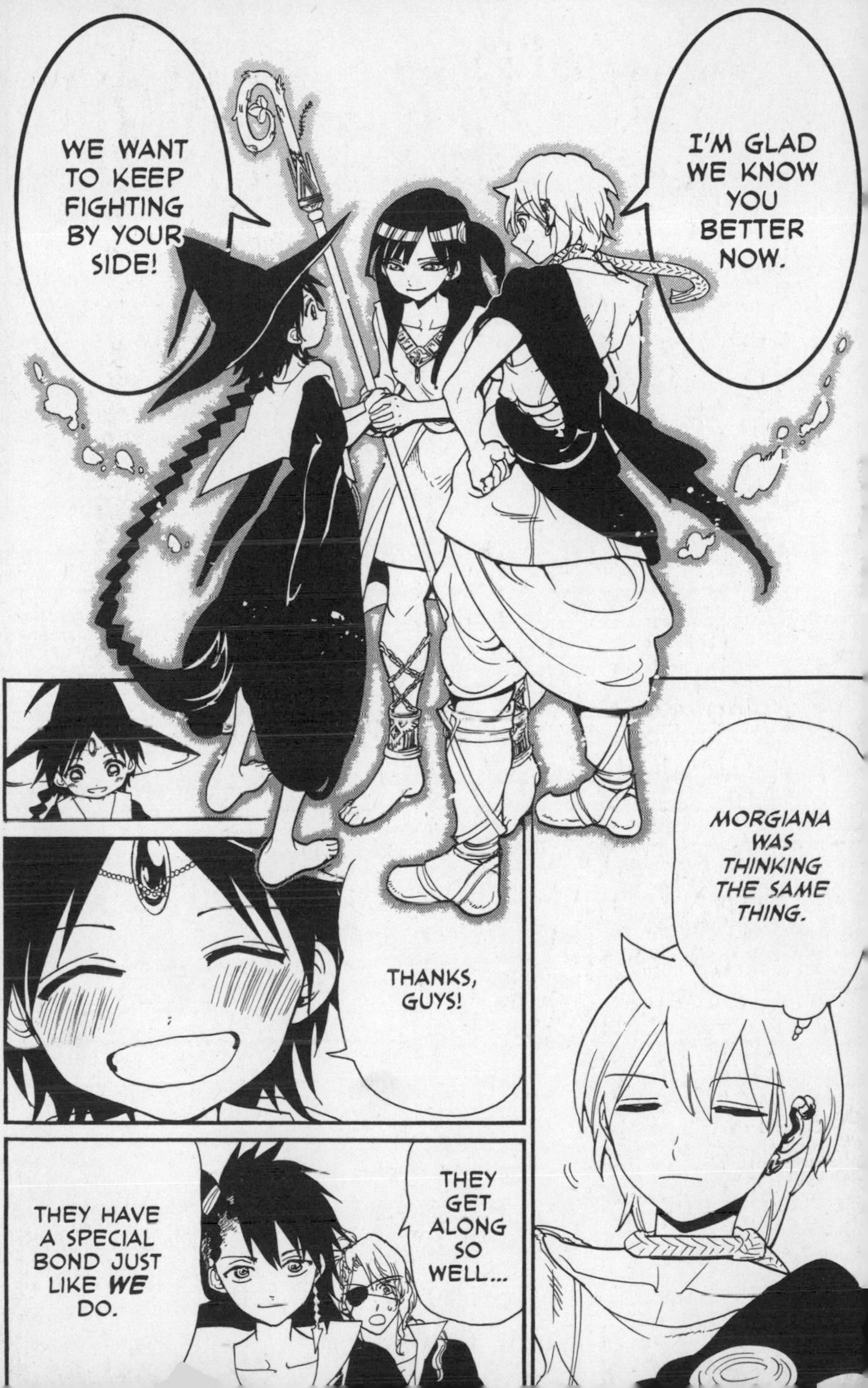
I'M GLAD WE KNOW YOU BETTER NOW.
WE WANT TO KEEP FIGHTING BY YOUR SIDE!
MORGIANA WAS THINKING THE SAME THING.
THANKS, GUYS!
THEY GET ALONG SO WELL...
THEY HAVE A SPECIAL BOND JUST LIKE *WE* DO.

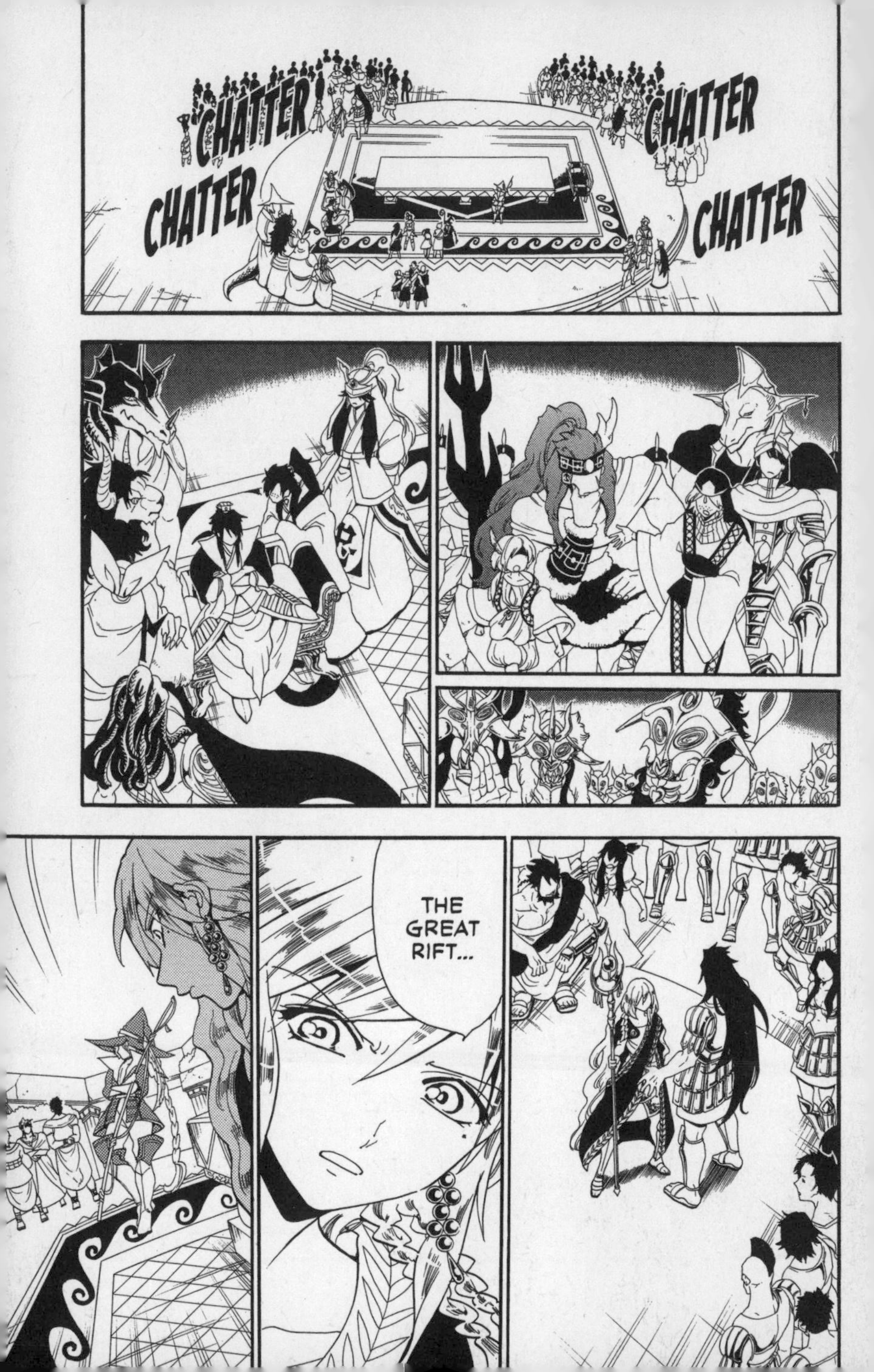
CHATTER
CHATTER
CHATTER
CHATTER
THE GREAT RIFT...

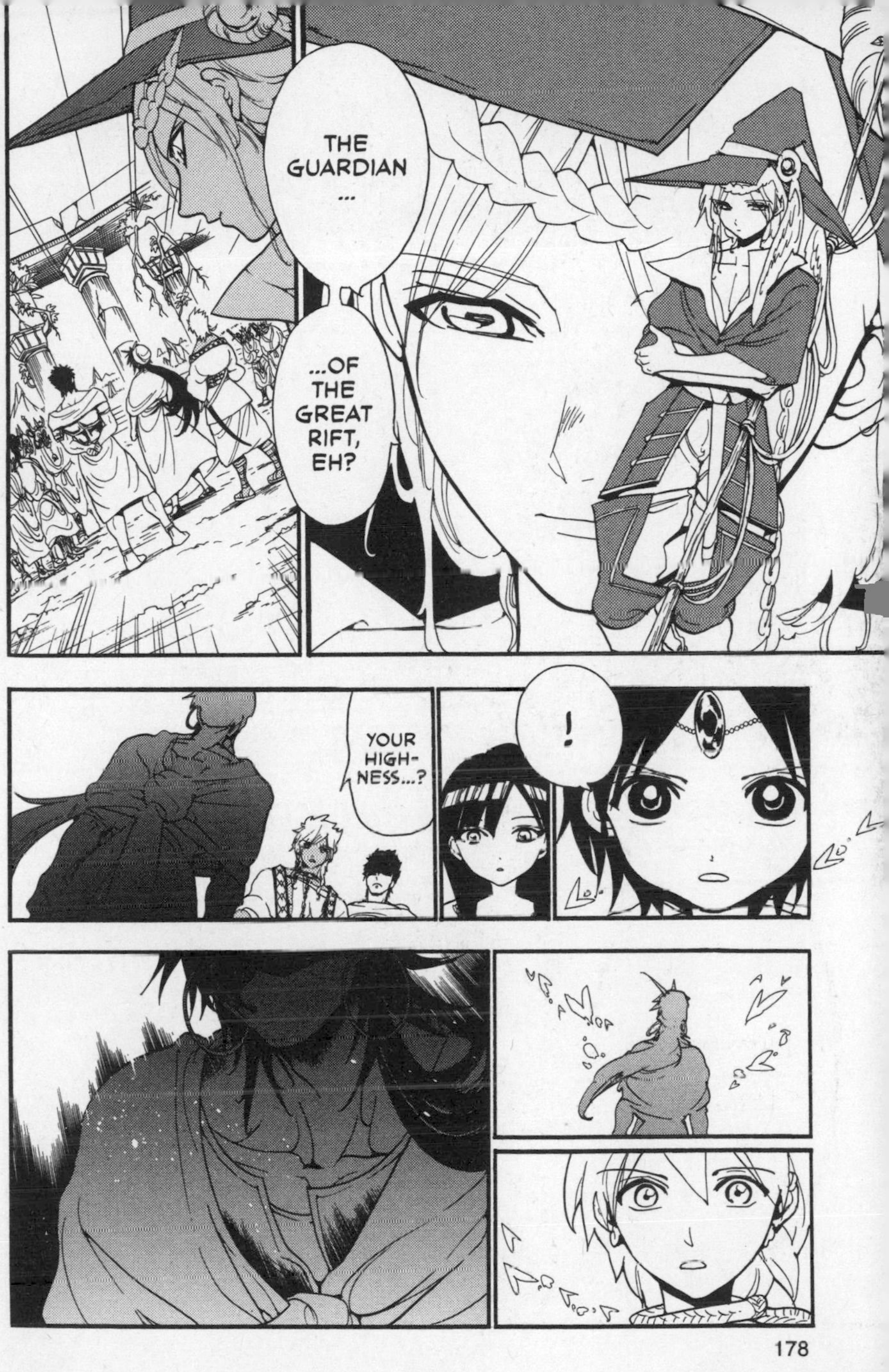
THE GUARDIAN ...
...OF THE GREAT RIFT, EH?
!
YOUR HIGHNESS...?

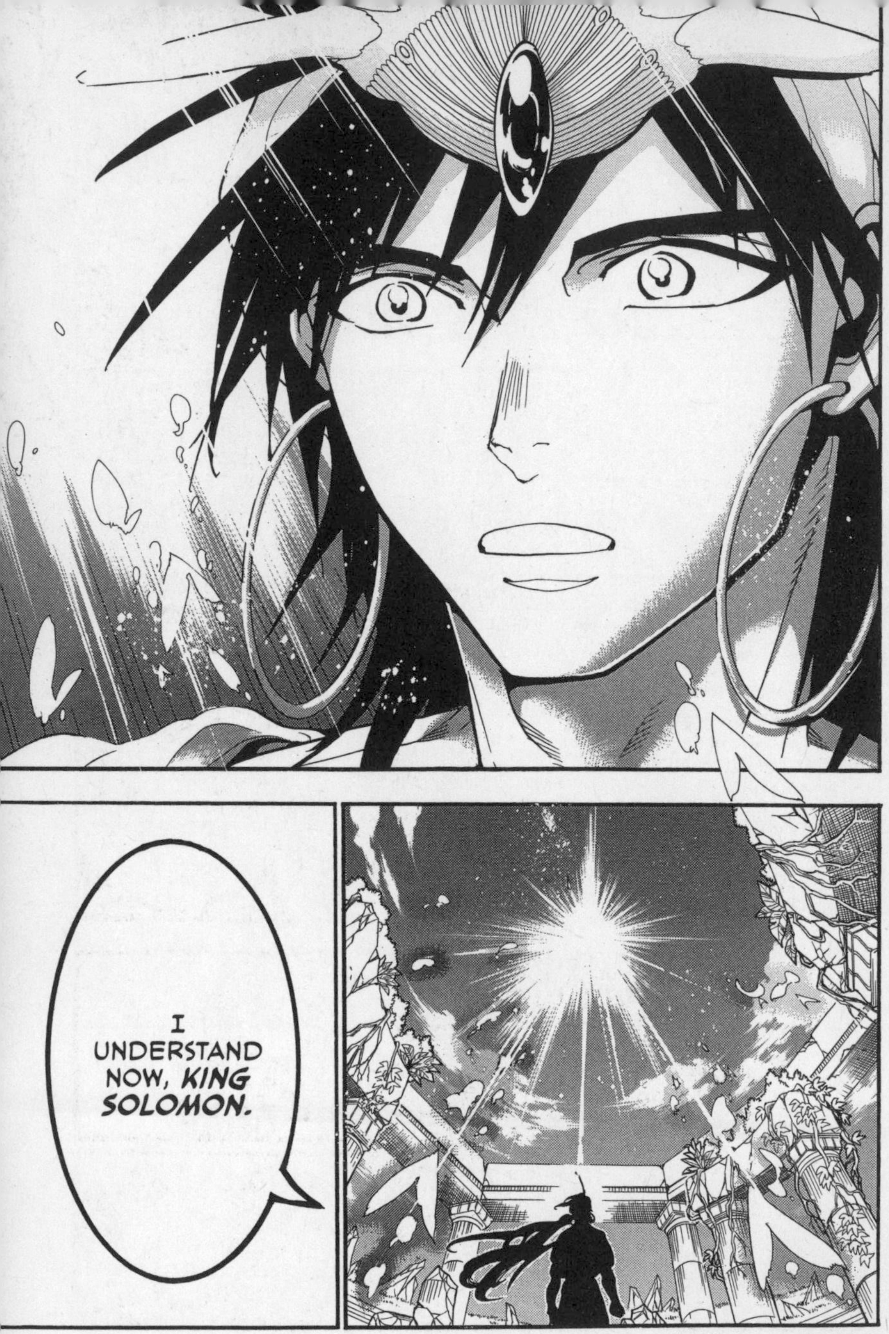
I UNDERSTAND NOW, *KING SOLOMON.*

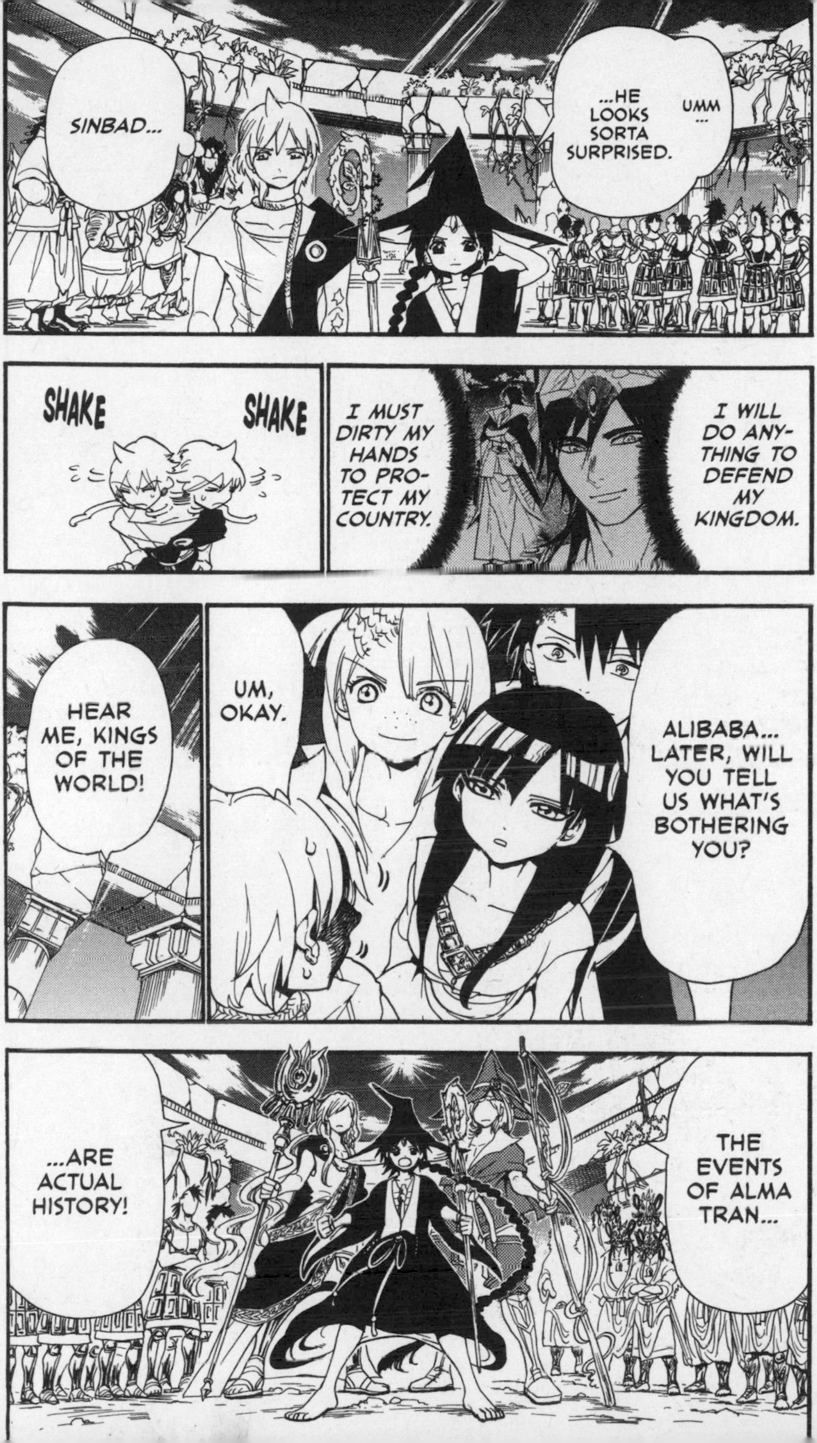
UMM ...
...HE LOOKS SORTA SURPRISED.
SINBAD...
I WILL DO ANY-THING TO DEFEND MY KINGDOM.
I MUST DIRTY MY HANDS TO PRO-TECT MY COUNTRY.
SHAKE
SHAKE
ALIBABA... LATER, WILL YOU TELL US WHAT'S BOTHERING YOU?
UM, OKAY.
HEAR ME, KINGS OF THE WORLD!
THE EVENTS OF ALMA TRAN...
...ARE ACTUAL HISTORY!

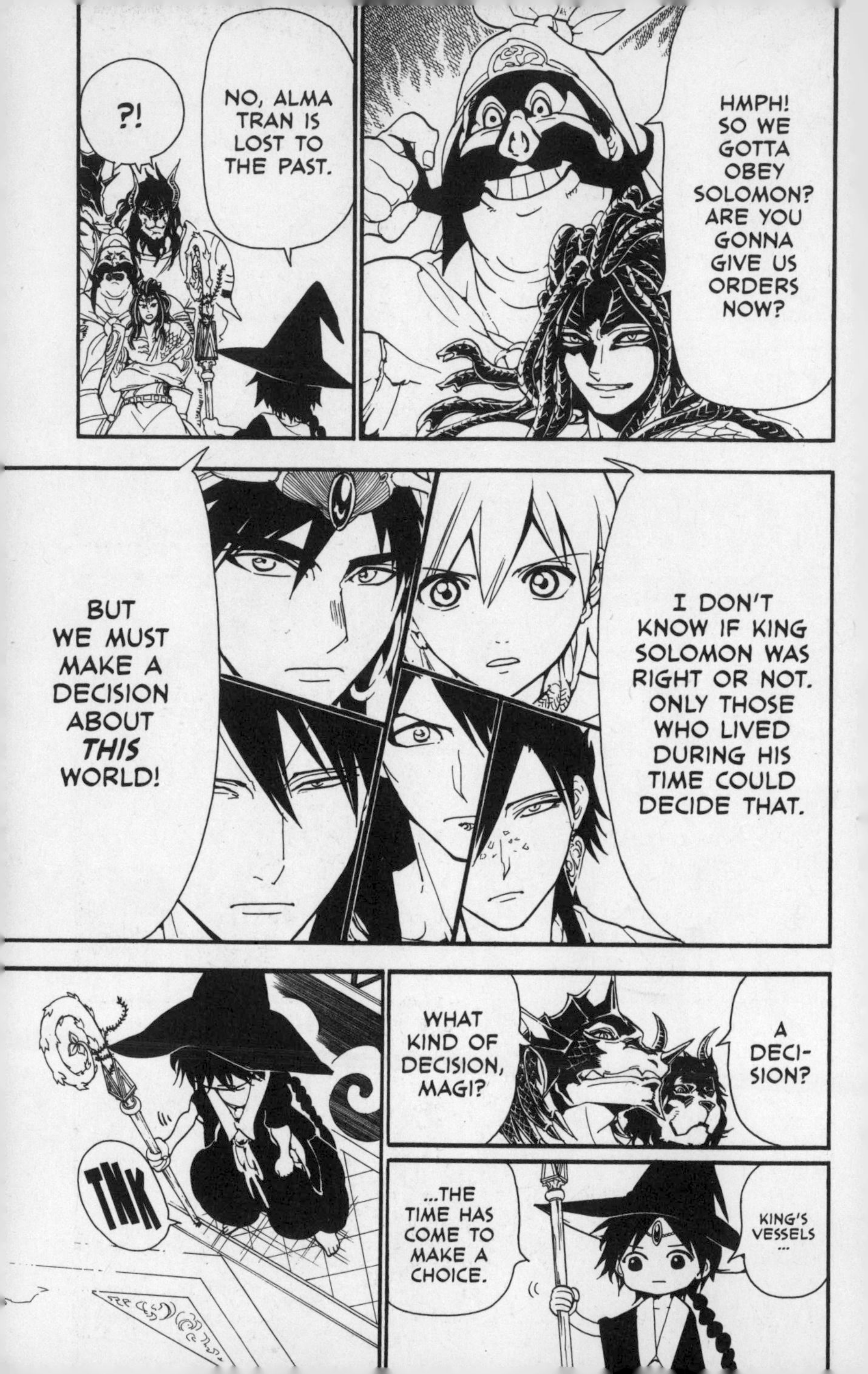
HMPH! SO WE GOTTA OBEY SOLOMON? ARE YOU GONNA GIVE US ORDERS NOW?
NO, ALMA TRAN IS LOST TO THE PAST.
?!
I DON'T KNOW IF KING SOLOMON WAS RIGHT OR NOT. ONLY THOSE WHO LIVED DURING HIS TIME COULD DECIDE THAT.
BUT WE MUST MAKE A DECISION ABOUT *THIS* WORLD!
A DECI-SION?
WHAT KIND OF DECISION, MAGI?
KING'S VESSELS ...
...THE TIME HAS COME TO MAKE A CHOICE.
TNK

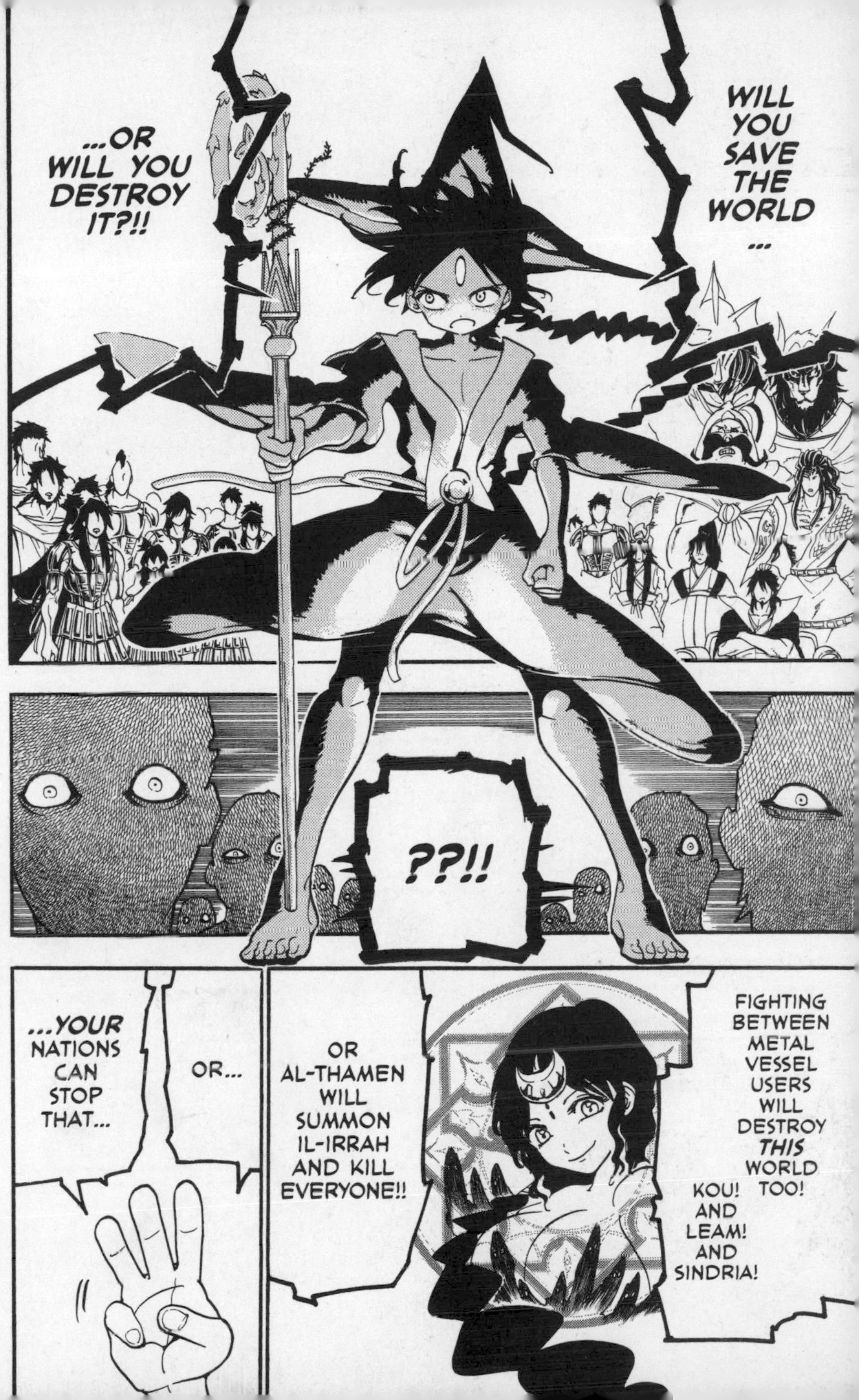

WILL YOU SAVE THE WORLD ...
...OR WILL YOU DESTROY IT?!!
??!!
FIGHTING BETWEEN METAL VESSEL USERS WILL DESTROY *THIS* WORLD TOO!
KOU! AND LEAM! AND SINDRIA!
OR AL-THAMEN WILL SUMMON IL-IRRAH AND KILL EVERYONE!!
OR...
...*YOUR* NATIONS CAN STOP THAT...

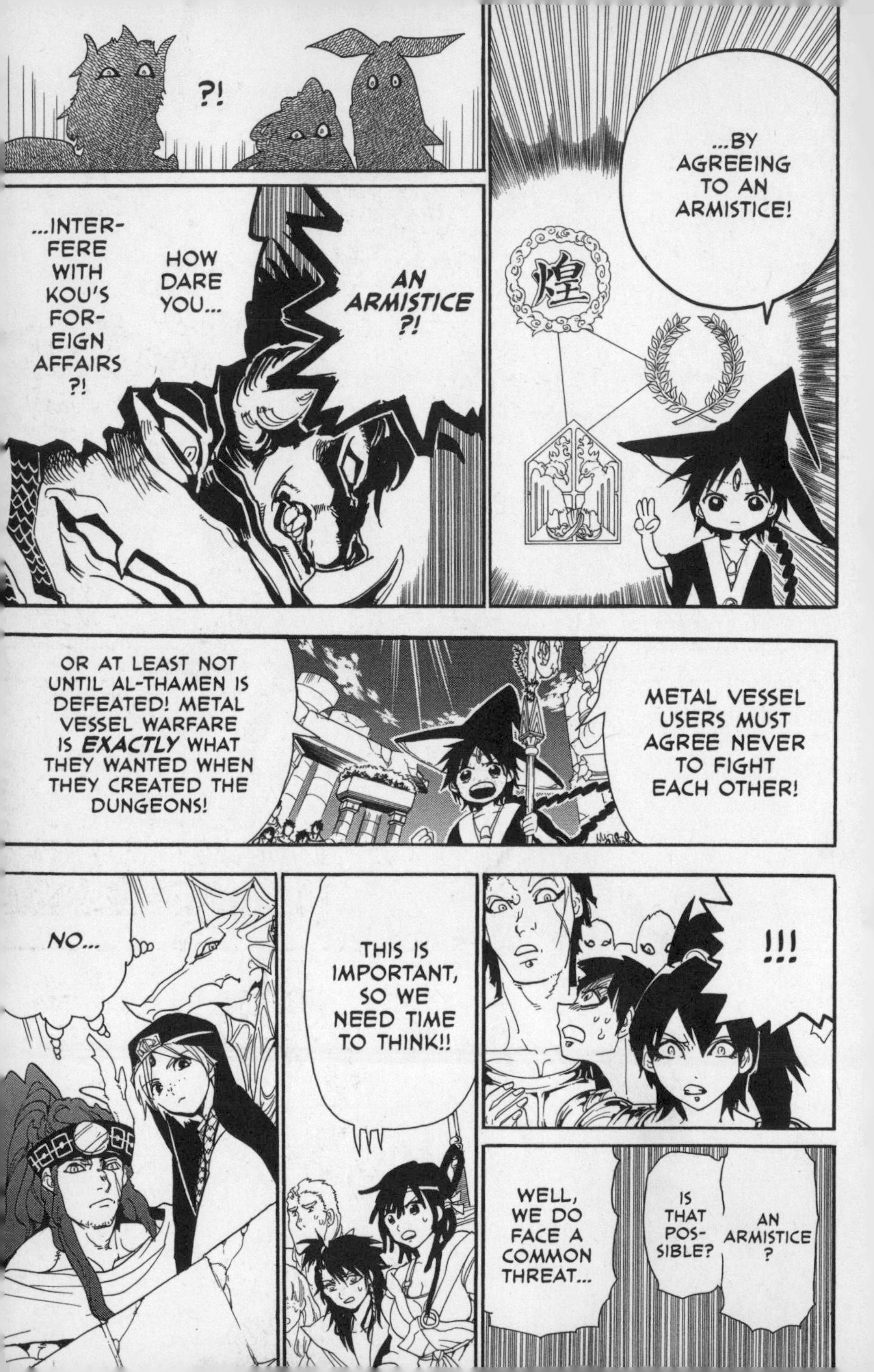
...BY AGREEING TO AN ARMISTICE!
?!
AN ARMISTICE ?!
HOW DARE YOU...
...INTER-FERE WITH KOU'S FOR-EIGN AFFAIRS ?!
METAL VESSEL USERS MUST AGREE NEVER TO FIGHT EACH OTHER!
OR AT LEAST NOT UNTIL AL-THAMEN IS DEFEATED! METAL VESSEL WARFARE IS *EXACTLY* WHAT THEY WANTED WHEN THEY CREATED THE DUNGEONS!
!!!
AN ARMISTICE ?
IS THAT POS-SIBLE?
WELL, WE DO FACE A COMMON THREAT...
THIS IS IMPORTANT, SO WE NEED TIME TO THINK!!
NO...

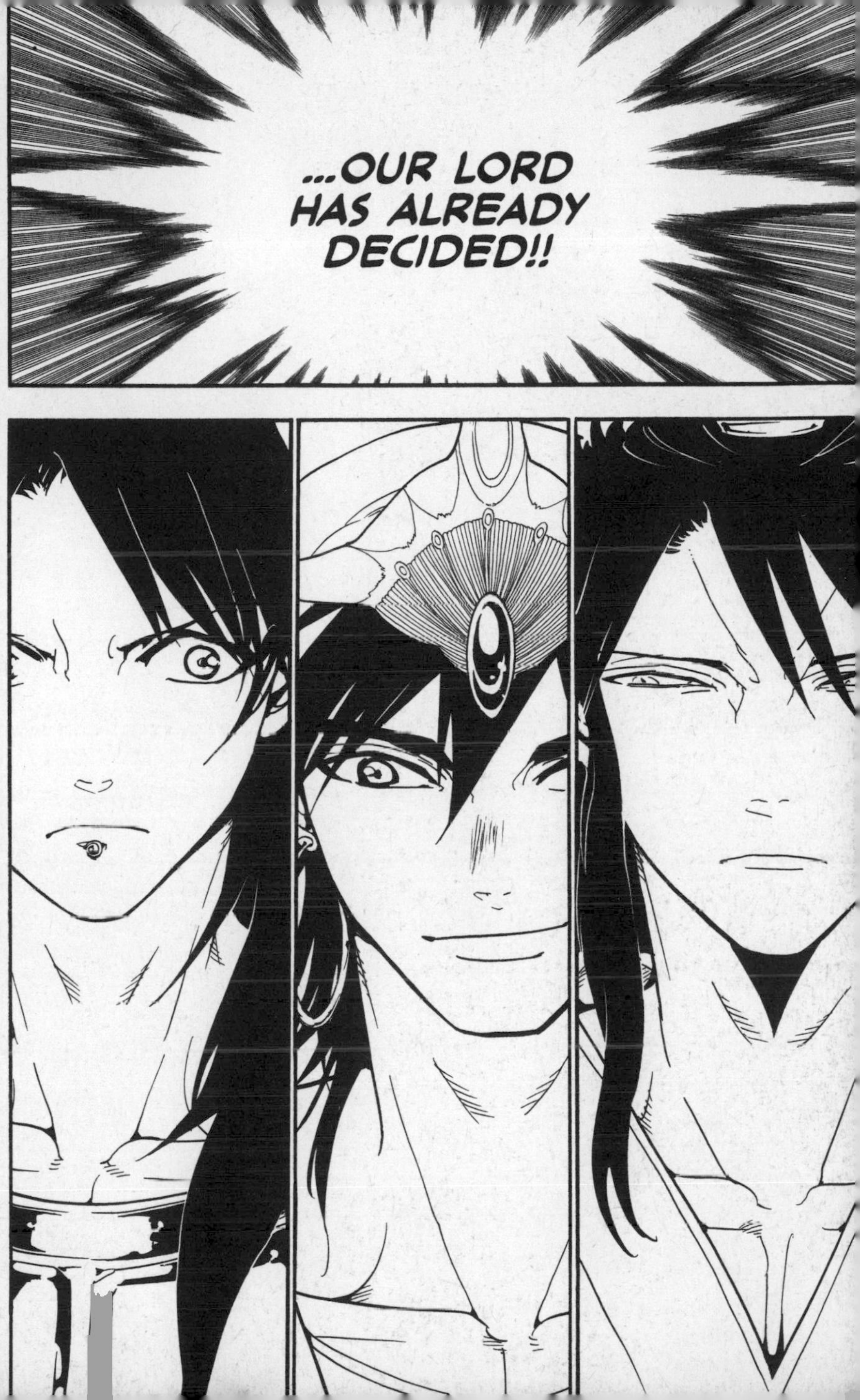
...OUR LORD HAS ALREADY DECIDED!!

MAGI
The labyrinth of magic **24**

Staff

■ **Story & Art**
Shinobu Ohtaka

■ **Regular Assistants**
Hiro Maizima

Yuiko Akiyama

Megi

Aya Umoto

Mami Yoshida

Yuka Otsuji

■ **Editors**
Kazuaki Ishibashi
Makoto Ishiwata

■ **Sales & Promotion**
Tsunato Imamoto

Yuta Uchiyama

■ **Designer**
Yasuo Shimura + Bay Bridge Studio

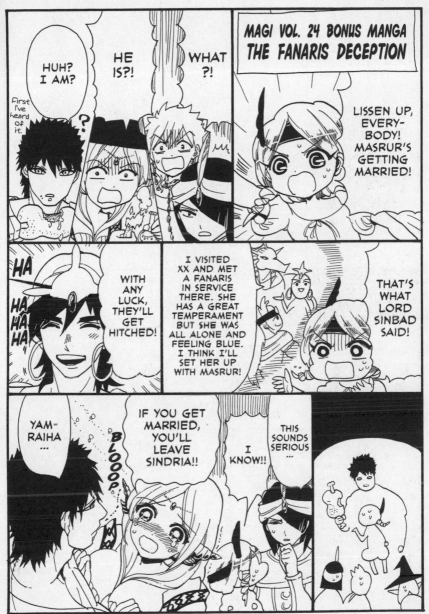

MAGI VOL. 24 BONUS MANGA
THE FANARIS DECEPTION
LISSEN UP, EVERYBODY! MASRUR'S GETTING MARRIED!
WHAT ?!
HE IS?!
HUH? I AM?
First I've heard of it.
THAT'S WHAT LORD SINBAD SAID!
I VISITED XX AND MET A FANARIS IN SERVICE THERE. SHE HAS A GREAT TEMPERAMENT BUT SHE WAS ALL ALONE AND FEELING BLUE. I THINK I'LL SET HER UP WITH MASRUR!
WITH ANY LUCK, THEY'LL GET HITCHED!
HA HA HA HA
THIS SOUNDS SERIOUS ...
I KNOW!!
IF YOU GET MARRIED, YOU'LL LEAVE SINDRIA!!
BLOOOP
YAM-RAIHA ...

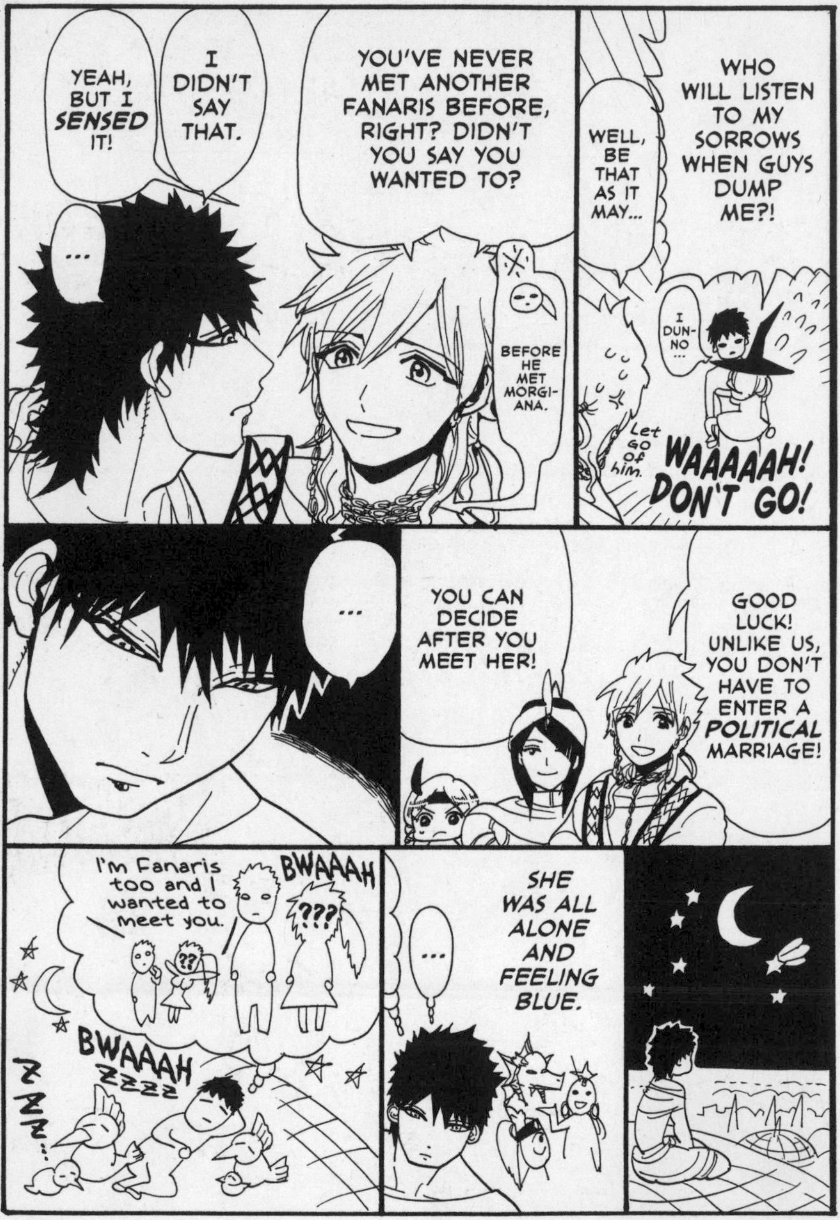

WHO WILL LISTEN TO MY SORROWS WHEN GUYS DUMP ME?!
WELL, BE THAT AS IT MAY...
I DUN-NO ...
Let go of him.
WAAAAAH! DON'T GO!
YOU'VE NEVER MET ANOTHER FANARIS BEFORE, RIGHT? DIDN'T YOU SAY YOU WANTED TO?
BEFORE HE MET MORGI-ANA.
I DIDN'T SAY THAT.
YEAH, BUT I SENSED IT!
...
GOOD LUCK! UNLIKE US, YOU DON'T HAVE TO ENTER A POLITICAL MARRIAGE!
YOU CAN DECIDE AFTER YOU MEET HER!
...
SHE WAS ALL ALONE AND FEELING BLUE.
...
BWAAAH
???
I'm Fanaris too and I wanted to meet you.
??
BWAAAH ZZZZ
ZZZ...

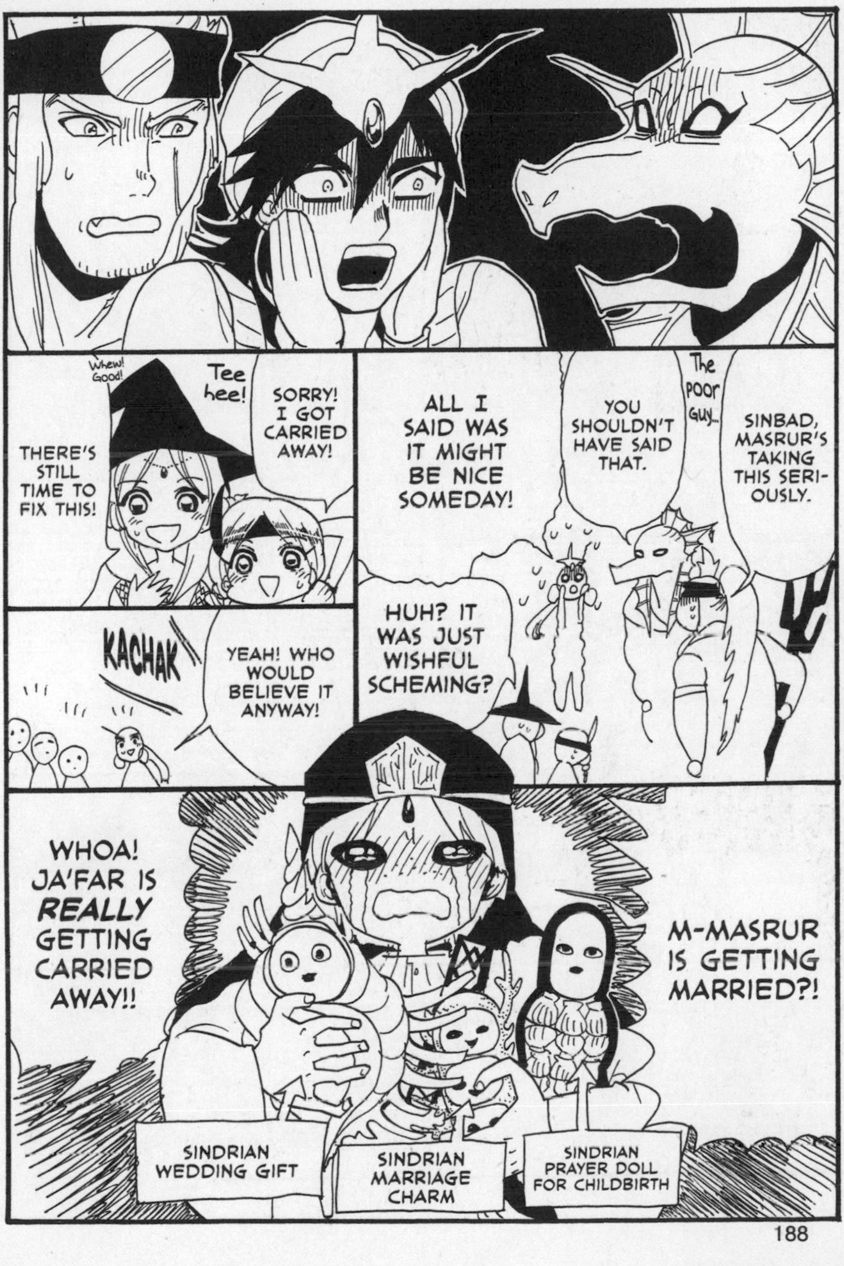
SINBAD, MASRUR'S TAKING THIS SERI-OUSLY.
The poor guy...
YOU SHOULDN'T HAVE SAID THAT.
ALL I SAID WAS IT MIGHT BE NICE SOMEDAY!
HUH? IT WAS JUST WISHFUL SCHEMING?
SORRY! I GOT CARRIED AWAY!
Tee hee!
Whew! Good!
THERE'S STILL TIME TO FIX THIS!
YEAH! WHO WOULD BELIEVE IT ANYWAY!
KACHAK
M-MASRUR IS GETTING MARRIED?!
WHOA! JA'FAR IS REALLY GETTING CARRIED AWAY!!
SINDRIAN PRAYER DOLL FOR CHILDBIRTH
SINDRIAN MARRIAGE CHARM
SINDRIAN WEDDING GIFT

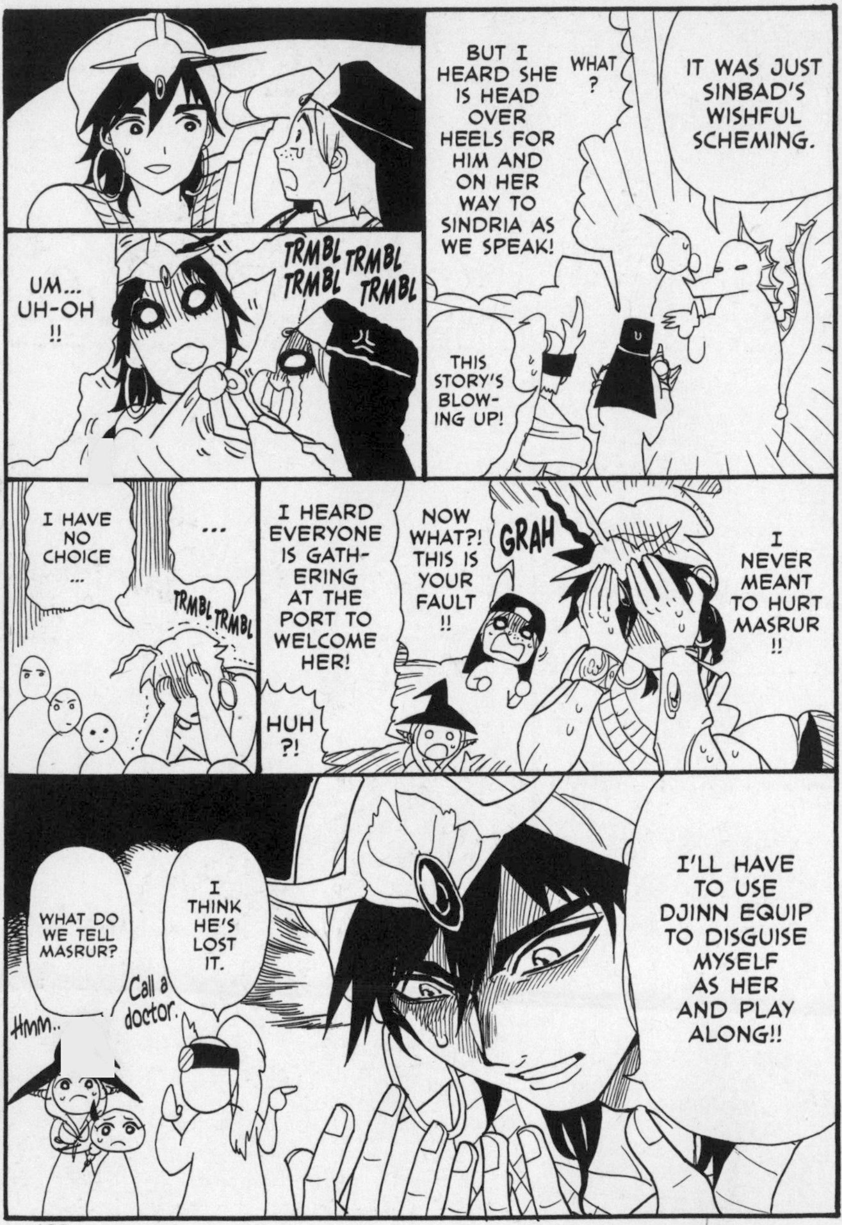
IT WAS JUST SINBAD'S WISHFUL SCHEMING.
WHAT?
BUT I HEARD SHE IS HEAD OVER HEELS FOR HIM AND ON HER WAY TO SINDRIA AS WE SPEAK!
THIS STORY'S BLOWING UP!
TRMBL TRMBL TRMBL TRMBL
UM... UH-OH!!
I NEVER MEANT TO HURT MASRUR!!
GRAH
NOW WHAT?! THIS IS YOUR FAULT!!
I HEARD EVERYONE IS GATHERING AT THE PORT TO WELCOME HER!
HUH?!
...
I HAVE NO CHOICE...
TRMBL TRMBL
I'LL HAVE TO USE DJINN EQUIP TO DISGUISE MYSELF AS HER AND PLAY ALONG!!
I THINK HE'S LOST IT.
WHAT DO WE TELL MASRUR?
Call a doctor.
Hmm..

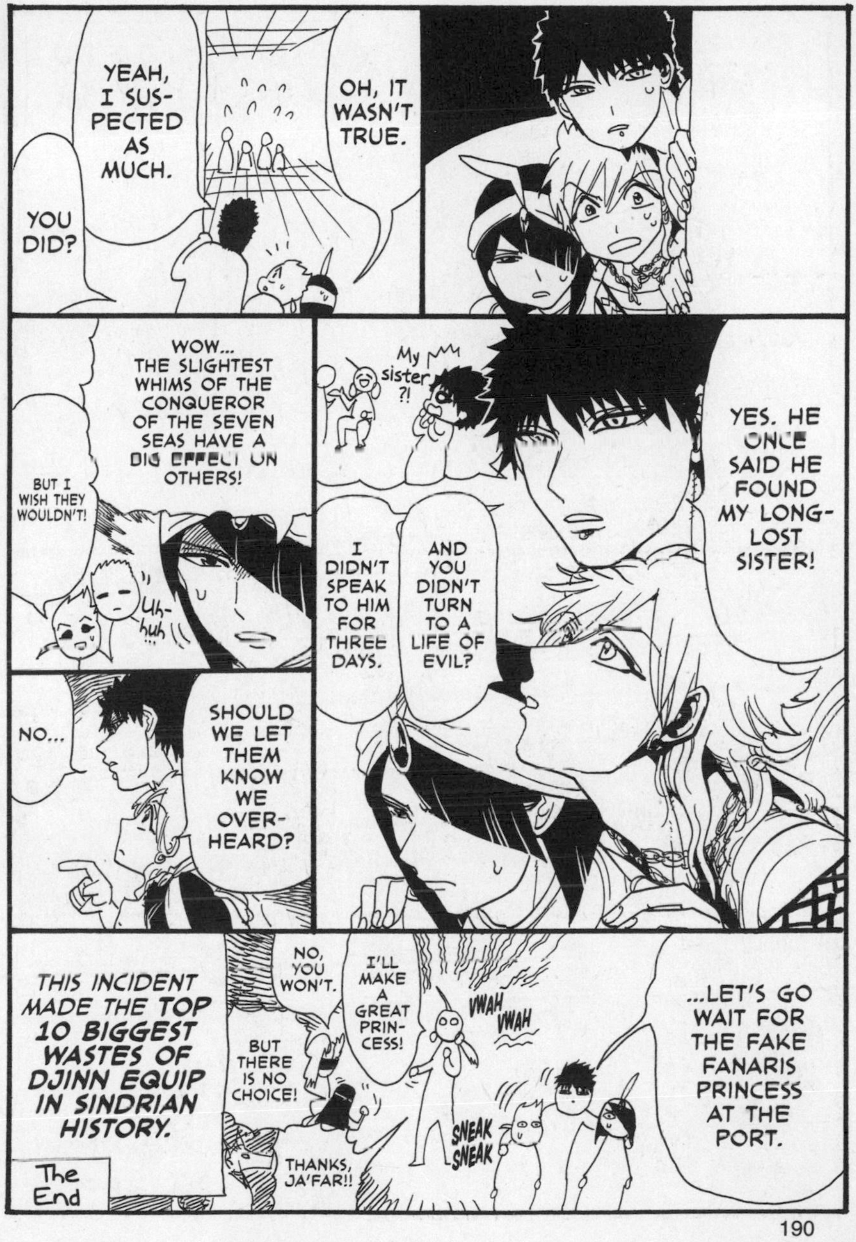
OH, IT WASN'T TRUE.
YEAH, I SUSPECTED AS MUCH.
YOU DID?
YES. HE ONCE SAID HE FOUND MY LONG-LOST SISTER!
My sister ?!
AND YOU DIDN'T TURN TO A LIFE OF EVIL?
I DIDN'T SPEAK TO HIM FOR THREE DAYS.
WOW... THE SLIGHTEST WHIMS OF THE CONQUEROR OF THE SEVEN SEAS HAVE A BIG EFFECT ON OTHERS!
BUT I WISH THEY WOULDN'T!
Uh-huh...
SHOULD WE LET THEM KNOW WE OVERHEARD?
NO...
...LET'S GO WAIT FOR THE FAKE FANARIS PRINCESS AT THE PORT.
SNEAK SNEAK
VWAH VWAH
I'LL MAKE A GREAT PRINCESS!
NO, YOU WON'T.
BUT THERE IS NO CHOICE!
THANKS, JA'FAR!!
THIS INCIDENT MADE THE TOP 10 BIGGEST WASTES OF DJINN EQUIP IN SINDRIAN HISTORY.
The End

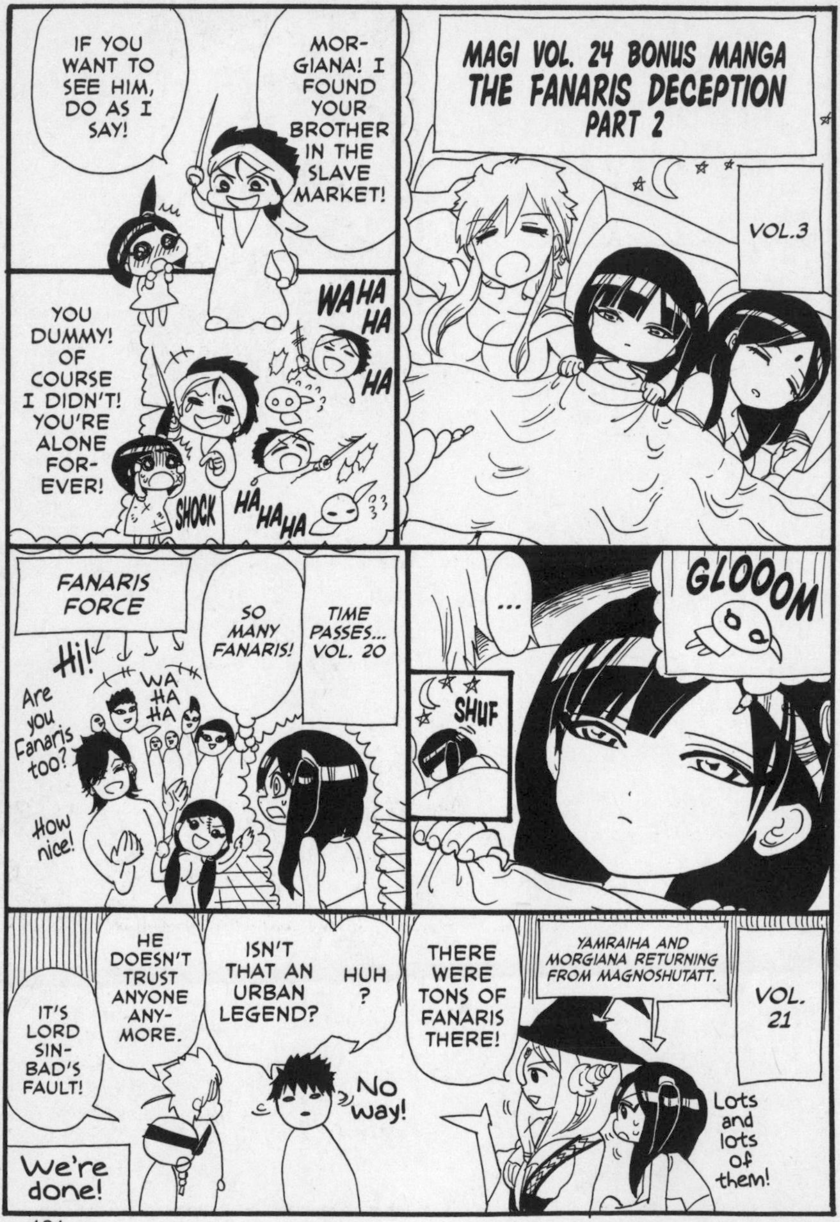
MAGI VOL. 24 BONUS MANGA
THE FANARIS DECEPTION
PART 2
VOL.3
MOR-GIANA! I FOUND YOUR BROTHER IN THE SLAVE MARKET!
IF YOU WANT TO SEE HIM, DO AS I SAY!
WAHAHA HA
HA
YOU DUMMY! OF COURSE I DIDN'T! YOU'RE ALONE FOR-EVER!
HAHAHA
SHOCK
GLOOOM
...
SHUF
TIME PASSES... VOL. 20
SO MANY FANARIS!
FANARIS FORCE
Hi!
WA HA HA
Are you Fanaris too?
How nice!
VOL. 21
YAMRAIHA AND MORGIANA RETURNING FROM MAGNOSHUTATT.
Lots and lots of them!
THERE WERE TONS OF FANARIS THERE!
HUH?
No way!
ISN'T THAT AN URBAN LEGEND?
HE DOESN'T TRUST ANYONE ANY-MORE.
IT'S LORD SIN-BAD'S FAULT!
We're done!

You're reading the
WRONG WAY

◇◇◇◇◇◇◇◇◇◇◇◇◇◇◇◇◇◇◇◇◇◇◇◇◇◇

MAGI reads from right to left, starting in the upper-right corner. Japanese is read from **right** to **left**, meaning that action, sound effects, and word-balloon order are completely reversed from English order.

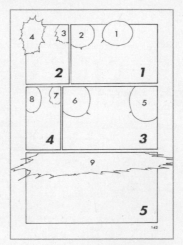